THE VICTIMOLOGY HANDBOOK

Garland Reference Library of Social Science (Vol. 605)

THE VICTIMOLOGY HANDBOOK

Research Findings, Treatment, and Public Policy

Edited by

EMILIO C. VIANO

School of Public Affairs,
The American University

and

Victimology: An International Journal,
Washington, D.C.

GARLAND PUBLISHING, INC.
New York & London
1990

Library of Congress Cataloging-in-Publication Data

Viano, Emilio
The victimology handbook : research findings, treatment, and public policiy / Emilio Viano.
p. cm — (Garland reference library of social science : v. 605)
ISBN 0-8240-4031-7 (alk. paper)
1. Victims of crimes—Congresses. 1. Title. II. Series.
Includes index.
HV6250.2.V515 1990 90-38717
362.88—dc20

Printed on acid-free, 250-year-life paper
Manufactured in the United States of America

Book interior and cover design by Julie Threlkeld
This book was designed using the Stone family of typefaces

To
SHERRY LEE ICENHOWER

whose abilities, dedication, and skills have made the World Congresses of Victimology successful and outstanding events that have greatly contributed to the international development and recognition of victimology.

Contents

PART III
PUBLIC POLICY

1

Introduction

Victimology: A New Focus of Research and Practice

Emilio C. Viano
School of Public Affairs, The American University
and
Victimology: An International Journal

The International Growth of Victimology

The last two decades have seen the development of a victim movement in various countries as a separate political force. In the United States the victim movement was begun in the 1970s. The women's movement, inspired by the civil rights movement, was its primary moving force. Also influential were the substantial efforts undertaken after the urban riots of the late 1960s to improve the operations of the criminal justice system and the consumer movement, which demanded more accountability not only of producers of consumer goods but also of the state and of the justice system.

Feminists forcefully pointed out the problems faced by women victims of sexual assault when they came in contact with the police, hospitals, and the courts. Practitioners and academics in the justice system realized that the system did not serve the victims of crime. Instead, it "used" them to obtain needed information, cooperation, and services, for example, as a witness without giving them any active role, respect, or consideration in return. In essence, it was said, the system "re-victimized" the victim.

Other groups founded in response to specific problems facing society also greatly contributed to the development of a general awareness of the concept of victim, of the plight of various victims, and of the need for support services and, most of all, appropriate legislative reforms. The best example of such a group is Mothers Against Drunk Drivers (MADD).

Child abuse and neglect, domestic violence, missing and exploited children, the elderly, the survivors of victims of homicide, date rape, sexual harassment, and patient abuse by therapists have also been added to the focus of concern of victimology as it grew.

The success of these groups concerned with particular crimes and crime victims has served to highlight the general importance of "victims" as an effective political symbol and as a rallying point for a variety of grievances, dissatisfactions, and political agendas.

The early 1980s saw several expressions of this political awareness and recognition: the establishment of a Victims of Crime Task Force (1980), subsequently called the Presidential Commission of Victims of Crime, and of the Family Violence Task Force (1984) and the passage at the federal level of the Victims and Witness Protection Act of 1982, of the Victims of Crime Act of 1984, and of the Justice Assistance Act also of 1984.

Several developments at the states' level also demonstrated the growth and importance of the victim movement in the United States. California voters approved in 1982 the widely publicized Victim's Bill of Rights or Proposition 8 amending the State Constitution. Florida voters passed a similar constitutional amendment in 1988. Twenty-eight states have enacted similar Bills of Rights.

The enactment of compensation for victims of crimes by forty states and the District of Columbia; the provision of funds to support domestic violence shelters by forty-nine states; the funding of victim-witness programs in countless jurisdictions and localities are other positive developments engineered by organizations, professionals, academics, and volunteers concerned about the victim.

While the growth of the movement and the proliferation of initiatives are impressive, there have also been setbacks. For example, the United States Supreme Court in 1989 in *South Carolina v. Gathers* reaffirmed the 1987 *Booth v. Maryland* decision banning the use of victim impact statements, at least in death penalty cases. Victim impact statements represent one of the major and most promising breakthroughs of the victims' rights movement. Mandated by law in some states, they inform the sentencing judge of the physical, financial, and emotional impact of the crime on the victim or the victims' survivors so that these elements can be taken into account when reaching a sentencing decision. Thirty-five states presently allow for some form of victim participation at sentencing. The future utilization of this important element in the sentencing process is now in jeopardy, even in those cases not directly affected by the Supreme Court's decision.

The field of victimology has also grown internationally. Victim services now exist at the national level in Canada, England and Wales, the Federal Republic of Germany, France, and The Netherlands. Some states in Australia have also made impressive strides in providing assistance to victims. Community-based or volunteer organizations offer services to victims, particularly of sexual assault and domestic violence, in several countries in Europe and elsewhere. One of the difficulties faced by the victims' movement in some countries is the complacent and convenient belief that the legal and social welfare systems of the country already provide more than adequately for the needs of the victim.

The growth and importance of victimology were officially recognized at the international level in the fall of 1985 when the United Nations General Assembly adopted Resolution 40/34 and the accompanying Declaration of Basic Principles of Justice for Victims of Crime and Abuse of Power, the first major pronouncement of the United Nations on the question of victims. Another international organization, the Council of Europe, has prepared and adopted in 1983 at its Committee of Ministers level a European Convention on Compensation of Victims of Crime which is now open for signature by the member countries. The Council of Europe also prepared and adopted in 1985 a Recommendation on Assistance to Victims and the Prevention of Victimization. Recommendations of the Council of Europe are addressed by the Council's executive organ, the Committee of Ministers, to the government of the member States and contain guidelines for national legislation and administrative and judicial practice.

While victims and witnesses of crime have received the most attention, victimology can and should also be concerned with other types of victims as well, for example, victims of earthquakes, natural disasters, occupational accidents and hazards, dislocation, and famine. In fact, the common denominator of victimological work is *crisis intervention* and the short- and long-term remedies that should be made available to victims.

Current and Future Research in Victimology

Theoretical Perspectives

It is said that victimology lacks a theoretical perspective and foundation. However, it is not necessarily improper or invalid for victimology to utilize and adapt to its needs and efforts the theoretical perspectives of social work, public administration, social policy, law, and justice. Victimology may simply represent a different focus of application of theoretical insights already developed by other disciplines which are germane because of their interest in people in crisis.

People who are *vulnerable* and/or *in crisis* may indeed constitute the common denominator linking victimology with other relevant disciplines and providing a focus of research and intervention. The uniqueness of victimology may stem from its focusing on populations and crises that have been neglected in the past by more established disciplines.

As we become increasingly aware of the complexities of life in society, a *new* discipline may be justified in existing not just because it is able to claim for itself a completely new area but also because it sees new relationships and dynamics and offers an integrated approach to research and intervention that transcend existing disciplines and utilize the best that each has to offer.

Abuse of Power and Collective Victimization

Governments, police and the military, multinational corporations, medical personnel, and parents have, in different degrees, power on the very existence, future and destiny of other human beings. In many nations of the world, laws have been enacted to control and neutralize the use of these positions as weapons against those whose lives can easily be affected by the powerful. Unfortunately, laws are often disregarded or not enforced and the resulting harm is similar to behavior that would definitely be considered criminal if engaged in by anyone other than those in control of the victims.

Examples of these victimizations are abundant: unlawful human experimentation, hostage-taking, random seizure and detention, genocide, apartheid, slavery, torture, serfdom, and forced prostitution. Many are at times targeted for mistreatment and abuse because of their membership in a certain group, like the poor, women, children, minorities, the homeless, political dissenters, religious minorities, and the elderly.

Amnesty International states that governments in some 98 countries use torture to combat insurgencies or as an administrative tool. The most insidious aspect of this inhuman practice is that the torturers are not necessarily or always sadistic psychopaths but ordinary state employees carrying out a state policy. Particularly troublesome is the reported or alleged collusion and collaboration of health professionals in physical and psychological torture.

In some countries, because of the resurgence of religious fundamentalism, forms of torture like flogging, stoning, and amputation are again legal. The fact that large regions of the world are controlled by dictatorships clearly indicates that serious or wholesale disregard for human rights and dignity is widespread and affects millions of persons. The expanded powers of police and the military and their use of intimidation and detention outside of court supervision is increasing in almost all countries. Reasons given at times are that these measures are necessary to combat growing terrorism, insurgency, and drug trafficking but the reality remains that state powers are greatly increased to the detriment of civil rights and civil liberties. The recent bloody repression of the student-led democracy movement in China offers dramatic evidence of how a "people's army" can be used against the people to support and maintain the entrenched power of the oligarchy. Moreover, even in democratic societies, delays and inequities in the administration of justice represent forms of effective victimization of defendants and victims alike and of their families.

Slavery is still a flourishing trade in many areas of the world but especially in certain countries of the Middle East and Asia. In particular, women and children have been collectively victimized throughout the centuries and still are. Thousands are kidnapped and sold into prostitution and slavery and traded in remote areas of the world, at times for the pleasure and entertainment of visiting tourists from Europe, North America, the Middle East, and Japan.

In many countries, especially in the Third World, children are still sold to work in factories, brothels, and massage parlors or for adoption in foreign countries. Child labor is a fact of life in many Third World countries, from the dump pickers of Mexico City, to the carpet weavers of the Middle East, to migrant field hands in farming societies around the world. In India alone, the last official census counted 11 million children under the age of fourteen in the labor force. Studies by nongovernmental groups put the figure at 40 million or higher. Ignorance, tradition, and—above all—a crushing poverty have forced these millions of children, some as young as five years old, into the workplace. Some are virtual slaves, bonded to a farmer or handicraft artisan or small shopkeeper by parents so desperate that, in effect, they sell their children so the family can eat.

Unfortunately, children are not even safe in their own homes as the statistics on child abuse and neglect and child sexual abuse indicate. In some developing countries, newborn babies are "dumped"—killed or left to die—when no one is willing or interested in raising them. Strict government enacted and enforced practices to limit family size, especially in China, have led to charges of widespread infanticide, particularly of baby girls; forced abortion; and violations of human rights. The murder, mostly by burning, of brides in India because of greed or dissatisfaction with the dowry paid to the husband's family appears to be a larger and more serious problem than anticipated or acknowledged by officials there.

In parts of Africa and the Middle East, young women suffer another form of violence, genital mutilation. This operation, often done in a crude, painful, and septic manner, removes all or part of the external female genitalia, including the clitoris. While this practice has its roots in the male desire to control female sexuality, it is sustained today by a host of other superstitions and mistaken beliefs, including that it is required by the Koran. Others defend it as an "important African tradition." According to the World Health Organization, more than 80 million women have undergone sexual mutilation in Africa alone. In all of these instances and more, women are the target of violence and repression because of their sex. This is no random violence. The risk factor is easy to identify. It is being female.

The adverse impact that multinational corporations can have on the life and health of people around the globe has been amply demonstrated in recent examples. Multinationals can easily alter traditional nutritional habits through full-scale advertising and promotional campaigns to the detriment of the long-range needs of the populations involved. For example, the introduction of baby formula for infants in the Third World as a more advanced means of raising them than utilizing the abundant supply of mother's milk led to widespread malnutrition, intestinal diseases, and death. It was only after a worldwide campaign and boycott that the offending companies agreed to stop their lucrative but deadly practices.

Even in advanced Western nations, the concentration of agribusinesses in the hands of few and powerful multinationals has created a situation where they vertically own and control every aspect of food production from the land to the machinery to the fuel to the seed patents to the fertilizer and are thus in a position to dominate the market and dictate what and how much people shall have to eat. The potential for abuse in such a situation is great.

Collective victimization has generally been neglected as a field of study and research. More attention should be directed at the effects and impact of white collar crimes; of corporate misconduct; of abuses of power on the part of the state; and of illegal business practices. The gross and pervasive *violations of human rights* that are occurring in several areas of the world and are affecting many millions of people should become a focus of increased inquiry.

Pervasive Cultural Values

Pervasive cultural values that create a climate that is permissive or conducive to victimization should be identified, examined, and targeted for change. Violent acts reflect environments of violence. It can be said that at the foundation of many patterns of abuse of the "weak" —children, women, the elderly, the mentally retarded—is the overwhelming acceptance of violence in our society as the legitimate and necessary means of solving problems at the personal, national, and international levels. This concept of dominance/submission, controller/controlled pervades parenting, relations between the sexes and the ages, and marital patterns.

For example, the fact that society has made women into sex objects in ads and other messages explains, among other things, in the opinion of some experts, the dramatic increase of teenage rape in the United States, especially among younger teens aged thirteen and fourteen. Crime statistics show that more rapes are being committed among seventeen- and eighteen-year-olds, but even more among thirteen- and fourteen-year-olds. The April 1989 attack on a New York City Central Park jogger by a pack of youngsters as young as fourteen, drew national attention to the reported increase in juvenile attacks.

While society at large and most of the research in the field focus on the more sensational, violent, or evident forms of victimization and on the more obviously distorted values, approaches, rationalizations, and beliefs that support them, there are in our society actually more insidious, pervasive, and widespread expressions of them, although they are less visible and objectionable.

The violent and victimizing behavior that is condemned and abhorred is often only the bolder, exaggerated expression of values and beliefs actually rooted and widespread in the larger culture. For example, the diffused pedophilia that transpires in advertisements which portray grown-up women as children and vice versa with an unmistakable sexual undertone; the pervasive exploitation and commoditization of the female body in commercials and advertisements, regardless of the item offered for sale; the violence and exploitation portrayed in detail in many television programs and films; the climate of ageism and sexism which permeates much of what our society does, all express and create a climate where victimizers express in a blunt, overt, and exaggerated manner what society at large believes and practices in a more subtle or carefully disguised fashion.

While research in the more obvious forms of exploitation and violence is easier to justify, obtain funds for, and even conduct, it will be research and intervention in the arena of the diffuse and camouflaged that will effectively attack the root of the problem.

Addiction and Compulsion

A better understanding of victimizing behavior, particularly in the area of sexual assault and exploitation, may be reached through the study of addictive, compulsive, and ultimately self-destructive behavior. Efforts should be undertaken to create a framework for understanding addictive behavior and to outline a model of the relationship among cultural, social, psychological, pharmacological, and other components of addictive motivation, based on the idea that addiction is a response to socially and individually conditioned needs for specific psychophysiological or experiential states.

This model should be designed to apply equally well to all areas of repetitive and compulsive behavior. Until now this approach has been used almost exclusively to study, analyze, and attempt to explain and treat various forms of drug addiction. It should be expanded to other types of compulsive behavior including those that lead to the criminal victimization of others. It should also address the larger issue of how our society is actually designed to encourage addictive behavior, filled as it is with pervasive and intrusive messages advertising or portraying certain addictions in a positive light—for example, when the drug or behavior in question is "legal"—while sternly and hypocritically condemning others.

Even more importantly, ours is an addictive society because, in many ways, we are taught to depend on large institutions for our ideas, our morality, even our survival. Modern culture has made the media, the school, the government, the church, the military, the corporations that produce and sell products, appear to be absolutely necessary for life itself. This fosters and even justifies feelings of dependency, powerlessness, helplessness, acceptance of substance use and abuse, and widespread habit reliance.

The linkages between this wider cultural context and compulsive behavior which victimizes and exploits others should be investigated and clarified. Thus, treatment and prevention efforts will focus not only on the individual offender but also on the cultural make-up that is equally to blame for its role in aiding and abetting the offending behavior and in creating a climate conducive to it. More obviously, many would agree that the abuse of alcohol and drugs runs like a very thick thread through the fabric of criminal violence.

The glorification of violence and the sexualization of everything in our society from toothpaste to shoes to wines to automobiles to travel also play a large part in creating an addictive and compulsive environment and should be taken into account for study and action.

While some resist this approach to the study of the dynamics of sexual assault, domestic violence, and sexual abuse of children, in particular, and advocate the mandatory imposition of criminal sanctions, it is important to keep in mind that—in the long run—locking up sexual offenders and spouse abusers in the hope that they will just go away will not work. It is also important to realize that, while some offenders have no real moral conflict between their sexual or violent desires and their personal convictions, others are very tortured by the fact that they are, for example, sexually attracted to children. For them it is a constant struggle to fight off temptation. At the same time, every person in prison because of such offense is an example of the failure of the fear of incarceration to deter.

It is essential that through research, discussion, and public education we look at these problems with a realistic and dispassionate attitude, stripping away the fear, prejudice, and loathing that often and quite understandably accompany their consideration and that we at least distinguish between political agendas fueled by predetermined objectives (and therefore uncompromising and narrowly focused) and a genuine and compassionate attempt at a fuller understanding of the dynamics at work here. Presently, the stigma that is attached particularly to the sexual abuse of children and that affects not only the offenders but also the victims and their families makes it very difficult to engage in open and dispassionate research and discussion addressing victims *and* offenders. This also stands in the way of developing and experimenting with treatment models.

Finally, one more cogent reason why such an approach is crucial is found in the often-mentioned fact that some of the offenders of today were victims yesterday and that some of today's victims will be tomorrow's offenders. If we truly believe and accept this fact, then we should be ready to follow it to its ultimate conclusions and therefore look at offenders in a different light because they, too, are or were victims.

Victims and Criminal Justice Reform

This approach—applicable to all types of victimization—would also be extremely useful in dispelling the perception that to be concerned about the victims entails an "offender be damned" attitude; that victimology is the antithesis of an enlightened and progressive movement in criminal justice, particularly corrections; and that victimologists want to dismantle reforms recently introduced in the administration of justice. It is true, of course, that some with a "right wing" political agenda have been exploiting victimological concerns for exactly those reasons. However, it does not have to be that way. Actually, it *cannot* be that way. Genuine victimology is perfectly compatible with and supports the efforts aimed at humanizing and improving the criminal justice system because it recognizes that the line distinguishing the victim from the offender is often blurred; that the scenarios of victimization are not starkly drawn in black and white; that offending behaviors are often the consequences of a normalization process steeped deep in an attempt to make sense of a nightmarish victimization experience.

In some cases more than others, of course, it is difficult to tell who is the victim and who is the offender. Certainly, the physical actions, the blows, the violence, the sexual assault, the improper fondling are carried out by one person while the other is at the receiving end but to stop there in the analysis of the situation is to offer only a "first impression" and at times a self-serving view of what is truly occurring.

The appearances indeed confirm the "black-and-white" approach but if we look deeper we may find a different reality. In this tragic ballet of fear, victimization, and exploitation both actors may be acting out parts they both learned as victims while assuming different roles as dictated by wider cultural beliefs. To approach one as the all-evil offender which deserves only punishment and the other as the all-innocent victim which only needs vindication is just too easy. Victimology should have reached by now a sufficient level of sophistication and assuredness to be able to reveal the complexity of the situation and to point the way to a truly healing process that encompasses both the victim and the victimizer.

To say that the offender needs treatment based on understanding and compassion is not to be "soft on crime"; to say that the victim needs treatment as well, for example, to snap out of self-destructive patterns, is not "blaming the victim." Those who maintain that it is so, may be more concerned about defending an ideological position than about truly serving the victim.

The "black-and-white" approach has been undeniably useful in the initial stages of the process of recognizing the reality and dynamics of victimization. At that point, it was important to "draw the line" so that society could be confronted with what had been overlooked and neglected for too long. The shock and outrage felt by those active in the field when they realized the depth and seriousness of the problem understandably contributed to this view of the problem. Political agendas also require that issues be simplified, that the right side be clearly distinguishable from the wrong side, and that battle lines be drawn. In the world of politics, there is no time or place for nuances, qualifiers, and niceties. However, the scholarly search for understanding should take responsibility for approaching the problem as a complex reality that defies easy description and solutions.

Victims' Wants and Needs

Another area needing more attention and effort is research directed at what victims want and need. Some feel that in this area the field in certain instances may be working under a set of assumptions and beliefs influenced by differing political and value orientations that do not necessarily reflect the actual desires and needs of victims.

Also, in order to combat society's pervasive apathy, prejudice, and outright hostility, there has been insistence that victims be assumed to be totally innocent, inherently good, with high standards of morality and civic duty. Some feel that this is an unrealistic and ultimately patronizing portrayal of victims of crime not unlike the "noble savage" stereotypes of colonial times or the "child savers" approach to solving juvenile delinquency.

The question raised here is that what victims really want or need may not necessarily be what people in the field assume it is, however disappointing this realization may be. Class, cultural, educational, and racial differences may play a part in creating different understandings and expectations.

Unrealistic expectations of the needs and wants of victims may also lead to the possible rejection of the needy victim who does not meet the preconceived notions of what he or she should feel, believe and want. While the concept of "deserving" victim has generally been attributed to the society that creates or supports victimization and then sits in judgment of the victim, those coming to the rescue of the victim may also have a preconceived notion of who deserves help and assistance. In this case, the victim would lose again but this time at the hand of those who are ostensibly there to help.

The need to guard against victim services operating under a set of values that may not reflect the true needs and desires of victims makes it important to carefully study this overall question, particularly in light of the currently increasing trend to institutionalize services. This will inevitably lead to the development of a bureaucracy that relies heavily on rules and regulations to screen potential clients against preconceived standards and on the basis of a pre-set allocation of resources.

International Contributions to the Field

The main purpose of this book is to bring together under one cover and to arrange coherently current and representative contributions in research, prevention, treatment, and public policy. The contributions for this volume, originally presented at a World Congress of Victimology, were especially selected because their authors were able to present their own ideas, research, or practical knowledge in a cogent and interesting way and also to address some of the more urgent and representative issues facing the field today. The book has been divided into three parts:

I. Research Findings
II. Prevention and Treatment
III. Public Policy

The book has been designed to provide a balance between practical and theoretical issues and concerns and to offer a sample of international perspectives and approaches. This way, the book will constitute a truly positive contribution to the development of the field. It will also be useful and appealing to students preparing for professional careers (e.g., in law, social work, administration of justice, or mental health fields) and to those already working in those fields.

The ultimate goal of all work in criminology, victimology, and related sciences is the establishment of a caring, fair, and just society. A society without violence, oppression, and suffering should be the ultimate goal of the process of social change generated by our concern for victims of crime.

The various facets of victimization emphasized by different groups are but variations on the same theme: a fundamental lack of understanding and appreciation of the commonality of our humanity, of what truly makes us human, of the bonds that support and nourish us. Patriarchy, sexism, machismo, ageism, and racism are different attempts to establish hierarchies; to inflate and exploit the importance of superficial differences; to mask one's weakness by denigrating others; to deny our interdependence and mutual linkages; to subdue, oppress, and take advantage of those conveniently declared to be inferior.

Thanks to the courage and dedication of reformers, feminists, scholars, and victims themselves, victims' voices are beginning to be heard. They certainly deserve to be. The work completed to date on various fronts has already had considerable impact and borne promising fruit. It is essential as we scan the future and chart the course for the decades ahead, that we maintain the momentum and forge onward towards a society without fear, violence, and oppression.

The victim movement holds great promise as a force of genuine change in society's attitudes and patterns of caring for its members. The publication of this volume is intended to be a useful contribution to help it gain momentum, reach its full potential, and become an integral part of the values, beliefs, and policies of our contemporary society.

This volume would not have been possible without the generous cooperation and commitment of its 36 contributors who took active part in the World Congress of Victimology and then prepared their presentations for publication. They have certainly earned the gratitude of the editor and of the readers for their willingness to share their work and to significantly contribute to the development of victimology through the publication of this anthology.

Part I

Research Findings

Introduction to Part I

While effective policymaking requires a background of knowledge about crime, research is likely to make a direct contribution to policy only if it concentrates on those causal factors which can be affected by administrative or legislative action. *Major topics* that can be identified under this perspective as having high priority for future study and research are:

- factors making people vulnerable to victimization
- the impact of crime on victims
- perceptions of crime seriousness
- fear of crime
- victims' experiences with the police
- short-term and long-term needs of the victims
- preparedness to participate in community crime prevention
- victims' needs for support schemes
- and the potential for victim-offender mediation and reparation programs.

One of these topics—*the impact of crime on victims*—reflects the growing awareness of researchers and practitioners of the psychological harm victims can suffer as a result of a criminal event. Crime victimization has traditionally been seen as a temporary experience of physical injury that is followed by relief and recovery. Society is finally beginning to recognize that this simplistic characterization is inaccurate. Psychological effects can be profound and long-lasting. However, little is known about the psychological responses to victimization or about the processes of secondary victimization sustained during the investigatory and judicial process and even at the hand of well-meaning doctors, friends, counselors, and clergy.

Several chapters in Part I address the issues of the *immediate and long-term effects of criminal victimization* and of the *response to the victim* by various professionals. However, the focus is expanded to *include natural and environmental disasters* as having similar impact on their victims. Today's worldwide concern about the looming environmental crisis is addressed by two selections which expand the traditional definition of victimization.

M. Jean Parks (chapter 3) reports on her study of rape victims' perceptions of long-term effects three or more years post-rape. Individual interviews focused on changes each victim perceived in herself as a result of the rape, particularly in the area of her relationships with men.

From the themes presented by the victims, a two-dimensional category system was derived which elucidates the nature of the changes they perceived. The similarities between the subjects' statements and David Shapiro's description of the paranoid style are discussed. The subjects also described their perceptions of men and of themselves in relation to men, using the Interpersonal Check List.

The victims and an undergraduate comparison group held common views of males as dominant, powerful, and aggressive. The victims differed from the comparison group in seeing themselves as less affiliative in relation to men. The victims' highest score on the SCL-90-R was on the Depression dimension. Clinical implications are discussed.

Helen W. Ross (chapter 11) interviewed handicapped persons who reported victimization in order to learn the unique problems posed by their victimization. The crimes included sexual molestation, fraud, larceny, and burglary. The Cambridge Victim Survey was used for the collection of the data.

Ranjana S. Jain (chapter 9) presents the results of a domestic violence study conducted in India. She highlights the different patterns of violence and victimization experienced or inflicted by males and females and stresses the factors and dynamics specific to Indian culture that impact family violence.

Bhanuprasad Pandya (chapter 15) takes a historical approach to examine in depth two major forms of victimization that have existed for centuries and still survive in India: the discrimination against Harijans and the dowry deaths. Their impact not only on their direct victims but also on society at large is examined as well.

Sarah R. Stanley (chapter 4) reminds us that in order to understand the issues and needs of the sexually molested victim we need to know normal child and adolescent development. The developmental issues for the molested child may differ greatly from chronological age expectations. A review of the general principles of development is presented. Physical and cognitive growth patterns with emphasis on perception, memory and language processes are illustrated.

Psychological and social stages are delineated from infancy through adolescence using an adaptation of Claire Fagin's work. Direct application to the management of cases of young victims of sexual molestation is made. General coping and adaptive behaviors of abused children are also explored.

Whether one comes from an investigative or clinical perspective, it is important to note that the child is not a passive being who is molded entirely by the environment. Understanding the internal operations of a child's thinking and communication abilities will promote more accurate assessments and facilitate advocacy for the child and the adolescent victim.

Rhoda Estep (chapter 2) compares data on crime victims appearing on prime time television between 1976 and 1981 with the images projected by soap operas in the same time period. Television's depictions are then contrasted with the profile obtained from the official records. Major discrepancies uncovered involve four basic demographic dimensions: race, class, age, and gender. In both time periods, there is an overrepresentation of white, middle-class, and middle-aged individuals as victims.

Soap operas have consistently portrayed murder and robbery victims as female. In contrast, until 1981, the most common prime time crime victim is inevitably male. Thus, the gender of the victim of murder and robbery has also recently emerged as a major discrepancy between real-life and televised portrayals of violence.

Considerable evidence is also accumulating that people who consume large quantities of mass media experience a heightened sense of being victimized or at risk. Estep reviews studies that provide this evidence and also two recent studies establishing that crime news can have an effect similar to entertainment television. Although the impact here is not due to actual but to vicarious victimization, it is nonetheless a real effect.

Frank Henry and **Susanne Chomicki** (chapter 6) address the long term results of a more subtle but no less real form of victimization: violence against children on the part of the pharmaceutical industry through the marketing and sale of poorly tested or known harmful drugs.

They examine the drug industry's role as chief educator of the medical profession on drug use and show how profit maximization has induced drug companies to use this position to promote a variety of inadequately tested drugs and also drugs whose harmful effects were well known before marketing.

The results have been disease, injury, and death for thousands of children in developed and underdeveloped areas of the world.

Stephen R. Couch and **J. Stephen Kroll-Smith** (chapter 13) contrast the patterns of victimization present in immediate impact natural disasters to those in long-term or chronic technological disasters. In the first type of catastrophe, physical damage to persons and property is clear. Victims and non-victims alike agree upon what happened and generally on what should be done to recover and rebuild. A "therapeutic community" forms by which the community draws together to aid the victims. The response of the government and of private agencies is victim oriented, being directed toward alleviating physical and emotional suffering and rebuilding damaged physical structures.

Conversely, the patterns of victimization associated with chronic technological disasters are much more ambiguous. The extent of physical injury, if any, is generally unclear, as is damage to physical property. Conflict also develops over who should be labeled a "victim." Agency response tends to be agent oriented, attempting to slow or stop the advance of the disaster agent itself rather than ameliorate the suffering of the victim population. Arguments over technical scientific questions on how to deal with the disaster agent increase conflict on several fronts. The most deleterious effect is the creation of a community in social turmoil in which the psychological stress of community conflict is sometimes greater than the stress caused by the disaster agent itself. The implications of this difficult situation for social service professionals are discussed.

Knowlton W. Johnson, Gerald Hutchins, and **Jim Phifer** (chapter 14) at the onset state that victims touched by natural or man-made disasters have been the subject of considerable study in recent years, but that there is still little evidence that this research has been beneficial to disaster victims.

To correct the situation, they propose a prototype disaster impact monitoring system (DIMS) that would generate information on a continuous basis which can be used by emergency managers to mitigate the short-term and long-term effects of disasters.

The conceptual discussion of the proposed system focused on the victims' quality of life as it might be affected by disaster stressors and environmental factors. In addition, implementation aspects of the model, including data collection, storage, and retrieval are discussed, with attention given to the results of a national survey of federal and state emergency agencies.

Analysis and reporting features of the model are also discussed. The highlight of the chapter is the concluding discussion of a paradigm which presents the prototype monitoring system in its entirety.

How victims react to their victimization and how various agencies and professionals in society respond to them is also an important area for research in order to more fully understand the dynamics of victimization and society's response to it. **Edward W. Gondolf, Ellen Fisher,** and **J. Richard McFerron** (chapter 10) studied the helpseeking behavior of battered women. They analyzed the intake and exit interviews of over 6,000 battered women who received shelter in Texas between 1983 and 1985. A comparison with previous battered women studies shows the Texas sample to have a greater percentage of minority, undereducated,

and low-income women. These battered women also received more life-threatening abuse.

The frequencies of four helpseeking variables show women to assertively respond to their batterers' abuse and use a variety of shelter services. Correlation matrices show that income, number of children, the severity of the abuse, and shelters services influence helpseeking behavior.

The results lend support to the survivor strategy hypothesis rather than the learned helplessness hypothesis, and demonstrate the important role of shelter in furthering helpseeking.

Sandra M. Stith (chapter 7) examined the relationship between the male police officer's individual and family characteristics and his responsiveness to female victims of domestic violence. Specific variables that were considered included the police officer's age and education; level of sex-role egalitarianism; reported level of stressful life events; attitude toward marital violence; and method of handling conflict in his own family. The results of this investigation emphasize the importance of the predictor variables in impacting police response.

Seth C. Kalichman and **Mary E. Craig** (chapter 5) investigated mental health professionals' patterns of responsibility attribution for incestuous abuse and their tendency to report incest cases. The results of their study indicate sex differences in clinicians' incest responsibility attribution to both daughter-victims and mothers in father-daughter incest families.

Responsibility attribution to the father and daughter was found to be a function of the victims' age: fathers abusing younger victims were blamed more, while the victim was blamed less. Also 40 percent of non-licensed clinicians were not aware of reporting laws and 25 percent indicated they would not report incest. The authors discuss their results with reference to the effectiveness of mandatory reporting laws.

Reactions to external factors that may lead to justifying and inflicting victimization in the family are examined by **Ronelle Pretorius** (chapter 8). Until recently, family murder was an unknown and exceptionally infrequent phenomenon in South Africa. The author argues that the realities of the war on South Africa's border, urban terrorism, political unrest, disinvestment and unemployment which began affecting whites since the 1980s as well as fear of sociopolitical change (Black majority rule) have created in South Africa a climate of hopelessness, insecurity, and fear among whites that may explain the dramatic increase of family murders especially among the Afrikaans-speaking whites.

Finally, **Irving Kaufman** (chapter 12) analyzes a major problem in our culture that results in severe victimization: arson. He states that arson is associated with an extraordinarily large and conflicting range of fantasies encompassing life, death, the most holy and the most profane.

2

Televised Victims of Murder and Robbery: Prime Time versus Soap Opera Portrayals

Rhoda Estep
California State University, Stanislaus

This study compares data on crime victims appearing on prime time television between 1976 and 1981 with the images projected by soap operas in the same time period. Television's depictions are then contrasted with the profile obtained from official records. Major discrepancies uncovered involve four basic demographic dimensions: race, class, age, and gender. In both time periods, there is an overrepresentation of white, middle-class individuals as victims. Also, while real-life victims are typically young, their televised counterparts tend to be middle-aged. Soap operas have consistently portrayed murder and robbery victims as female; in contrast, until 1981, the most common prime time crime victim was inevitably male. Thus, the gender of the victim of murder and robbery has also recently emerged as a major discrepancy between real-life and televised portrayals of crime.

Considerable evidence is accumulating that people who consume large quantities of the mass media experience a heightened sense of being victimized. Gerbner (1977) was one of the first to document that heavy TV viewers tend to inflate the level of violence and are more likely to believe in the concept of a "mean world." As a consequence, heavy television viewers are more wary of strangers (Karmen, 1984). This exaggerated fear of being victimized has been found even among residents of relatively safe communities (Jaehnig et al., 1981).

Two recent studies establish that crime news can have an effect similar to that of entertainment TV. An experimental approach to studying the impact of crime news (Wakshlag et al., 1983) found that those most apprehensive about being victimized also found crime news to be extremely exciting, possibly due to some type of "vicarious victimization" (Elias 1986, 43). From a large representative sample of Syracuse adults, researchers (Einsiedel et al., 1984) documented that those persons who had greater exposure to crime news also feared being victimized more. This relationship held even when controlling for the amount of crime experience. However, when Gerbner and colleagues (1980) controlled for age, only older viewers believed that their age group was the most victimized. In contrast, this media message did not generate a similar perception among young and middle-aged viewers. Overall, then, knowing how the media portrays crime and its victims is essential in order to assess the impact of the media's message.

Both newspapers and television have been subject to analyses of their crime content. There is widespread consensus that both news and entertainment concentrate on murder and other serious crimes involving victims, such as robbery and assault, and virtually ignore property crime (Dominick, 1973; Einsiedel et al., 1984; Mawby and Brown, 1984; Sherizen, 1978). With respect to content analyses of newspapers, there is also some agreement on the characteristics of victims. In systematically examining a year's coverage of crime by the *Chicago Tribune*, Graber (1980) reported that the majority of crime victims were white males under the age of twenty-five. Similarly, Pritchard (1985) found that homicides allegedly committed by blacks or Hispanics were covered much less extensively than those done by whites in Milwaukee's newspapers. In a well-done study focusing on eight national newspapers in Britain, Mawby and Brown (1984) document that females, young people, and those with high status were overrepresented as victims. They also maintain that about twice as many negative as positive portrayals were found in British newspapers. Negative or unsympathetic images consisted mainly of blaming the victim, implying that they precipitated the attack. This overemphasis on high status and victim blaming has been found in the *L.A. Times*' coverage of female victims as well (Estep, 1982).

In studying television images of victims, there is little doubt that Gerbner and colleagues (1977, 1978, 1979, 1980) have been the front-runners. Gerbner's method of reporting (1977) has been to calculate a "victimization ratio." The ratio is computed by comparing the number of violent characters to the number of victims in a variety of demographic categories. For the most part, Gerbner and associates (1977, 1978, 1979, 1980) discuss victimization ratios without differentiating prime time television from children's programs on the weekends such as cartoons. One exception is Gerbner and Signorielli's 1979 report based on ten years' study of prime time television. Based on the victimization ratios found, they conclude "If and when involved in violence, women and minorities, and especially young and old as well as minority women characters, are more vulnerable than their majority counterparts" (p. 26). Tedesco (1974) agrees with Gerbner and Signorielli by reporting that more women than men are killed in their study of dramatic programs in prime time. There is, however, considerable dissent from Gerbner's overall findings expressed by other researchers. Lowery and DeFleur (1983) maintain that middle-aged men, not women, and nonwhites are most likely to be killed. Several others (Cumberbatch and Beardsworth, 1976; Dominick, 1973; Lemon, 1977; Schneider, 1982) argue that in crime dramas, regardless of whether in suspect or victim roles, white, middle-aged, middle-class men predominate.

These contradictory findings can possibly be explained by a closer look at Gerbner's method of reporting via "victimization rates." As Comstock and colleagues (1978) have commented, victimization ratios are basically pretty arbitrary. They fail to give the actual number or percentage of persons who are victims in any one demographic category and, thus prohibit any true comparison between groups. Moreover, Gerbner divides those killed from those hurt but never separately analyzes victims of different crimes. To further add to the confusion, Gerbner almost always fails to compare televised victims with estimates of victims in real life. For example, he reiterates that young boys have a high rate of victimization on TV. If these young boys were victims of violent crimes, then such a portrayal is both accurate and realistic ("Teens Face More Crime," 1987). Thus, even though Gerbner has done extensive studies on televised victims, his analysis seriously limits any conclusions that can be drawn about victims on television. This study proposes to help fill the gap by comparing televised victims of murder and robbery on both prime time and daytime soap operas with official estimates of victimization.

Methodology

With respect to prime time television, three television seasons were sampled over a period of five years: 1976–1977, 1978–1979, and 1980–1981. Sampling in the first two seasons was purposive, focusing on prime time (8–11 p.m., E.S.T.) programs that dealt with either murder or robbery. In the third season, a complete or saturation sample for all prime time programs on the three main commercial networks in November 1980 was completed.

The content of each program featuring a murder or robbery was analyzed. Any person receiving the direct impact of these crimes was classified as a victim. Where it was possible, the victims' gender, race, age, and social class were coded. Intercoder reliability coefficients (Holsti, 1969, pp. 139–140) were calculated for the second and third seasons. All coefficients surpassed .75 with the highest ratio of agreements found for gender and race, followed by class and age.

A different methodology was employed to capture crime victims on soap operas. The rationale for the switch was due to the nature of crime on soap operas. While prime time crime usually takes a single episode for resolution, soap opera crimes may take months or even years to end. In order to obtain information on soap opera crime and its victims, 315 soap opera viewers were interviewed. Like most soap opera viewers, the sample was composed mainly of females (84%) and whites (85%). On the average, these respondents had watched between two and three soap operas for over seven years. They produced data on the 12 most popular soap operas in proportions similar to those indicated by Nielsen (Cantor and Pingree, 1983).

The information from the respondents provided details on 80 murders and 78 thefts, spread over an eight-year period, between 1977 and 1984. Reliability coefficients were again calculated, finding .78 overall for murder and .76 for robbery. Like prime time, the highest level of agreements between interviewers' accounts were found for race and gender of the victims.

In order to compare television with real-life victims, the Federal Bureau of Investigation's (FBI) Uniform Crime Report for murder and victimization studies for robbery and other theft were used. Despite acknowledged difficulties with official sources of information (Booth et al., 1977; Kitsuse and Cicourel, 1963), they are still very accurate for murder because of its high rate of reporting. Victimization studies on robbery were used to compare with prime time crime. Although median years were used in two of the three comparisons, it can be noted that these types of statistics rarely demonstrate even one or two percent differences from year to year. Because soap opera respondents often confused robbery with other types of theft, a combination of robbery, burglary and larceny was constructed to compare with soap opera victims of theft.

Findings

In the first two seasons of prime time television sampled, the profile of the average murder victim is similar—a white, middle-class man in his mid-thirties (see Table 2.1). However, the predominant gender of the murder victim changed to female in the '80–'81 prime time television season. The image of the murder victim in soaps corresponds

Table 2.1

Murder Victims of Murder and Robbery: Prime Time Versus Soap Opera Portrayals

		Prime Time Television			Daytime TV Serials	Official Records*
		1976–1977 (n=44)	1978–1979 (n=55)	1980–1981 (n=17)	1977–1984 (n=80)	1981 (n=27, 860)
GENDER	Male	70%	76%	35%	46%	77%
	Female	30%	24%	65%	49%***	23%
RACE	White	84%	73%	71%	94%	53%
	Black	2%	9%	18%	0%	42%
	Other	5%	13%	12%	0%	1%
	Unknown	9%	5%	0%	6%	3%
AGE	Average	37 years	35 years	36 years	36 years	35 years
CLASS	Average	Middle	Middle	Middle	Middle	Lower**

* F.B.I.'s Uniform Crime Report

** Since no national data are collected on the socioeconomic status of murder victims, this designation is based on other studies, cf. Wolfgang, 1958; Hindelang, 1978; Hindelang et al., 1979.

*** Percentages do not total 100% due to respondent disagreement five percent of the time.

closely to prime time in three dimensions—race, age, and class. Unlike prime time, however, about half of all murder victims on soaps are females. While this may be partially explained by the fact that half of the actors on soaps are female (Downing, 1974), it vastly overrepresents the number of females victimized by murder. If prime time continues the latest trend studied here, these hours will also feature more females killed than official records indicate.

However, the most systematic discrepancy between television and official records is the race of the victim. While prime time and especially daytime soaps portray victims as being white at least three-quarters of the time, official records indicate that close to half of all those murdered in the United States are nonwhite. The other consistent difference in television and real life is the murder victim's social class. As found in previous studies (Dominick, 1973; Schneider, 1982), television depicts members of the middle class at most risk of being killed. Sociological studies of homicide (Hindelang, 1978; Hindelang et al., 1979; Wolfgang, 1958) have consistently documented the lower-class nature of the crime. With respect to the age of murder victims, both television and official sources place the victim in their mid-thirties.

As found with murder, the characteristics of a robbery victim on prime time television have been relatively constant between 1976 and 1981. The average prime time robbery victim is a white, middle-class man around forty (see Table 2.2). One significant trend is a steady decrease in the age of the robbery victim, from a high of 48 in the first season sampled to a low of 34 in the last season sampled.

In contrast, victimization studies reveal the person who is usually robbed to be a black, lower-class male in his early teens. The only characteristic agreed upon by prime time television and official records is the victim's gender—male. In all other categories, prime time television diverges from the official image. In regard to race, prime time TV has over three times as many robbery victims being white as official records would indicate. Also, the class of a robbery victim in reality would be much lower than indicated by evening television programs. Finally, young teens, not forty-year-old adults, are most commonly at risk for being robbed.

Daytime television's victim of theft is almost always white, usually upper-middle class and around forty (see Table 2.3). Victims of theft on soap operas are equally as likely to be male as female. The official image

Table 2.2

Robbery Victims: A Comparison of Prime Time TV and Official Records

		Prime Time Television			Official Records*	
		1976–1977 (n=17)	1978–1979 (n=11)	1980–1981 (n=20)	1977	
GENDER	Male	71%	64%	65%	46%	(8.7/1000)
	Female	29%	36%	35%	32%	(4.0/1000)
RACE	White	82%	82%	90%	24%	(5.4/1000)
	Black	6%	0%	10%	58%	(13.0/1000)
	Other	0%	18%	0%	18%	(4.1/1000)
	Unknown	12%	0%	0%	—	—
AGE	Average	48 years	45 years	34 years	12–15	(10.9/1000)
CLASS	Average	Middle	Mid/Upper	Middle	Middle	Lower

* *Criminal Victimization in the United States, 1977: A National Crime Survey Report*

Table 2.3

Victims of Theft: A Comparison of Daytime TV Serials and Official Records

		Daytime TV Serials* 1977–1984 (n=107)	Official Records** 1980	
GENDER	Male	50%	55%	(108.1/1000)
	Female	50%	45%	(89.1/1000)
	Unknown	1%	—	—
RACE	White	97%	33%	(98.0/1000)
	Black	2%	34%	(99.6/1000)
	Other	0%	33%	(96.4/1000)
	Unknown	1%	—	—
AGE	Average	40 years	28 years	
CLASS	Average	Upper-Middle	Middle (burglary) Middle (larency) Lower (Robbery)	

* In asking the question about most memorable robbery in a soap opera, some respondents replied by giving burglaries or larencies rather than robberies. Consequently, this category represents three types of theft rather than robbery by itself.

** Based on data from *Criminal Victimization in the United States*, 1977.

derived from victimization studies differs from daytime television serials in three of the four categories studied. The only similarity is the gender of theft victims. Like daytime television, official records also show a pretty even split between males and females. Like prime time television, daytime serials cast three times as many whites in the role of theft victim as warranted by official sources, which indicate that two-thirds of all theft victims are nonwhite. In reality, victims of theft are about 12 years younger than soaps would suggest. Finally, the victims of theft on soaps are more wealthy than their real-life counterparts.

Discussion

In comparing television's images of both murder and robbery victims with official sources, conflicting evidence has been uncovered on each of the four demographic characteristics studied. First, whites are vastly overrepresented as both murder and robbery victims on television. Second, the average TV victim, whether due to murder or theft, is shown as wealthier than they are in real life. Third, while the age of the average murder suspect on television agrees with official estimates, the average robbery victims on television is portrayed as being much older than s/he is in real life. Fourth, with respect to televised victims of theft, gender representations correspond rather closely to official figures. However, females on soap operas and more recently in prime time programming as well are killed more frequently than warranted according to official sources.

Typical of the trend of feminizing the victim was a "Charlie's Angels" episode appearing during the prime time sample period. The plot revolved around a college professor whose Robert Redford looks predisposed his female students to get a "crush" on him. Charlie's Angels assumed undercover roles following the disappearance of two college coeds, both of whom were members of his class. Not surprisingly, the professor was fingered when he attempted to kidnap one of the Angels. This story illustrates Mawby and Brown's (1984) earlier finding of a negative image of the victim. The coeds, it is implied, are at fault for not instinctively distrusting the motives of such a good-looking teacher. The plot also exemplifies a cursory look at certain victims. For example, as the story unfolds, it is revealed that at the professor's former university, two girls were kidnapped and taken out of the country. Such coverage of victims makes them "invisible" as Sherizen (1978) discovered in his study of four major Chicago newspapers. In addition, multiple victims given little, if any, attention may understate the victim's plight (Karmen, 1984).

Another point illustrated by this episode as well as the statistical findings is the suggestion that motivation for crime stems from individual decisions of good and evil. Murdock and Golding maintain that the media's image of violence may immobilize the public for it suggests "a nonpolitical explanation which minimizes societal factors" (as cited in Sherizen, 1978, p. 207). The fact that middle-class white males are television's typical victims of serious, violent crimes means the public must resort to some type of psychological explanation of crime (Estep and Macdonald, 1983). Instead, if televised victims more often resembled official images—poor, black and young—then social causes of strife, such as unemployment and poverty, would be more logical explanations for theft and blood.

Finally, as found in many other previous media studies (Dominick, 1973; Einsiedel et al., 1983; Mawby and Brown, 1984; Sherizen, 1978), entertainment television appears to be fixated on the most violent crimes with victims. Murders frequently feature multiple victims and people who are robbed are also often killed. As Karmen (1984) has pointed out, an overemphasis on homicide or robbery victims who are killed may lead the public to overestimate the risk of becoming a victim.

In an earlier study, half of all the rapes reported in the *L.A. Times* were found to end in death as opposed to less than one percent of all rapes reported to the police (Estep, 1982). The media's overconcentration on murder and its misrepresentation of the circumstances involved may not only create unnecessary alarm in consumers but also ill prepare them to cope with crime as it typically occurs.

Bibliography

Booth, A., D. R. Johnson, and H. M. Choldin

1977 "Correlates of City Crime Rates: Victimization Surveys Versus Official Statistics." *Social Problems,* 25: 187–197.

Cantor, Muriel G., and S. Pingree

1983 *The Soap Opera*. Beverly Hills, CA: Sage.

Comstock, George, Steven Chaffee, Natan Katzman, Maxwell McCombs, and Donald Roberts.

1978 *Television and Human Behavior.* New York: Columbia University.

Cumberbatch, Guy, and Alan Beardsworth

1976 "Criminals, Victims and Mass Communications." In E. Viano, ed. *Victims and Society*. Washington, DC: Visage Press.

Dominick, Joseph R.

1973 "Crime and Law Enforcement on Prime-Time Television." *Public Opinion Quarterly,* 37: 241–250.

Downing, M.

1974 "Heroine of the Daytime Serial." *Journal of Communication,* 24(2): 130–137.

Einsiedel, Edna F., Kandice L. Salomone and Frederick P. Schneider

1984 "Crime: Effects of Media Exposure and Personal Experience on Issue Salience." *Journalism Quarterly,* 61(1): 131–136.

Elias, Robert

1986 *The Politics of Victimization: Victims, Victimology, and Human Rights*. New York: Oxford University Press.

Estep, Rhoda

1982 "Women's Roles in Crime as Depicted by Television and Newspapers." *Journal of Popular Culture,* Winter: 151–156.

Estep, Rhoda, and Patrick T. Macdonald

1983 "How Prime Time Crime Evolved on TV, 1976–1981." *Journalism Quarterly,* 60: 293–300.

Gerbner, George, Larry Gross, Michael F. Eleey, Marilyn Jackson-Beeck, Suzanne Jeffries-Fox, and Nancy Signorielli

1977 "TV Violence Profile No. 8: The Highlights." *Journal of Communication,* Spring: 171–180.

Gerbner, George, Larry Gross, Marilyn Jackson-Beeck, Suzanne Jeffries-Fox, and Nancy Signorielli

1978 "Cultural Indicators: Violence Profile No. 9." *Journal of Communication,* Summer: 176–207.

Gerbner, George, Larry Gross, Nancy Signorielli, Michael Morgan, and Marilyn Jackson-Beeck

1979 "The Demonstration of Power: Violence Profile No. 10," *Journal of Communication,* Summer: 177–196.

Gerbner, George, and Nancy Signorielli

1979 *Women and Minorities in Television Drama, 1969–1978.* Philadelphia, PA: University of Pennsylvania, The Annenberg School of Communications.

Gerbner, George, Larry Gross, Michael Morgan, and Nancy Signorielli

1980 "The 'Mainstreaming' of America: Violence Profile No. 11." *Journal of Communication,* Summer: 10–29.

Graber, Doris A.

1980 *Crime News and the Public.* New York: Praeger.

Hindelang, Michael J.

1978 "Race and Involvement in Common Law Personal Crimes." *American Sociological Review,* 43: 93–109.

Hindelang, Michael J., Thomas Hirschi, and J. G. Weis

1978 "Correlates of Delinquency: The Illusion of Discrepancy Between Self-Report and Official Measures." *American Sociological Review,* 44: 995-1014.

Holsti, Ole R.

1969 *Content Analysis for the Social Sciences and Humanities.* Reading, MA: Addison-Wesley.

Jaehnig, Walter B., David H. Weaver, and Frederick Fico

1981 "Reporting Crime and Fearing Crime in Three Communities." *Journal of Communication,* 31: 88-96.

Karmen, Andrew

1984 *Crime Victims: An Introduction to Victimology.* Monterey, CA: Brooks/Cole.

Kitsuse, John I., and Aaron V. Cicourel
1963 "A Note on the Uses of Official Statistics." *Social Problems,* 11: 131–139.

Lemon, Judith
1977 "Women and Blacks on Prime-Time Television." *Journal of Communication,* 27: 70–79.

Lowery, Shearon, and Melvin L. DeFleur
1983 *Milestones in Mass Communication Research: Media Effects.* New York: Longman.

Mawby, Rob I., and Judith Brown
1984 "Newspaper Images of the Victim: A British Study." *Victimology,* 9(1): 82–94.

Pritchard, David
1985 "Race, Homicide, and Newspapers." *Journalism Quarterly,* 62(3): 500–507.

Schneider, Ursula
1982 "The Presentation of Victims of Crime in Television Movies Documentaries." In Hans Joachim Schneider, ed. *The Victim in International Perspective.* Berlin: Walter de Gruyter.

Sherizen, Sanford
1979 "Social Creation of Crime News: All the News Fitted to Print." In Charles Winick, ed. *Deviance and Mass Media.* Beverly Hills, CA: Sage, pp. 203–224.

Tedesco, Nancy S.
1974 "Patterns in Prime Time." *Journal of Communication,* 24: 119–123.

"Teens Face More Crime"
1987 *NCTV News,* 9(1–2): 3.

Wakshlag, Jacob J., Leonard Bart, John Dudley, Gary Groth, John McCutcheon, and Cheryl Rolla
1983 "Viewer Apprehension about Victimization and Crime Drama Programs." *Communication Research,* 10(2): 195–217.

Wolfgang, Marvin E.
1958 *Patterns of Criminal Homicide.* Philadelphia, PA: University of Pennsylvania Press.

3

Rape Victims' Perceptions of Long-Term Effects Three or More Years Post-Rape

M. Jean Parks
Trinity University

To contribute to the knowledge of long-term effects of rape, ten women who had been raped three or more years earlier participated in this study. Individual interviews focused on changes each victim perceived in herself as a result of the rape, particularly in the area of her relationships with men. From the themes presented by the victims, a two-dimensional category system was derived which elucidates the nature of the changes they perceived. The similarities between the subjects' statements and David Shapiro's description of the paranoid style are discussed. The subjects also described their perceptions of men and of themselves in relation to men, using the Interpersonal Check List. The victims and an undergraduate comparison group held common views of males as dominant, powerful, and aggressive. The victims differed from the comparison group in seeing themselves as less affiliative in relation to men. The victims' highest score on the SCL-90-R was on the Depression dimension. Clinical implications are discussed.

Rape Victims' Perceptions of Long-Term Effects Three or More Years Post-Rape

More research has been conducted on victims' response to sexual assault than to any other crime (Burt and Katz, 1985). The majority of the research on rape victims has focused on the immediate and short-term effects during the first year after the rape (e.g., Burgess and

Holmstrom, 1974; Kilpatrick et al., 1979; McCahill et al., 1979; Sutherland and Scherl, 1970).

Although most researchers in the field would agree that rape may affect the victim's life for years, the effects after the first year are not as well documented. Some studies have focused on specific topics such as sexual functioning and satisfaction (e.g., Becker et al., 1982; Feldman-Summers et al., 1979) or marital problems (e.g., Miller and Williams, 1984) but have often included subjects who had been raped less than a year prior to the study, making if difficult to distinguish effects that occur years after the assault.

Efforts to describe effects a year or more after the rape have included both longitudinal studies (e.g., Burgess and Holmstrom, 1979) and retrospective studies (e.g., Ellis et al., 1981). While these reports have contributed greatly to the field, much more information is needed on how victims perceive the effects of rape on their lives and how those effects may evolve over time. For example, increased distrust of men is often mentioned as a long-term effect (e.g., Holmes, 1979; Medea and Thompson, 1974; Notman and Nadelson, 1976), but the nature of that distrust and the effect it has on the lives of the victims has not been fully explored.

The present study sought to isolate the long-term effects of rape by including only victims who had been raped three or more years before. The study emphasized victims' perceptions of men and their interactions with men. The thrust of the effort was to document a range of long-term effects and to develop an organizing system to guide further research as well as clinical interventions.

Method

Subjects

For the purposes of subject selection, rape was defined as the forced sexual penetration of any body opening of a female by a male. Spousal rape was not excluded by this definition, but none of the subjects reported a spousal rape as the "target rape." (The term "target rape" refers to the rape incident which a subject identified as the primary focus of the interview.) Several subjects reported more than one rape in their history and several others reported additional sexually coercive experiences.

A total of ten volunteers served as subjects for the interview and other procedures. Three responded to a description of the study which was distributed to female clients at mental health facilities. The other seven responded to appeals to the general public, including notices at a rape crisis center. A small sample size was chosen to allow in-depth analysis of the extensive interview data.

All the subjects were white women. Their mean age at the time of the interview was thirty years (range sixteen–forty-two), the mean age at the time of the target rape was twenty-one (range nineteen–twenty-six), and the mean number of years since the target rape was nine (three–seventeen). Volunteers were not accepted for the study if they had been victims of incest or sexual abuse before age sixteen.

At the time of the target rapes, seven of the subjects had never been married, two were divorced, and one was separated. At the time of the interviews, the annual family incomes of the subjects ranged from $1,440 to $50,000, with a median of $8,250. Their occupations included homemaker, nurse, college student, clerical worker, factory supervisor, and administrator.

A comparison group of ten white, single, female undergraduate students (mean age of 18.6 years, range eighteen–twenty) were recruited from psychology classes to take the Interpersonal Check List.

Instruments and Procedures

The Interpersonal Check List (ICL), developed by Rolfe LaForge and Robert Suczek (Leary, 1957: 455–463), is a list of 128 adjective phrases that can be used to measure how a subject perceives herself and other people she is asked to describe. Leary (1957) incorporated the ICL into his system of interpersonal diagnosis of personality which emphasizes interactional patterns. Scores on two dimensions may be derived from the pattern of ICL responses. The "Dominance" score represents the subject's relative placement of self or other on a power dimension, ranging from dominance to submission in relationships with others. The "Love" score represents placement on an affiliation dimension, ranging from hostility to affection. This instrument and scoring system were chosen because the two dimensions reflect issues often discussed in relation to rape such as power, anger, hostility, attraction, domination, and submission.

The subjects were asked to use the ICL to describe their perceptions of the following people or groups of people:

- general description of men (over age sixteen) you know, other than your current or latest boyfriend or spouse;
- yourself in relation to the men you know with the same qualifications as on the previous page;

- ➢ your current or latest boyfriend or spouse, if you have one;
- ➢ yourself in relation to the person you described on the previous page;
- ➢ general description of men (over sixteen) who are strangers to you;
- ➢ yourself in relation to men (over sixteen) who are strangers to you;
- ➢ male involved in the coercive event you will be discussing;
- ➢ yourself in relation to the male involved in the coercive event; and
- ➢ yourself in general.

In addition, to provide a standard stimulus for the subjects to rate with the ICL, the investigator produced a videotape. Two graduate students, one male and one female, were actors seated and engaged in apparent conversation. The 2-minute silent videotape was presented to the subjects, who were then asked to rate each actor using the ICL. The videotape was presented without sound to allow for maximum projection on the subject's part.

The comparison group of undergraduate women completed the ICL for the same groups and individuals, except for a male involved in the coercive event and themselves in relation to such a male.

The second instrument, the SCL-90-R, is a 90-item self-report inventory designed to measure symptomatic psychological distress. Each subject was asked to respond to each item, indicating how much discomfort it had caused her during the past 7 days, including the day of the interview. The response for each item is made in on a 5-point scale ranging from "not at all" to "extremely." The SCL-90-R yields scores on nine primary symptom dimensions and three global indices of distress. Of the several sets of norms published, the two relevant for present purposes are Norm A—Outpatient Females and Norm B—Nonpatient Females (Derogatis, 1977). The SCL-90-R was chosen because the primary symptom dimensions (such as Somatization, Depression, Anxiety, and Interpersonal Sensitivity) tap symptoms that have been reported by rape victims in the first year post-rape (Kilpatrick et al., 1979).

After completing the pencil and paper measure, each subject participated in a semistructured, 60- to 90-minute interview. Questions early in the interview were designed to gather information concerning the rape itself and were selected to reflect factors which have been identified in the literature as related to victims' short-term responses. Later questions were designed to tap the victim's perception of the impact the rape had on her life, particularly in regard to her relationships with men and the course of change over time, i.e., whether the victim still feels the effect(s) of the rape or feels she has recovered.[1]

Data Analysis and Results

ICL: *T*-scores for both the Dominance and Love dimensions were obtained for each of the twenty subjects' ratings of the various categories of males and self-ratings. To determine if the victims' response patterns were unique to their group, their mean *T*-scores were compared to the means obtained for the comparison group. Four two-way analyses of variance were used. The two groups' ratings of males (videotape male, known males, strangers, and current or past boyfriend or spouse) were compared first on the Dominance dimension and then on the Love dimension. Similarly, the two groups' self-ratings (in relation to known males, to strangers, to current or past boyfriend or spouse, and themselves in general) were compared on the Dominance and Love dimensions.

Three of the eight main effects were found to contribute significantly ($p < .02$) to the variation in scores, but none of the interactions was significant (Table 3.1). Each of the three main effects was examined to identify the significant variable.

In the ratings of males on the Dominance dimension, the victim and comparison groups did not differ significantly from each other. When they were considered as one group, however, the women did rate the various males differentially. A post hoc test, the Least Significant Difference Test (LSD), revealed that the overall mean Dominance score for the male in the videotape was significantly lower than the other three ratings of males, none of which was significantly different from another (Table 3.2). All the means, except for the rating of the male in the videotape, were greater than the midscale score of 50, suggesting that women in general perceive males in their environment as dominant and that rape victims are not significantly more likely to do so.

As on the Dominance dimension, the victim and comparison groups did not differ significantly from each other on their ratings of males on the Love dimension however, the combined group did differentiate between the males. The LSD test revealed that the overall mean Love score for strangers was significantly lower than the other three ratings of males, none of which was significantly different from another (Table 3.2). This pattern suggests that both victims and nonvictims perceive men who are unknown to them as significantly more aggressive and exploitive relative to the other men in their environment.

There was a significant difference ($p < .02$) between the victim and comparison groups on their ratings of themselves on the Love dimension but not on the Dominance dimension. As determined by the LSD test, the rape victims perceived themselves as consistently less affiliative than did the comparison group, except in relation to their boyfriends or spouses, where the groups' means were not significantly different (Table 3.3).

The means of the victims' Dominance and Love ratings of the males involved in the rape, 61.2 and 36.9 respectively, closely paralleled their ratings of male strangers, even though seven of the ten target rapes involved friends or acquaintances.

Table 3.1

Analysis of Variance Summaries for Victim vs. Comparison Group by Persons Rated

Source	df	Mean square	F
RATINGS OF MALES—DOMINANCE			
Between groups	1	82.02	0.8503
Between treatments (males)	3	906.41	9.3967*
Interaction	3	96.51	1.0005
Error	72	96.46	
RATINGS OF MALES—LOVE			
Between groups	1	82.02	1.1108
Between treatments (males)	3	700.65	9.4886*
Interaction	3	87.74	1.1882
Error	72	73.84	
RATINGS OF SELF—DOMINANCE			
Between groups	1	168.20	0.7092
Between treatments (males)	3	159.08	0.6708
Interaction	3	139.77	0.5893
Error	72	237.16	
RATINGS OF SELF—LOVE			
Between groups	1	833.05	7.2295*
Between treatments (males)	3	310.45	2.6942
Interaction	3	69.59	0.6038
Error	72	115.23	

*$p < .02$.

Table 3.2

Overall Means for Victims' and Undergraduates' Ratings of Males

	Male in Videotape	Current or past Boyfriend or Spouse	Strangers	Known Males
Dominance	48.7[a]	60.2[b]	61.9[b]	63.5[b]
Love	49.7[c]	48.0[c]	36.4[d]	45.4[c]

Note. The higher the Dominance score, the more powerful the person is perceived as being; the higher the Love score, the more affiliative the person is perceived.
For each row, means with different superscripts differ significantly at $p < .02$.

SCL-90-R: Mean *T*-scores for each of the nine symptom dimensions and for the three global indices were obtained for each of two subsamples of victims corresponding to the two sets of norms, female psychiatric outpatients (used for the three subjects recruited from the mental health center) and female nonpatients (used for the seven subjects recruited from the general population). None of the means for the outpatient group was significantly different from the test mean of 50. The Depression dimension mean for the seven subjects from the general population was significantly greater than the nonpatient test norm (M=61.57, $p < .05$). The Positive Symptom Distress Index (a measure of the intensity of distress, adjusted for the number of symptoms endorsed) was also significantly higher than the test mean for the subsample of nonpatients (M=63.43, $p < .02$).

Interviews

The interviews were the heart of the study. The analysis of the interview was designed to identify the rape victims' perceptions of the long-term impact of the rape on their lives, especially their interpersonal relationships with men, and whether the effect(s) had changed over the years. Because of the paucity of information available on long-term effects, a phenomenological, descriptive approach (Colaizzi, 1978) to analyzing the interviews was chosen. It was hoped that the victims' statements on these issues would suggest a category system which would in turn suggest new ways of understanding their experiences.

"Significant statements" were extracted from each victim's interview. Statements were deemed significant if they referred to a change or condition which the victim attributed to the rape and which she was either experiencing at the present time or had experienced sometime after three years following the rape. Excerpts were as long as necessary to fairly represent the nature and complexity of what the victim was saying and varied in length from one to about a dozen sentences.

Once the significant statements had been identified, the investigator grouped them in several ways, searching for the most coherent thematic structure. When a satisfactory system had been identified, it was refined through collaborative efforts to sort the statements into categories. The resulting system contained two dimensions; the first consisted of three categories, the second had four. Each statement received a score on each dimension.

To determine whether the category system could be used to reliably score the statements, two independent raters, graduate students in clinical psychology, were trained to score the items. When agreement between these two raters reached approximately 80 percent in training sessions, the raters independently scored 70 statements they had not seen previously. The investigator also scored each of the statements. Reliability measures were significant at the .01 level for agreement on all the categories for each pair of raters, indicating that the category system can be learned and applied reliably.

Dimension I, Nature of Change Attributed to Rape, reflects the victims' perceptions of the changes they attributed to the rape (Table 3.4). The three categories within Dimension I pertain to different points

Table 3.3

Love Score Means of Self-Ratings by Victims and Undergraduates

	Means	
	Victims	Undergraduates
Self in relation to strangers (males)	38.4^{a}	48.5^{b}
Self in general	45.0^{c}	51.5^{d}
Self in relation to known males	46.3^{e}	54.2^{f}
Self in relation to current or past boyfriend or spouse	51.1^{g}	53.4^{g}

Note. For each row, means with different superscripts differ significantly at $p < .02$.

Table 3.4

Nature of Change Attributed to Rape (Dimension I)

A. Heightened awareness of or sensitivity to the aggressive and exploitative potential of the other, primarily male

Associated affect: tension, anxiety, anger

- ➢ more sensitive, reactive to others
- ➢ description of angry, tense interactions
- ➢ issues of power, dominance, and control figural in interactions, including sexual ones
- ➢ description of hostile or indifferent responses on victim's part, hostility likely to be seen as justified by victim
- ➢ victim may move against or away from the other

B. Heightened awareness of one's own vulnerability in relation to the other, primarily male

Associated affect: fear

- ➢ more distrustful
- ➢ more defensive, closed off, less open to others
- ➢ fears of abandonment, insecurities in relationships, need for reassurance
- ➢ amorphous or specific fears, which may limit activities
- ➢ anticipation that bad things happen to one
- ➢ sexual difficulties related to impaired trust
- ➢ avoidance of other in interest of self-protection

C. Self-focus, self-reflection or commentary

- ➢ unresolved emotions
- ➢ different perspective on life
- ➢ negative self-concept, view of self as bad, worse, unhappier
- ➢ feelings about discussing the rape
- ➢ frequency of thoughts about the rape and intensity of associated feelings
- ➢ sexual difficulties related to internal issues rather than to issues of control or distrust

on a continuum from other-focus to self-focus. The first two categories, A and B, are both interpersonal in nature. In Category A, the primary emphasis and focus is on the Other in the relationship. The content is related to the increased awareness of or sensitivity to the aggressive and exploitive potential of the Other. This category represents changes having to do with a new awareness of the potential harm others, primarily males, are capable of causing. Several victims became more sensitive to the issues of power, dominance, and control in relationships and remained easily angered by actions they perceived as men's attempts to control them in any way, including sexually. At the time of the interviews, many of the victims still experienced anxiety and tension when they were in the presence of men. Some of the victims reported responding by angrily confronting the men or by withdrawing from the interaction.

Category B is juxtaposed with the first; however, the emphasis is on the Self. The content is related to heightened awareness of one's own vulnerability in relation to the Other, specifically, a perception of the Self as more vulnerable than before the rape. The associated affect is usually fear, either amorphous or specific. Relationship problems were reported in the areas of feeling insecure, fearing abandonment, needing reassurance, and having great difficulty in trusting and accepting the love of another. Several victims reported avoiding relationships in an effort to protect themselves, and some felt they were more closed off emotionally and less likely to get close to another person than they had been previously.

Category C involves changes or effects that are primarily intrapersonal in nature, such as changed perceptions of the self, changed perspectives on life, and unresolved emotions and memories related to the rape. Some victims felt they were "bad" people because they had been raped. Most still experienced some uneasiness when discussing their rapes. Sexual difficulties were included in this category if the victim described them as internally determined rather than interpersonally determined.

Dimension II, Subsequent Course of Change Attributed to Rape, represents the victim's experience of the change or effect over time (Table 3.5). Categories 1 and 2 involve the perception of some transition or relief over time, such as a transition from guilt to anger or to less frequent thoughts of the rape. The distinction between the first and second categories is based on whether the victim identified any factor as a mediator of the transition or recovery. If the victim mentioned no specific mediator other than the passage of time, Category 1 was assigned. Here, there was a sense of the rape fading from figure to ground over time, with no apparent effort involved. If a specific process or mediator was identified as having facilitated the transition or recovery, Category 2 was applicable. Examples of mediating factors are relationships with patient, caring lovers or spouses, relationships with counselors, and the victims' own efforts to work through problems caused by

Table 3.5

Subsequent Course of Change Attributed to Rape (Dimension II)

1. Time or unspecified mediator important in victim's sense of recovery, relief, improvement or transition in a problem or affect related to the rape
   - ➢ decreased frequency of problem occurrence
   - ➢ decreased intensity of affect associated with rape or problems due to rape

   Sense of rape fading from figure to ground

2. Specified process important in victim's sense of recovery, relief, improvement or transition in a problem or affect related to the rape
   - ➢ decreased frequency of problem occurrence
   - ➢ decreased intensity of affect associated with rape or problems due to rape
   - ➢ reference to working through, working on, or working out a problem
   - ➢ experiences with others, especially specific relationships, including therapy relationships, seen as helpful
   - ➢ increased action or initiative on victim's part seen as helpful

   Sense of rape remaining a figural event to be addressed, yet some relief is obtained from doing so

3. Explicit statement that problem persists without any sense of relief or recovery
   - ➢ "I still . . . ," "never recover," etc.

4. Implication that problem persists without any sense of relief or recovery
   - ➢ present tense used in describing problem, with no reference to improvement

Note. Expression of a positive feeling about a change due to the rape does not necessarily imply improvement. To be included in Category 1 or 2, total recovery need not be present. If the victim states she feels partially or mostly recovered and then elaborates, base sorting on the nature of the elaboration rather than on the introductory statement. If the problem is described in past tense with no reference to current experience, assume some improvement is implied.

the rape via introspection and reflection or via dialogue with others. There was a sense that the rape had remained a figural event to be addressed, yet some relief was obtained from doing so actively.

Categories 3 and 4 reflect no sense of transition or relief from the changes or effects brought about by the rape. Category 3 includes explicit statements that the problem persists and implies a comparison to the past or future. Such statements included phrases such as, "I still . . .," and "you never recover from. . . ." Category 4 includes statements which imply the problem persists through the use of present tense verbs but which involve no explicit time reference such as "still." An example of a Category 4 statement is, "I'm much less tolerant of things men do and say. . . ."

Several of the significant statements were quite complex. Because the categories of Dimension I are not mutually exclusive, raters had the option of coding a statement in one, two, or all three categories; however, the categories within Dimension II are mutually exclusive, so only one score from this dimension could be assigned for each statement.

Table 3.6

Statement Score Frequencies and Category Totals

Statement Score	Frequency	Category	Total	Percent
A1	4	Dimension I		
A2	5	A	24	25.5
A3	1	B	28	29.8
A4	9	C	49	52.1
				107.4[a]
B1	3			
B2	4			
B3	6			
B4	9	Dimension II		
		1	33	35.1
C1	25	2	19	20.2
C2	7	3	15	16.0
C3	8			
C4	6	4	27	28.7
				100.0
AB2	2			
AB4	2			
AC4	1			
BC1	1			
BC2	1			

Note. Only scores which occurred at least once were included. Thus, no statements were scored AB1, AB3, AC1, etc.

[a]The total percentage is greater than 100 because several statements were scored in more than one category.

The frequencies of the various statement scores and score totals by category are presented in Table 3.6. The highest frequencies were found in Categories C (intrapersonal) and 1 (time or unspecified factor as mediator of improvement) and the largest group of scores was C1. Many of the statements in this group concerned a reduced frequency in thoughts about the rape and increased comfort in discussing it.

Statements classified in Categories A and B (interpersonal) occurred in approximately equal proportions across the subjects as a whole. These statements were more likely than C (intrapersonal) statements to be classified in Category 3 or 4 (no sense of recovery), indicating that the interpersonal problems were more likely to be seen by the victims as persisting unabated (x^2=7.9280, $p < .05$). There was considerable variation among the victims in their emphasis on interpersonal versus intrapersonal effects and in their perceptions of the extent of their recovery.

Discussion

An initial hypothesis was that rape victims would perceive men as more dominant, hostile, and aggressive than would women who have not been raped. It is an important finding that the victims did not differ significantly from the comparison group on their ICL ratings of males on either the Dominance or Love dimensions. This indicates that women, whether they have been raped or not, tend to have similar views of men, seeing them as managerial, competitive, and aggressive. The victims, however, rated themselves as less affiliative and less likely to be congenial to those men than did the comparison group.

Because there were differences between the victim and comparison groups in addition to rape, it is unclear whether the victims' self-perception of being less affiliative was caused by the assault. For example, the victims were older, seven of them were married, and five of them reported at least one incident of being physically abused by men other than the rapists. Thus the victims have had more time and potentially more opportunities than the undergraduates to become disillusioned in relationships with men. Although the interview data show that some victims attributed some of their feelings about interacting with men to factors other than the rapes, all stated explicitly that they believed the rape was associated with their feelings to a significant degree. The victims' disaffiliativeness may then reflect a self-protective gesture on their part. That is, their experiences with men may not have substantially altered their perceptions of men (as compared to the undergraduates), but the victims may have changed their own behavior to reduce the possibility of being victimized again.

Depression was the only SCL-90-R symptom dimension for which the nonpatient victims' mean score was significantly greater than the normed mean. This would suggest that victims who were raped years earlier may not initially present a unique clinical picture and that counselors should be alert to the possibility of sexual assault in the histories of all their clients.

The primary contribution of the interview data is the elucidation it provides of the victims' difficulties in heterosexual relationships. The identification of two related but distinguishable modes of relating to other people (Categories A and B) offers a more complete way of understanding victims' feelings about and behavior around men. The two modes, heightened awareness of the other's aggressive and exploitive potential and heightened awareness of one's own vulnerability, will be discussed in the context of a theory of personality style.

Shapiro (1965) described various modes of human functioning by delineating characteristic styles of cognition and perception as well as subjective experiences and activity. Among the styles he identified was the paranoid style, a key element of which is a suspicious mode of thinking and perceiving, including hyperalertness for clues in the environment which will confirm pre-existing notions. Several victims reported hyperalertness to signs of a male's readiness to take control. Three stated that they had become more sensitive to sexual aggressiveness and antifemale attitudes. The ICL data indicates that victims' perceptions of men were not significantly different from other women's, but the ICL and interview data do indicate that some victims were acutely sensitive and reactive to those perceptions and tended to be constantly on the lookout for potential threats to their autonomy.

The paranoid person's attention is rigid and biased. Evidence contradictory to expectation is likely to be dismissed as "'mere appearances'" (Shapiro, 1965: 57). Two of the victims discussed having great difficulty trusting a male's statements that he cares for them. They expected to be exploited sexually and the rigidity of this expectation precluded the relaxation necessary for emotional intimacy to develop. Efforts to take control of the sexual interaction and lack of arousal sometimes resulted.

Shapiro wrote that much of the paranoid's rigidity reflects an effort to compensate for the lack of an adequately developed sense of autonomy. The paranoid's constant apprehension about external control is accompanied by an acute sensitivity and resistance to external authority. Internal impulses and desires can also be threats to security if they lead to vulnerability to subjugation by others, so spontaneity and playfulness are almost nonexistent for the paranoid person and the range of affect is constricted. Victims in this study reported a constriction of affect and lack of spontaneity in social as well as sexual arenas. One victim articulated this clearly: "I think the fear comes from the rape. I don't like to be in a room with men I don't know because you don't know what they're going to do. . . .You don't know how they're going to turn on you. . . . That's why I'm not very sociable to men. . . . If I see them and they look my way, I'll just give a half grin and drop my head. . . . I don't think it's for shame. . . . I think it's . . . I know what they can do."

Shapiro distinguished two manifestations of the paranoid style: "furtive, constricted, apprehensively suspicious individuals and rigidly arrogant, more aggressively suspicious, megalomanic ones" (1965: 54). Although these are rather extreme descriptions for the victim population, the distinction is a useful one and closely parallels Dimension I Categories B and A, respectively. Category B highlights one's own vulnerability and the associated fear and distrust, while Category A highlights the other's potential aggressiveness and exploitiveness with the associated tension, anger, and hostility. Thus, it appears that the rape victims' descriptions of their interpersonal coping behaviors parallel Shapiro's paranoid style. The victims' behaviors and thought processes are, however, characteristic of the milder ranges of the style, rather than the psychotic loss of touch with reality that can take place in the more severe cases.

The degree to which the findings of this study may be generalized to rape victims as a whole is unclear. The group was heterogeneous in socioeconomic level but not in race. While avoiding the sampling biases of groups recruited from emergency rooms or rape crisis centers, the recruitment method used in the present study had its own bias because only women who were willing to spend time and risk emotional upset in discussing the rape volunteered. Perhaps those who believe they do experience long-term effects were more motivated to volunteer than those who do not. Thus, the findings should be considered tentative but they do warrant further study, preferably with the addition of a control group. The category system should be further developed and refined with larger and more heterogeneous samples.

Clinical Implications

Analysis of the interviews resulted in the identification of themes relevant to clinical work with rape victims. It is important, however, to remember that each victim responded to her rape in a unique way and that the adaptations she made are not necessarily problems that need to be resolved. For instance, perhaps the paranoid stance adopted by some victims may actually reflect a more realistic awareness of the possibilities in the world. If so, the victim may need to become reconciled to this world view rather than stripped of her "healthy paranoia" (C.P. Cohen, personal communication, 1984). Thus, the counselor should avoid making assumptions about what kinds of help the rape victim wants or needs. If the victim is unable to articulate how she would like to deal with the rape, a collaborative effort may be needed to identify troublesome areas and the ways she would like things to be different.

Depression and other presenting complaints may not readily distinguish victims of long-ago rapes from other clients. Counselors should therefore make inquiry about sexual assault part of their usual intake assessment. In this way, they invite the victim to reveal and work through whatever issues remain as a result of her victimization.

Reference

1. Copies of the interview format are available from the author.

Bibliography

Becker, Judith V., Linda J. Skinner, Gene G. Able, and Eileen C. Treacy
1982 "Incidence and Types of Sexual Dysfunctions in Rape and Incest Victims." *Journal of Sex and Marital Therapy,* 8: 65–74.

Burgess, Ann W., and Lynda L. Holmstrom
1974 "Rape Trauma Syndrome." *American Journal of Psychiatry,* 131: 981–986.

Burgess, Ann W., and Lynda L. Holmstrom
1979 *Rape: Crisis and Recovery.* Bowie, MD: Brady.

Burt, Martha R., and Bonnie L. Katz
1985 "Rape, Robbery, and Burglary: Responses to Actual and Feared Criminal Victimization, with Special Focus on Women and the Elderly." *Victimology,* 10: 325–358.

Colaizzi, Paul F.
1978 "Psychological Research as the Phenomenologist Views It." In Ronald S. Valle and Mark King, eds. *Existential-Phenomenological Alternatives for Psychology.* New York: Oxford University Press.

Derogatis, Leonard R.
1977 SCL-90: Administration, Scoring and Procedures Manual I for

the R(evised) Version and Other Instruments of the Psychopathology Rating Scale Series. Unpublished manuscript, Johns Hopkins University School of Medicine, Baltimore.

Ellis, Elizabeth M., Beverly M. Atkeson, and Karen S. Calhoun
1981 "An Assessment of Long-Term Reactions to Rape." *Journal of Abnormal Psychology*, 90(3): 263–266.

Feldman-Summers, Shirley, Patricia E. Gordon, and Jeanette Meagher
1979 "The Impact of Rape on Sexual Satisfaction." *Journal of Abnormal Psychology*, 88(1): 101–105.

Holmes, Karen A.
1979 "Rape-as-Crisis: An Empirical Assessment." *Dissertation Abstracts International*, 40: 1685-A (University Microfilms No. 7920134).

Kilpatrick, Dean G., Lois J. Veronen, and Patricia A. Resick
1979 "The Aftermath of Rape: Recent Empirical Findings." *American Journal of Orthopsychiatry*, 49: 658–669.

Leary, Timothy
1957 *Interpersonal Diagnosis of Personality*. New York: Ronald Press.

McCahill, Thomas W., Linda C. Meyer, and Arthur M. Fischman
1979 *The Aftermath of Rape*. Lexington, MA: D.C. Heath.

Medea, Andra, and Kathleen Thompson.
1974 *Against Rape*. New York: Farrar, Straus, and Giroux.

Miller, William R., and Ann Marie Williams
1984 "Marital and Sexual Dysfunction Following Rape: Identification and Treatment." In Irving R. Stuart and Joanne G. Greer, eds. *Victims of Sexual Aggression: Treatment of Children, Women, and Men*. New York: Van Nostrand Reinhold.

Notman, Malkah T., and Carole C. Nadelson
1976 "The Rape Victim: Psychodynamic Considerations." *American Journal of Psychiatry*, 133: 408–413.

Shapiro, David
1965 *Neurotic Styles*. New York: Basic Books.

Sutherland, Sandra, and Donald J. Scherl
1970 "Patterns of Response Among Victims of Rape." *American Journal of Orthopsychiatry*, 40: 503–511.

4

Developmental Issues and the Sexually Abused Child and Adolescent

Sarah R. Stanley, M.S., R.N., C.N.A., C.S.
American Nurses' Association

It is essential to have knowledge of normal child/adolescent development to understand the issues and needs of the sexually molested victim. The developmental issues for that child may differ greatly from chronological age expectations. A review of the general principles of development is presented. Physical and cognitive growth patterns with emphasis on perception, memory, and language processes are illustrated. Psychological and social stages are delineated, from infancy through adolescence. Direct application to the management of cases of young victims of sexual molestation is made. General coping and adaptive behaviors of abused children are also explored.

Whether one comes from an investigative or clinical perspective, it is important to note that the child is not a passive being who is molded entirely by environment. Understanding the internal operations of a child's thinking and communication abilities will promote more accurate assessments and facilitate advocacy for the child/adolescent through the multiperson/systems that impact on the sexual victim after disclosure.

"The adult who is interested in knowing what abused children are like would be advised to know what children are like" (Martin and Beezley, 1977). It is essential to have knowledge of normal child development to understand this special group. Only with such a background can one appreciate how sexually abused children *differ* and *do not differ* from other children (Martin and Beezley, 1977; Hartman and Burgess, 1985; Mrazek and Mrazek, 1981).

This chapter will briefly review the general physical and cognitive developmental stages of mental processes such as memory, perception, characteristics of thought and language development for every child. In addition, psychological issues and fears of the sexually victimized child will be presented. Whether one comes from an investigative or clinical discipline, an understanding of the physical, cognitive, language growth and the impact of sexual victimization is critical to helping the victim and family (Pothier, 1980; Smetana et al., 1984; Kagan, 1971; Finkelhor and Browne, 1985).

The working assumptions of this presentation are basic and not divided into medical or legal definitions.

- ➢ Sexual misuse, abuse, assault is defined as all sexual exploitation of a child, male or female, who is not developmentally capable of understanding or resisting the contact.
- ➢ All degrees of sexual activity, fondling, sodomization, vaginal penetration, pornography are included.
- ➢ The child who reports sexual misuse is assumed to be telling the truth unless there is clear evidence otherwise.
- ➢ Protection of victim and other siblings is a primary concern.
- ➢ Without intervention sexual victimization will continue.
- ➢ The abuser is frequently uncooperative and will not voluntarily seek help.
- ➢ There is still not enough known about effective treatment.

It is hoped that through the information provided here, there will follow practical application to questions such as: What developmental factors would contribute to a five-year-old changing his statement about his sexual abuse?; How might a seven-year-old react if interviewed multiple times about her incestuous sexual abuse of two years?; how would one defend the position that family members (parents, siblings, and/or grandparents) should be present at the interview of a ten-year-old?

Principles of Child Development

There are several general principles of childhood development. These may be summarized as follows:

1. Development is a continuous process from conception to maturity, not to be thought of in terms of mere milestones. Before any milestones are reached, a child goes through many preceding stages. It is not what a child does but how he does it that is of importance.
2. Development depends on maturation and myelination of the central nervous system. Until this occurs, no amount of practice can make a child learn a relevant skill. When practice is denied, the ability to perform the skill lies dormant, but it is rapidly learned when opportunity is given.
3. The sequence of development is the same for all children, but the rate of development varies from child to child. The child learns to sit before walking, but the age of each accomplishment may vary considerably.
4. The direction of development is cephalocaudal (head first). The acquisition of head and neck control is the first task. Next, the spinal muscles develop and the child is able to sit. The use of hands comes before legs, therefore, the child can crawl by pulling himself and the legs trail.
5. Generalized mass activity gives way to individual response. To express pleasure a baby's eyes widen, legs and arms move vigorously and respirations will increase, while an older child or adult shows pleasure simply by facial expression or words.

Much of the general physical development is visible and specific. The cognitive/intellectual functioning, however, is not always as evident.

Cognitive Development

Cognition describes all mental processes entailed in thinking. If a problem is central to the child's concern, the processes will be activated naturally; if not, he may not work to problem solve. The child develops concrete thoughts using basic cognitive units, schematas, symbols, concepts, and rules. With growth the child tries to assimilate new experiences with old ideas. He/she will stubbornly resist retiring old beliefs that work. These will not be replaced by criticism alone but by recognition of a better set of rules. Every new event creates a state of uncertainty, which the child wants to resolve and understand. The child will dip into reserves in an active attempt to make sense of an experience, e.g., a toddler sees mother crying and automatically thinks of what makes him cry, physical pain, fear, loneliness. He then checks the plausibility of each. He rejects fear and loneliness—adults are never afraid, adults are never lonely, but adults can feel pain. Therefore, he asks, "What hurts Mommy?"

The child is not a passive being whose desires, skills, and ideas are molded by environment alone. At four to five years, a set of *executive processes* emerge and are in place by age eleven. These relate past experiences and future possibility to the present. The child can then select best strategies to solve problems. This permits the child to be self-consciously aware of his/her own thinking. It also allows him/her to be more flexible, more playful, more aware of his/her talents, and more sensitive to his/her cognitive inadequacies. He/she becomes more apprehensive about making mistakes. From four to twelve years the child becomes increasingly concerned with degree of agreement between his/her concepts and those of other children and adults. In the United States and Europe, the greatest cognitive growth is between five to ten years, but it can be delayed until adolescence in isolated, rural, subsistence communities. Conditions of rearing do have influence on rate of cognitive growth; however, the major cognitive processes are inherent and mature in an orderly way among children growing in a reasonable environment, even if the adult knows little of what the child requires.

Of the many cognitive processes, the focus of this chapter will be on perception and memory. These are critical issues for the clinician and investigator working with child victims. If one ignores the child's perception of the victimization and expected outcomes after disclosure, a great deal has been missed.

In perception, the goal is to understand events through detection of critical features. The organization and interpretation of information from the outside world and external environment are vital. The ability to perceive objects, space and dynamic events is natural to all children (Kagan, 1984, Piaget, 1969). At age five or younger the child is easily distracted, unable to direct the focus of his/her attention, or to shift focus rapidly, even though the number of sensory events that can be attended to at one time may be the same. Between four to ten years important reorganization of the central nervous system occurs. The child's expectations or selective attention shows rapid increase. If a child five to seven years knows what events are about to happen, he/she can prepare for the event. Preparation will then aid the accuracy of perception. Basically, the difference of perception performance is due to variance with initial taking in, coding, or memory.

Memory, the storage and retrieval of information, is one of the most important cognitive processes. Yet, it is most elusive, fragile, and vulnerable to the slightest interference. There are three types of memory—sensory, short term, and long term. Each of these is a label for how long information must be available to be stored. Sensory memory is the term which describes something remaining for one-fourth of a second or less in vision. It is difficult to retain the complete memory sensation. This is the same for child and adult. With short-term memory one must be able to trace available information for a maximum of 30 seconds and must actively transfer to long-term storage or it will be lost, e.g., a friend's new phone number. A child is tested based on what has been registered and stored by recognition or recall. For recall the child must retrieve all information from storage. The efficiency of the retrieval process will affect memory, e.g., the child is asked to recall names of twenty classmates. This will be vulnerable to names of all children known. On the other hand, if the child is given names and asked to recognize if a person is in the class, there is much more accuracy. Recognition is far superior to recall and the differences become more dramatic with age (Illingsworth, 1983). For example, the ten-year-old can recall 8 of 12 items but can recognize all 12. The four-year-old can recall 3 of 12 items and recognize 10 of 12.

The difference in the quality of memory can be attributed to motivation, anxiety, or distraction. The retrieval of information requires work. The motivated child will work longer and is likely to ferret out more information. This skill improves with age after seven years. Before six or seven years, the child can hold only a few words or ideas in his/her mind when someone is speaking. The younger child is easily bored with memory tests and unconcerned about ability to recall all information. Anxiety also can have a strong impact on memory and is the most frequent cause of interference. Feelings and thoughts that comprise anxiety are distracting and deflect attention from information to be remembered. Distraction is a very strong deterrent to the memory process. Multiple sensory stimuli, i.e., noise, people, etc., can interfere also. The recognition/recall differences and the interference factors of memory are very important and have serious implications in relation to the child victim and the facts they can provide to interviewers.

The acquisition of language is one of the young child's most complex accomplishments. It enables him/her to communicate information, meanings, intentions, and requests. The child's attempts to communicate begin by one year of age with gesturing, pointing, and vocalizing sounds. Age, however, is not a good index of linguistic level. Young children comprehend much more than they can produce. They can understand and react to relatively complex requests, questions, negative statements, and commands long before they can produce these.

Cognitive processes are linked but not dependent on language, e.g., deaf children can learn without speech. Authorities say language development is part of cognitive growth, reflecting rather than determining levels of achievement. "It's learning how, what you already know, is expressed in your native tongue" (Kagan, 1971). Children learn language through reward and punishment, direct training exercises, and imitation. Chomsky theorizes that human beings possess some kind of built-in pre-wired structure that enables the child to process language heard, to construct rules, to understand, and to generate appropriate grammatical speech. There is no single teaching/training technique which by itself has significant impact on language development. A mother will speak to a two-year-old using repetition, restricted concrete vocabulary, shorter and less complex sentences, and more attention-getting words. A four-year-old sibling will do the same thing when talking to the two-year-old.

Between one and six years, a child's vocabulary grows dramatically. A child under three understands "where" questions but "what" questions bring irrelevant answers. At age three grammar becomes more complex and the child asks many who, where, and how questions. "Why" questions are not understood and are responded to as "what" or "where" questions. The principal grammatical rules are acquired by four to five years. Comprehension and flexibility in use of language appears at ages five to six years. This age child uses "because" and "then" to express time rather than casual relationship. At age six, most U.S. children have a vocabulary of 8,000 to 14,000 words. From kindergarten to ninth grade his vocabulary grows enormously, syntax is complete, and thirty months after a child says his first sentence, he is capable of using full complex adult-like sentences.

There have been comparison studies done of language environments of middle and lower socioeconomic groups. It was suggested that deficits in language accounted for poor performance of lower socioeconomic children on cognitive functioning tests. Current thinking is that competence (knowledge necessary to use language) not performance needs to be the measurement criteria. Children from lower socioeconomic groups were found to have fluent, highly structured grammatical systems through which logical thoughts and emotions were expressed. They have no difficulty being understood in their own family and neighborhood (Kagan, 1971).

Psychological Development

A child's cognitive development includes many complex processes. Perception, language, memory, and thought patterns may be very different for each individual. Along with the general physical and cognitive processes, the psychological or personality development is also taking place (Maier, 1969; Fagin, 1972; Mussen et al., 1979). The child develops a sense of belonging, based on his/her self-concept of things done rather than things felt. He/she also bases an assessment of self and how he/she fits into the world from external factors and development of a sense of right and wrong. The child needs to take part in new experiences; to be praised for trying something new and making progress, not criticized for not doing it perfectly; to be compared with self only, not measured against others; to have toys and games that allow experimentation and risk; to be aware of solid consistent limits that are reasonable, applied fairly, and enforced; to have appropriate and congruent affect with verbal messages and punishment that "fits the crime" (Babich, 1982).

In their psychological development, children develop patterns of coping to ward off responses to stress and the sense of failure (Josselyn, 1978; Barahal and Waterman et al., 1981). Their behaviors are seen as obvious adaptations and reactions to the environment. Adapt he must, cope he will, but how? If a stressor is more than the child can cope with successfully, he may develop a maladaptive response. Psychological responses work to reduce anxiety but are maladaptive if they interfere with continued mastery and growth, bring negative feedback, or result in lowered self-esteem. Factors contributing to adaptive coping include environmental support systems and past successful coping experiences which stimulate trust, autonomy, initiative and a positive view of the world. Adaptation of the abused child may take the form of apathy, depression, oppositional behavior, and immaturity. The child victim lives with a sense of uncertainty, impermanence, disorganization, and loss of control.

Coping Mechanisms

The coping mechanism a sexually abused child may choose can be one of several. *Identification* may occur with the offender who is the source of the victim's conflict, and one can find a nine-year-old victim who has sodomized a five-year-old sibling. There may be coping through *Regression*. Because adaptation to the abuse has been difficult a six-year-old will begin bed-wetting and display the clinging behaviors of a much younger child. There is often *Denial* and *Repression* when the experiences are excluded from consciousness. *Isolation* can occur which allows the child to separate his feelings from the source of trauma. There may be *Intellectualization* where the older child will use books, diagrams, or a diary to cope with crisis. Finally, there can be *Turning Against Self* rather than the object of conflict, and one finds running away, substance abuse, and suicidal and other damaging behaviors. Studies show that physically abused children display tremendous orality, indiscriminate affectional behavior with strangers, hypervigilance and extreme sensitivity to cues from adults (Beezley and Martin, 1976; Rodeheffer, 1976).

Younger children often use magical thinking. This may be in the form of *animism*, the belief that there are no accidents or impartial events but that everything occurs by intent; or *omnipotence*, the belief that thoughts are as powerful as deeds. Children also may use rituals as a way of warding off bad things or *denial*: if one doesn't think about things, they won't be real.

Assessing a Child's Development

Claire Fagin (1972) has described principles to guide assessment of a child's development. She proposes that at each stage "tools" emerge for the child to accomplish the "tasks" of that period. Once accomplished, these become the tools for the following stage in learning. The periods are infancy (birth to two), childhood (one-and-a-half to six years), juvenile (six to nine years), preadolescence (nine to twelve years) and early adolescence (twelve to fifteen years).

In the infancy period, the individual proceeds from birth to the emergence of a capacity for communication through speech. The main task of this age is learning to count on others to gratify needs and satisfy wishes. The tools are crying and other prespeech vocalizations.

For the sexually abused child from birth to approximately three years there are several key issues. Dependence on the adult for protection, a need for adult approval, and the inability to verbalize or generalize, significantly increases the vulnerability for victimization and reabuse. The basic fears of this age sexually abused child are of losing protection or "caring" of the adult and fear of painful assault (Ludwig, 1983).

As the child progresses to childhood or preschool period one finds the development of communication through speech. The general psychological tasks are learning to accept interference, to separate from parents, and to develop a sense of autonomy and initiative. The tools used are language, autistic invention (magical power of thoughts) and experimentation. With the latter there is refinement of aggressive behavior, imitation, curiosity, increased locomotion, masturbation, and parallel play. For the sexually abused child from three to five years, the ability to sequence events is present, gender differentiation is established, and although this age may not be specific about time, the child can tell before or after. Modesty develops, as does sexual curiosity, and there may be masturbation and sexualized play after abuse. The preschool child has significant confusion about abuse incidents. He/she may be frightened by the parent's anxiety or anger and have strong feelings of being "bad" or causing upset in the family. Behavior changes and phobias can develop. The four- to five-year-old preschooler tends to be protective of parents, begins to know right from wrong and to separate fantasy from reality. This child can be very talkative and generally responds well to praise and encouragement.

The middle childhood period begins with the need for association with age mates and ends with the capacity to love according to Fagin. The general tasks of a six- to a nine-year-old are learning to form satisfying relationships with peers, to win recognition by producing, to intellectually move from egocentricity to the abstract, and to see self in relation to others. The tools utilized are competition, compromise, cooperation, and exploration. This child begins accepting responsibility and learns to take consequences for his/her behavior. He/she can distinguish the differences in his/her own role in various social and authoritative situations.

In preadolescence, nine to twelve years, the child moves to a fully social state. Here emerges the capacity to love, a tool which enables the child to express himself/herself freely because he/she thinks as much of someone else as he/she thinks of himself/herself. Tolerance, sympathy, generosity, and optimism also appear. A value system develops in this period, and the mores of his culture are important. The school-age child can be summarized as an individual diffusing into the large world and achieving compromise between home and the larger world.

The sexually abused developmental issues for the school age child are several. The abuse is perceived as sexual, there are feelings that "sex is wrong" and there are often threats by the perpetrator to maintain the secret. There is often guilt about incident(s) and impact of disclosure on family members (Summit, 1983). The child has discomfort discussing his or her body, especially with persons outside the family. The abusive incident may have been pleasurable and nontraumatic which is difficult for many adults to hear and accept (Rosenfeld, 1982). The child will have fears that his or her body "feels dirty" and "different" after sexual abuse.

Early adolescence begins with first signs of puberty to the completion of mature body changes. The main psychological areas of focus are a struggle for independence, an acceptable body image, a search for self-identity, and the mastery of abstract thinking. This may be a time of highs and lows and frequent mood shifts for the maturing child. Peers are of critical importance, and anxiety is the tool used to learn the establishment of relations with members of the opposite and same sex. The issues with the sexually abused adolescent are multiple and complex. There is a strong need to conform and be "normal." With sexual victimization there is grief over loss of virginity, feelings of abnormality and of being dirty, as described with the used goods syndrome (Sgroi, 1983). The abused adolescent often doesn't feel understood and may withdraw into depression by running away, substance abuse, or suicide gestures.

To summarize development, the child from birth is growing, evolving, changing physically, cognitively, and psychologically. He/she is mastering a sense of belonging. Recent knowledge in childhood growth and development has changed the notion of the child as a blank slate to be filled in and shaped by parents, environment, and community. An understanding of the uniqueness of childhood as a special time of change is needed by all who plan to work with children. This paper presents normal growth and development with allowance for variation. Children, especially the tragic victims of sexual abuse, need to be understood, taught and dealt with differently from adults. The United Nations Declaration of Rights of the Child states "the child shall enjoy special protection and shall be given opportunities and facilities by law and other means to enable him/her to develop physically, mentally, morally, spiritually and socially in a healthy and normal manner in conditions of freedom and dignity. . . . the child shall be the paramount consideration. . . . Mankind owes the child the best it has to give" (Wilkerson, 1973). This challenge is clear to all who work with child victims.

Bibliography

Babich, Karen
1982 "Assessing the Mental Health of Children" Monograph, WICHE, NIMH.

Barahal, Robert M., Jill Waterman, and Harold P. Martin
1981 "The Social Cognitive Development of Abused Children." *J. of Consul and Clin. Psychology,* 49(4): 508–516.

Beezley, Patricia, Harold P. Martin, and Ruth Kempe
1976 "Psychotherapy." In Harold P. Martin and C. Henry Kempe, eds. *The Abused Child.* Cambridge, MA: Ballinger, pp. 201–214.

Fagin, Claire M.
1972 *Nursing in Child Psychiatry.* St. Louis: C.V. Mosby, pp. 13–27.

Finkelhor, David, and Angela Browne
1985 "The Traumatic Impact of Child Sexual Abuse." *Amer. J. of Orthopsychiatry,* 55(4): 530–451.

Hartman, Carol R., and Ann Wolpert Burgess
1985 "Child Sexual Abuse: Generic Roots of the Victim Experience." *J. of Psychotherapy and the Family,* 2(2): 77–87.

Illingsworth, Ronald
1983 *The Normal Child.* New York: Churchill-Livingstone.

Josselyn, Irene
1978 *Psychosocial Development of Children.* New York: Family Serv. Assoc. of Am.

Kagan, Jerome
1971 *Understanding Children.* New York: Harcourt Brace.
1984 *The Nature of the Child.* New York: Basic Books.

Ludwig, Stephen
1983 "Child Abuse." In Gerald Fleisher et al., eds. *Textbook of Pediatric Emergency Medicine.* Baltimore: Williams & Wilkens, pp. 1027–1049.

Maier, Henry W.
1978 *Three Theories of Child Development.* New York: Harper and Row.

Martin, Harold P., and Patricia Beezley
1977 "Behavioral Observations of Abused Children." *Developmental Medicine and Child Neurology,* 19: 373–387.

Martin, Harold P., Patricia Beezley, et al.
1974 "The Development of Abused Children, Part I: Review of Literature. Part II: Physical, Neurologic, and Intellectual Outcome." *Advances in Pediatrics,* 21: 25–73.

Mrazek, Patricia, and David Mrazek
1981 "The Effects of Child Sexual Abuse." In Patricia Mrazek and C. Henry Kempe, eds. *Sexually Abused Children and Their Families.* New York: Pergamon, pp. 235–245.

Mussen, Paul H., John J. Conger, and Jerome Kagan
1979 *Child Development and Personality.* New York: Harper and Row.

Piaget, Jean, and Barbara Snhelder
1969 *The Psychology of the Child.* New York: Basic Books.

Pothier, Patricia
1980 "Issues and Influences in Infancy and Childhood." In Marion Kalkman and Anne Davis, eds. *New Dimensions in Mental Health and Psychiatric Nursing.* New York: McGraw-Hill.

Rodeheffer, Martha, and Harold P. Martin
1976 "Special Problems in Development Assessment of Abused Children." In Harold P. Martin and C. Henry Kempe, eds. *The Abused Child.* Cambridge, MA: Ballinger, pp. 113–128.

Rosenfeld, Alvin A.
1982 "Sexual Abuse of Children: Personal and Professional Responses." In Eli Newberger, ed. *Child Abuse.* New York: Little, Brown, pp. 57–87.

Sgroi, Suzanne M.
1983 *Handbook of Clinical Intervention in Child Sexual Abuse.* Lexington, MA: Lexington Books.

Smetana, Judith, Mario Kelly, and Craig Twentyman
1984 "Abused Neglected and Non-maltreated Children's Conception of Moral and Social-conventional Transgressions." *Child Development,* 55: 277–287.

Summit, Roland
1983 "The Child Sexual Abuse Accommodation Syndrome." *Child Abuse and Neglect,* 7: 177–193.

Wilkerson, Albert E.
1973 "United Nations Declaration of Rights of the Child." In Albert Wilkerson, ed. *The Rights of Children.* Philadelphia: Temple, pp. 3–6.

5

Victims of Incestuous Abuse: Mental Health Professionals' Attitudes and Tendency to Report

Seth C. Kalichman
University of South Carolina
and
Northside Community Mental Health Center
Tampa, Florida

Mary E. Craig
University of South Carolina

This study investigated mental health professionals' patterns of responsibility attribution for incestuous abuse and their tendency to report incest cases. The purpose of the study was to: (1) investigate mental health professionals' patterns of attributing responsibility for incestuous abuse, (2) observe how responsibility attribution to the father and daughter may be affected by changes in victim's age, (3) investigate professionals' tendency to report incestuous abuse. Results indicated sex differences in clinicians' incest responsibility attribution to both daughter/victims and mothers in father-daughter incest families. Responsibility attribution to father and daughter was found to be a function of the victim's age: fathers abusing younger victims were blamed more, while the victim was blamed less. Also, 40 percent of non-licensed clinicians were not aware of reporting laws, and 25 percent indicated they would not report incest. Results are discussed with reference to the effectiveness of mandatory reporting laws. Suggestions for future research are offered.

The authors wish to thank Northside Community Mental Health Center, Tampa, Florida, Hillsborough County Sexual Abuse Treatment Center, and Broward County Mental Health Division for their participation in this project. Tony Broskowski, Rita Kalichman, and Linda Steinman are also acknowledged for their support in this research.

Incestuous abuse is known to occur across all segments of society at higher rates each year (Finkelhor, 1984). Recent social awareness of incest has led to an increase in empirical research. One important direction this research has taken is in the study of incest's impact on those involved (Courtois, 1979). Victims of father-daughter incest are known to develop a number of emotional and social problems, including depression, social skills deficits, sexual dysfunction, substance abuse, and higher rates of suicide attempts (Browne and Finkelhor, 1986; Spencer, 1978). Ruch and Chandler (1982) reported that child incest victims suffer a greater degree of trauma than both adult and child rape victims. It is, therefore, no surprise that incest victims are seen so frequently as mental health clients. Husain and Chapel (1983) found that 14 percent of adolescent girls admitted to a psychiatric in-patient facility had been incestuously abused, a finding replicated by other studies (e.g., Rosenfeld, 1979; Spencer, 1978).

Although victims of incest are frequently seen in mental health centers, the question of mental health professionals' attitudes toward incest and incest victims has not been addressed in the literature. Attitudes and beliefs held by professionals about clients are known to affect treatment procedures. For example, Alexander (1980) cites a number of studies demonstrating that the quality of care offered by professionals working with a number of different populations may be affected by their attitudes. Attribution of responsibility is one area of attitude research which lends itself well to the study of victims because of the underlying theoretical constructs which account for such attributions. For example, a person who ascribes to a "just world hypothesis" may attribute substantial levels of responsibility to victims for their circumstances (Alexander, 1980). Further, attributing responsibility to a person may imply causality or moral responsibility for the situation (Schneider, Hastorf, and Ellsworth, 1979).

As a particular case of child abuse, father-daughter incest is included under the child abuse reporting laws in all fifty states (Finkelhor, 1984). Despite the legal obligations involved, Swoboda, Elwork, Sales, and Levine (1978) found that 66 percent of licensed psychologists surveyed would not report a hypothetical case of child abuse. Other studies have obtained similar results with psychologists (Muehleman and Kimmons, 1981), teachers, family physicians, clergy, and psychiatrists (Williams, Osborne and Rappaport, 1985). Research has not addressed the possibility that professionals may treat different types of abuse in different ways. With many professionals stating that they are not likely to report cases of child abuse and the overrepresentation of incest victims seen in psychiatric settings, a study of mental health professionals' attitudes towards incest and their tendency to report incest seems of value.

Table 5.1

Licensed and Non-Licensed Professionals by Sex (n=71)

	Licensed		Non-Licensed	
	Psychologists and Social Workers	Psychiatrists and Nurses	Adult Counselors	Adolescent Counselors
Male	10	3	10	10
Female	10	9	10	9

In the present study, mental health professionals' patterns of attributing responsibility for incestuous abuse and their reporting of incest are investigated. The attribution of responsibility to the mother in a father-daughter incest family is also explored. To our knowledge, no study has considered the mother as a factor in incest responsibility attribution. Finally, the effect of the victim's age on levels of attributed responsibility is also investigated. It is hypothesized that mental health professionals will alter their responsibility attribution as a function of victim age and, therefore, demonstrate a differential attitude system.

Method

Subjects

This study was conducted in two mental health centers in Florida. The centers are relatively similar in services provided, clients served, and setting. The subjects were thirty-three male and thirty-eight female licensed and non-licensed mental health professionals working with either adolescents or adults in an in-patient or out-patient setting. Table 5.1 presents the distribution of subjects within the different professional categories. Subjects participated voluntarily and were assured of anonymity and confidentiality.

Procedures

Data were collected through surveys distributed to subjects on their job sites and completed in private rooms. Each questionnaire consisted of four parts. First, the Jackson Incest Blame Scale (JIBS) was adminstered. The JIBS is a factor-analytically derived, twenty-item, six-point Likert-type scale measuring father/offender, daughter/victim, situation, and society responsibility attribution (Jackson and Ferguson, 1983). Scores on each factor of the JIBS could range from 5 to 30. A second measure of responsibility attribution was used which involved assigning relative percentages of responsibility for father-daughter incest to the father, mother, daughter, situation, and society (Alexander, 1980; Steinman, 1981). Responsibility was assigned to each source of attribution under three conditions of victim age: when the victim was referred to as a child, an adolescent, and no specific age. Part Three consisted of two open-ended questions asking subjects their tendency to report a case of incestuous abuse and their awareness of state mandatory reporting laws. The first question asked "hypothetically, if you were working with a child and she told you in confidence that she was being sexually abused by her father, how would you handle that? What would you do?" The second question continued "do you know of any law which might pertain to such a situation?" Responses were judged by two independent raters for likelihood of reporting a particular case and demonstrating knowledge that reporting suspected child abuse is mandatory in Florida. Disagreements were settled by discussion. Finally, Part Four consisted of a brief history of the subject's background and professional history.

Results

Mental health professionals attributed the greatest degree of responsibility to the father and the least to the daughter on both measures of

Table 5.2

Means and Standard Deviations of Jackson Incest Blame Scale Scores by Clinician Sex

	JIBS Factor			
Clinician Sex	Father	Daughter	Society	Situation
Males	21.6 (3.7)	11.2 (2.9)	15.1 (5.1)	18.1 (3.1)
Females	22.1 (4.1)	9.4 (2.8)	16.2 (5.5)	17.8 (3.4)

Table 5.3

Means and Standard Deviations of Relative Percentages of Responsibility Assigned as a Function of Clinician Sex

	Sources of Responsibility				
Clinician Sex	Father	Mother	Daughter	Society	Situation
Males	63% (20.2)	22% (14.3)	5% (6.9)	4% (6)	5% (8.2)
Females	64% (27.1)	16% (13.4)	8% (17.1)	3% (4.6)	7% (8.1)

responsibility attribution. Clinicians were also found to attribute a substantial amount of responsibility to the mother in these families (19 percent). Tables 5.2 and 5.3 display male and female clinicians' mean JIBS scores and relative percentages of responsibility, respectively.

Analyses of variance indicated that male clinicians attributed significantly greater responsibility to the mother than did female clinicians [F (1,68) = 3.94, p<.05]. Analyses also indicated significant sex differences in subjects' scores on the Jackson Incest Blame Scale. On the JIBS, male clinicians were found to attribute significantly more responsibility to the daughter in a father-daughter incest family [F (1,68) = 7.4, p<.01].

Manipulation of the daughter's age did not affect levels of responsibility attributed to the mother, situation, and society. However, the father was attributed significantly greater levels of responsibility when the daughter was referred to as a child [t (70) = 5.4, p<.001]. Table 5.4 presents mean percentages of responsibility attribution as a function of victim age.

Results also indicated significant differences between licensed and non-licensed clinicians in their knowledge of reporting laws and their tendency to report incest. Forty percent of non-licensed clinicians were unaware of the reporting laws, and 25 percent responded that they would not report a case of incest as presented in the question. In contrast, all licensed clinicians responded that they knew the reporting laws and would report cases of incest.

Discussion

Mental health clinicians' patterns of attributing responsibility for incestuous abuse are very similar to the patterns of college students reported by Steinman (1981) and Jackson and Ferguson (1983). This finding was unexpected, given that more than 90 percent of the sample had had contact with sexually abusive persons or victims. While disproportionate cell sizes precluded statistical testing, there were no apparent differences between those having had contact and those who had none in their attribution of responsibility. However, there were significant sex differences in responsibility attribution. Males attributing greater levels of responsibility to the daughter/victim were found both in this study and in a study of college students (Jackson and Ferguson, 1983). Therefore, the social values reflected in levels of responsibility attribution do not seem to change with experience in working with abusers and victims. This result suggests that the effects of experience on professionals' attitudes towards child abuse are different from those of rape (Alexander, 1980).

Our results also found that clinicians attributed a substantial degree of responsibility to the mother in a father-daughter incest family. The mother in these families is clinically important due to the number of cases referred to family therapy and the importance of family dynamics in the treatment of families and victims. Male clinicians attributing a greater degree of responsibility to the mother may reflect a sex difference in the perception of the mother's role in the family. One possible explanation of this result is that males are more inclined to believe that mothers should be highly attentive to family interactions and are, therefore, accountable for what happens within the family. This belief appears to be related to traditional sex roles ascribed to family members.

Table 5.4

Mean Relative Percentages of Responsibility Assigned as a Function of Victim Age

	Sources of Responsibility				
Victim Age	Father	Mother	Daughter	Society	Situation
Child	68%	19%	2%	4%	5%
Adolescent	63%	18%	8%	4%	5%
Not Specified	63%	19%	6%	3%	6%

Mental health professionals systematically altered their attribution of responsibility to the father and daughter as a function of the daughter/victim's age. Clinicians held father/offenders more responsible for committing incest when the daughter was younger. That adolescent victims are held accountable for their sexual victimization has direct clinical implications for the treatment of adults who have been victimized in adolescence and for adolescents who are currently being abused (Courtois, 1979; Gelinas, 1983). Interestingly, responsibility attributed to the mother did not change as a function of the victim's age. This result suggests that the non-abusive mother's role is viewed as a constant throughout a child's development.

With respect to reporting, in contrast to previous studies, all of the licensed professionals in this study stated that they knew the law and that they would report a case of incestuous abuse. This finding is contrary to previous research in which many licensed professionals did not know the reporting laws and would not report child abuse. The discrepancy suggests that clinicians view incestuous abuse differently than physical abuse and, therefore, respond to it differently. Alternatively, this difference may be due to sampling. This study investigated only clinicians employed by mental health centers while other studies sampled clinicians randomly through professional associations (Muehleman and Kimmons, 1981; Swoboda et al., 1978). It is possible that clinicians working within agencies are facing multiple consequences if they fail to report a case of child abuse and may, therefore, be more motivated to report.

The large number of non-licensed clinicians in this study failing to report incestuous abuse deserves consideration. Non-licensed clinicians commonly stated that they were more likely to console and comfort the child victim and find out what she would like to have done about the situation. The majority of subjects not reporting incest stated they were unaware of the reporting laws. However, knowledge of the law did not necessarily correspond with reporting. A number of non-licensed clinicians who did not know the law stated they would report, while others who did know the law would not. It seems likely that non-licensed clinicians are somewhat misinformed over issues of confidentiality. They appear to be facing the dilemma of maintaining confidentiality and following the law, both of which have ethical constraints. Therefore, it seems essential to provide training programs to educate all mental health providers about the existence of reporting laws, as well as the reality of the affects of reporting on the child, family, and subsequent treatment.

Further Research

There can be no question of the relevance and importance of clinicians' decision making in child abuse reporting. Given that there have been few studies conducted investigating this area, there are numerous questions which remain to be answered. Below we offer some possible directions for future research.

First, it remains unclear what it is that clinical service providers are considering when they fail to report suspected abuse. For example, suspected abuse may not be well enough defined to warrant reports for some clinicians; that is, what constitutes suspicion has not been clarified. If clinicians believe that a minimum degree of information is required to justify a report, they may fail to report until such information is gathered. Clearly, the law would read that if a suspicion warrants the gathering of further information, it would warrant reporting. Thus, researchers may attempt to investigate clinicians' interpretations of the law and how interpretations relate to decision making. In addition, the degree to which clinicians believe they must be correct in their suspicion before reporting should be assessed. Thus, the relationship between degree of confidence the clinician has in abuse occurring and deciding to report should be investigated.

A second area that should be addressed in future research is the effect of training on reporting decisions. As seen in the present study, professionals of varying levels of education differ in their approach to reporting. Also, the setting within which the professional works should be investigated as an influencing factor. Do professionals working within institutions and for agencies differ from those who work in private practices? In addition, specific training programs for professionals of various levels and settings should be designed, implemented, and evaluated.

Finally, the role of responsibility attribution in clinical settings will require careful study. While the present study and others have identified patterns of responsibility attribution for child abuse, the relationship of these attitudes to clinically relevant factors has not been demonstrated. Also, the precise meaning of attributed responsibility needs clarification. For example, it is not clear what 19 percent of responsibility attributed to the mother in incestuous families means. While potential interpretations have been offered, these are tentative and will require controlled research for greater confidence. In addition, the JIBS will require further validation, and it, too, should be investigated for application.

It is suggested that future researchers in child abuse reporting carefully look at a variety of professionals using a multimethod approach. The use of analogue methods, such as vignettes and scenarios depicting abusive situations, may provide insight into the factors which influence reporting. These studies will need to be carefully controlled and experimentally designed to provide clear answers (Alexander, 1980; Finkelhor, 1984). Interviews and various survey formats may also be employed to assess views and interpretations of reporting laws. Finally, field experiments may be conducted in various clinical settings to investigate factors influencing reporting within an ecologically valid context. Such studies will provide further understanding of how clinicians approach cases of child abuse and will move us closer to improving the quality of services provided to cases of child abuse.

Bibliography

Alexander, C.
1980 "The Responsible Victim: Nurses' Perceptions of Victims of Rape." *Journal of Health and Social Behavior,* 21: 22–23.

Browne, A., and Finkelhor, D.
1986 "Impact of Child Sexual Abuse: A Review of the Research." *Psychological Bulletin,* 99: 66–77.

Courtois, C.A.
1979 "The Incest Experience and Its Aftermath." *Victimology: An International Journal,* 4: 337–347.

Finkelhor, D.
1984 *Child Sexual Abuse: New Theory and Research.* New York: Free Press.

Gelinas, D.J.
1983 "The Persisting Negative Effects of Incest." *Psychiatry,* 46: 312–332.

Husain, A., and J.L. Chapel
1983 "History of Incest in Girls Admitted to a Psychiatric Hospital." *American Journal of Psychiatry,* 140: 591–593.

Jackson, T.L., and W.P. Ferguson
1983 "Attribution of Blame in Incest." *American Journal of Community Psychology,* 11: 313–322.

Muehleman, T., and C. Kimmons
1981 "Psychologists' Views on Child Abuse Reporting, Confidential-

ity, Life, and the Law: An Exploratory Study." *Professional Psychology,* 12: 631–637.

Rosenfeld, A.A.
1979 "Incidence of a History of Incest Among 18 Female Psychiatric Patients." *American Journal of Psychiatry,* 136: 791–795.

Ruch, L., and S.M. Chandler
1982 "The Crisis Impact of Sexual Assault on Three Victim Groups: Adult Rape Victims, Child Rape Victims, and Incest Victims." *Journal of Social Service Research,* 5: 83–100.

Schneider, D.J., A. Hastorf, and P. Ellsworth
1979 *Person Perception.* Reading, MA: Addison-Wesley.

Spencer, J.
1978 "Father-Daughter Incest: A Clinical View from the Corrections Field." *Child Welfare,* 9: 581–591.

Steinman, L.M.
1981 "Attribution of Responsibility to Differing Aged Victims as a Function of Beliefs Concerning the Scope, and the Effects of Incestuous Abuse." Unpublished manuscript, Pennsylvania State University.

Swoboda, J., A. Elwork, B.D. Sales, and D. Levine
1978 "Knowledge of and Compliance with Privileged Communication and Child Abuse Reporting Laws." *Professional Psychology,* 9: 448–458.

Williams, H., Y. Osborne, and N. Rappaport
1985 "Child Abuse Report Law: Differences Among Professional Groups in Tendency to Report and Knowledge of Law." Paper presented at the meeting of the Southeastern Psychological Association, Atlanta.

6

Violence Against Children: The Pharmaceutical Industry

Frank Henry
McMaster University
Hamilton, Ontario,
Canada

Susanne Chomicki
Wilfrid Laurier University
Waterloo, Ontario, Canada

This chapter examines the drug industry's role as chief educator of the medical profession on drug use and shows how profit maximization has induced the drug companies to use this position to promote a variety of inadequately tested drugs and drugs of which the harmful effects were well known before marketing. The results have been disease, injury and death for thousands of children in developed and underdeveloped countries. This violence begins before birth with drugs such as thalidomide and Bendectin, continues through early childhood with such drugs as Chloromycetin and Lomotil (especially in the Third World) and into later childhood with psycho-active drugs such as Ritalin for which a specific behavioral disorder, minimal brain dysfunction, was invented.

Companies in the pharmaceutical industry engage in violence by promoting drugs for which the known harmful effects far outweigh the possible benefits, by promoting drugs for inappropriate uses, by promoting drugs without adequate warnings of their harmful side effects and by promoting drugs for which the harmful effects have purposely been inadequately investigated. This chapter will examine a number of cases of this pharmaceutical violence against children but to appreciate the extent to which drug companies are able to promote the misuse of their products it is helpful to have some understanding of how completely information and misinformation regarding drugs is under the control of the drug industry. A physician's education in medical school does not ordinarily include many hours in the use of drugs. According to testimony at a Senate hearing in 1974, fewer than 10 percent of the medical schools in the United States provided any courses in drug therapeutics. On the other hand after graduation all medical societies in the United States require physicians to take courses in continuing medical education and by 1978, drug companies were yearly spending up to fifteen hundred dollars per office-based physician to sponsor symposia for which doctors could get continuing education credit. Naturally, they select speakers and panel members who are known to be sympathetic to the drug industry point of view (Hughes and Brewin, 1979: 194–205).

One of the most important sources of information about drugs is the battery of sales representatives who call on doctors, druggists and hospital and clinic personnel to promote their company's products. In the United States there is about one drug company sales representative for every ten doctors (Silverman, 1976: 122). According to a Pharmaceutical Manufacturers Association survey, 53 percent of physicians considered the sales representatives a very important source of information about drugs and 31 percent considered them a somewhat important source of information; only 16 percent considered them an unimportant source (Hughes and Brewin, 1979: 209). Sales representatives tend to favor the heavy prescription writers with more visits and probably their more frequent visits also tend to encourage greater use of prescription drugs. One survey found that doctors who received fewer than four visits a week from drug company sales representatives wrote on the average less than fifty prescriptions per week; whereas doctors who had more than eight visits per week, wrote more than one hundred and fifty prescriptions per week (Braithwaite, 1984: 213–214). It was also noted that the heavy prescribers were more dependent on drug information supplied by drug manufacturers. Only 40 percent of doctors who wrote fewer than thirty prescriptions per week reported that the drug industry was their most important source of information about drugs, compared with 75 percent of those who wrote from fifty to one hundred prescriptions per week and 100 percent of those who wrote one hundred and fifty or more (Braithwaite, 1984: 213–214). Since those doctors who prescribe more are more dependent on industry sources for their drug information, it seems that something like 85 percent of all prescriptions in the United States are based on information and misinformation supplied by drug manufacturers and in particular by their personal agents, the sales representatives.

In most countries, sales representatives work on a salary plus commission basis. Their commissions or bonuses are based on the analysis of sales to pharmacies, hospitals and clinics within each sales region. Drug company representatives are usually cautioned to be truthful but as one medical director explained to John Braithwaite, "Our great concern is not so much avoiding misrepresentation, though that's important for its own sake, but avoiding those kinds of misrepresentation which upset doctors. The company's credibility is all important" (1984: 223). The usual response to a complaint about an over enthusiastic sales person is a transfer to a region where sales are lagging (Braithwaite, 1984: 223–225).

Another important source of information about drugs for prescribing physicians is the *Physicians' Desk Reference* which is distributed free of charge to 340,000 physicians in the United States. Other countries have similar reference books, for example, the *British Monthly Index of Medical Specialties* (MIMS UK). Surveys show that doctors typically refer to the *Physicians' Desk Reference* seven or eight times a week. Information for the PDR is supplied by the drug companies and constitutes an important type of paid advertising. Drug indications, contraindications and warnings generally adhere fairly well to Food and Drug Administration regulations, although the 1978 edition, for example, contained some descriptions that the FDA considered incomplete, inadequate and misleading (Hughes and Brewin, 1979: 217).

For some doctors at least, articles in medical journals are an important source of information about drugs but here, too, drug company influence is not lacking: Their advertisements are colorful and striking and constitute a considerable proportion of most medical journals. The only medical publication in the United States that does not accept drug advertising is *The Medical Letter*, which is published by an independent non-profit organization and contains evaluations of drugs by various specialists (Silverman, 1976: 123). The American Medical Association once set up a committee of distinguished physicians to check the accuracy of ads submitted to the *Journal of the AMA*. Advertising revenue dropped as the drug companies switched their promotional money elsewhere, where such restrictions did not exist, and the committee was disbanded (Braithwaite, 1984: 218).

Some of the articles in medical journals are written by drug company employees, not always under their own name. For example, an article defending thalidomide published in the *American Journal of Obstetrics and Gynecology* under the by-line of Dr. R.O. Neilsen was actually written by Dr. Raymond Pogge an employee of Richardson-Merrell, the American licensee for thalidomide (Dowie and Marshall, 1980). Physicians who have done clinical trials on a drug and have achieved favorable results are also urged to publish their findings. One use of journal articles is to advertise drugs not yet approved for marketing. FDA commissioner James Goddard complained of "The planting in journals of articles that begin to commercialize what is still an investigational drug" (Silverman and Lee, 1974: 105).

Drug industry domination of drug information would present little problem if this information were consistently accurate. One indication of the degree of accuracy of drug industry information is provided by the results of the studies of drug efficacy carried out by the National Academy of Sciences-National Research Council. The 1938 Food, Drug and Cosmetic Act had required evidence of safety before a drug could be approved for marketing but the act did not require evidence of efficacy. The 1962 Kefauver-Harris Amendments to the act made it necessary to check the efficacy of all drugs approved for marketing between 1938 and 1962. FDA commissioner Goddard arranged for the National Academy of Sciences and its research arm, the National Research Council, to make the necessary studies. Two hundred experts constituted thirty panels to consider the evidence for the efficacy of some four thousand products which were being prescribed or sold over the counter at that time. Of the sixteen thousand therapeutic claims submitted for these drugs, 66 percent were rejected for lack of evidence. The drug companies were given additional time to prove that their products were effective for the purposes indicated, that their claims were true, but in the end most of them were withdrawn from the market or the excess claims were dropped (Silverman and Lee, 1974: 115–124).

Considering the domination of drug information by the drug industry, it is not surprising that some medical educators have expressed concern regarding the drug education of physicians and the rationality of their prescribing. Dr. Jan Koch-Weser of Harvard, for example, expressed her belief that "lack of knowledge in the proper therapeutic use of drugs is perhaps the greatest deficiency of the average American physician today" (Silverman and Lee, 1974: 282). Rational prescribing may be defined as "the right drug for the right patient, at the right time, in the right amount and with due consideration of relative costs." A study of the rationality of the prescribing of physicians in private practice in the U.S. found that the percentage of irrational prescriptions varied from 57 for hypertension to 86 for anemia. A Canadian study reported somewhat better results: Irrational prescribing varied from 15 percent for cardiac failure to 75 percent for hypertension (Silverman and Lee, 1974: 282, 299–300). A more recent study in the Netherlands found, on the average, 52 percent of prescriptions were irrational (Haayer, 1982).

Cases of Violence Against Children

When administered during the fifth to eighth week of pregnancy, when the limbs began to form, thalidomide is nearly 100 percent teratogenic. Some thalidomide children were born with no arms, just flippers; some have no legs, only toes from the hip; some are deaf or blind (Knightley et al., 1979: 91; Dowie and Marshall, 1980). All these children were victims of the lie that thalidomide was a completely safe, completely non-toxic, tranquilizer (Knightley et al., 1979: 1–2). Thalidomide was invented by the German firm, Chemie Gruenthal. Although most of Gruenthal's records disappeared sometime before their 1968 trial, it seems quite clear that thalidomide was very inadequately tested. With regard to effectiveness, when standard tests showed no effect, Gruenthal devised new tests; their researchers are the only ones who have ever been able to show a sedative effect of thalidomide. For example, when Smith, Kline and French were offered the U.S. license, they checked the sedative effect of thalidomide and found that the drug had no effect and rejected the offer to be the U.S. licensee (Knightley et al., 1979: 15–19).

Although a sedative would likely be used over the long-term and although thalidomide was advertised as safe on a long-term basis, no tests were made of its long-term effects. Also, although thalidomide was advertised as safe for pregnant women, no tests were ever performed with pregnant animals until a few days before the drug was removed from the market. Then Dr. George Somers, pharmacologist at Distillers Company, the British licensee, used four sets of rats, including a control set, to investigate the effect of thalidomide administered during pregnancy. He found that the litter size varied inversely with the dosage level. At the highest dosage level about half the pups were apparently reabsorbed into the placenta because they were deformed: This is the way the bodies of mice and rats respond to deformed pups (Knightley et al., 1979: 49–58). A short time later he administered thalidomide to four pregnant white rabbits. Thirteen of the sixteen kits were born with the horrible deformities associated with thalidomide. New Zealand white rabbits were a standard item in Distiller's laboratories (Knightley et al., 1979: 108–110, 271). These experiments should have been performed years earlier, but presumably if thalidomide were teratogenic, Gruenthal and Distillers and Richardson-Merrell and other licensees preferred not to know. And so they would do no safety testing not required by their regulatory agencies.

When the advertising people at Chemie Gruenthal had said that thalidomide was astonishingly safe, fully harmless, completely non-toxic and exhausted all of the synonyms for safe and non-toxic, they would likely think of other ways of expressing the same idea: That thalidomide was safe on a long-term basis, or that it was safe even for infants or the very old, or that it was safe even for pregnant women. Just doing their job of promoting thalidomide. A few weeks before Distaval (Distiller's trade name for thalidomide) was removed from the market an ad read: "Distaval can be given with complete safety to pregnant women and nursing mothers without adverse effect on mother or child" (Teff and Munro, 1976: 2).

When Smith, Kline and French turned down the license for thalidomide, Gruenthal made an arrangement with Richardson-Merrell. Even before Richardson-Merrell made application to the FDA to market thalidomide in the United States, the company sent out over two and a half million thalidomide tablets to 1,267 physicians. What were supposedly clinical trials were run not by the medical department but by the sales department using physicians selected by the sales representatives. No placebos or consent forms were supplied except by request. When the horrors of thalidomide became evident, several hundred patients could not be contacted because the doctors had kept no records of to whom the tablets had been given (Knightley et al., 1979: 70).

Dr. William McBride witnessed the birth of several deformed babies to mothers who had taken no drug during their pregnancies except thalidomide. He communicated his observations to the office of Distillers in New South Wales, but nothing was passed on to the head office in London until four months later. In the meantime investigation in Germany spurred on by a young lawyer whose wife and sister both gave birth to deformed babies, was reaching a similar conclusion. By 1960, nearly every pediatric clinic in Germany had at least one case of missing or shortened limbs (Teff and Munro, 1976: 5). Although a 1949 study, before the advent of thalidomide, found only one such case in 4,000,000 births, there were an estimated fifty cases of phocomelia in Hamburg alone between September 1960 and October 1961 (Knightley et al., 1979: 97). The initial reaction of Gruenthal executives to the investigations of the effects of thalidomide was to threaten to sue the investigators for slander, but eventually pressure from the health authorities brought the withdrawal of thalidomide from the market in Germany and Britain (Knightley et al., 1979: 86–106). However, other licensees continued to market thalidomide. In some countries, it was still being sold as much as a year later (Knightley et al., 1979: 2).

Bendectin is prescribed to pregnant women for the nausea and vomiting which not infrequently occurs in the first few months of pregnancy. Although four medical reviewers for the FDA reported that the studies submitted by Richardson-Merrell did not show the drug to be either safe or effective, the FDA approved Bendectin and it has been prescribed to millions of pregnant women. In spite of the fact that the drug was marketed only for nausea and vomiting in pregnancy, it was not tested for teratogenicity until after the thalidomide disaster. In 1963, Richardson-Merrell asked Dr. Robert Staples to test Bendectin with pregnant rabbits. When he found no deformities in the kits of two rabbits, he repeated the experiment and found deformities in two of the forty-eight kits. He concluded that this was not statistically significant proof that Bendectin caused birth defects. His study was not reported to the FDA. When seventeen years later, Dr. Roger Palmer, head of the Department of Pharmacology at the University of Miami School of Medicine, gained access to Dr. Staple's raw data, he found that one-half of the litters contained at least one abnormal kit and that the total number of deformed kits was not two out of forty-eight but six out of forty-eight. The company has not been charged for the criminal offense of withholding the Staple's results from the FDA (Dowie and Marshall, 1980).

In 1981, Dr. Reimar Roll conducted a study for the West German Health Ministry in which dexylamine succinate, the antihistomine in Bendectin, was fed to Wistar rats. Six percent of the bucks were born with diaphragmatic hernia (a hole in the diaphragm which allows the intestines to enter the chest and put pressure on the lungs). A study of one million American hospital births showed that the rate of diaphragmatic hernia increased 64 percent from 1970 to 1980, a period during which American Bendectin prescriptions approximately doubled (*Insider*, Winter 1983). Bendectin sale increases and diaphragmatic hernia increases were found to be roughly parallel. Dr. Rolf Bass found eleven times as many cases of diaphragmatic hernia among the sons of Bendectin users than among the sons of non-users in a study of 50,282 pregnancies in West Germany (Mintz, 1982).

Preliminary results of a study at the University of California at Davis suggest a link between Bendectin and a hole in the wall of the heart called ventricular septal defect, a deformity which has increased almost 300 percent among American women since 1970 according to the National Center for Disease Control (*Insider*, Summer 1982). The West German and California studies are the first two animal studies of Bendectin done independently of Richardson-Merrell. Richardson-Merrell knew of the Roll's study but did not submit it to the FDA until two weeks after Representative Steve Walgren (D-Pa.) sent a copy to FDA commissioner Arthur Hayes, Jr. (Mintz, 1982).

One of the clinical studies of Bendectin was conducted by Dr.

Richard Smithells of the University of Leeds. His research was supported by a grant of twenty-six thousand dollars from Richardson-Merrell. The company further showed its gratitude by depositing fifteen hundred dollars in Dr. Smithell's Canadian bank account. His report was rejected by the *British Medical Journal*, the *Lancet*, and the *New England Journal of Medicine* but accepted by *Teratology*, a journal on which Dr. Smithell is an associate editor. In a letter to Merrell, Dr. Smithell stated that he thought it was understood when he undertook the study that the published results would probably save the company a great deal of money in products liability suits and that the company would likely be generous to him as a result (Dowie and Marshall, 1980).

Of twenty-three clinical studies reviewed at the trial of Cordova and Merrell-Dow (formerly Richardson-Merrell) in Palo Alto, California; only two apparently showed more defects among the offspring of mothers in the control group than among the mothers administered Bendectin. While none of the other studies, considered individually, showed a statistically significant relation between Bendectin and birth defects, a simple sign test for the set of studies as a whole gives overwhelming evidence of such a correlation (Henry, 1985). There is, however, a difficulty with all of these imperfectly controlled clinical tests and that is that it may be the vomiting itself that is related to birth defects rather than the anti-nausea drugs. Evidence for this hypothesis is provided by studies such as those that show that rats which were fasted for twenty-four to forty-eight hours gave birth to litters with a variety of birth defects (Henderson, 1977: 722).

Not long after Bendectin came on the market, doctors began contacting Merrell describing birth defects in children born to women who had taken the drug during pregnancy. According to doctors interviewed for an article in *Mother Jones*, the set procedure when such a report was received was to have a medical officer from Merrell contact the doctor to see if the adverse reaction report could not be rephrased as an inquiry. (Drug companies are legally required to report adverse reaction reports to the FDA but not inquiries.) Richardson-Merrell would then respond to the doctor's inquiry by stating that no similar adverse reaction reports had been received. For example, in March 1971 an English doctor reported a case of a baby born with two missing fingers to a mother who had been prescribed Bendectin during her pregnancy. A Richardson-Merrell medical officer's reply was "I should like to reassure you that there is no record of Bendectin being associated with such abnormalities." By that date Richardson-Merrell files contained eleven cases of children born without fingers to mothers who had been prescribed Bendectin (Dowie and Marshall, 1980).

Dr. Bernard St. Raymond was the first FDA official to review

Richardson-Merrell's data on the safety of Bendectin. He reported that their study was "of practically no value." His report was ignored. Dr. Tom Anderson was asked to review a study of Bendectin's efficacy but he wanted rather to see all of the data on Bendectin and congenital abnormalities. Dr. Barrett Scoville was the next FDA official to evaluate Bendectin. He doubted that the drug should be "allowed to remain on the market" (Dowie and Marshall, 1980: 49, 54). Dr. E. DeVaughn Belton evaluated the studies on Decapryn, the antihistamine in Bendectin, which was also marketed separately. He advised Merrell that a warning would have to be given on the label that adequate reproduction studies had not been made of the drug. After a visit from Dr. Thomas O'Dell, a Merrell official, Dr. Marion Finkel, acting director of New Drug Evaluation, ruled that the warning was unnecessary. When Dr. Carol Kennedy, the next review official for Bendectin suggested that Merrell do a follow-up of the babies born to mothers who had participated in the efficacy study, Merrell resisted and Dr. Kennedy was given another job. When Dr. Frances Da Costa, another of the reviewers of Bendectin, was asked about FDA approval of the drug she described the review "as a kind of charade in which scientists who refused to play by company rules were simply pulled off the review" (Dowie and Marshall, 1980: 55). After the most recent FDA evaluation in 1981, Dr. A. T. Gregoire, executive secretary to the review panel, reported that because of the inadequacies of the studies presented, "There's uncertainty still, and Bendectin should only be used when everything else fails to stop pernicious vomiting" (*Insider*, Winter 1981: 1). Following a jury award in a Bendectin case of $750,000 in May 1983 (eventually overturned), Merrell-Dow announced plans to stop production of the drug (*The Spectator*, 1983).

Diethylstibestrol (DES) is a synthetic estrogen approximately two and one half times as powerful as natural estrogen. It was invented in the late 1930s in England and never patented. In 1941 a committee of twelve drug companies headed by Eli Lilly submitted applications to the FDA to market DES for a variety of conditions unrelated to pregnancy. These applications were approved. Beginning in 1947, applications were made and approved to market DES for the prevention of miscarriage. Although in this new use, DES was specifically aimed at the unborn child, and although it was well known that such drugs would pass the placental barrier, and although there were animal tests available that would have demonstrated in six weeks time that cancer was likely to develop in female offspring when they reached maturity, no such tests were made. The drug companies also should have been aware that in 1939, three prominant Chicago physiologists had experimented with DES on rats and mice and concluded that it was teratogenic.

Until the middle of the 1960s, cancer of the vagina or cervix was a relatively rare disease; radical surgery or radiation are the only possible treatments and if they are unsuccessful, death usually results (*Payton v. Abbott Laboratories*, 1982). Since 1965 there have been thousands of cases of vaginal and cervical cancer. Joyce Bichler was one such case. Joyce Bichler's mother was prescribed DES when she was pregnant with Joyce. At seventeen Joyce was diagnosed as having cancer of the cervix and vagina. Her life was saved by surgical removal of her ovaries, fallopian tubes and two-thirds of her vagina. Following the Kefauver-Harris Amendments to the 1983 Food, Drug and Cosmetic Act and the NAS-NRC evaluation of the efficacy of drugs approved prior to 1968, DES was decertified as a preventive of miscarriage, having been found to be both ineffective and teratogenic (*Bichler v. Eli Lilly*, 1981).

There are a number of other drugs with similar histories. For example, Pfizer was required to notify physicians that advertisements for the tranquilizers Atarax and Vistaril, and the antinauseants Bonamine and Bonadoxine, recommended to control the nausea of pregnancy, were inaccurate and gravely misleading in that they failed to mention that the drugs produced abnormal offspring in experimental animals (Silverman and Lee, 1974: 64). And drug companies are sometimes able to get around bans on the marketing of their products. For example, after the connection between oral pregnancy tests and deformities in the unborn child became well known and the pregnancy tests were withdrawn from the market, they continued to be sold as contraceptives. Duogynon was removed but five Anovlar tablets contain as much norethisterone as the two Duogynon tablets taken for the test and six times as much ethinyloestradiol as two Duogynon tablets. So a woman on Anovlar takes the equivalent of two Duogynon tablets every five days. There is a failure rate with contraceptive pills, especially if there is gastric upset, and some women menstruate once or twice after conception. Although the risk is low, the problem is great for any woman who bears a deformed child. She is given no warning so that she could decide for herself whether the risk is worth taking (Gorring, 1978).

From a financial point of view, the number of mass disasters that involve pregnant women and their unborn children is perhaps not too difficult to understand. On the one hand there is the traditional caution against prescribing any but absolutely necessary drugs to women during pregnancy, but on the other hand there is the fact of a more-or-less captive set of customers and the improbability of tracing the cause of the disaster to the drug company. The traditional reluctance of doctors to prescribe drugs to pregnant women has been overcome to a considerable extent by advertising them as absolutely safe during pregnancy, as in the case of thalidomide, or as specifically related to pregnancy as in the cases of Bendectin and DES. That the claims for the drugs were false, that thalidomide was not an effective sedative, Bendectin an effective antinauseant nor DES effective in preventing miscarriage, was regrettable, but from a financial point of view, largely irrelevant so long as doctors could be persuaded that the drug companies' claims were true. The traditional caution of physicians in prescribing drugs during pregnancy simply meant that a more intense advertising campaign would be involved. The drug companies faith in the likely success of their promotional schemes was proven by sales to be well founded. As Dr. Dale Console, former director of research at Squibb, told a Senate committee:

> With a little luck, proper timing, and a good promotion program, any bag of asafoetida with a unique chemical side-chain can be made to look like a wonder drug. The illusion will not last, but it frequently lasts long enough. By the time the doctor learns what the company knew at the beginning, it has two new products to take the place of the old one. . . . The pharmaceutical industry is unique in that it can make exploitation appear a noble purpose. (Silverman and Lee, 1974: 40)

The great majority of women in developed countries pay many visits to a doctor's office during pregnancy. Even with declining birth rates in first world countries these women constitute an enviable market for drugs. The doctor is the usual link between the drug company and the patient. Since the typical doctor's information regarding drugs is largely supplied by drug companies and the doctor is the one who decides on drug use, the doctor is, in a sense, an agent of the drug companies. Pregnancy is an occasion for repeated contact with this agent. Too good an opportunity, too big a market, to be missed. And the fact that the injury occurs, not to the patient herself, but to the unborn child, makes it somewhat less likely that the cause of the injury will be discovered, particularly if the injury is not apparent at birth. If cancer of the vagina and cervix had not been a relatively rare disease before the advent of DES, it seems doubtful that the thousands of cases of this disease initiated when the victim was in utero, would have been traced to the drug. Proof of injury is also especially difficult with a drug like DES. In the case of *Mink v. University of Chicago*, for example, it was held that the drug company could not be held liable on a theory of strict liability because it was not the women who had taken the drug who suffered physical injury (1978). And in several New York cases it was held that the time span relative to the statute of limitations began at the time the drug was ingested and it had therefore already elapsed when the cancer was discovered (*Johnson v. Eli Lilly*, 1983; *Fleishman v. Eli Lilly*, 1984).

Chloromycetin was developed at Yale with a grant from Parke, Davis and the company took out a seventeen year patent on it. It is a specific for typhoid fever, Rocky Mountain spotted fever and a rare urinary infection. In 1969, one hundred and seventy cases of typhoid fever were reported in the United States; at most there might be one thousand cases per year in the United States for which Chloromycetin would be the drug of choice. At twenty dollars per one hundred capsules that would have meant a gross income for Parke, Davis of twenty thousand dollars per year. The first year on the market (1949) sales were $9,000,000 and this had increased to $52,000,000 by 1951. Parke, Davis achieved this level of sales by promoting Chloromycetin not only for its appropriate uses but for a wide variety of inappropriate uses as well (Fuller, 1972: 65–70).

Aplastic anemia is one of the serious blood diseases caused by Chloromycetin. The bone marrow of a person suffering from this disease ceases to produce white and red blood cells and platelets; the result is frequently fatal. Extrapolating from California State Department of Health figures, Mintz estimated in 1979 that approximately 1,200 Americans had died of aplastic anemia caused by Chloromycetin. A Senate committee in the same year estimated the total number of Americans who were suffering severe adverse reactions from Chloromycetin to be two thousand per year (Muller, 1982: 31). Aplastic anemia did not kill Timothy Salmon but it did leave him permanently and seriously disabled. When Timothy was two years old, a physician prescribed Chloromycetin for an injury to his palate and again, later that year, for bronchitis. He developed aplastic anemia shortly thereafter (*Salmon v. Parke, Davis*, 1975).

Besides the dangers of aplastic anemia and other serious blood diseases, indiscriminate use of an antibiotic like chloramphenicol is likely to result in the development of resistance among some bacteria. When an epidemic of typhoid fever raged in Mexico in 1972–73, Chloromycetin, which had previously been the drug most effective against typhoid fever, was found to be of little use because the particular typhoid bacteria involved had, through long exposure to Chloromycetin, built up resistance against it. Some twenty thousand people, mostly children, died as a result (Mintz, 1979).

When Parke, Davis' patent on chloramphenicol ran out in 1973, McKesson Laboratories put out its brand (Chloramfenicol), and these two companies continued to market and promote chloramphenicol in the Third World with very inadequte warnings (Silverman, 1976: 13–14) and for a wide variety of inappropriate conditions, some of them ones that they were specifically forbidden to advertise the drug as appropriate for in the United States (Muller, 1982: 31).

Valium and its predecessor, Librium, have been advertised for children frightened by the dark, by school, by dental visits or by monsters. They were also advertised for college students facing a new environment, learning about national and world conditions, facing exams or unrealistic parental expectations (Braithwaite, 1984: 214–215). The National Institute on Drug Abuse estimates that from one to two million women in the United States are hooked on prescription psychoactive drugs like Valium. NIDA estimates the total number of people in the United States who are hooked on heroin as fewer than half a million.

Studies by the National Institute of Drug Abuse's Drug Alert Warning Network based on coroner's reports estimated nine hundred deaths yearly associated with Valium singly or in combination with other drugs; an estimated fifty deaths associated with Valium alone. And it was not until 1976 that the FDA finally required a warning label for pregnant patients on all minor tranquilizers, although, for years before this reports of birth abnormalities associated with Miltown, Librium and Valium had been sent by doctors to the drug manufacturers (principally Wallace Laboratories, Wyeth Laboratories and Hoffman-LaRoche) and to the FDA. Another adverse effect is that the unborn children of mothers addicted to drugs like Valium also become addicts and experience the horrors of withdrawal the first days after birth (Hughes and Brewin, 1979: 8–11, 62, 83, 110).

One form of drug misinformation is supplied by inventing an imaginary illness for which your company's drug is the remedy. For example, until taken to task by the FDA, Eli Lilly advertised that its tranquilizer, Aventyl, was effective in the treatment of "behavioral drift" (Silverman and Lee, 1974: 65). Another example of this form of promotion is the invention of the phrase minimal brain dysfunction as a diagnostic term for children who were, from an adult point of view, behavior problems. Ciba-Geigy's Ritalin was offered as the cure. Ciba-Geigy estimated that "one out of every twenty school children has MBD—three quarters of them boys." Company sales representatives showed films at teachers' meetings and PTA meetings describing the symptoms of MBD and pushing Ritalin. Adverse reactions to Ritalin include nervousness, insomnia, skin rash, anorexia, nausea, abdominal pain, dizziness, headache, angina, blood pressure and pulse changes, heart beat disturbances, and toxic psychosis (Hughes and Brewin, 1979: 115–125). In 1975, lawyers from the National Center for Youth Law in San Francisco brought suit on behalf of a number of school children and their parents against the Taft City School District and various employees to force them to stop "coercing children into taking a psychoactive drug commonly referred to as Ritalin as a condition of attending public school." In 1980 a settlement was reached in which the Taft board agreed to stop coercing children into taking Ritalin and to pay $210,000 in damages (*Benskin v. Taft City School District,* 1980). In the late 1970s the FDA ordered Ciba-Geigy to stop advertising directly to parents and school administrators and in 1979 it ordered the term minimal brain dysfunction eliminated as a diagnostic term (Hughes and Brewin, 1979: 117–118).

Ritalin is one of a number of drugs that can create some of the very symptoms it is supposed to cure. It is possible to increase a boy's nervousness by giving him Ritalin to reduce his nervousness. It is ideal from a profit point of view, if when the normal nervousness for which a boy may have been prescribed Ritalin disappears, Ritalin induced nervousness remains and prompts the prescribing of still more Ritalin. Bendectin works the same way with the nausea and vomiting of pregnancy. Likewise anxiety is one of the common side effects of Valium (Mendelsohn, 1981: 13–15; Hughes and Brewin, 1979: 17).

One of the most violent drug promotions in the Third World is that involving antidiarrhoeals. In underdeveloped countries, diarrhea is a leading cause of death especially among children. Antidiarrhoeals like Searle's Lomotil and Ciba-Geigy's Mexaform work by stopping the large intestine from pushing its contents along. However, the danger of diarrhea is not in the diarrhea itself but in dehydration, in too little fluid being available for the various body functions, and once the liquid has reached the large intestines it is completely unavailable. There is no advantage to retaining it there and if the antidiarrhoeal dose is too large, it can paralyze the gut and poison the patient. With children a fatal dose is not much larger than the recommended one. In Britain the doctor is warned, "Lomitil should be used with caution in young children . . . accidental overdosage may produce unconsciousness with respiratory depression, particularly in children, or atcopine poisoning, or both." No such warnings are given to Third World doctors (Melrose, 1982: 99). The important treatment for a child with diarrhea is replacement of lost fluid and this can be accomplished safely and inexpensively with a home mixture of salt, sugar, orange juice (or some other source of potassium) and water. Commercial antidiarrhoeals, by attacking only the most obvious symptom, retain the organism causing the diarrhea, further the harm they are supposedly intended to cure and increase the probability of the child's death (Muller, 1982: 50–61; Melrose, 1982: 98–100).

Bibliography

Benskin v. Taft City School District
1980 "Settlement Agreement." Mimeographed.

Bichler v. Eli Lilly and Company
1981 *North Eastern Reporter*, 436: 182–190.

Braithwaite, John
1984 *Corporate Crime in the Pharmaceutical Industry*. London: Routledge & Kegan Paul.

Dowie, Mark, and Carolyn Marshall
1980 "The Bendectin Cover-up," *Mother Jones*, 5 (November): 42–56.

Fleishman v. Eli Lilly and Company
1984 *Atlantic Reporter* (2nd), 94: 556–590.

Fuller, John G.
1972 *200,000,000 Guinea Pigs; New Dangers in Everyday Foods, Drugs, and Cosmetics*. New York: Putnam.

Gorring, Pam
1978 "Multinationals or Mafia: Who Really Pushes Drugs?" In Paul R. Wilson and John Braithwaite. *Two Faces of Deviance*. St. Lucia: University of Queensland Press, pp. 81–100.

Haayer, Flora
1982 "Rational Prescribing and Sources of Information." *Social Science and Medicine*, 16(23): 2017–2023.

Henderson, Ian W.
1977 "Statement of the Subcommittee on Pharmacotherapy." *Canadian Medical Association Journal*, 117: 721–722.

Henry, Frank
1985 Notes taken at *Cordova v. Merrell-Dow* trial, 25 April.

Hughes, Richard, and Robert Brewin
1979 *The Tranquilizing of America*. New York: Harcourt, Brace, Jovanovich.

Insider (Mother Jones Investigative Fund)
Winter 1981 "Drug cleared (If You Ignore the Fine Print)," p. 1.
Summer 1982 "Bendectin Cover-up," p. 2.
Winter 1983 "It's Still on the Shelf," p. 2.

Johnson v. Eli Lilly and Company
1983 *Federal Supplement,* 577: 174–180.

Knightley, Phillip, Harold Evans, Elaine Potter, and Marjorie Wallace
1979 *Suffer the Children: The Story of Thalidomide.* New York: Viking Press.

Melrose, Dianna
1982 *Bitter Pills: Medicine and the Third World Poor.* Oxford: Oxfam.

Mendelsohn, Robert S.
1981 *Male Practice: How Doctors Manipulate Women.* Chicago: Contemporary Books.

Mink v. University of Chicago
1978 *Federal Supplement,* 460: 713–765.

Mintz, Morton
1979 "The Dump That Killed Twenty-thousand." *Mother Jones,* 4: 43–44.
1982 "Warning Eyed on Anti-nausea Drug Bendectin." *Washington Post,* 25 June, pp. A1, 8.

Muller, Mike
1982 *The Health of Nations.* London: Faber & Faber.

Payton v. Abbott Laboratories
1982 *North Eastern Reporter* (2nd), 437: 171–194.

Salmon v. Parke, Davis and Company
1975 *Federal Reporter* (2nd), 520: 1359–1362.

Silverman, Milton
1976 *The Drugging of the Americas.* Berkeley: University of California Press.

Silverman, Milton, and Philip R. Lee
1974 *Pills, Profits, and Politics.* Berkeley: University of California Press.

The Spectator (Hamilton, Ontario)
1983 "Experts Say Drug Victim of Bad Publicity." 22 November, p. B10.

Teff, Harvey, and Colin R. Munro
1976 *Thalidomide: The Legal Aftermath.* London: Gordon and Cremonesi.

7

The Relationship Between the Male Police Officer's Response to Victims of Domestic Violence and His Personal and Family Experiences

Sandra M. Stith, Ph.D.
Virginia Polytechnic Institute and State University, Falls Church

Police officers have a unique opportunity to interrupt the cycle of violence within marital relationships. In order to add to the existing information on police officer decision-making, the current investigation examined the relationship between the male police officer's individual and family characteristics and his responsiveness to female victims of domestic violence.

Specific variables which were considered included the police officer's (1) age and education, (2) level of sex-role egalitarianism, (3) reported level of stressful life events, (4) attitude toward marital violence, and (5) method of handling conflict in his own family. The results of this investigation emphasize the importance of the predictor variables in impacting police response.

Violence against wives is a crime of enormous proportions, both in number of people involved and in long-term consequences. A clear link has been reported between observing or experiencing violence as a child and participating in a violent family as an adult (Straus et al., 1980).

Data for this paper came from the author's dissertation at Kansas State University, Manhattan, Kansas. The author wants to acknowledge the contribution of her major professor, Dr. Candyce Russell, and her committee members, Dr. Anthony Jurich, Dr. Walter Schumm, and Dr. Fred Bradley.

Research has also been reported which suggests that each year 1.8 million wives are severely assaulted by their husbands in this country (Straus et al., 1980), and that 30 percent of female homicide victims are killed by their husbands or boyfriends (FBI, 1982). Therefore, it should be evident that marital violence is a major national problem demanding national attention.

When violence in the home reaches an intensity that the privacy of the home is invaded and service providers are called upon to intervene, one of the first providers to be called is the law enforcement officer (Berk and Loseke, 1981). As probably the first group outside the family to intervene in domestic violence situations, police officers have a unique opportunity to assist victims of spouse abuse and to intervene in the cycle of violence. The response of the police officer may give the victim the assurance that help is available and may encourage her to seek help again if the violence should recur. Likewise, police response which is perceived as hostile or threatening to victims may encourage battered wives to remain in abusive marriages.

A number of investigators have noted that police officers see domestic violence calls as among their most stressful. For example, Russo, Engel, and Hatting (1983) administered questionnaires to 173 police officers in the Midwest in order to examine police stress. Domestic violence calls were treated among the most stressful calls they answered. The authors suggest that these data support the established police view that domestic violence situations are unpredictable, high-risk, and have a high potential for injury or death.

The importance of effective police response is emphasized by research funded by the Police Foundation in Detroit and Kansas City. These studies found that in the two years preceding the targeted domestic assault or homicide, police had been at the address of the incident for disturbance calls at least once before in about 85 percent of the cases and at least five times previously in about 50 percent of the cases.

In addition, police frequently find that responding to domestic violence calls is frustrating. Roger Loeb (1983) surveyed a group of 54 police officers from 22 police departments. Loeb asked the respondents to list the two most frustrating things about dealing with spouse abuse calls. Police officers rated frustration with the unresponsiveness of victims in terms of prosecuting, carrying through with prosecution, or doing anything to get out of the situation, and the officer's feeling of helplessness and hopelessness as the most frustrating aspects of intervening in domestic disturbances (p. 249).

Anna Kuhl (1982) examined battered women's perception of police response as a part of her investigation of the community's response to battered women. Her subjects were 420 women who sought assistance at a domestic violence program. The women in Kuhl's (1982) study reported that 5 percent of the officers believed the woman, while 5 percent did not believe her. Five percent blamed her, and 5 percent blamed her spouse. Five percent did not want to get involved. Eleven percent listened, 19 percent offered information, and 41 percent intervened. Although these results suggest that the majority of the police officers responded at least somewhat supportively, the fact that the battered women reported that 15 percent of the police either did not believe the victim, blamed the victim, or did not want to get involved, indicates that there is still room for improvement in police response. In addition, unanswered questions remain as to why some police remain unsupportive to victims of domestic violence.

Albert Roberts (1984) also investigated the perceptions of battered women about police response. He conducted a nationwide study of 89 emergency shelters for battered women. He asked the shelter personnel to report their client's experiences with police officers. He received reports from 79 of the 89 shelters. Thirty-four programs reported having generally positive experiences with the police; 10 had mainly negative experiences; and 35 reported mixed experiences.

Of the 30 women who had called the police in an unpublished survey conducted by Saunders and Size (reported in Saunders, 1980), half saw the police as indifferent and not helpful or concerned in general. However, when they rated specific encounters, they reported higher ratings: 54 percent helpful and 66 percent concerned. Nevertheless, Saunders (1980) emphasizes that the police were rated by the battered women as the least concerned and helpful out of a group of eight formal and informal helpers.

In summary, although the battered women in the studies reported had a variety of reactions to the police response they received, in general their reactions were not as negative as might have been assumed, given the prevailing negative attitudes about police response. However, concern remains as to why some officers remain unsupportive of victims of domestic violence at least some of the time. This unanswered question is an important theoretical and practical consideration.

The present investigation was undertaken because there was limited research dealing with predicting police officer response to victims of domestic violence. The attitudes and other characteristics of police officers which may influence their response to battered women were chosen for study because, although police officers do have a unique opportunity to intervene in the cycle of violence, they have often been criticized for their approach to the problem (Dobash and Dobash, 1979; Roy, 1977).

An additional important question which has not yet been addressed is, "Does the harmony or disharmony of the family influence the officer's ability to perform at work?" (Ellison and Genz, 1983). Little empirical research to date has investigated this question. Thus, the current investigation is designed to answer specific questions previously unaddressed in the police literature.

The possibility that family problems may affect police officers' work performance underlies the establishment of programs for police families. Niederhoffer and Niederhoffer (1978) report that the majority of police wives surveyed would like police organizations to provide services which include family or marital counseling, orientation programs for wives, and social activities. The Niederhoffers further report that, in their study of 94 police departments, 40 percent have responded to the needs of police families. In most cases, these services included brief orientations for wives. More comprehensive programs are rare.

More research is clearly needed to examine the link between police officers' individual and family stress and the effects of this stress on police officer functioning. This research would give a stronger theoretical basis for developing additional programs to reduce police officer stress and support police families.

The present investigation examined the response of male police officers to domestic violence rather than that of female officers because previous research (Homant and Kennedy, 1985) has suggested that female officers (as a group) generally respond to victims of domestic violence differently from the way male officers respond. The response of only policemen were examined in order to eliminate a potential confounding variable (that of sex of the officer).

Specific variables to be considered included the police officer's (1) age and education, (2) level of sex-role egalitarianism, (3) reported level of stressful life events, (4) reported level of marital stress, (5) attitude toward marital violence, and (6) method of handling conflict in his own marriage. These factors were linked by a regression analysis with the officer's likelihood of responding negatively to the victim. These factors are viewed as theoretically and conceptually relevant predictors of police response. Rationale for the choice of these specific variables and the predicted direction of influence grew out of a review of the literature.

Hypotheses

The following seven hypotheses were tested:

1. Police officers who behave more violently in their own marriages respond more negatively to victims of domestic violence than do officers who behave less violently in their own marriages.
2. Police officers who approve more strongly of marital violence respond more negatively to victims of domestic violence than do officers who approve less strongly of marital violence.
3. Police officers who are more sexist respond more negatively to victims of domestic violence than do officers who hold more egalitarian attitudes.
4. Police officers who report more stress in their lives respond more negatively to victims of domestic violence than do officers who report less stress in their lives.
5. Police officers who report more stress in their marriages respond more negatively to victims of domestic violence than do officers who report less stress in their marriages.
6. Police officers who are younger and those who have more education respond less negatively to victims of domestic violence than do officers who are older and have less education.
7. The police officer's response to victims of domestic violence is predicted from his age, education, reported level of stressful life events and marital stress, his attitude toward marital violence and his use of violent conflict tactics in his own marriage.

Methods

The data for this investigation came from questionnaires which were distributed to 240 law enforcement officers from three sheriff departments and four police departments in northeast Kansas. Ninety-seven completed questionnaires were returned, which represented a 40 percent return rate. Seventy-two of the questionnaires were returned by officers who met the criteria for inclusion in the study (married men). Thus, the sample consisted of 72 married male law enforcement officers.

The mean age of the officers was thirty-five years. Sixty-four percent of the officers were currently married to their first wife, while 36 percent were remarried. The sample appeared to be highly educated, with the majority having had at least some college courses (92 percent) and only 6.9 percent reporting only a high school education. The average years of police experience reported by the officers was 9.5.

Predictor Variables

The predictor variables were chosen on the basis of their anticipated relationship with the officer's response to victims of domestic violence. Means, standard deviations, ranges, and alpha scores for the criterion and predictor variables are included in Table 7.1. Further details concerning each of the scales, including specific items, factor matrices, etc. with this sample are reported in Stith (1986).

Table 7.1

Means, Standard Deviations, Ranges, and Alpha Scores for Criterion and Variables (n=72)

Variables	No. of Items	Possible Range	M	SD	Reported Range	Alpha
Predictor Variables						
SRE	25	1–125	96.76	10.70	68–125	.89
MSTRESS	7	7–28	12.08	5.24	7–28	.92
STRESS	44	0–1466	192.45	131.18	4–634	NA
AMV*	8	8–56	50.16	7.80	8–56	.84
CTS	9	0–45	0.83	2.38	0–22	.84
SO.DESIRE	18	18–36	25.52	2.38	20–30	.63
AGE			35.47	7.69	23–56	NA
EDUCATION**		2–6	3.31	.91	2–6	NA
Criterion Variables						
ARREST	2	0–20	13.77	5.20	0–20	.58
MEDIATING	4	0–40	25.68	11.80	0–40	.88
ANTIVICTIM	6	0–60	9.90	11.47	0–51	.76

* High scores = Low Approval of Marital Violence

** Scale: 2=High School, 3=Some College, 4=Bachelor's Degree, 5=Some Graduate Courses, 6=Graduate Degree.

NA = Not Applicable

Sex-Role Egalitarianism

Sex-role egalitarianism is defined as "an attitude that causes one to respond to another individual independently of that other individual's sex" (Beere et al., 1984: 564). A variable measuring the officer's level of sex-role egalitarianism was selected because the literature on family violence suggests a relationship between "their male dominant nature of the family system and a corresponding tendency to use physical force to maintain that dominance when it is threatened" (Straus, 1978: 449). In addition, this measure was chosen because it was thought that it might help to explain the behavior of the officer toward battered women as a part of his general beliefs about male-female relationships.

Each officer was asked to complete the short form of the Sex-Role Egalitarianism Scale (Beere et al., 1984). This form contained 25 items which assessed attitudes toward nontraditional role behaviors of both sexes. Low scorers are viewed as traditional in their sex-role attitudes, while high scorers are considered tolerant of both males exhibiting traditionally female role behaviors and females exhibiting traditionally male role behaviors. The alpha measure of internal reliability for this scale with this sample was .89.

Stressful Life Events

This variable was selected because of concern that "pile up" of normative and non-normative life events may explain why some families may lack the regenerative power to recover and adapt to a family crisis (McCubbin and Patterson, 1983). It was hypothesized that officers who were under more stress in their lives may lack the strength to support others in crisis and may respond negatively as a result of their own problems. The Social Readjustment Rating Scale (Holmes and Rahe, 1967) was used to evaluate the amount of stressful life events which the officer had experienced in the year preceding this investigation.

Approval of Marital Violence

The officer's attitudes as to the acceptability of marital violence were also examined in this investigation. The scale used to measure approval of marital violence was adapted from one developed by Saunders (1980). The current version of this scale asked the respondents to rate how "justified" or "acceptable" the husband and wife were to "slap" or "severely bruise" their spouse in response to a variety of situations ranging from verbal insults to infidelity or self-defense. High scores indicated low approval of marital violence. The measure of internal reliability of this scale for this sample was .84.

Use of Violence in the Police Officer's Marriage

One of the most consistent conclusions of previous research on family violence has been that violence breeds violence (Straus et al., 1980). Police officers who have learned violent responses to conflict in their own homes may have a hard time being sensitive to the needs of abused wives in other homes. The physical violence scale of the Conflict Tactics Scale developed by Straus (1979) was used to measure the officer's use of violence in his marriage. This scale asks the officers how often they used various tactics to resolve conflicts last year. The possible responses ranged from 0 to 5, "never" to "more than once a month." Items included in the scale ranged from "threw something but not at spouse" to "used a gun." Although, on each item, from 81 percent to 100 percent reported never using the suggested conflict tactic, at least one officer reported using every violent tactic except "used a gun" and "hit spouse with something hard." The internal reliability for this scale with this sample was .84.

Social Desirability

In order to measure the tendency of the respondents to answer in socially desirable directions, each participant of this study was asked to

Table 7.2

Intercorrelations of Predictor and Criterion Variables

Variables	1	2	3	4	5	6	7	8	9	10
1. SRE	1.00									
2. MSTRESS	-.01	1.00								
3. STRESS	-.11	.04	1.00							
4. AMV	.34**	-.24*	.05	1.00						
5. CTS	-.18	.25*	-.00	-.66****	1.00					
6. SO.DESIRE	-.14	-.17	-.16	-.02	-.01	1.00				
7. AGE	.04	.19*	-.15	-.18	.03	-.06	1.00			
8. EDUC	.08	.14	-.29**	-.26**	.31**	-.20*	.07	1.00		
9. ARREST	.14	-.13	.01	.14	-.30**	-.11	.00	-.01	1.00	
10. MEDIATING-	.10	-.07	-.01	-.20*	.18	.01	-.03	-.02	-.21*	1.00
11. ANTIVICTIM	-.31**	-.02	.12	-.36***	.17	.00	.18	.03	-.16	.26*

*$p < .05$.

**$p < .01$.

***$p < .001$.

****$p < .0001$.

complete the Marlowe Crowne measure of social desirability (Crowne and Marlowe, 1964). As indicated in Table 7.2, this instrument was not correlated with the criterion measure or any of the predictor measures except education (r =-.20, p = .045). Thus, relationships involving the officer's level of education must be viewed cautiously.

Police Officer Response to Victims

In order to measure the response of the police officers to victims of domestic violence, police officers were asked to rate their likelihood of responding in certain ways (from 0 percent to 100 percent) to two vignette descriptions of domestic violence incidents developed by Saunders (1980). The response was coded as "antivictim" if the officer reported that he would "arrest the woman," "warn the woman of arrest," or "discourage the woman from seeking arrest." The alpha reliability for this scale was .76. Analysis Pearson Correlation Coefficients were calculated among all variables (see Table 7.2). In addition to examining zero correlations, multiple regression analysis was used to estimate the contribution of each of the predictor variables to police response to victims of domestic violence (antivictim response). All of the predictor variables were placed in the regression equation simultaneously. An estimate of the net effect (a beta, or standardized partial regression coefficient) of each predictor variable is reported in Table 7.3.

Results

In order to examine the relationships among the variables in this investigation, Pearson Correlation Coefficients were calculated. Table 7.2 reports the intercorrelations among the predictor and criterion variables. Eleven significant correlations out of a possible 36 were found. Approximately two correlations would be expected to be significant by chance (at the .05 level of significance). Thus, the number of significant correlations is greater than the number expected by chance.

In addition to significant relationships which were noted among the predictor variables, correlations between the criterion variable (antivictim response) and the predictor variables were also noted. From this analysis the first six hypotheses were tested. The results are as follows:

I. The officer's use of violence in his own marriage (CTS) is not significantly related to antivictim response. However, it should be noted that the correlation between CTS and antivictim response was .17, which approached significance. This may indicate a nonsignificant tendency for the officer to increase his negative response to victims as his level of violence in his own marriage increases.

II. Approval of Marital Violence is significantly related to antivictim response ($p < .001$). It appears that the more the officer believes that violence in marriage is sometimes justifiable or acceptable, the more likely he is to respond negatively to victims of domestic violence.

III. Egalitarianism is significantly related to antivictim response ($p = .01$). Thus, the more egalitarian the officer is, the less likely he is to respond negatively to victims of domestic violence.

IV. Stressful life events are not significantly related to antivictim response ($r = .12$).

V. Marital stress is not significantly related to antivictim response ($r = .02$).

VI. Age ($r = .18$) and education ($r = .03$) are not significantly related to antivictim response ($r = .18$). However, it should be noted that the relationship between age and antivictim response approached significance. Thus, older officers seemed to have a nonsignificant tendency to behave more negatively toward victims of domestic violence. In addition to examining the correlations between various independent variables and the dependent variable (antivictim response), each independent variable was entered simultaneously in a regression equation. Results of this analysis are presented in Table 7.3. These results support hypothesis VII.

VII. Age, education, egalitarianism, marital stress, stressful life events, approval of marital violence and use of violence in the officer's marriage, together predict a significant amount of the variance in the officer's use of antivictim response ($r2 = .23$; $p = .02$). Thus, 23 percent of the variance in the officer's use of hostility to victims of domestic violence is predicted by the combined effect of each of the predictor variables. In addition, it is noted that approval of marital violence bears a stronger zero-order relationship and a stronger partial relationship to antivictim response than do any other predictor variables.

Table 7.3

Multiple Regression of Antivictim Response upon Seven Independent Variables

Independent Variables	B	Beta	*t*
Stress	.01	.15	1.31
CTS	-.34	-.07	-.49
Egal	-.22	-.21	-1.81
Age	.25	.17	1.47
Mstress	-.30	-.14	-1.19
Educ	.42	.03	.28
AMV	-.50	-.34	-2.26*
	r	.48	
	r2	.23	
	r2 Adjusted	.14	
	F 2.68		
	df (7.64)		
	p .02		

Note: B = Unstandardized Partial Regression Coefficient
Beta = Standardized Partial Regression Coefficient
*p < .05.

Interaction Effects

In order to determine the extent to which there were indirect and interactive relationships within the predictor and criterion variables, 21 two-way interaction effects were tested. The only significant interaction effect with antivictim response was with egalitarianism and stress (B = 2.48, t = 3.61, p>.005). Figure 7.1 graphically depicts this relationship.

Under conditions of low stress, a highly significant relationship appeared between antivictim response and egalitarianism (B = -.51, p = .00009). However, when the officer was under high stress, a slight (non-significant) tendency existed for him to increase his level of antivictim response with increasing egalitarianism (B = .13, p = .31). Thus, it appears that stress suppresses the relationship between egalitarianism and antivictim response. If the police officer is under low stress, increasing levels of egalitarianism seem to be related to decreasing levels of negative response to victims, whereas under high stress, egalitarianism does not appear to be significantly related to police officer behavior toward victims.

Discussion

The results of this study must be viewed with caution because of the limitations of the study. The first limitation has to do with the fact that neither the police departments nor officers were selected randomly. This may have introduced a nonrandom bias into the results. The policies of the departments selected with regards to domestic violence may have impacted the results. In addition, those officers who chose to volunteer to participate in the study and to share private parts of their lives may be different from those who chose not to participate. It is likely that volunteer subjects may be among the best educated, least stressed, and least maritally violent. Thus, this data may represent only the tip of the iceberg with regards to stress, marital stress, and marital violence within police officers' lives.

In addition to limitations resulting from sampling procedures, limitations must be noted resulting from the small sample size. Previous

Figure 7.1

Interaction Effect of Stress and Egalitarianism on Antivictim Response

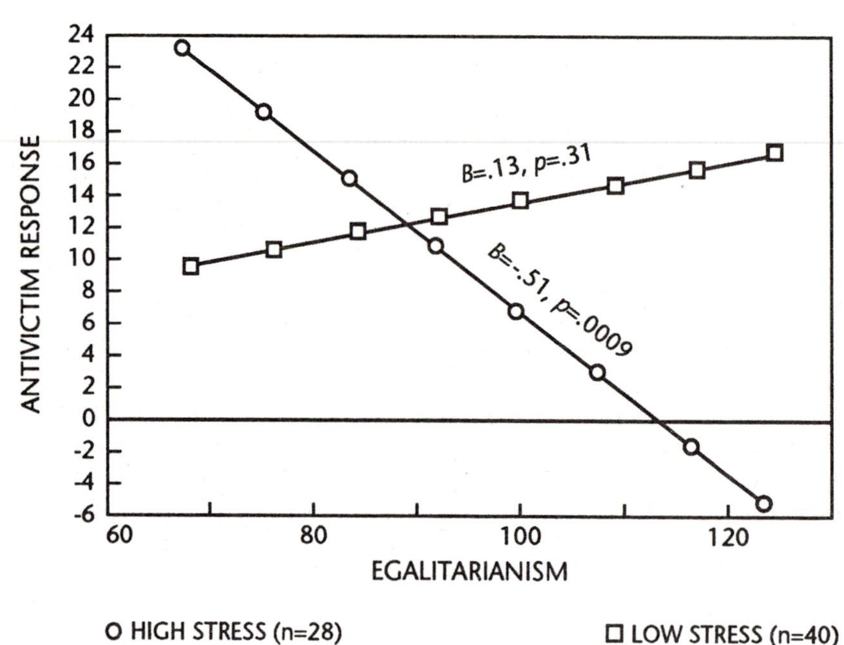

investigators (Schumm et al., 1980) have suggested that a minimum of ten subjects should be available for each variable in a regression analysis. With seven predictor variables, this sample size barely meets the suggested criteria.

Finally, limitations may have resulted from the nature of the questionnaire methodology and the scales used to assess the variables. Self-report data may have been biased, although efforts were made to control for social desirability. In addition, the criterion measure of police response to vignettes of domestic violence situations can only be said to represent a tendency to respond. The validity of these measures, as far as predicting the police officer's response in actual domestic violence incidents is concerned, has not been established. Thus, extreme caution must be exercised in generalizing from this data.

Implications for Further Research

These findings accentuate the need for further study of the effects of the police officer's attitudes and personal experiences on his response to victims of domestic violence. This research should include measures of other sources of stress in the police officer's life, including his job stress. Further research is needed to examine the impact that the officer's attitudes and experiences have on his response to perpetrators of domestic violence. Future research should involve a larger, more representative sample of police officers. Inclusion of data from the police officer's wife would add validity to the officer's self-reported level of stress and violence in his marriage and would provide a more systemic approach. Future investigations might use a multi-method approach, including field observations, questionnaires completed by officers and family members of officers, and interviews of victims and perpetrators of domestic violence.

Implications for Training and Policy

The present investigation has some implications for training of law enforcement officers and for the development of supportive programs for officers and their families. These implications will be strengthened if the results are corroborated with further investigations.

1. Training programs designed to improve police officer's response to victims of domestic violence should include activities designed to increase the officer's level of sex-role egalitarianism.

   In particular, training materials need to be inspected for sexist biases. Saunders (1980: 189) has suggested that consciousness-raising exercises about sex roles might enhance the officer's sensitivity to female victims. Films, speaking to battered women who are not in crisis, and other exercises designed to help the officer to understand the plight of the battered woman need to be included in training programs.

2. Training programs designed to improve police officer responses to victims of domestic violence should include activities designed to decrease the officer's level of approval of marital violence. Training programs must emphasize that violence within marriage is a crime and is not appropriate or acceptable.
3. Decreasing sexist attitudes and attitudes approving of marital violence may not be sufficient to change police officers' behavior unless the level of stress in the officers' lives is also reduced. The present investigation suggested that stress seemed to suppress the relationship between the officer's attitudes and his behavior. Thus, when stress is high, previous training attempts to develop nonsexist attitudes may be nullified. If the effect of attitudes is suppressed by stress in the police officers' lives, then training designed to change attitudes will have little effect on changing behaviors. Therefore, more effort needs to be directed toward decreasing stress in police officers' personal lives. Police practices which may decrease stress may need to be instituted. In addition, it may prove cost-effective to increase supportive programs, such as provision of family counseling, family support programs, etc., for police officers and their families.

In conclusion, law enforcement officers have the opportunity to have a major impact in the reduction of domestic violence, not just today, but for future generations. In order to provide officers with the tools and the ability to use the tools to make an impact, we must consider the officer as not just an enforcer of laws, but as a whole person. Through our research efforts, policy development and provision of services, we must consider, not just the law enforcer, but the individual person, the person within the family system, the police system, and the law enforcement system.

Bibliography

Beere, C., D. King, D. Beere, and L. King

1984 "The Sex-Role Egalitarianism Scale: A Measure of Attitudes Toward Equality Between the Sexes." *Sex Roles,* 10 (7–8): 563–567.

Berk, S., and D. Loseke

1981 "Handling Family Violence: Situational Determinants of Police Arrest in Domestic Disturbances." *Law and Society Review,* 15(2): 318–345.

Crowne, D., and D. Marlowe

1964 *The Approval Motive: Studies in Evaluative Dependence.* New York: Wiley.

Dobash, E., and R. Dobash

1979 *Violence Against Wives: A Case Against Patriarchy.* New York: The Free Press.

Ellison, K., and J. Genz

1983 *Stress and the Police Officer.* Springfield, IL: Charles C. Thompson.

Federal Bureau of Investigation

1982 *Uniform Crime Reports* 1982. Washington, DC: U.S. Department of Justice.

Holmes, T., and R. Rahe

1967 "The Social Readjustment Rating Scale." *Journal of Psychosomatic Research,* II: 213–218.

Homant, R., and Kennedy, D.

1985 "Police Perceptions of Spouse Abuse: A Comparison of Male and Female Officers." *Journal of Criminal Justice,* 13: 29–74.

Kuhl, A.

1982 "Community Responses to Battered Women." *Victimology: An International Journal,* 7(1–4): 49–59.

Loeb, R.

1983 "A Program of Community Education for Dealing with Spouse Abuse." *Journal of Community Psychology*, 11: 241–251.

McCubbin, H., and J. Patterson

1983 "Family Transitions: Adaptions to Stress." In H. McCubbin and C. Figley, eds. *Stress in the Family: Volume I: Coping with Normative Transitions*. New York: Brunner/Mazel, pp. 5–25.

Niederhoffer, A., and E. Niederhoffer

1978 *The Police Family: From Station House to Ranch House*. Lexington, MA: D.C. Heath.

Pearlin, L., and C. Schooler

1978 "The Structure of Coping." *Journal of Health and Social Behavior*, 19: 2–21.

Police Foundation

1977 *Domestic Violence and the Police: Studies in Detroit and Kansas City*. Washington, DC: The Police Foundation.

Roberts, A.

1984 *Battered Women and Their Families: Intervention Strategies and Treatment Programs*. New York: Springer.

Roy, M.

1977 "A Current Survey of 150 Cases." In M. Roy, ed. *Battered Women: A Psychological Study of Domestic Violence*. New York: Van Nostrand Reinhold, pp. 25–44.

Russo P., A. Engel, and S. Hatting

1983 "Police and Occupational Stress: An Empirical Investigation." In R. Bennett, ed. *Police at Work: Policy Issues and Analysis*. Beverly Hills, CA: Sage.

Saunders, D.

1980 "The Police Response to Battered Women: Predictors of Officers' Uses of Arrest, Counseling and Minimal Action." *Dissertation Abstracts International*, 40: 6466A (University Microfilms No. 80-08840).

Schumm, W., W. Southerly, and C. Figley

1980 "Stumbling Block or Stepping Stone: Path Analysis in Family Studies." *Journal of Marriage and the Family*, 42(2): 161–207.

Stith, S.

1986 "Police Officer Response to Marital Violence Predicted from the Officers' Attitude, Stress, and Marital Experience: A Path Analysis." *Dissertation Abstracts International*, 47(7): 240–252.

Straus, M.

1978 "Wife Beating: How Common and Why?" *Victimology: An International Journal*, 2(3–4): 443–458.

1979 "Measuring Intrafamily Conflict and Violence: The Conflict Tactic (CT) Scales." *Journal of Marriage and the Family*, 41: 75–88.

Straus, M., R. Gelles, and S. Steinmetz

1980 *Behind Closed Doors: Violence in the Family*. Garden City, NY: Anchor Press.

8

Family Murder in the Republic of South Africa—A Case of Misguided Family Rights and Responsibilities?

Ronelle Pretorius
University of Pretoria, South Africa

Family murder, in this chapter, refers to a situation where a person kills his/her spouse and some or all of the children and then almost immediately thereafter commits suicide. A review of literature on homicide followed by suicide indicates that this type of family murder is extremely rare, if not unknown, in most societies. More frequent and well known, however, is the murder of a spouse or a child, followed by the suicide of the offender at a later stage.

Until recently family murder, as defined above, was an unknown and exceptionally infrequent phenomenon in South Africa. However, since 1983 this society was struck by a spate of family murders, and what makes this phenomenon more exceptional is the fact that it is almost exclusively limited to the White population—more explicitly to the Afrikaans-speaking than to the English-speaking group. The inevitable question arises whether an explanation of this kind of family victimization does not lie in the country's sociopolitical structure and in the Afrikaner's culture.

We argue that the realities of a war on the country's border, urban terrorism, political unrest, disinvestment and unemployment which began affecting Whites seriously since the 1980s as well as fear of sociopolitical change (Black majority rule and socialism/communism) created a sense of hopelessness, insecurity, pessimism and even fear about the future among many Whites. Family murder can be related to this condition.

An analysis of the manner in which victims of family murders were slain suggests that they were not killed in rage or out of revenge but rather that the offender acted out of some positive interpretation of death. It is postulated that a misguided sense of one's duties and rights as head of a family drives some people to commit a family murder in a rescue fantasy: the offender wishes to save him/herself and the family through death from some existential crisis.

Following from this argument is an analysis of the possible influence of a number of factors which affect the right and duty of the head of a household to decide on the life and fate of family members, i.e., legitimization of violence by society under certain conditions (e.g., political violence), positive definitions of death by religion, intensely close knit family ties and family isolation, existential crises and definitions of the family's situation as hopeless.

Family Murder—A Rare Phenomenon

In this chapter, family murder refers to a situation where a person murders his/her spouse and one or more of the children and then virtually immediately thereafter commits suicide. The reality of such a family murder is illustrated by the following case: On November 30, 1984, the South African press gave extensive prominence to a family tragedy during which seven people died. A farm laborer, one morning, summoned the police after becoming suspicious when his employer and family did not make an appearance. The forty-three-year-old mother and her five children, two girls of five and seven years and three boys of nine, eleven and thirteen years, respectively, were found dead in their bedrooms. The father of the family, aged 43, was found with a bullet through the head and a heavy caliber pistol in his hand on the bathroom floor. Circumstantial evidence indicated that the man murdered his family while they were asleep and then committed suicide. Neighbors, family and friends described the family as a happy one. However, family members claimed that shortly before the tragedy the man was seriously concerned about his health and the fact that doctors had not been able to diagnose his problem.

A review of the literature dealing with murder followed by suicide reveals that this type of family murder is very rare, if not virtually unknown, in most societies. A phenomenon which does occur relatively often and about which substantial research has been done, is the murder of a spouse or child, followed by the suicide of the offender, usually at a later stage. Among the most well-known research on this type of murder-suicide is that of Ruth Cavan (1928) in Chicago in 1923; Wolfgang's (1958) investigation in Philadelphia in 1948 to 1952; West's (1965) study in England and Wales during 1954 to 1961, and the more recent investigation of Nancy Allen (1983) covering a ten-year period from 1970 to 1979 in Los Angeles. Virtually all the cases in these investigations relate to the murder of a spouse or lover. In the odd case where an entire family was wiped out, it was not dealt with as a separate category. This suggests that they were in fact exceptional cases and evidently the authors did not consider them to be categorically different to other murder-suicide cases.

The South African Scene

Until recently, family murders that include both parents and children, as defined at the outset of this chapter, were unknown in South Africa. Between 1983 and 1986, however, the country has actually been hit by a wave of family murders. In this period there were 23 such cases in which a total of 96 persons died. What makes the phenomenon exceptional is the fact that, in a country with a population of 25 million people, family murders occur exclusively amongst the approximately four-and-a-half million White South Africans, and more specifically, only amongst the approximately 2.7 million Afrikaans-speaking White South Africans, who make up approximately 56 percent of the White population, as opposed to none among the English-speaking Whites, who constitute approximately 44 percent of the White South African population. An inevitable question is why this phenomenon only made its appearance in the 1980s and only amongst Afrikaans-speaking White South Africans? Does the explanation lie partly in the country's socio-economic and political structure—and in the culture and perception of social reality of the Afrikaner?

Popular and Traditional Explanations of Family Murder

A number of popular explanations of family murder that have been offered at the same time mirror some of the foundations upon which well known sociological and psychological theories of violence rest. The most well-known of these that will receive attention are mental derangement as an explanation for family murder, frustration-aggression and the interactional perspective approach to family murder.

Mental Derangement as Explanation for Family Murder

At times it is argued that a family murderer must be temporarily or permanently insane to commit such a deed. Psychiatric disorders that can be associated with family murder are, for example, paranoid schizophrenia coupled with pathological jealousy and neurotic pride. Delusions of persecution can, for example, lead to suspicion and outbursts of rage with fatal consequences. A number of researchers like Revitch (Roy, 1982), and Morgan (1982) have, for example, found that paranoia may play a role in the murder of a spouse.

According to official reports on the family murders covered in this paper, no evidence of a diagnosed psychiatric problem was found in any of the cases. Furthermore, there are also problems in general with this theory of the diagnosis of psychiatric problems, particularly in the case where both the offender and the victims died. Theological arguments for the existence of mental disorders are also often put forward. It is argued, for example, it is argued that the behavior of the murderer is evidence of the fact that he is mentally deranged.

The Frustration-Aggression Theory as Explanation for Family Murder

A seemingly logical and popular question is, what did the family do to deserve murder at the hands of the husband or wife? The question presumes that the offender, due to frustration, lost all self-control and destroyed the entire family; that the human psyche rests on a stimulus-response basis and that the victims, by provoking violence, are in fact actually responsible for their destruction. Dollard (in Hirsch, 1981: 25) laid the foundations of this theory in 1939 and showed that the blocking of goal attainment leads to frustration which is expressed by means of, inter alia, feelings of futility and explosions of rage and aggression that could culminate in murder followed by suicide.

This theory could in fact explain some family murders, but the circumstances in which the majority of victims referred to in this chapter were found to suggest that they were shot while they slept or murdered after being awakened by the shots aimed at other family members. In one case the parents and their two infants were found gassed in their car. These circumstances indicate that the murder and suicide is at least not directly preceded by a quarrel or struggle. A further problem with this theory is that aggression or murder followed by suicide is not the only possible reaction to frustration and that family members may help someone cope with his/her frustration.

The Situational/Interactional Approach to Family Murder

According to the situational approach, one could argue that within a specific situation, having dimensions of time, place, and circumstances, "something" must have taken place between offender and victims that gave rise to the murder and suicide. At a certain stage in the succession of interaction patterns between family members, there would then be a trigger factor provoking a struggle, during which the opponents try to retain their status/honor at all costs. The struggle then culminates in murder followed by suicide. It is argued that in families where a love-hate interaction pattern is present, behavior follows a cybernetic model: each person's behavior carries a message to which others respond and the trigger factor instigating the fatal confrontation lies in the negative interpretation of a family member's behavior (Gulotta in Viano, 1976: 53). A husband will hit his wife during an argument, for example, following which she will throw an object at him because he is attacking her. He then gets hold of a gun because he feels his life is in danger—in this way, the confrontation ends in tragedy.

One contribution of this approach is that it points to the part played by circumstances, such as time, place and incidents, in the course of a violent confrontation. Family murders are actually difficult to reconstruct when all the members of the family have died. The explanation does not take account of the personality differences of family members. This interpretation also tends towards determinism. To judge by newspaper accounts, family murders seldom seem to be the result of an argument or fight. This interpretation also does not explain why the murder is extended to innocent (sleeping) children or the rest of the family who were possibly not even involved in an argument at all.

Concluding Remarks on Popular and Traditional Explanations for Family Murder

The interpretations that have just been discussed would appear to be too narrow and probably only offer an explanation for a limited number of cases. They do not provide an explanation as to why family murder (as defined) has suddenly appeared at this particular time in the history of South African society and why it is noted only amongst one specific sector of society. It furthermore does not account for the diverse nature and circumstances of persons involved in family murder. The problem is too complicated to be explained by any single-factor approach. The question arises whether there is not a more fundamental factor in society that makes it possible or even easier for people with a particular personality composition and/or existential problem to commit family murder.

A Misplaced Sense of Duty and Responsibility as Possible Basis for Family Murder

In view of the fact that family murder is apparently a phenomenon that is unique to South Africa and is apparently only evident amongst Afrikaans-speaking Whites—the question arises as to whether there is not something present in this country's social structure and/or culture of the Afrikaner which would explain this phenomenon. It would seem as if we are probably dealing with a misplaced sense of duty and responsibility which makes a person a family murderer. A family with a strong patriarchal or matriarchal basis can create a climate in which it is considered not only the right but also the duty of one person to decide on the life and destiny of his/her family. An analysis of the total situation in which family murders occur, may perhaps cast some light on this hypothesis.

The Society Surrounding the Family Murderer

Family murder takes place within a violent society—South Africans are confronted daily with reports on violence in newspapers, magazines, radio and television. In addition, the country is fighting a war on its borders and with conscription, few White families do not have a family member who at some time or other performs military border duty. Such violence is positively defined because it is taking place for a so-called "honorable cause," for example, to prevent crime or destroy the enemy. We therefore have a situation in which, under certain circumstances, it is the right and the duty of one person to decide on the lives of other people. When self-defense, the control of crime, and a war situation legitimizes the killing of people, such circumstances could possibly work through to a personal level to cause a family murder.

The Culture in Which Family Murder Takes Place

Within a religious context death is often portrayed in a positive light. Christianity has had a great impact on the culture of White South Africans, and death is associated with the resurrection of Christ and regarded as a deliverance. The following Bible verses portray death very positively.

"Death is swallowed up in victory. O death, where then your victory? Where then your sting?" (1 Cor. 15, 54–55);

"For to me, living means opportunities for Christ, and dying—well, that's even better!" (Phil. 1, 21);

"Sometimes I want to live and at other times I don't, for I long to go and be with Christ. How much happier for me than being here!" (Phil. 1, 23).

Van Arkel (1985: 140–148), on the grounds of similar biblical viewpoints on death, contends, "Besides the Christian 'no' to murder (and suicide) there is still an underlying invitation to die." The belief that after death a person is united with deceased loved ones, together with the conviction that death releases or relieves one of an existential problem, could act as contributing factors in the case of family murder. Thus, someone with a serious life problem and a misplaced sense of responsibility could, if he has a positive attitude towards death, grasp at family murder to release himself and his family from misery.

The Marriage and Family Relationship of Family Murderers

Research on murder followed by suicide indicates that the bonds between those involved are intense and closely knit (West, 1965). The same intense involvement is evidently also the case with members of a family murder. Such close family ties are accentuated by Christian values and norms and are further strengthened by a patriarchal family system which endorses the authority and power of the father as head of the household. His right to make decisions regarding family matters is therefore sanctioned by culture and religion, or at any rate, such is the interpretation by some persons of the Scripture of the husband and the husband as head of the household. Research alone will determine whether such extreme domination over family members, based in a misplaced view of power and authority, plays a part in family murder. Judging by newspaper reports on family murders, it would seem as if these families in fact were very close and a hypothesis of a pathological involvement of family members in the welfare of members as a factor in this type of murder would seem to be feasible.

Circumstances of Families Who Become Victims of a Family Murder

The biographies of victims of family murders, as reported in the press, are very fragmented and possibly also speculative regarding the personal crises of the deceased. It is nonetheless noteworthy that family murders have in fact made their appearance during an unstable and turbulent period in South African socioeconomic and political history. In this period many White South Africans, especially among the right-wing Afrikaners, feared that a Communist or Black takeover of the country was imminent. Prior to 1983, family murder as defined was an unheard of occurrence in the Republic of South Africa, and the appearance of this phenomenon on the South African scene coincides with the economic recession which made its mark with large scale unemployment among Whites during 1984. In addition, political unrest, which was sparked by the riots in Soweto in 1976, together with the threats and realities of economic boycotts against the country, which culminated in a rush of pessimism and uncertainty in the 1980s about the future of White South Africans, could have led some insecure or desperate persons with some existential problems to lose all hope in life and commit family murder—possibly stems out of a sense of responsibility to spare loved ones the unpleasantness of a hopeless future.

The State of Mind of the Perpetrator

Research on suicide has revealed that a feeling of hopelessness or the conviction that there is no solution to a problem is a more reliable indicator of suicide than depression (Kovacs et al., 1974: 102). The question arises whether family murderers do not also experience an intense feeling of hopelessness. In the light of the previous point regarding the socioeconomic and political circumstances present in the country, Srole's concept of anomia (in Smigel, 1971: 97) could offer a possible explanation of the mental state and behavior of family murderers.

On the grounds of the following possible perceptions held by such persons, Srole's concept of anomia may point to characteristics of alienation/estrangement from others by family murderers.

1. A feeling that community leaders are *insensitive* to his/her problems and are not genuinely interested in the well-being of the ordinary person. In the period under discussion the government was persistently accused, especially by the right-wing Afrikaans press, of only looking at the interests of Black South Africans.
2. The perception that the *social order is fragile* and unpredictable. It is therefore difficult or impossible to reach one's goals in life. The social construction of South African realities, as reflected by the right-wing Afrikaans press and political parties and representing the mood of many Whites in the late 1970s and early 1980s was (or still is) that a takeover of the government by radicals is imminent because of concessions towards Blacks.
3. The belief that a person's circumstances in life only get worse, that one only moves backwards and the *the ordinary individual's position gets progressively worse.* It is striking that during the period under discussion South Africa experienced its highest inflation and unemployment rate in the past four decades.
4. The feeling that *life becomes meaningless,* inter alia, because values and norms lose their power. Many Afrikaners experienced the government's "reform policies" concerning the dismantling of apartheid as extremely traumatic. This reaction to what is perceived as a dramatic change is perhaps somewhat reflected in the gains of the Conservative Party in the 1987 elections. Interestingly enough, the item according to which Srole proposes to measure this component reads, "It's hardly fair to bring children into the world with the way things look for the future" (in Smigel, 1976: 97).
5. The impression that a person's network of friends and interpersonal *relationships are no longer predictable and reliable*—the feeling that you can no longer trust anyone.

Someone subject to anomia may experience his/her circumstances as extremely hopeless and can become morbidly depressed—it is not unknown for depressed persons to commit seemingly senseless deeds, often out of desperation.

Conclusion

In the light of the foregoing discussion, I would like to propose that individuals experiencing existential crises and who are in a society where violence is not only rampant but, under certain circumstances, is also culturally legitimized, on the grounds of a pathological involvement in family circumstances, may destroy him/herself and his/her family out of a feeling of hopelessness and a misplaced feeling of responsibility.

Bibliography

Allen, Nancy H.
1983 "Homicide Followed by Suicide: Los Angeles 1970–1979." *Suicide and Life-threatening Behavior,* 13(3): 155–166.

Cavan, Ruth S.
1928 *Suicide.* Chicago: University of Chicago Press.

Hirsch, Miriam F.
1981 *Women and Violence.* New York: Van Nostrand Reinhold.

Kovacs, M., et al.
1974 "Hopelessness: An Indicator of Suicidal Risk." *Suicide,* 5: 98–103.

Morgan, S.M.
1982 *Conjugal Terrorism: A Psychological and Community Treatment Model of Wife Abuse.* Palo Alto, CA: R & E Associates.

Roy, Maria
1982 *The Abusive Partner: An Analysis of Domestic Battering.* New York: Van Nostrand Reinhold.

Shneidman, E.S.
1957 *Clues to Suicide.* New York: McGraw-Hill.

Smigel, E.O., ed.
1971 *Handbook on the Study of Social Problems.* Chicago: Rand McNally.

Van Arkel, W.T. de J.
1985 *A Pastoral Theology: Perspective on Family Murder.* Pretoria: University of South Africa.

Viano, E.C.
1976 *Victims and Society.* Washington, DC: Visage Press.

West, D.J.
1965 *Murder Followed by Suicide.* London: Heinemann.

Wolfgang, M.E.
1958 "An Analysis of Homicide-Suicide." *Journal of Clinical and Experimental Psychopathology*, 19: 208–218.

9

The Victim-Offender Relationship in Family Violence

Ranjana S. Jain
University of Rajasthan, India

This chapter presents the results of a domestic violence study conducted in India. It highlights the different patterns of violence and victimization experienced or inflicted by males and females. It also stresses those factors and dynamics specific to Indian culture that impact family violence.

The family is regarded as the most important of all the institutions. Institutionally, the family is considered functional to the society and its individual members as it serves such certain fundamental needs as protection, affection, security, socialization along with other biological functions like sexual gratification, reproduction, economic function of division of labor, inheritance, rearing and care of children and spouse. Being a universal institution without any alternative which could substitute for it, it is considered functional for its individual members and society at large. This naturalistic tendency has created built-in academic pressures to neglect the areas of violence and overt conflicts of a serious nature in the family.

But the facts tend to provide an opposite picture. When we look closely at the family, we find conflicts, tensions, frustrations, bitter feelings, quarrels, rivalry, jealousy, and even cases of violence between close family members. Violence within the family is not abrupt. It is the result of a sequence of events where bitter feelings are nursed within the hearts of family members to such an extent that one starts hating the other and, as a consequence, one becomes the victim and the other becomes the offender. Regarding the victim-offender relationship Wolfgang and Ferracuti (1967) state, "As a rule the two individuals are friends or acquaintances and often they are biologically related or marital partners." Among 550 Philadelphia cases he studied, Wolfgang (1967: 207) found that victim and offender were close friends in 28.2

percent of the killings, in 24.7 percent they were relatives, in 13.5 percent they were acquaintances, in another 9.8 percent they were paramours, and in 12.2 percent they were strangers (the remaining percentages included homosexual partners, police officer–felon encounters, and so on). Stuart Palmer's (1965) cross-cultural study indicates that in the vast majority of non-literate societies he analyzed, 41 out of 44 homicidal victims and offenders are rarely if ever strangers.

The above data reveal that family members can, under most provocations, become violent towards each other. The family provides a framework of a more or less permanent relationship which is not voluntary. This permanance of the relationship puts pressure on members to tolerate each other despite differences, dislike and distrust. The close proximity to each other and the openness of spontaneous reactions tend to create situations of exposure of real self. Its positive dimensions lead to love, affection, care and security, while its negative aspects lead to hatred, dislike, and violence—both verbal and physical. As Steinmetz and Straus (1973) put it, "Some form of physical violence between family members is so likely to take place at some point in the life cycle that it can be said to be almost universal. Violence seems to be at least as typical of family relationships as love."

The nature of the relationship significantly determines the form and type of violence. This chapter tries to analyze the victim-offender relationship within the family. It shows how and why some family members resort to violence. It can be said that the most intimate relationships are institutionally possible within the family and that, if they are not properly managed, they can lead to intense mutual dislike. Since the relations within the family cannot be willfully or easily broken, the pressure to live together further creates serious problems of adjustment between family members. The situation at times becomes so tense that one tries to do away with the other because of emotional imbalance.

The Study

This study utilized 50 male and 50 female family offenders as the sample and focused on the victim-offender relationship in family violence. The data revealed that violent behavior in the family springs from all kinds of negative emotions like fear, jealousy, frustration, anger, irritation, unforgiven humiliations, and rivalries in almost every sphere of life. The respondants revealed that when two individuals in the family cannot get along well together they are at times in conflict with one another. Sometimes they may be verbally aggressive which further increases hostility in both members. As one is exposed to these actions more and more, it leads to further disagreements, tensions, frustrations, and escalation to the point of attack. As a consequence, as one thinks about all the humiliations and injuries suffered in the past, one is at times unable to control his or her emotions and resorts to violence. Thus both the individuals, i.e., the victim and the offender, contribute to violence not only over the the long run, but also during the ultimate conflict situation of violence.

The motives of violence in the family ranged from domestic quarrels to mental disability. Despite great efforts to know the exact and precise factors involved in domestic quarrels or any other such dispute, we were unable to acquire information other than the fact that a trivial argument developed or an insult was suffered by one or both of the parties which resulted in violent behavior. The present data revealed that 46 percent of males and 4 percent of females had been involved in violence because of domestic quarrels. Fourteen percent of the males resorted to violence on account of property disputes because it is the male who has the legal right to inherit the property of his parents. On the other side, we found that 10 percent of males and 2 percent of females had been involved in violence on account of jealousy; 10 percent of males and 18 percent of females had taken to violence because of infidelity of the spouse; 6 percent of males and 6 percent of females had been violent because of dislike for the spouse.

Females in India have to make more adjustments with the family members after their marriage than males do. We found that 8 percent of women had been violent due to maltreatment by the husband, 14 percent because of maltreatment by in-laws, 4 percent because of problems related to childbearing, 2 percent for self-defense, and 18 percent on account of the habits of drinking or gambling. There were 22 percent female and 6 percent (male) of respondents who were falsely implicated in crime. Four percent of males had also been involved in violence on account of mental disability. Four percent of males and 2 percent of females had been violent in what was considered the heat of passion.

The problem of utter mutual hatred, maladjustment and complete break up between family members led one to do away with the other and we found the closest kin had been violent towards one another. The following table shows the victims and the offenders in our study of family violence.

Table 9.1

The Offender

The victim of crime	Male	Female	Total
Husband	—	38 (76%)	38
Wife	32 (76%)	—	32
Mother	5 (10%)	—	5
Brother	11 (22%)	—	11
Daughter	—	5 (10%)	5
Father-in-law	1 (2%)	—	1
Mother-in-law	—	4 (8%)	4
Brother-in-law (Dewar)	—	1 (2%)	1
Sister-in-law	—	2 (4%)	2
Daughter-in-law	1 (2%)	—	1
Total	50 (100%)	50 (100%)	100

The present study shows that violence between spouses was most common and the next most predominant familial violence was that between parents and children and violence related to siblings. In the third category we can put violence related to in-laws. Males usually killed their wives, mothers, brothers, or in-laws in exceptional cases. Females, though, usually killed their husbands, daughters, or one of the in-laws. We found that only males had been violent in their family of origin. On the other hand, violence in the family of procreation is prevalent among both males and females. Violence related to in-laws is more common among females than males because it is the wife who has to make more adjustments with her in-laws in the Indian family structure.

Conclusion

On the basis of the foregoing discussion we may state that the highest frequency of crimes of violence is found in relationships characterized as relatively close, intimate, personal and direct, in short, primary contacts. In almost all cases analysed, the family relationship was quite close. Usually the victim and the offender had strained relations with each other. They claimed that they tried to adjust to each other, but in a fit of passion and anger one killed the other. In other words, the constant arguments and quarrels in which the family members are often engaged lead to the emotional outburst leading to the murder of one. The dissatisfaction with each other continues for months and sometimes years when finally one of them cannot control his emotions any further and resorts to violence under the pressure of extreme frustrations and disappointments.

Extramarital relations, sexual promiscuity, faithlessness, or sexual perversion have been identified as serious causes of friction. Other reasons for domestic quarrels like shortages of money, disagreements over the expenditure of money, habits such as drinking or gambling, problems of maladjustment in families made mother and son the victim and offender. We also found that property disputes cause serious jealousy and rivalry between brothers, often with violent results. Victim-offender relationships were also found between in-laws and their young married children. The conflict was usually more common between the mother-in-law and the daughter-in-law because their adult roles contribute to the frequency of conflict in their relationship since they are individuals with many differences in their role experience. In general when there is a conflict of roles, and when the expectations of the family members are not duly fulfilled, differences and friction develop. This gulf becomes wider and wider with the passage of time. Thus one could say that it is the familial structure that puts constraints on role relationships and creates patterns of interactions leading to violence.

Bibliography

Palmer, Stuart

1965 "Murder and Suicide in Forty Non-literate Societies." *Journal of Criminal Law, Criminology and Police Science*, 320–324.

Steinmetz, Suzanne K., and Murray Straus

1973 "The Family as a Cradle of Violence." *Society*.

Wolfgang, Marvin E., and Franco Ferracuti

1967 *The Subculture of Violence*. New York: Barnes and Noble.

10

The Helpseeking Behavior of Battered Women: An Analysis of 6,000 Shelter Interviews

Edward W. Gondolf
Indiana University of Pennsylvania

Ellen Fisher
La Casa de las Madres, San Francisco

J. Richard McFerron
Indiana University of Pennsylvania

This chapter reports on the analysis of intake and exit interviews of over 6,000 battered women who received shelter care from 1983 to 1985. A comparison with previous battered women studies shows the Texas sample to have a greater percentage of minority, undereducated, and low income women. These battered women also received more life threatening abuse. The frequencies of the four helpseeking variables show women to assertively respond to their batterers' abuse and use a variety of shelter services. Correlation matrices computed for background, abuse, and other helpseeking variables show income, number of children, the severity of abuse, and shelter services influence helpseeking behavior. The results lend support to the survivor strategy hypothesis, rather than learned helplessness hypothesis, and demonstrate the role of shelters in furthering helpseeking.

NOTE: The authors wish to thank the Texas Council on Family Violence and the Texas Department of Human Services for their cooperation in collecting and sharing the data. We are particularly grateful to the shelter staff and battered women who completed the intake interviews at a time of crisis. The Graduate School of Indiana University of Pennsylvania generously provided funding for the initial data analysis.

The Hypotheses

The research on battered women has proliferated in recent years. Clinical, incidence, and explanatory studies have established the severity and extent of abuse rooted in a sexist and violent society. With the development of shelter services has also come studies of the helpseeking behavior of battered women. Unfortunately, most of these studies have been of small samples and limited outcome variables.

In an effort to understand better the helpseeking behavior of battered women and particularly its relationship to shelter services, we have analyzed the intake and exit interviews from over 6,000 sheltered battered women in Texas. Our research question is essentially: What factors contribute to the helpseeking behavior of sheltered battered women? Four helpseeking variables were identified: the women's general response to abusive incidents, the shelter services they obtained, the shelter services they plan to continue, and their living arrangements upon leaving the shelter.

Our preliminary analysis of the Texas data base serves also to clarify the prevailing hypotheses about the helpseeking behavior of battered women. These hypotheses are summarized as follows:

1. *Learned helplessness.* The more severely battered the woman, the less likely she is to seek help. The severe abuse fosters a debilitating sense of fear and self-blame (Walker, 1979, 1984). This victimization as an adult may be related to violence experienced as a child, as intergenerational theory suggests (Straus et al., 1980).
2. *Resource deprivation.* The battered woman with limited resources will display less helpseeking in part because she must depend on her husband for financial support (Pagelow, 1981). The status imbalance between the man and the woman contribute to this state of economic dependence (Straus et al., 1980).
3. *Violent-prone men.* The battered women with more generally violent batterers will show less helpseeking behavior. Their tremendously jealous and dangerous batterers make it virtually impossible for the women to escape them completely. This general violence is learned largely from the abuse that the men witnessed or suffered during

childhood (Stacey and Shupe, 1983; Walker 1984).

4. *Survival strategy.* The more intensified and prolonged the abuse, the greater the variety and extent of helpseeking in order to assure one's survival (Bowker, 1983). Also, there is some indication that the helpseeking increases as the positive reinforcements within the relationship decrease (Walker, 1984).

Our preliminary findings suggest that women's helpseeking is influenced most by the severity and extent of abuse, income of the client, the number of children, and the amount and extent of shelter services received. The status and background of the sheltered women and their batterers appear to contribute very little. These tendencies have been further substantiated in a structural equation model reported elsewhere (Gondolf with Fisher, 1988). The results lend support specifically to the survivor strategy hypothesis and suggest that shelters reinforce and extend the helpseeking behavior of their clients.

Methodology

The questionnaire. This research is a secondary analysis of intake and exit interviews of battered women who entered Texas shelters from 1983 to 1985. The interviews entailed the completion of a three-part, 84-item questionnaire designed jointly by the Texas Council on Family Violence and the Texas Department of Human Services. Staff in each of the state's 50 shelters administered the questionnaire to the women who received residential or non-residential service from their shelter. The questionnaire included a general background section (administered at first contact, i.e., intake), a second section exploring the nature and extent of abuse (administered shortly after the onset of service), and a third section inquiring about services received and expected (administered at the termination of service, i.e., exit).

For the purposes of this study, only the women who reported having been physically battered and who used residential services were considered. This group constituted a sample of 6,612 "sheltered battered women," which was 73 percent of the original interview population of 9,076. The non-residential respondents (1,605) were deleted to avoid duplication that would occur from the many non-resident respondents who later became shelter residents. Women who did not report physical abuse (512) or did not complete the second section of the questionnaire

(347) were also deleted in order to assure a sample of physically battered women.

Variables. The items on the questionnaire were sorted into three categories for analysis: background variables on the present family and parental family, the nature and extent of abuse, and helpseeking behaviors. The family status variables are continuous ordinal responses on income, education, number of children, etc. The parental family variables are largely dichotomous variables based on the presence or absence of spouse abuse, child abuse, and alcohol/drug abuse in the client's family of orientation. The total number of the kinds of parental family abuse (spouse, child, and alcohol and drug abuse) was computed as an indicator for "exposure to abuse." Also a total for the differences between the batterer and the client (in terms of age, income, occupational status, education, and times married) was computed and used as an indicator for "status imbalance."

The abuse variables, which include the kinds of abuses, injury, and care received (excepting duration and frequency of the abuse), are ranked behavioral responses with as many as twelve categories per variable. The rankings were determined by a group of shelter residents and shelter staff using the specified criteria. For instance, "physical abuse" is measured using less severe to most severe abuse: "If you were physically abused, which of the following happened?" (1) threw things at you, (2) confined or held against your will, (3) threw you around, (4) slapped, (5) choked, (6) pulled hair, (7) burned, (8) punched, (9) kicked, (10) used a weapon or object. (The 2% "other" responses were considered "missing.") This particular abuse ranking also parallels the widely used Conflict Tactics Scale (Straus et al., 1980) and the severity ratings of Walker Violent Acts Scale (Walker, 1984).

A value score for each of the principal variables was calculated by summing the ranks of each kind of physical abuse mentioned. The value score for physical abuse was highly correlated with the most severe abuse mentioned (.80), and the total number of kinds of abuses mentioned (.96). Value scores for the other principal variables of abuse and helpseeking displayed even higher correlations with the most severe and total number of responses mentioned, suggesting validity in using the value scores as indicators for their respective variables. Interestingly, "injury" and "care" only moderately correlated to physical abuse (.54, .35) and to each other (.58); that is, the impact of abuse was not necessarily proportionate to the kind of abuse, and that the care sought was not always proportionate to the injury.

Lastly, the principal helpseeking variables included ranked behaviors for "the response to abuse," "the shelter services received," "continued services," and "living arrangements." The response to abuse ranged from the least to most assertive acts toward the batterer: "attempted suicide" to "take legal action." The shelter services ranged from the least intensive service to the greatest, from "referral" to "counselling"; and living arrangements reflected increased independence in the responses: "return to partner," "undetermined," "live with relatives," "live with friends," and "live on own."

Analysis. First, a comparative descriptive analysis was conducted by contrasting frequency distributions of the Texas sample to similar but much smaller samples of battered women.[1] The principal analysis reported in this chapter is the bivariate correlation of background, abuse, and other helpseeking variables with the four major helpseeking variables. Matrices of the nonparametric Tau-b coefficient are used to identify the variables that most influence helpseeking.

This approach is comparable to that employed in the helpseeking studies of Bowker (1983) and Pagelow (1981). Those variables with a coefficient above (+).15 ($p<.001$) are considered influential for the purposes of this study, as is the case in the Bowker and Pagelow studies. The relatively low coefficients are a reflection of the complex nature of the variables which confound the variance and of the complex nature of helpseeking. Helpseeking is no doubt laden with a diversity of motivational factors that elude our behavioral and situational measures.

Qualifications. There are, of course, several other qualifications to this research. One, it is preliminary in nature in that it seeks to sort and clarify an extensive secondary data base. Ideally, a multivariate analysis might be developed but this would involve further manipulation that might decrease the validity. Two, as is the case with much of the research in this field, our analysis lacks a control group that would enable more reliable hypothesis testing. The contrast to other studies' samples offers at least some semblance of comparison.

Three, the essentially categorical nature of many of the variables, especially those related to abuse, make it difficult to develop measures that weight severity and count. Our effort to establish a ranked order of the responses at least approximates more developed scales but must be used with caution. Moreover, the variables for "parental family" abuse are dichotomous (with a "yes" or "no" response) and are therefore relatively insensitive measures of past abuse. This may account for the very small coefficients derived from these variables. Four, a follow-up study particularly of the helpseeking variables identified as "living arrangements" and "services to be continued" would, of course, be ideal. The information collected during the exit interviews form the shelter expresses only intentions and cannot be accepted at face value.

The findings, however tentative, consider a greater breadth of variables and larger sample than most of the previous research.

Findings

Sample description. The sheltered women in our sample appeared to be largely undereducated and underemployed, compared to Bowker's study of formerly battered women (1983), Pagelow's study of California shelter women (1981), Stacey and Shupe's study of Dallas sheltered women (1983), and Walker's study of Rocky Mountain battered women (1984). This might reflect the disproportionate number of Texas women from minority, lower working class, and larger sized families. For example, nearly half of the Texas women had only some high school education, as opposed to 39% of the Stacey and Shupe sample, 32% of the Pagelow sample, and 29% for the national average. The majority of the women's husbands (75%) made $15,000 or less a year, contrasting to 69% in the Stacey and Shupe sample and a $15,000 average in the Walker sample and $23,000 average in the Bowker sample. Notably 30% of the batterers were currently unemployed (only 15% of the Stacey sample and 14% of the Walker sample were unemployed). Only 54% of the women were anglo in contrast to 64% of the Stacey sample, 80% of the Walker sample, and 78% of the Pagelow sample.

The physical abuse inflicted on the Texas women, furthermore, appears to be more severe than for the other samples. Forty-one percent of the women had been abused with weapons or objects; 16% with a gun and 17% with a knife. Additionally, two-thirds (67%) of the batterers had threatened to kill their wives. In the Stacey and Shupe sample of Dallas battered women, only 21% reported being abused with a weapon. Nearly three-quarters (72%) of the Texas sample were punched and over half (58%) kicked at some time. Other kinds of abuse were inflicted as well: sexual abuse (27%), pregnancy abuse (53%), and child abuse (56%). The wife abuse had been occurring for a year or more in 65% of the cases; in 24% of the cases for more than five years (74% and 26% respectively in the Stacey and Shupe sample).

The physical abuse caused head injuries for half (51%) of the Texas women and broken bones for 13% of the sample. Forty-two percent sought medical care for their injuries at some time during the relationship; 10% required hospitalization. Interestingly, more of our sample reported receiving bruises and cuts than the Stacey and Shupe sample, but fewer reported broken bones. An indicator of the psychological impact may be the portion of women who attempted suicide; this was

14% of our sample.

The abuse appears to come largely from generally violent or criminally prone batterers, as Walker (1984) and Stacey and Shupe (1983) have observed. Over one-third of the Texas batterers (37%) had abused people outside the home. In fact, 15% of the sample had been arrested for assault against non-family members. The overall arrest rate (56%) was, however, much less than the Walker sample (71%) and the Stacey and Shupe sample (81%). The majority of the Texas men (62%) reportedly had alcohol problems, as well.

Helpseeking. The first of the helpseeking variables is the women's "response to the abuse." This is indicated in the respondent's answer to the question: "In general, immediately after abusive incidents, what have you done?" The sheltered women generally responded with actions ranked more assertive. Their assertiveness contrasts to the self-reports of passivity in 44% of the Walker sample. Specifically, the majority of the Texas women (71%) had previously left home before becoming shelter residents, as in the Bowker sample of women who had stopped the abuse (75%). In 63% of the cases, the women had contacted the shelter or a lawyer; and over half (53%) had called the police at least once (45% in the Stacey and Shupe sample). A substantial portion of women had evidently pressed charges against their batterers, since 11% of the men had been arrested for assaulting the client. Also, 47% had called their family about the abuse, 35% had threatened the batterer, and 19% had taken legal action.

Interestingly, the least mentioned responses were visiting a social service agency (11%) or visiting a shelter (14%). The formerly battered women in the Bowker study found the shelters to be the "most helpful" and the clergy to be the least helpful (only 17% of our sample contacted the clergy). The Texas women's responses were diverse in that half of the women noted a mean of five helpseeking contacts out of a possible thirteen ($\bar{x}$=4.6, s.d.=2.7).

Once in the shelter, the Texas women drew primarily on the following "shelter services": counselling (85%), transportation (73%), and referral (67%). They used an average of 4.3 (s.d.=2.0) of twelve categories of service. The majority of the women (72%) brought children to the shelter; in fact 21% were accompanied by three or more children. The women when leaving the shelter noted that they would continue to use primarily the crisis hotline (70%), counselling (61%), and referral services (52%) of the shelter (total number of mentions $\bar{x}$=1.7).

Interestingly the child, employment, and legal services were less mentioned as "services to be continued." This might be because of the increased financial support the women obtained, while in the shelter, or the lack of such services for non-residents. Forty-three percent of the women indicated no income at intake and only 29% indicated no income when leaving the shelter. The significant increases were in AFDC and spousal support. Half of the women indicated that they had their own car, and 17% could afford babysitters or day care services.

Shelter workers are perhaps most concerned with "the living arrangements" of the abused women after leaving the shelter, since living separate from the batterer implies greater independence and relative safety. In our sample, only a quarter (24%) of the women *planned* to return to the batterer, and another quarter (26%) *planned* to live on their own. (27% planned to live with relatives, 15% with friends, and 8% were undecided.) If these plans were enacted, about twice as many Texas women did not return to the batterer as is commonly reported. (89% of the women were living with the batterer at the time of the intake.)

Background with helpseeking. The background variables appear to contribute very little to the helpseeking variables (Table 10.1). There is little evidence to support the hypothesis that learned helplessness derived from childhood exposure to violence (parental family variables) differentiates the helpseeking behavior of the sheltered women. (Walker, 1984, also disproves the notion of a victim prone personality.) Similarly, the hypothesis of status imbalance, represented here in the "difference" variables, has little influence. The notion that the better educated and more occupationally experienced women are better equipped to be helpseekers is also not supported. Also of note, the presence of alcohol and drug problems did not appear to influence the helpseeking or, for that matter, the severity of abuse.

The correlations with the client's income and children can be explained in practical terms. The women's response to abuse is positively correlated to the severity of discipline (.23, .23) suggesting perhaps the more assertive responses to the man are in part an attempt to improve circumstances for the children. The slight correlation of the women's response to the severity of child abuse (.15) and child injury (.27) lend support to this notion. The shelter service is surprisingly not influenced by education (.01) or income (-.07), dispelling any myth about "freeloaders" or the more savvy obtaining the bulk of the service. The number (.16) and age (.18) of children appear influential in part because one possible kind of service is childcare and because of the additional referral and transportation needed for extra children.

The future living arrangements of the women appear sensitive to the women's income (.20). The more money she has available the more independent she is able to become. Also the number (.17) and age (.22)

Table 10.1

Coefficient Matrix for Family Status (Background) Variables

	Response to Abuse	Shelter Services	Services Continue	Living Arrangements
Age-Client	.05**	.03	.06**	.11**
Age-Batterer	.06*	.06	.05	.06**
Age-Difference	.03	-.02	-.03	.05
Race-C	-.07	.07	.05	.04
Race-B	-.06	.05	.05	.06*
Education-C	.09**	.01	.01	.07**
Education-B	.06	.07	-.01	.08
Education-D	-.03	.06	-.02	-.05**
Income-C	.05*	-.07	.09**	.20**
Income-B	.01**	-.03	.01	.02
Income-D	.03	-.04	-.04	-.08**
Occupation-C	.02**	-.07*	.06**	.14**
Occupation-B	.07*	-.02	.01	.02
Occupation-D	.02	.04	-.04	-.11**
Unemployment	-.01	.05	.02	.06
Times Married-D	.04	.05	.01	-.01
Long in Relationship	.14**	.12**	.05*	.14**
Number of Children	.07	.16**	.02*	.17**
Age of Oldest Child	.07*	.18**	.09**	.22**
Alcohol-C	.00	-.03	.01	.08
Alcohol-B	-.05	.04	.01	-.08
Composite Difference B-C	.03	.03	-.04	-.13**
Composite Parental Family Abuse-C	.08*	.05	.01	.01
Composite Parental Family Abuse-B	.14**	.10**	.07*	.05

KEY: C=Client; B=Batterer; D=Difference between Batterer and Client

** $p<.001$

* $p<.01$

of the children are correlated to living arrangements. The women with less dependent, older children may have more mobility and be more likely to move out to protect and better care for a greater number of children.

Abuse with helpseeking. As mentioned, the variables for helpseeking were most sensitive to the abuse variables (see Table 10.2). Interestingly, the women's response to abusive incidents is most influenced by the severity of abuse (.26, .27, .24). This moderate correlation of the women's response to the abuse variables and lower correlation of living arrangements to abuse (.13, .22, .15) may suggest that women are more eager to stem the abuse than end the relationship. The women's future living arrangements are less influenced by the physical abuse (.13) and more influenced by the practical concerns of money (.20), children (.17, .22), and the shelter services (.26).

Table 10.2

Coeffecient Matrix for Abuse Variables

	Response to Abuse	Shelter Services	Services Continued	Living Arrangements
Physical Abuse	.26**	.10**	.05	.13**
Verbal Abuse	.27**	.16**	.09	.22**
Sexual Abuse	.11*	.16**	.04**	.16**
Pregnancy Abuse	.14**	.13**	.01	.04
Child Abuse	.15*	.08*	-.15*	.18**
Others Abuse	.24**	.09	.05	.15**
Injury-C	.27**	.08	.06	.10
Care Received-C	.28**	.11	.05	.08
How Long Abused-C	.18**	.13**	.07*	.10**
Recent Frequency-C	.01	.07*	.01	.11**
Response to Abuse-B	.34**	.10**	.10**	.10*
Arrested-B	.22**	.08*	-.01	.02
Convicted-B	.13**	.04	-.04	.02
Jailed-B	.14**	.06	.04	-.05

KEY: C=Client; B=Batterer; D=Difference between Batterer and Client

** $p<.001$

* $p<.01$

More specifically, the women's response to abuse is not only influenced by physical (.26), verbal (.27), and other abuse (.24) but also by the impact of the abuse in terms of injury (.27) and care required (.28). How long the abuse has been occurring is also related to the women's response (.18). The severity of the batterer's response, however, contributes the most to the assertiveness of the women's response (.34). In essence, the more intensive and extensive the abuse, the more likely the woman is to respond assertively in order to protect herself and her children.

The living arrangements, on the other hand, are not only less influenced by the abuse but also much less influenced by the impact. In fact physical abuse (.13) is much less influential than verbal abuse (.22) and sexual abuse (.16), perhaps suggesting the long-term degrading effect of, particularly, verbal abuse has in ending a relationship. The provision of shelter services and continuation of services are not substantially affected by the abuse variables.

Other helpseeking with helpseeking. The women's response to abuse is not correlated to the other helpseeking variables (see Table 10.3). That is, the previous assertiveness does not appear to influence the amount of service that a battered women obtains from the shelter (.08). There are probably a number of factors unique to the shelter that are more influential in this regard: the number of shelter residents, the competence of the staff, the development of the program, and the facility itself. Also, the assertiveness (implied in "the response to abuse" variable) may be confounded by some women's attempt to improve the relationship as opposed to other women's desire to leave the relationship. Therefore, equally assertive women could be receptive to very different levels of shelter service.

As for the continuation of services, the client's income (.22) when exiting the shelter contributes to her continuing use of some shelter services. This finding counters the notion that the poorer clients are likely to be more dependent on the shelter and continue to draw on its services. Perhaps the income signifies greater mobility to reach the shelter or is the product of employment counselling or job training to be continued through the shelter. The continuation of services, most importantly, is correlated to the service obtained while a shelter resident (.18). In other words, the involvement of the client in the shelter activity appears to have some carry-over effect. This is notable given there are no other correlating variables to continuation of services.

The living arrangements after shelter are moderately related to the services obtained in the shelter (.26). It appears, therefore, that the shelter experience does contribute to the women's "getting free."

Table 10.3
Coefficient Matrix for Other Helpseeking Variables

	Response to Abuse	Shelter Services	Services Continued	Living Arrangements
Response to Abuse	—	.08*	.06	.07
Shelter Services	.08	—	.18**	.26**
Service Continued	.06	.18**	—	.22**
Living Arrangements	.07	.26**	.10**	—
Income at Exit	.04	.06**	.22**-	.11**
Transportation	.01	.13	.01	.15**
Child Care at Exit	.02	-.07	.03	.20**
Batterer in Counselling	-.04	.01	.07*	-.17**

** p<.001
* p<.01

	Response to Abuse	Shelter Services	Services Continued	Living Arrangements
Age-Client	.05**	.03	.06**	.11**
Age-Batterer	.06*	.06	.05	.06**
Age-Difference	.03	-.02	-.03	.05
Race-C	-.07	.07	.05	.04
Race-B	-.06	.05	.05	.06*
Education-C	.09**	.01	.01	.07**
Education-B	.06	.07	-.01	.08
Education-D	-.03	.06	-.02	-.05**
Income-C	.05*	-.07	.09**	.20**
Income-B	.01**	-.03	.01	.02
Income-D	.03	-.04	-.04	-.08**
Occupation-C	.02**	-.07*	.06**	.14**
Occupation-B	.07*	-.02	.01	.02
Occupation-D	.02	.04	-.04	-.11**
Unemployment	-.01	.05	.02	.06
Times Married-D	.04	.05	.01	-.01
Long in Relationship	.14**	.12**	.05*	.14**
Number of Children	.07	.16**	.02*	.17**
Age of Oldest Child	.07*	.18**	.09**	.22**
Alcohol-C	.00	-.03	.01	.08
Alcohol-B	-.05	.04	.01	-.08
Composite Difference B-C	.03	.03	-.04	-.13**
Composite Parental Family Abuse-C	.08*	.05	.01	.01
Composite Parental Family Abuse-B	.14**	.10**	.07*	.05

KEY: C=Client; B=Batterer; D=Difference between Batterer and Client
** p<.001
* p<.01

Conclusion

According to our secondary analysis of shelter interviews, the battered women from Texas shelters are not that dissimilar from other samples of battered women. A greater percentage, however, are from lower incomes and racial minorities and are less educated and their husbands are less employed. In terms of abuse, the Texas sample reported more life threatening abuse than the earlier Dallas sample (Stacey and Shupe, 1983), suggesting perhaps more severe cases are being admitted to shelters or the severity itself is increasing over time.

In general, the battered women in our shelter sample appear to act as *survivors*, escaping an increasingly abusive relationship with generally violent men. In a sense, the battered women are comparable to the innocent residents in a war-torn city like Beirut, who fend off the imposing enemy as best as possible but appear reluctant to evacuate their home despite the danger. Their helpseeking is influenced more by the behavior of the batterer (or advancing enemy) and the support of the shelter than by their background or that of the batterer. There is in fact little support for the learned helplessness and intergenerational hypotheses.

The sheltered woman's helpseeking, therefore, appears to be a coping response to her batterer's unrelenting abuse. For instance, the increase in the batterer's severity of arrest, violence to others, and response after the abuse all correlate to helpseeking variables. As Walker (1984) points out, battered women tend to leave when the reinforcements for staying (like occasional affection or financial support) are diminished and/or outweighed by pervasive abuse. The Texas women suggest, in fact, that the man's response to his abuse is very inconsistent. The "honeymoon" phase of the cycle of violence, which purportedly lures some battered women into staying, is at best occasional.

Moreover, the learned helplessness hypothesis supported by Walker's findings (1979, 1984) did not receive much support from our analysis. The Texas women in fact tended to intensify their responsiveness as the abuse became more severe, rather than become more weakened and passive before it. Moreover, the more abuse women experienced as children did not appear to make them vulnerable to more severe abuse or less likely to seek help as some versions of the learned helplessness hypothesis might imply (Straus et al., 1980). While background variables, like a violent parental family, may differentiate battered women from non-battered women, they do not differentiate battered women from other battered women, as Bowker's (1983) study on formerly battered women asserts. Helpseeking did, however, reflect the income of the client and the number of children, as Pagelow (1981) indicates in her examination of resource deprivation. Status imbalance between husband and wife, which Straus et al. (1980) suggest is a factor, did not prove to be influential.

Lastly, the shelter service appears to further helpseeking behavior. The more services a battered woman receives, the more likely she is to intend to continue service and live more independently. Interestingly, the post-intake helpseeking does not reflect the assertiveness of the women prior to entering the shelter. This may suggest that shelter services help promote independence regardless of a woman's prior assertiveness.

These preliminary findings imply that shelters do play an important role in the battered woman's move toward safety and independence. In the process, the violent background and supposed helplessness of battered women do not need to be treated as much as income and child needs. The long-term severe abuse from which these women come reinforces, however, the need for earlier intervention. Considering their previous police, doctor, and shelter contact, battered women should be easy to identify and direct toward shelter service. This would require, however, more outreach workers and more shelter space, as well as a more responsive community. This prerequisite is unfortunately sorely lacking, especially amidst the current funding cuts.

In sum, the aspects of helpseeking identified in this study are situationally based. That is, they are more a response to immediate income and abuse, than background factors including previous helpseeking. Most importantly, the shelter experience furthers this helpseeking process as it moves from assertiveness and coping to independence and safety.

Reference

1. The comparison draws on five other major studies of battered women and a subsample of shelter non-residents from our all Texas sample. The Stacey and Shupe (1983) sample (N=542) of shelter women in Dallas area from 1980 to 1982 uses a shorter version of our questionnaire administered at intake. The Pagelow (1981) study offers another sample of sheltered women (N=350), in this case volunteers largely from California shelters and a Florida shelter. The Walker (1984) sample (N=400) presents a quasi-control of volunteer non-randomized respondents from the Rocky Mountain region who were both in and out of shelters and more likely to not be in a battering relationship at the time of the interviews. The Bowker (1983) sample (N=1,000) poses the other extreme of recruited for-

merly battered women who had been free of abuse for at least a year. The Bowker and Pagelow studies are the only one's that include specific correlations for helpseeking behavior. Unfortunately, the existing comparison groups do not have a complete set of matching variables. Also there is as yet no distinct control group of battered women who have not gone to a shelter.

Bibliography

Bowker, Lee

1983 *Beating Wife Beating.* Lexington, MA: D.C. Heath.

Gondolf, Edward, with Ellen R. Fisher

1988 *Battered Women as Survivors: An Alternative to Treating Learned Helplessness.* Lexington, MA: Lexington Books.

Pagelow, Mildred Daley

1981 *Woman-Battering: Victims and Their Experiences.* Beverly Hills, CA: Sage Publications.

Stacey, William, and Anson Shupe

1983 *The Family Secret: Domestic Violence in America.* Boston: Beacon Press.

Straus, Murray, Richard Gelles, and Susan Steinmetz

1980 *Behind Closed Doors: Violence in the American Family.* New York: Anchor/Doubleday.

Walker, Lenore

1979 *The Battered Woman.* New York: Harper and Row.

1984 *The Battered Woman Syndrome.* New York: Springer.

11

The Criminal Victimization of the Physically Challenged*

Helen W. Ross, Ph.D.
San Diego State University

The Cambridge Victim Survey was used to interview nine handicapped persons (requiring wheelchairs) who reported victimization. The population was divided by gender, and the mean age was 41.7 years. The crimes included sexual molestation, fraud, larceny, and burglary. We concluded that this population is understudied and has unique problems of victimization.

Definitions

The original meaning of *victim* is defined by *Webster's Third International Dictionary* (1971) as "apart, singled out as a person subjected to oppression, deprivation, or suffering"—"someone tricked, duped, or subjected to hardship; someone badly used or taken advantage of." Thus, a victim may suffer at the hands of another; a victim may either be victimized for causes beyond his or her control—natural disasters, accidents of birth—or suffer as a result of his/her own actions (e.g., a victim of one's own ambition).

Our population is doubly victimized. First, they have been singled out by the nature of a handicap—a victim of physical limitations that result in psychological and social consequences that do set him/her apart. Second, at the hands of another, they have been made a victim by being duped, tricked, or badly used. They have so defined themselves by volunteering for the study as handicapped victims of crime.

Crime, in the broadest sense, refers to an offense against public law, either the *commission* of an act that is forbidden or the *omission* of a duty that is commanded by a public law.

---

*This study was supported by a Faculty Grant-in-Aid from the Graduate Division and Research, San Diego State University. I wish to thank L. Riehman, Professor Emeritus, School of Social Work, for her able assistance in the original design of the project and the collection of data.

Statement of the Problem

Victimization research has focused primarily on the elderly, on women, and on children (Balkin, 1981), and we have been unable to locate even *one* study directed specifically toward the physically disabled as victims of crime. Despite extensive victim survey data (Hindelang, 1976; Hindelang et al., 1978; Organization for Economic Cooperation and Development, 1976; Sparks et al., 1977; Williams, 1976), a literature review failed to reveal data on the frequency of crime against the physically disabled. According to Robert Gorski, of the President's Commission on the Employment of the Handicapped (personal communication, July 18, 1986), there are no figures on the frequency of crime against the handicapped, much less the visibly physically disabled. Therefore, no evidence is available to indicate that a proportionately greater incidence of crime is committed against the physically handicapped than against the nonhandicapped.

There are, however, innumerable psychological studies on behavior and attitudes toward the physically disabled (English, 1977; Katz, Glass, Lucido, and Farber, 1977; Katz, Farber, Glass, Lucido, and Emswiller, 1978; Katz et al., 1979). However, a review of the literature regarding the disabled as crime victim provides a focus on prevention, and there are minimal data on the extent of the problem. Studies related to the disabled victim are not empirically based. They provide either suggestions for the victim regarding how to cope (Stuart and Stuart, 1981) or manuals to aid the peace officer with the recognition and handling of the developmentally disabled. Thus, in spite of the lack of data, there is a tacit assumption that crime against the handicapped poses a problem.

The present study focuses on the visibly physically disabled as victims of crime. In recent years, persons with physical disabilities have become more evident and more geographically mobile. Reasons for this include educational and legislative efforts (e.g., removal of architectural barriers, exhortations to hire the handicapped, and media campaigns to educate the public). These factors have precipitated a change in public perception of persons with physical handicaps. Law enforcement agencies and community groups sponsor educational programs on crime prevention and self-defense techniques for the physically disabled.

Nonetheless, according to Gunnar Dybwad (Park, 1977), *normalization* of the lifestyles of the disabled includes the right to be exposed to "trouble, strife, trial and tribulation." Normalization includes the dignity of taking risks. As the visibly physically disabled become better integrated into the community, they take greater risks, becoming more vulnerable to crime victimization. They probably become even more vulnerable than the nondisabled population by virtue of the handicap that targets them as easy victims.

We suggest the following:

1. The increasing mobility of the physically disabled exposes them to much greater than normal risk of becoming victims of crime (*exposure*).
2. The inability to protect themselves makes them more vulnerable (*vulnerability*).
3. Adaptive housing for physically disabled persons is usually located in low-income, high-crime neighborhoods (*environment*).

We further suggest that two additional factors increase the likelihood that the physically handicapped may become victims of crime:

1. Physically disabled persons who have made the transition to the open community from previously protected environments often lack the skills and information to enable them to live safely in the community (*inadequate preparation*).
2. Their dependence on attendants increases their risk of being victimized by crime (*dependence*).

Moreover, the physically disabled population is reported to experience feelings of powerlessness, helplessness, and guilt; and they are stigmatized (English, 1977; Geis, 1977; Shontz, 1977; Stuart and Stuart, 1981; Tussman, 1975). When victimized by crime, these preexisting feelings may be accentuated by the victimization so that they may even more intensely experience the usual responses to victimization: a feeling of being stigmatized, powerless, helpless, and a sense of self-blame (Bard and Sangrey, 1986; Miller and Porter, 1983; Perloff, 1983). Research on victims of crime is important not only because we are concerned for the victim but also because without knowledge of the victim, we have incomplete knowledge of the crime (Sparks, 1982).

Survey

In order to ascertain the extent of locally available data, we surveyed San Diego County law enforcement agencies and any community groups who focus on crime prevention and information for the physically disabled as potential victims. Additionally, we consulted San Diego State University law enforcement specialists. Our survey revealed the following:

1. There are no city, county, state, or national police statistics on the physically disabled as victims of crime.
2. The crime reports refer to the type of crime committed, but they do not indicate whether the victim was physically disabled unless the disability was a primary factor in enabling criminal access (e.g., an elderly disabled bedridden person living alone).
3. The crime reports do indicate whether the person became disabled as a result of the crime.
4. There are no statistics for the state of California specifically addressing the physically disabled as victims of crime.
5. The FBI's *Uniform Crime Reports* include limited kinds of data on all crimes reported to the police nationwide, but they rarely specify whether the victim is physically disabled.
6. Data in crime reports reflect entirely different kinds of information than victim surveys, and the information that overlaps often reports different results (e.g., rate of crime victimization).

Additionally, two groups address the issue of criminal victimization of the physically handicapped. The Victim's Assistance Program of San Diego focuses on persons who are injured and disabled as a result of a crime. The San Diego Coalition for the Prevention of Crime against the Physically Disabled comprises law enforcement officers and representatives from community agencies, and their function is primarily crime education and prevention. The coalition assists disabled persons to prevent their becoming victims of crime. The coalition also strives to increase the police officers' awareness regarding the special needs of disabled persons. According to the coalition, approximately 200,000 disabled persons live in San Diego, or 10.3 percent of the total population. Unfortunately, the coalition specifies neither a demographic breakdown on the disabled population nor which kinds of disabled persons may be excluded from this percentage.

Available Data on Victims of Crime (San Diego Crime Prevention Survey)

Victim surveys, first implemented in the mid-1960s, reflect a wide variety of data concerning a *representative sample* of victims. These surveys indicate that rates of victimization are closely tied to such victim characteristics as age, gender, marital status, family income, and race. The victim surveys have been made in *many* large American cities and in a number of cities in Europe. Though the findings are not equivalent, similar patterns arise in the relationships among these characteristics across cities (Hindelang et al., 1978; Mowbray, 1986; OECD, 1976; Sparks et al., 1977).

These surveys measured the extent to which city residents (age 12 and over), households, and commercial establishments were victimized by selected crimes, whether completed or attempted. The offenses committed against individuals included rape, robbery, assault, and personal larceny. The surveys covered several crimes against households: burglary, household larceny, and motor vehicle theft. Burglary and robbery against commercial establishments were also surveyed.

San Diego data (Gregg, Bratt, and Renshaw, 1977) are derived from victimization surveys conducted in 1974 under the National Crime Survey program. This report supplements criminal victimization surveys in 13 American cities and presents more-comprehensive survey results and additional technical information.

Household and commercial surveys revealed that an estimated 203,900 criminal victimizations were committed against San Diego residents in 1973. Fifty-two percent involved individuals, 44 percent households, and 4 percent commercial establishments. Personal crimes of theft outnumbered personal crimes of violence by about 2.7 to 1. We realize that current data would indicate changes.

In 1973, 53 of 1,000 San Diego residents (age 12 and over) were victimized by personal crimes of violence. This rate was lower than the average reported in the other cities, and there was no significant difference between the rates for whites and blacks—a finding different from most cities surveyed. As in other major cities, the young (12–34 years), the poor (less than $3,000 per year), and those from households of six or more persons were most likely to become victims of personal crime (Hindelang, 1976).

The reports from all cities indicated that a staggering number of crimes go unreported, and only three-tenths of all personal crimes were reported to the police. Sparks et al. (1977) note that only 1 crime in 11 is reported. The most common reasons for not reporting personal, household, and commercial crimes were the victim's beliefs that nothing could be done and that the crime was not important enough. Of major significance, information concerning health, physical, or mental status of the victim was not available from victim surveys.

Victims socialize largely with persons who share similar lifestyles and with nonfamily members (Greenberg and Shore, 1984). Hindelang et al. (1978) and Williams (1976) conclude that the victims' lifestyles expose them to vulnerability, and the victim appears vincible. In general, our findings are consistent with Hindelang's (1976) review of victim surveys, despite the lower rate of victimization in San Diego than in other major cities.

We suggest that the visibly disabled person certainly appears vincible and may be more likely than the average person to exhibit the characteristics of the victim. Thus, the disabled person may be a more likely target than a nonhandicapped counterpart. We originally intended to test the hypothesis that the visibly physically handicapped may be more vulnerable to crime victimization than their nonhandicapped peers. Difficulties in locating victims, however, limited our population size. With constraints on time and money, we decided to look at our limited data based on nine respondents.

Method

Definitions

The following definitions were used throughout the study:

- *Victims*: All respondents are crime victims, as self-defined.
- *Crime*: The reports of criminal victimization surveys in 13 American cities were used for crime classification in conjunction with the glossary defining specific terms. Crimes were classified as crimes against persons, including crimes of violence (i.e., rape, personal robbery, and assault), all of which bring the victim into direct contact with the offender; crimes against households (i.e., burglary, household larceny, and motor vehicle theft), which do not involve personal confrontation.

➢ *Incident*: A criminal act involving one or more victims and offenders. The incident must have occurred within 12 months prior to the interview (see Gottfredson, 1977). All subjects reported being victimized by more than one crime. In our calculations, we used the crime the subject targeted as the crime reported to us.

Subjects

Both male and female subjects (interviewed in 1982–1984) were visibly physically disabled persons who met the following criteria:

1. Between 18 and 65 years of age.
2. Visibly physically disabled (i.e., having a disability readily apparent to a casual observer).
3. Self-identified as a victim of a crime within the past year, with a visible physical disability existing prior to the crime.
4. Victimized by a crime committed within San Diego County within the 12 months prior to their participation.

To reach the subjects, we contacted social service agencies in San Diego serving physically disabled persons. The project was described, and a brief description was sent, along with a poster with the investigators' names and phone numbers. We also posted flyers on campuses and in areas we deemed likely to be frequented by the disabled. Several newsletters included a description of the study, with requests for disabled volunteers who had been victims of crime. We contacted the following agencies and requested their assistance with our study: Community Service Center for the Disabled, Deaf Association, Blind Association, Multiple Sclerosis Association, Cerebral Palsy Association, Veteran's Associations, members of the San Diego Coalition for Prevention of Crime against the Physically Disabled. We received approximately 26 responses, 9 of which met the criteria.

Despite the limited number, our subjects represented a fair ethnic and educational cross section of the San Diego residents. One subject was self-identified as Afro-American, one as Mexican-American, and the remaining seven as Caucasians. The majority had some college, one respondent had postgraduate work and two were high school graduates. Our population included five females and four males whose average age was 41.7 years (range 31–57). Four subjects were married (two to each other and two separated from their spouses). Subject incomes ranged from none reported to more than $35,000 per year, with a median of $4,700 per year. Five subjects lived in public housing in high-crime areas. One couple and a single resided in middle-class neighborhoods, and the remaining unit was in a low-income area.

Disability

All subjects were in wheelchairs, and six subjects had received attendant care. Diagnosis was difficult because several were multihandicapped. Briefly, three suffered from an impairment that has affected their lives from infancy (i.e., cerebral palsy or infantile polio), four from a disease with onset in later life (i.e., polio or multiple sclerosis), and two from accident or trauma.

Instrument

Interviews were conducted with a modification of the University of Cambridge Crime Victim Survey (Sparks et al., 1977).

The questionnaire selected for modification can be found in Sparks, Genn, and Dodd (1977). It was selected because Sparks et al. specifically addressed the methodological problems of validity and reliability, and the instrument was developed to overcome flaws cited in previous victim surveys. This questionnaire is too lengthy for inclusion, but it requests the following information in an interview format:

- Lifestyle patterns such as frequency of outings, mode of transportation, and type of establishment frequented.
- Attitudes toward rehabilitation and neighborhood.
- General questions about frequency of crime in own and other neighborhoods.
- Feelings of safety versus vulnerability.
- Contact with police and attitude toward police.
- Measurement of the respondent's assessment of the seriousness of the crime, and assessment of moral attitudes.
- Specific questions concerning their own victimizations.

This questionnaire includes 102 questions covering lifestyle patterns, attitudes, and demographic material, plus an additional 40 questions that cover the reported crime. We judged interrater reliability, established after the interview, to be near 90 percent.

Procedure

After each subject agreed to participate, two trained interviewers conducted the interview in the subject's home. The Cambridge form was filled out, and a tape was made of the interview. Each interview lasted approximately 2 hours.

Tentative Findings

Overview

In terms of lifestyle, this group reported that they frequently attended or visited church and meetings for the handicapped, as well as clinics and doctors, family and friends. They occasionally went to the movies and to bars. Not one member reported leaving home to go to work. Several did not go out at night; of those who did, they traveled by taxi, car, or transportation provided for the handicapped. The group was split in terms of feeling "at home" in their current neighborhood, but they were all attached to at least one other area of the city (e.g., church, mother's or sister's home). All but three lived in high-crime neighborhoods. Despite this, they suggested that they would miss the neighborhood should they have to leave. In the neighborhood where they resided, they reported a high incidence of theft, burglary, assault, and drug usage. They attributed these crimes largely to drug addicts and teenagers. Only one person responded with a racial stereotype—"uneducated blacks." All respondents expressed concern about the increasing rate of crime.

This questionnaire includes 23 questions that deal with the values of the individual. On the dimensions of control over external events and pessimism versus optimism, the group was evenly distributed.

Crimes committed against this sample included sexual molestation, fraud, larceny, burglary, and assault. All but one attendant was reported to have committed a crime against his/her employer. A notable finding, even with such a small sample, is that all reported being victims of more than one crime incident.

Their attitudes toward the police ranged from hostile to positive. Seven of the victims reported at least one of the crimes by which they were victimized, but only one of the persons who were multiply victimized reported all of the crimes. Of those crimes that were reported to the police by our subjects, only one subject reported satisfaction with the manner in which the police handled the crime. The relative dissatisfaction with police handling of the crime was frequently mentioned as a factor in subsequent nonreporting.

The most ambivalent set of responses concerned the use of violence in response to crime. There was unanimous agreement that "one should turn the other cheek" on the one hand, while there was almost unanimous agreement that "violence deserves violence." The response to using violence to prevent violence was divided, but a conservative value system is the consensus of this group.

Unique Experiences of These Subjects

Our sample differs from other victim samples in age, education, and lifestyle. This sample is older and better educated, and their lifestyle clearly differs from many victim samples.

The majority of our sample feel that the physically handicapped are more likely to be victimized than their more physically able peers. The aftermath of the crime changed the behavior of all respondents, but the attitudes and personality of the victim determined the reaction to the crime. The following synopses illustrate some of the differences.

Susan: After her first victimization (breaking and entering into her home), Susan's family tried to force her to move into their home. Susan (cerebral palsied) refused but could neither sleep nor feel comfortable in her home alone. The police had been highly inefficient in investigating the crime, and they treated her as though she were mentally retarded, so she did not report additional uninvited, unlawful entries into her home. She briefly sought psychiatric help, but she was unsatisfied with the result. A while after the interview, she moved to a new, more secure apartment and felt safer and more comfortable thereafter.

Kay and Jack: This married couple's attendant embezzled more than $1,500 from them. A previous attendant had stolen some personal property from them. The couple reported neither of the crimes to the police, but the bank reported the embezzlement. After the embezzlement, the couple hired their youngest son as their caregiver, and they decided not to hire future attendants until they had seen a driver's license and had checked the potential attendant's records for prior criminal activity.

Genevieve: Genevieve's specially designed van had been stolen from outside her parent's home. Her father reported the theft to the police, and the van was found later, somewhat damaged. The thieves were never apprehended. Prior to this time, however, Genevieve had been victimized by two different attendants. One attendant threatened her life and the other left her with more than $200 in unauthorized phone bills. Just before the interview, a radio was stolen from Genevieve's van, and Genevieve suspected a friend of the son of one of Genevieve's friends. Additionally, the screen was torn on her apartment window. After the victimizations by attendants, Genevieve asked her sister to help her screen applicants. These victimizations and the theft of the radio led Genevieve to feel hurt that the disabled are so easily victimized and to lose trust in other people.

Juanita: Juanita was robbed of her entire SSI (Social Security Income) check, was unable to pay bills, lost several irreplaceable photos, and had her electricity turned off. Additionally, her 10-year-old son's toys and bicycle were vandalized. On a previous occasion, when there had been a knife fight in her home "over money," she had called "911" and had been asked to "please hold." Juanita feels frustrated and vengeful as a result of her crime victimizations.

Tom: When Tom and his attendant were away from the house, Tom's $1,300 video system had been stolen. Tom suspected a neighbor to whom he had previously lent a key. Tom reported the theft to the police, but they did little to investigate despite Tom's full cooperation. Tom's insurance covered the loss of the video system. A previous robbery of tools from his car was not reported to the police and was not reimbursed by his insurance company. On two previous occasions, his home had been broken into, but nothing had been stolen. One occasion was reported to the police and the other was not. Tom was dissatisfied with the police handling of his victimizations and responded by making his apartment more secure at his own expense. Additionally, Tom planned to purchase a weapon and to obtain a "house sitter" for any absences of more than a day.

Arthur: Arthur's attendant committed fraud against him, costing Arthur $700. When Arthur, who has a degree in criminal justice, called the police, they informed him that it was a civil matter and did nothing. Additionally, Arthur was robbed four other times, once from his person and three times from his home, including a manuscript that he considered to be of no monetary value though it had taken him many years to write it. After one of the robberies was reported to the police, Arthur was sufficiently disappointed in their handling of it that the other crimes were not reported. The major consequence of the fraud was that Arthur felt very foolish. The robberies caused Arthur to feel unsafe in his apartment, and he began searching for a more secure residence.

Liz: Liz was sexually molested by a man in her apartment building. She had been trained as a paralegal and had a restraining order served against him. Nonetheless, when she called the police to have them enforce the injunction, they did little to reassure her of their protection against the man. Prior to this crime, Liz had been robbed by two different attendants. She reported all three crimes to the police, but she claims that she has never received any satisfactory results from the police. She feels very uncomfortable in any of the public areas of her apartment building and has been taking Valium ever since the sexual assault. Her efforts to handle the crimes through legal channels have offered Liz little reassurance or recompense.

John: While John was away from his home, a leather jacket, his stereo, and the keys to his van were stolen. When he noticed the robbery, he did not check on the whereabouts of his van. Later that night, he noticed that the van had been stolen. He reported the theft to the police and filed a claim with his insurance company. Later, his almost-stripped van was found, and the insurance company paid to have it repaired. The thieves were never apprehended, and John felt dissatisfied with the police handling of the matter. Earlier, John had been threatened by a robber who had a knife in a public park. Despite his wheelchair confinement, he was able to defend himself—his call for help was not heeded. He considered theft to be a fact of life and did not believe that the theft had altered his behavior or his attitudes. He did, however, install a burglar-proof ignition system on his van.

Discussion

Trends and impressions: Because this population is so small, we feel it more accurate to present our findings in terms of trends and impressions rather than to use percentages on any specific variable studied. We do feel that this population does, in fact, meet the criteria for being "at risk" for victimization. As a group, they do not go out at night (with two exceptions), but they do go to movies and to visit friends. Their disability makes them less able to protect themselves than more physically able peers, and with three exceptions, they live in low-income, high-crime areas.

Study limitations: A self-reported population is always suspect. Unfortunately, we had no other way to collect data. In an attempt to use self-report measures to enhance validity vis-a-vis the victim, our findings become suspect. However, according to Hindelang, Gottfredson, and Garofalo (1978), it is erroneous and naive to conclude that victimization survey results represent a true rate of crime. There are several sources of error: overreporting (erroneous victimization reporting), underreporting (nonreporting of victimization), memory decay, and telescoping (Gottfredson and Hindelang, 1977). Because there is limited research on this question, we must assume that these respondent characteristics are randomly distributed.

Our research design was unorthodox (by virtue of the topic selected for study) and posed problems in validity and reliability. For example, crime self-reports are after the fact, and the accuracy of reportage may be psychologically affected. This population sample was self-selected. It is impossible to make comparisons and generalize to the population at large, based on the wide parameters in sampling criteria. In this pioneer effort, however, the sampling criteria enabled us to assess the problem deductively and then begin to infer as we classified and compared.

Further, to enhance our assessments, we interviewed 10 additional disabled persons' crimes who were victimized too long ago to include in our study. All 10 of these persons had attendants and reported attendant abuse, including sexual assault and theft. Victimization of the disabled by attendants has also been documented in the *Los Angeles Times* (Banks and McGraw, 1984).

Inferences from the Study: From interview responses, we inferred that the visibly physically disabled

- are understudied
- are vulnerable, underprotected, and easy targets for crime
- have unique problems
- may be demographically distinct from other victim populations
- are at risk for victimization.

We further deduced that

- the outcome or response to the crime is a function of the individual's prior adjustment
- the sequelae of victimization may depend more on personality variables than on the disability or the nature of the crime
- the nature of the crime in this population is often a function of the person's dependence on others for care.

Implications for attendant care: All the subjects who had attendants received state funds with which to pay the attendant. In order for a disabled person to qualify for funds for attendant care, he or she must qualify as being "in financial need" under Social Security Income (SSI) guidelines. To qualify as being *in financial need*, the disabled person can neither earn more than $300 per month in gainful employment nor have more than $1,500 in assets. On the basis of an interview, a social worker establishes the eligibility for care and the number of attendant hours required. In California, the program that actually disburses funds for attendant care is separate from SSI. The state fund (with matching federal dollars) is administered by individual counties. The disabled person may receive the money directly and then locate and hire an attendant. Or the county may contract for and provide the disabled person with the specified number of hours of attendant care.

The state provides $3.78 per hour for the attendant, and 251 hours per month is the maximum number of hours allowed for care. The attendants are not state employees; they receive neither benefits nor unemployment protection; nor are they licensed or bonded. The meager salary and nonexistent benefits do little to attract responsible, sensitive, intelligent caregivers. In 1983, a law was passed in California to make it a criminal offense for an attendant of a disabled person to abuse this person psychologically or physically, but it is small wonder that victimization of the disabled by their caregivers continues to be a problem.

The original purpose of this exploratory study was to test the interview instrument. We believe, however, that the limited information we have gathered is important, and we have, as a result, been able to generate ideas both for research and for reviewing current policies. Sparks (1982) suggests that because victimization is rare, surveys of the victim population may not be cost effective and that we target populations at risk for victimization. We largely concur with this suggestion, but this small study has led us to suggest that this at-risk population may differ in demographic characteristics and that the crimes committed against them may be of a different nature than crimes against other populations. Additionally, Sparks (1982) adds that though victimization is a rare event, once a person becomes a victim, the probability of being victimized again increases. Therefore, more research efforts should be addressed toward the at-risk populations. The victims in our population all reported more than one event, and we urge that more study be made of the disabled as victims. We were unprepared for the extent of crime perpetrated by those whose duties are to administer care to the disabled. This finding in such a small sample suggests a larger problem demands a review of our current policies which govern the hiring and placement of attendants for the disabled as well as an investigation into the nature and extent of the problem.

Bibliography

Balkin, S.

1981 "Towards Victimization Research on the Mentally Retarded." *Victimology*, 6: 331–337.

Bard, M., and D. Sangrey

1986 *The Crime Victims Book*. New York: Bruner/Mazel.

English, R.W.

1977 "Combatting Stigma toward Physically Disabled Persons." In R.P. Marinelli and A.E. Dell Orto, eds. *The Psychological and Social Impact of Physical Disability*. New York: Springer.

1977 "Correlates of Stigma toward Physically Disabled Persons." In R.P. Marinelli and A.E. Dell Orto, eds. *The Psychological and Social Impact of Physical Disability*. New York: Springer.

Geis, J.H.

1977 "The Problem of Personal Worth in the Physically Disabled Patient." In R.P. Marinelli and A. E. Dell Orto, eds. *The Psychological and Social Impact of Physical Disability*. New York: Springer.

Gottfredson, M., and M. Hindelang

1977 "A Consideration of Memory Decay and Telescoping Biases in Victimization Surveys." *Journal of Criminal Justice*, 5: 205–216.

Greenberg, M.S., and S. Shore, eds.

1984 "Criminal Victimization." *Journal of Social Issues*, 40: 1–182.

Gregg, J.M.H., H. Bratt, and B.H. Renshaw

1977 *Criminal Victimization Surveys in San Diego*. Washington, DC: U.S. Government Printing Office.

Hindelang, M.

1976 *Criminal Victimization in Eight American Cities: A Descriptive Analysis of Common Theft and Assault*. Cambridge, MA: Ballinger.

Hindelang, M., M. Gottfredson, and J. Garofalo

1978 *Victims of Personal Crime: An Empirical Foundation for a Theory of Personal Victimization*. Cambridge, MA: Ballinger.

Katz, I., D. Glass, D. Lucido, and J. Farber

1977 "Ambivalence, Guilt and the Denigration of a Physically Handicapped Victim." *Journal of Personality* 45, 419–429.

Katz, I., J. Farber, D. Glass, D. Lucido, and T. Emswiller

1978 "When Courtesy Offends: Effects of Positive and Negative Behavior by the Physically Disabled on Altruism and Anger in Normals." *Journal of Personality*, 46: 506–518.

Katz, I., et al.

1979 "Harm-doing and a Victim's Racial or Orthopedic Stigma as Determinants of Helping Behavior." *Journal of Personality*, 47: 340–364.

Miller, D.T., and C.A. Porter.

1983 "Self-blame in Victims of Violence." In R. Janoff-Bulman and I.H. Frieze, eds. *Reactions to Victimization. Journal of Social Issues*, 39: 1–228.

Mowbray, R.

1986 "The Victim-Offender Relationship and Its Implications for Policies: Evidence from the British Crime Survey." Paper presented at the Second World Congress of Victimology, Orlando, Florida, July 9–13.

Organization for Economic Cooperation and Development

1976 "OECD Data Sources for Social Indicators of Victimization Suffered by Individuals." 3. Paris.

Park, L.D.

1977 "Barriers to Normality for the Handicapped Adult in the United States." In R.P. Marinelli and A.E. Dell Orto, eds. *The Psychological and Social Impact of Physical Disability*. New York: Springer.

Perloff, L.S.

1983 "Perceptions of Vulnerability to Victimization." *Journal of Social Issues*, 39: 41–61.

Shontz, F.C.

1977 "Physical Disability and Personality: Theory and Recent Research." In R.P. Marinelli and A.E. Dell Orto, eds. *The Psychological and Social Impact of Physical Disability*, New York: Springer.

Sparks, R., H. Genn, and D. Dodd.

1977 *Surveying Victims: A Study of the Measurement of Criminal Victimization, Perceptions of Crime, and Attitudes to Criminal Justice*. New York: Wiley.

Sparks, R.

1982 "Research on Victims of Crime: Accomplishments, Issues, and New Decisions." DHHS Publication No. (ADM) 82-1091. Washington, DC: Government Printing Office.

Stuart, C.K., and V.W. Stuart.

1981 "Sexual Assault: Disabled Perspective." *Health and Rehabilitation Services,* 21: 246–253.

Tussman, N.

1975 "An Exploration of Feelings of Aggression and Helplessness as Manifested in the Dreams of the Physically Disabled." *Dissertation Abstracts International*, 36(3-B): 1463.

Williams, K.M.

1976 "The Effects of Victim Characteristics on the Disposition of Violent Crime." In W. F. McDonald, ed. *Criminal Justice and the Victim.* Beverly Hills, CA: Sage.

12

Arson—From Creation to Destruction

Irving Kaufman, M.D.
Auburndale, Massachusetts

Arson is the fastest growing crime in the United States and is extremely difficult to prevent and treat.

The setting of fires has many healthy as well as pathologic meanings. The focus of this chapter will be the underlying meaning of fire to an individual when arson is the objective.

Persons who set fires for pathologic reasons are communicating the meaning of fire to them. The most extreme message expressed by both male and female firesetters is a wish to destroy, annihilate, or murder.

Differences in attitudes of males and females towards fire have been observed over the course of time. For example, in Roman times males were not entrusted to care for and perpetuate fire. That task was assigned to the vestal virgins.

Although both males and females tend to direct the aggression associated with firesetting out onto the environment, many female firesetters also direct their destructive aggression inward onto the self in reality or fantasy. Some females actually set their clothes or themselves on fire. Other females may view the fire as a cleansing, purifying or a rebirth ritual—like the Phoenix fantasy.

Study of mythologic meanings of fire often reveal similar fantasies occurring in the minds of modern day arsonists. In a previous paper we described how fire, wind, water, and earth fantasies recur over and over again in the thinking of arsonists.

This chapter will present (1) incidence, (2) developmental diagnosis, including libidinal and aggressive drives, (3) thought processes and fantasies, (4) family interaction, (5) male and female arson, and (6) implications for treatment and prevention.

Arson is a major problem in our culture and can result in severe victimology. Arson refers to the setting of serious fires. Despite a wide range of often apparently conflicting fantasies expressed by the arsonist, the end result is generally some form of destruction. The target can be things, such as buildings, or it can be directed at people or animals. Unlike controlled fires, for warmth or cooking, arson and the associated uncontrolled fire is a complex process often reflecting an external representation of the all-consuming force felt by the ego when it is flooded by the terrorizing sensations of primary anxiety. Expression of the fantasies accompanying arson can range from such basic opposites as lofty ideals to the most depraved motives. The combination of lofty and depraved motives is seen in burning witches or Jews to rid the culture of contaminating evil forces. Arson, as will be discussed, is associated with an extraordinarily large and conflicting range of fantasies encompassing life, death, the most holy and the most profane.

This presentation will discuss (1) incidence of arson; (2) the developmental diagnosis of arsonists including some of the complexities of their libidinal and aggressive drives; (3) a brief compilation of some recurring fantasies and associated thought processes; (4) their family patterns and interaction; (5) similarities and differences in male and female arsonists; (6) a brief discussion of the implications for treatment and prevention.

Incidence

Wooden (1985) stated that the United States has the highest rate of arson in the world. Arson is the fastest growing crime. Six thousand civilians and one hundred fire fighters die in a year. The number of individuals requiring treatment for burns and their associated physical and psychological traumas are enormous. Wooden stated that property loss has increased to a billion dollars a year. Because arson often occurs within a destructive personality, it can be part of victimizing and terrorizing the community. An example which Wooden cited was that of David Berkowitz (Son of Sam), who was acknowledged to be a mass murderer and had set more than two thousand fires.

It is extremely interesting that such a major type of crime, victimization, and misery has received so little public attention and concern.

In contrast to Wooden's observations of the excess of middle class children as firesetters, my research in such facilities as state hospitals, courts and correctional institutions has revealed a predominance of children and adults of all socioeconomic levels with an unusually high representation of socially and economically deprived persons.

Developmental Diagnosis Including Libidinal and Aggressive Drives

The early psychoanalytic literature placed arson as a disturbance associated with a fixation at the phallic-urethral stage of development. This conceptualization views arson closer to the neurotic level than I found in my cases which had a much more serious disturbance. As a further validation of their phallic-urethral view of arson, Freud (1964) and Michaels (1953) discussed the subject in some fascinating ways with which I take exception.

Freud (1961) stated that "Man after he had captured fire, placed woman by the hearth to guard the fire, since her anatomy makes it impossible to extinguish it." It was also noted that historically the tenders of fire have been women such as the vestal virgins. Although the aim of this argument is interesting, my cases do not support this chauvinistic point of view.

Michaels' (1953) book focused on the relation between eneuresis and delinquency including arson-again connecting arson with the phallic-urethral state of development. I found less than half of my cases of arson to be eneuretic. Another dimension to this psychoanalytic point of view is the utilization of a biologic frame of reference to understand behavior. This historical and still fascinating conceptualization implies that behavior and emotions have a related biologic base. In the above mentioned book by Michaels, he connected many problems of impulse control including delinquency in general and arson to the developmental issues of gaining sphincter control. While there still may be some usefulness in relating the sequences of biologic mastery over one's body to behavior, the focus of this chapter will be based on developmental frame of reference more closely allied to the effects of object relationships on personality.

Reviewing the literature discussing the diagnosis of arsonists gave a very mixed picture. Lewis and Yarnell (1951) described their cases of adolescent female arsonists as primarily retarded. A few of the researchers, including Bender (1959) and Kaufman et al. (1961), described the arsonists as schizophrenic. Most researches view arsonists at either a neurotic or characterologic level. This topic is stressed because management and treatment must be based on diagnosis.

Personality diagnosis of the arsonists may be difficult and take time to clarify. In a previous publication Kaufman et al. (1963) described most of the patients who committed crimes of violence such as arson as a type of schizophrenic. Part of the problem in determining their diagnosis is that their symptoms of gross schizophrenia could be episodic and alternated with periods of personality reintegration.

We found that the arson was associated with the oral stage of development and not the genital as described by Freud (1961), who said that setting a fire and putting it out was a symbolic sexual act. Although in some cases there may be sexual implications to the setting of a fire, the sexual components were the least significant. The oral characteristics demonstrated at the deepest level by these patients were manifested by a cry for help or nurturance associated with rage at not receiving it. Both the beacon or signal for help and the rage took the form of light-fire arson. The behavior of these patients was complex and included other pathologic and often complicated ways to signal their oral needs as well as their violent rage. The choice of symptom is a difficult topic. Some attempt to describe some of the facets that go into symptom choice will be discussed later in this paper. Amongst the recurring components that emerged was some relation between the consuming oral need to be nurtured, fear of consuming-engulfing or being consumed and viewing fire as consuming what it burned.

Our above observations are in total agreement with those of Lauretta Bender (1953 and 1959) who said that children set fires to destroy. They are consumed with rage. The reason for the rage is the feeling that some family member has withheld love from the child in a very major way and that family member should be destroyed by burning.

At the same orthopsychiatric meeting in San Francisco in which Lauretta Bender presented the above material, Kaufman et al. (1963) presented a paper describing children who committed crimes of violence such as arson and labeled them "pseudodelinquent schizophrenia." Unknown to either of us, Lauretta Bender was simultaneously presenting a paper on children who murdered, committed arson and other acts of violence. She labeled her cases as a type of schizophrenia entitled "pseudopsychopathic schizophrenia."

The desire for nurture and the rage and resulting arson at not receiving it can take many forms. One example of an unusual expression of this phenomenon was described by Geller (1984). He described seven male and seven female patients who committed arson upon their release from an institution. I have seen many examples of institutionalized prisoners or patients who view the institution as the secure nurturant home. Unless there is a well thought out plan for home care on their release, they may steal or behave in some antisocial way in order to be returned to the jail or hospital.

In some of our cases children struggling with feelings of being unloved and not nurtured when they set fire to a home or a building reveal that they view the fireman as the idealized father who will rescue them.

The cases described by Geller illustrate an example of the above process which I have repeatedly observed.

Thought Processes and Fantasies

Understanding the core dynamics of the arsonist who feels deprived of the most basic care and nurturance and copes with those feelings by setting a fire to destroy is essential. However, in dealing with individual patients or cultural patterns such as burning Jews in ovens, more complex defense upon defense types of fantasies need to be understood in order to relate in a therapeutically useful way. For example, lighting a candle to ask for God's blessing is a "normal" expression of the wish "to be in Grace." Setting a home, school, church or other building on fire may also be a way of asking for help and dealing with the feelings that all is not right. It is important to know that there are general and often specific fantasies associated with the arson.

It is impossible to do more than give some representative examples of thoughts and fantasies which recur sufficiently to warrant considering them. In all cases the ultimate answer to an understanding of the meaning of the specific act of the arson resides within the patient.

Many of the universal concepts appear in mythology, the Bible and in literature. For example, the novel *She* by Haggard (1976) contains fascinating description of the range of thoughts and fantasies about fire including life, death and power.

Light and fire as a beacon or signal for help is illustrated both by the torch in the Statue of Liberty and the description in the Holy Bible of the "fire by night and smoke by day" which would lead the Israelites from their potential destruction to the "land of milk and honey" (from destruction to nurture). These examples relate to an emphasis on the "wish" side of the arsonist who is struggling with feelings symbolized by the lack of "milk and honey."

On the evil-shadow-destruction side, fire is more directly connected with punishment and destruction and ruled by Satan, who presides over the fires of Hell. Combinations of the above two sides can occur in such situations as burning witches to protect the community or burning Jews to destroy what was viewed as an evil force capable or harming the pure Aryans. All the above kinds of thinking can exist in the minds of the arsonists and must be reckoned with in order to treat them. Being saved or being destroyed share with birth purification and creations as recurring fantasies. Although many of the female firesetters are preoccupied with deprivation and revenge like "She," one needs also to be aware of purification and reproduction fantasies.

Two major examples of reproduction fantasies associated with fire occur in the Greek myths about Prometheus and the Phoenix. Bulfinch (1978) and Freud (1964) described the Greek myth where Prometheus and his brother Epimetheus were sent to Earth by Zeus to create people. Epimetheus took earth and water and somehow the breath of life was instilled and in this way men were created. Prometheus felt something essential was missing in them and in their lives—fire. He returned to the Gods and with the special aid of Apollo he went to the sun to bring back a burning brand. Zeus became enraged both at Apollo's gift of fire and the fact that his orders were not followed and planned to alter the process of creation. Zeus had a woman created, and the Gods endowed her with special attributes such as intelligence, beauty, musical ability, etc. Despite Prometheus' warning, when Pandora arrived Epimetheus found her irresistible and married her. Because of fire, creation was changed, and from Pandora's box came all kinds of problems. However, there was also hope. Perhaps this symbolizes the idea that immortality resides in creation, and a perpetual fire often symbolizes that concept in such places as religious shrines.

The other major myth about creation and fire is the Phoenix fantasy. This fantasy is worldwide. The Greeks stated that the Phoenix lived for five hundred years, built its own funeral pyre, and from the ashes came the new Phoenix. In this way, the Phoenix goes from destruction to creation. Included in this fantasy is the use of fire to deal with the above two great mysteries—life and death.

Freud pointed out that over the course of history the acquisition of fire has been viewed as theft and frequently led to punishment. Prometheus was punished for stealing fire by being tied to a rock and having his liver (which regenerated) eaten each day by a bird. The bird is not only part of this myth but reappears in the Phoenix myth. Freud said the liver was viewed as the place of intense feelings, and the bird was a symbol of a penis—saturation, depletion and renewal. These Freudian concepts again place these myths in the context of instinctual sexual fantasies. In the arson cases I have seen, the patients appear to be operating at a much more primitive oral, life, death, creation, destruction set of fantasies. I will illustrate these concepts in later case studies.

Family Interaction

Arson, like other violent acts, is often a reflection of shared family pathology. In child abuse, for example, either one or both parents can do the abusing with support or opposition of the other spouse. As with physical abuse, the underlying delusion in the aggressive act of arson is the concept that the victim or what is symbolized is evil and dangerous and has to be destroyed by fire. We also noted that many of the arsonists had suffered physical abuse and become abusers themselves.

A representative example of this kind of family pathology was described by Tucker and Cornwall (1977). They presented a case report of a mother who viewed her husband as the embodiment of evil and believed that the only solution was to destroy him by fire. She took her ten-year-old son from their home on the East Coast and moved him to the West Coast. There she indoctrinated him with her ideas about his father, trained him to become a firesetter, and put him on an airplane to visit his father. This ten-year-old boy did set a fire which burned down his father's house. The father almost died. The mother and son were institutionalized. With treatment the boy recovered from this imposed delusion and returned to the community.

Arson, battering, murder, and other interpersonal violence within a family can include any combination or permutation of alliance and victimization. Therapists have to be aware of this phenomenon. Treatment needs to include all the participants and an awareness of the various and often shifting roles they can play.

Male and Female Arson

Both boys and girls use fire as an expression of an outwardly directed act of aggression. There is evidence of different underlying fantasies in some cases.

John, an eleven-year-old boy, was ordered by the court to be interviewed by the court psychiatrist. He had set fire to and burned down several buildings including a school, a church and finally his home. His family could not manage their lives or control their impulses and were chronically economically deprived and were on welfare. His father was unemployed, alcoholic and abusive, and his mother was abusive and promiscuous. John, in addition to his arson, stole, truanted, and was a behavior problem at home and at school.

During the interview he freely talked about the fires along with his feelings of rage at his parents. In his drawings and in his dreams he visualized witches and devils pursuing him. He was preoccupied with wind, storms and hurricanes. He was afraid to be near water because he thought he would drown.

Themes of fire, wind, earth and water recur in the Bible, literature, art and astrology. However, for many of the arsonists these themes become entwined with dangerous destructive forces.

John illustrates a boy who dealt with the aggression and violence he feared and often experienced by identifying with the aggressor. During the course of his therapy it eventually became possible to help him see how threatened and frightened he felt and how much he hoped someone would notice. He also felt flooded by his rage which he had to externalize by setting fires or he would feel overwhelmed and consumed by these massive forces. This was all in the context of a lack of loving object constancy to give him any semblance of emotional security. Treatment needs to provide both containment and a restitutional experience to protect him from his parents and himself as well as protect the community.

Although there are many more male than female arsonists, there is a significant number of females who set fires. Lewis and Yarnell (1951) were amongst the earliest researchers to include females in their studies of firesetters. In my opinion, in their text they hesitated to view these girls as suffering from the degree of pathology they described. Instead, they identified these adolescent girls as primarily retarded. In my experience there are some cases of retardation, but these retarded cases were a minority. In addition, some of the retarded functioning appeared to be related to their traumatic life experiences and reflected the severity of their emotional disturbances.

For example, an adolescent girl, Margaret, was apprehended for shoplifting. While in the detention center she had an altercation with another adolescent girl. Margaret grabbed the other girl's sweater and set it on fire. Later when she was brought to court she became extremely aggressive and had to be restrained. She managed to break free long enough to obtain some matches and set herself on fire.

During her therapy sessions, she, too, revealed depriving and abusing parents. She was consumed with rage at those who abused and deprived her. She had fears and fantasies that she would burn in Hell. She said that if she could only become a witch she would feel less helpless and be able to get revenge on those who had hurt her.

Although Margaret directed her rage and the setting of fires out onto the environment, she also tried to burn herself. Turning the fire onto oneself appears to occur much more frequently in female than male arsonists. The self-directed fire can also be an acting out of parental destructive wishes against the child, who is seen as not nurturing them. This self-destructive pattern can also occur in various forms of juvenile suicide.

Sometimes the self-directed fire contains a cleansing, purifying or rebirth fantasy. The next case illustrates these concepts.

Elaine, an obese, promiscuous seventeen year old, was hospitalized because she had paranoid delusions that she was pursued by unknown enemies who were trying to harm her and ultimately destroy her. She came from a wealthy, highly educated Jewish family. They reacted to all her transgressions with lengthy lectures, complaints about her disgracing the family and predictions of her ultimate failure. No one considered that she was miserably unhappy and had unfulfilled needs. Sometimes the family wrath would become physical, but it primarily took the form of systematic degradation.

Elaine felt trapped, imprisoned, and fearful that her desires and impulses would lead to dangerous consequences. She sought comfort and relief in overeating and obtaining physical responses to her seductive behavior. The latter resulted in several abortions. When she developed psychotic delusions, she was placed in a psychiatric hospital. There she could no longer act out her ways of getting supplies. Deprived of these outlets, her conflicts intensified. She became increasingly frantic and one day went to her closet and burned all her clothes. She said she hated herself and wanted to get rid of her badness so she could start over again. When the clothing fire led to further restrictions by the hospital staff, she tried to set herself on fire.

Elaine illustrated her orality and neediness by trying to fill herself with food, sex and babies. Thus failing to relieve some of her emptiness and self-hatred, she tried to place the badness outside herself as dangerous forces trying to harm her. These became her paranoid delusions. Still struggling with herself about her devalued worthless image, she tried to cleanse and purify herself by first burning her clothes and then attempting to burn herself. Included were verbalized fantasies that she would return a better and more lovable person. For Elaine fire was one of the agents designed to achieve her goals.

Implications for Treatment and Prevention

This chapter has partially presented some of the core issues found in cases of arson. Treatment should include the individual and the family whenever possible. Recognition of both the deep longings for nurturance and the accompanying rage at being deprived and devalued makes for a very complex treatment problem. Because of the seriousness and danger of the symptom of arson, the individual and the community need to be protected. There is often an unexplainable denial of this danger. Sometimes it is only after a repeated series of fires with property damage, personal injury and possible loss of life that the arsonist is placed in a protected and therapeutic environment.

Basically, treatment has to deal with the core pathology. Before the arsonist can begin to face the overwhelming fears and anxieties that threaten to overwhelm him, he needs a sufficiently lengthy period of restitution, of caring, constancy, and limit setting to fill in the gaps in his development. Short-term containment and treatment fail to meet the needs of the arsonist, the family or the community. Prevention of arson is even more complicated.

There have been some serious attempts to try to identify and predict potential arsonists. I will briefly refer to three such endeavors. Jacobson (1985) in London studied and tried to list what he felt were specific antecedents to arson. Sackheim (1985) developed a predictor equation to try to define potential arsonists. Kolko and Kazdin (1986) attempted to outline a tentative model of firesetting risk. These fell within three major domains: (1) Learning experiences and cues; (2) Personal repertories; (3) Parental and family influences and stresses.

While the three above examples are ways to attempt to identify and predict potential arsonists are excellent beginnings, they have not been sufficiently pursued, nor do I believe they address enough of the core issues. This area also requires more careful research and could well be the topic of a future presentation.

Bibliography

Bender, Lauretta, ed.

1953 *Aggression Hostility and Anxiety in Children.* Springfield, IL: Thomas, pp. 116–137.

Bender, Lauretta

1959 "The Concept of Pseudopsychopathic Schizophrenia in Adolescents." *Amer. J. of Orthopsychiatry,* 29: 491–508.

Bradford, J.M.

1982 "Arson: A Clinical Study." *Can. J. Psychiatry,* 27: 188–193.

Bulfinch, Thomas

1978 *Bulfinch's Mythology.* New York: Avenal Books, pp. 12–19, 310–312.

Freud, Sigmund

1961 *Civilization and Its Discontents.* Standard Edition. Vol. 21. Toronto: The Hogarth Press, p. 90.

1964 *The Acquisition of Power over Fire.* Standard Edition. Vol. 22. Toronto: The Hogarth Press, pp. 185–193.

Geller, Jeffrey

1984 "Arson: An Unforeseen Sequela of Deinstitutionalization." *Amer. J. Psychiatry,* 141: 504–508.

Herjanic Henn, F.A., and R.H. Vanderpearl

1977 "Forensic Psychiatry: Female Firesetter." *Amer. J. Psychiatry,* 134: 556–558.

Jacobson, R.R.

1985 "Child Firesetters: A Clinical Investigation." *J. Child Psychology-Psychiatry,* 26: 759–768.

Kaufman, I.

1962 "Crimes of Violence and Delinquency in Schizophrenic Children." *J. Amer. Acad. Child Psychiatry,* 1: 269–283.

Kaufman, I., L. Heims, and D. Reiser

1961 "A Re-evaluation of the Psychodynamics of Firesetting." *Am. J. of Orthopsychiatry,* 31: 123–136.

1963 "Delineation of Two Diagnostic Groups Among Juvenile Delinquents: The Schizophrenic and the Impulse Ridden Character Disorders." *J. Amer. Academy Child Psychiatry,* 2: 292–318.

Kaufman, I., T. Frank, J.G. Friend, L. Heims, and R. Weiss

1963 "Adaptation of Treatment Techniques to a New Classification of Schizophrenic Children." *J. Amer. Acad. Child Psychiatry,* 2: 460–483.

Kolko, D.J., and A.E. Kazdin

1986 "Conceptualization of Firesetting in Children and Adolescents." *J. Abnorm. Child Psychology,* 14: 45–61.

Lewis, N.D.C., and H. Yarnell

1951 "Pathologic Firesetting (Pyromania)." N.Y. Nervous and Mental Disease Monographs (no. 82). *Female Firesetters,* 13: 346–375.

Michaels, J.J.

1953 *Disorders of Character.* Springfield, IL: Thomas.

Sakheim, G.A., et al.

1985 "Psychological Profile of Juvenile Firesetters in Residential Treatment." *Child Welfare,* 64: 453–476.

Tucker, L.S., and T.P. Cornwall

1977 "Mother-Son Folie a Deux: A Case of Attempted Patricide." *Am. J. of Psychiatry,* 134: 1146–1147.

Wooden, W.S.

1985 "The Flames of Youth." *Psychology Today,* 19: 22–28.

13

Patterns of Victimization and the Chronic Technological Disaster

Stephen R. Couch
Pennsylvania State University, Schuylkill

J. Stephen Kroll-Smith
Pennsylvania State University, Hazelton

In a recent lecture, Professor Rustum Roy, director of Penn State's Science, Technology and Society Program, asked students how they wished to die. Once resigned to the unpleasant assignment of having to make a choice, most responded that they wished a quick, painless death. Roy then pointed out how the government spends millions of dollars a year in research to reduce the risks of relatively quick and painless deaths (such as heart attacks), so that chronic diseases like cancer eventually take us!

Research on disasters and government disaster preparedness are somewhat analogous to this. Until recently, the study of disasters centered almost exclusively on immediate impact natural disasters (such as tornados and hurricanes). Lately, however, scholars and social service practitioners have begun to focus attention on long-term man-made disasters. Increasingly it is recognized that the slow seepage of toxic waste into groundwater or the long-term poisoning of the air by asbestos provokes structured responses and requires social agency intervention very different from those engendered by hurricanes and tornados.

Since 1981, we have been studying the effects of a long-burning underground coal mine fire on the small town of Centralia, Pennsylvania. Nobody died in Centralia because of the fire. No one knows for certain if residents have experienced any adverse health effects due to the blaze. But what is certain is that much suffering occurred. Victimization occurred in Centralia—physical problems, perhaps; social and emotional loss, absolutely. One would expect the disaster agent itself to be the main source of this loss. But our work in Centralia, as well as a close study of the literature on the Love Canal toxic waste disaster, indicated to us that a second order victimization occurred in which community and governmental response to the problem was itself the major stressor.[1]

This fact is best expressed in the words of victims. Let us consider what residents of Centralia, and of the poisoned community of Love Canal, New York, had to say.

> "Centralia is like someone you know who is slowly dying of cancer; I mean every time you turn around there is another part of the town that's infected. If we would just get together we could fight this cancer. But people around here are more concerned with themselves than with their neighbors. Rumors, hostileness, prejudice, backbiting . . . this town's more sick than the fire." (Centralia resident)

> "It was just that group over there. They got everybody so wound up, scared, that would be a good word, scared. . . . Then they really went ape, they were leaving like flies. . . . I think they left because they wanted the money." (Love Canal resident)[2]

> "My family lives every day with poisonous gases; I'm very scared, everybody is. . . . Some people in (the government) try to tell us it's okay here, it's safe. We know it's not safe here. . . . If it wasn't for God or dumb luck, I don't know which, we probably would fall in a hole like Todd did. . . . I don't trust the government anymore." (Centralia resident)

> "I can see their point as far as not trusting the government. . . . I think at one time people felt, well, if the government says something, it's God's law, where it's not that way anymore. . . . Well, as far as the government, they're going to give you what they want." (Love Canal resident)[3]

> "This fire has affected me terribly. Not because of fear of the fire itself, but (because of) the threat of the community being torn apart. . . . We're scared really of what's going to happen to us. It's a great, great emotional trauma on us." (Centralia resident)

> "Nobody was calm about anything. I came to find out everybody over there was nervous. You'd hear fights and stuff like that. It just wasn't a normal neighborhood. . . . You could feel tension in the air. There was a lot of hyper people, very hyper." (Love Canal resident)[4]

> "Centralia went from a community that was almost placid . . . to a community that's in constant turmoil. It's divided neighborhoods. It's created groups that work against each other. It's made me cynical in lots of ways. It's made me doubt the intentions of people. . . . I'm sick to death of it."(Centralia resident)

> "I think the only ones we really trusted was ourselves, because I felt we'd seen a lot of the true colors of people." (Love Canal resident)[5]

The suffering expressed in these passages is of a different kind than that which takes place following immediate impact natural disasters. Instead of having to deal with clear-cut and final destruction (e.g., physical loss of life or property, personal injury, and the like), the suffering expressed above was ongoing, chronic, as social as it was physical, less visible but just as real. Instead of the typical social response which follows most immediate impact natural disasters in which neighbor helps neighbor to cope and rebuild, the above passages indicate community conflict and upheaval, situations in which the basic communal infrastructures collapsed at a time when they were needed most. Indeed, in interview after interview, as well as in a more formal stress study, Centralians told us that the hardest thing for them, the source of their greatest anxiety, was not the fire itself, but the destruction of their social community—the loss of friends, the loss of neighbors, the loss of trust in others.

In a previously published paper, we argued that due to their distinct characteristics, chronic technological disasters (such as mine fires and toxic waste dumps) cause very different social consequences than do immediate impact natural disasters.[6] In this chapter, we consider how patterns of victimization differ depending on the type of disaster involved. Specifically, we seek to explain why, in chronic technological disasters, instead of providing a source of solace and aid, the social community breaks down, creating a milieu that for many people proves more threatening than the aversive agent itself. To do this, we will examine differences between immediate impact natural disasters (IINDs) and chronic technological disasters (CTDs) in six areas: the nature of loss; individual reactions; extra-local agency response; knowledge and information use; blame; and pre-disaster community structures.

Patterns of Victimization

The Nature of Loss

In an IIND, loss of life, health and property is clear. There is a high level of agreement over what was lost and what caused that loss. Visible physical evidence creates consensus over what damage was done and therefore over who should be labelled a victim. The boundaries of loss are well defined—a tornado strikes one block and not another; a swollen river floods one neighborhood and not another. There is little question as to what happened, the types and extent of loss, and who are "victims."

With a CTD, the situation is very different. What happened (or is happening), the types and extent of loss, and who are "victims" are ambiguous. The disaster agent is much less visible—in some cases, invisible (e.g., radiation, toxic gases or chemicals). Detecting it and understanding its qualities and dangers require a high degree of technological sophistication and often scientific knowledge beyond our present capabilities. Therefore, even experts disagree over the existence and/or extent of danger. While the loss caused by CTDs may be just as great as that due to IINDs, establishing a cause-effect relationship often is impossible, especially in individual cases (e.g., was a cancer developed in 1980 caused by radiation received in the 1950s? Are headaches due to toxic gases or something else?). Also, even when the existence of risk is established, its geographical boundaries are unclear.[7]

All of this creates a situation of uncertainty over who should be labelled and treated as a victim. Since physical evidence is unclear or lacking, and even experts disagree over causal linkages between the disaster agent and physical loss, each individual must decide who is and who is not a victim. This leads to nonconsensual conflict, as some attempt to convince others to accept their victim status, while others see those attempting to promote that label as not being in danger at all. Contradictory appraisals of the threat place the basic consensus of the community or neighborhood in question. One side believes the other side is underestimating the probability of loss or endangerment; likewise, those accused of underestimating the risks are themselves accusing others of exaggerating the threats. Each side is supported by an array of contradictory and confusing evidence, frequently coming from the same source. The intensity of emotions surrounding the conflict is based on an assessment of the stakes involved: the preservation of health and safety *versus* the preservation of the community and its way of life. Residents come to believe that success in one area can be achieved only at the expense of the other area. In fact, since the breakdown of community adversely affects those on both sides of this issue, *all* can be seen as victims.[8]

Individual Reactions

Shock, disbelief, numbness, relief for being alive, grief over loss, guilt—these are some of the reactions individuals typically experience after having lived through an IIND.[9] A hurricane or a tornado may well provoke psychological difficulties, but by and large, they are of relatively short duration and are in response to a past, not an ongoing, catastrophic event. In addition, the psychological responses of individuals to such disasters generally are accepted by others as being understandable, authentic and valid, generating empathy and desires to help. After the initial reaction wears off (or sometimes even during it), victims become involved with the jobs of cleaning up and rebuilding. This has been characterized as "situational coping," in which the problems at hand are dealt with directly in attempts to solve them.[10]

CTDs, however, evoke very different responses from affected individuals. Since they are long-term in duration and since no one knows for certain what the adverse health effects may be, CTDs produce chronic worry, anxiety and strain. The ongoing nature of CTDs leave people wondering if the worst is over or is yet to come. (Will I die in my sleep tonight because of gases from the mine fire? Will I develop cancer in ten years, thanks to toxic chemicals?) Individuals develop a pervasive feeling of uncertainty, of a lack of control over their own lives and over their own and their family's safety. As with IINDs, the disaster agent seems out of control, but unlike IIND situations, it is believed that people and technology *should* be able to control the disaster agent.[11] With IINDs, people tend to underestimate the risks they face. However, since the health effects of the CTD are ambiguous, individuals who possibly are in danger tend to develop a set of threat beliefs wherein they believe that the worst case scenarios are likely to come to pass.[12] Individuals in similar positions *vis-à-vis* the disaster agent share their fears with each other, reinforcing the notion that the worst case is, or will probably become, the typical case. A kind of "hysterical contagion" may develop wherein possibly exaggerated threat beliefs are passed among those living in the affected area.[13] These "victims" may then reach out to the rest of the community, expecting that their plight will be immediately understandable to all rational, caring people.

However, reactions of those who believe themselves to be unaffected by the disaster are not usually what the "victims" expect. To them, the claims of catastrophic danger made by the "victims" are seen as exaggerated. Indeed, those claiming victim status may be seen as threatening the security and way of life of the "non-victims"; for example, in the cases of Love Canal and Centralia, the "victims" succeeded in gaining a substantial relocation, something which was by no means favored unanimously. Those who do not see themselves as in danger due to the disaster develop their own set of threat beliefs in which the threat is to their way of life and the agent is the "victim" group. "Victims" are seen by some as out only for personal gain and by others as hysterical or crazy. This in turn encourages the "victims" to rely only on themselves and members of their small group, creating a "we *versus* them" situation which isolates the different segments of the community from each other. What develops are two very different, conflicting views of reality upon which action is based.[14] Add to this the high stakes involved, and uncompromising, nonconsensual conflict is likely to result.

For those attempting to attain victim status, then, chronic fear and anxiety produced by the disaster agent is exacerbated by rejection by and conflict with the rest of the community. For those who believe they are not in danger due to the disaster agent, there is the threat that, should the claims of the "victims" be believed and their wishes honored, the homes, neighborhoods and way of life of *all* in the community would be threatened. For individuals in both camps, there is a social victimization which takes place, one due to the loss of belief in the ability of their community to survive and in the benevolent intentions and trustworthiness of friends and neighbors.

Extra-Local Agency Response

IINDs strike quickly, do their damage, and are gone. Except, for example, in sandbagging the banks of a rising river, government and social service agencies are not expected to deal with the disaster agent itself. Agency response can be characterized as "victim-directed." While extra-local agencies cannot be expected to stop a hurricane, they *can* aid the victims, help clean up the mess, and assist in the rebuilding. Given the type of loss and beliefs governing appropriate response, structures exist by which to respond quickly to the emergency situation with food, blankets, housing, and medicine. In the longer run, victims often are aided with low-interest loans, counseling, and other services. Mechanisms exist whereby once a "disaster" is declared by the President, emergency federal aid of various types follows directly. While conflict often develops between the various political actors over power, jurisdiction, and so on, this conflict is after the disaster itself has subsided; initially, during the immediate post-disaster period, outside aid is welcomed. In addition, the conflict may be constructive from the perspective of reestablishing the structure of the community.[15]

In contrast to most IIND situations, extra-local (particularly governmental) agency response during a CTD tends to be "agent-directed."

Since the disaster agent is man-made and/or technological in nature, the government is expected to bring modern technology to bear on the disaster agent in order to stop or abate it. Questions of how to do this, instead of questions of human safety and concern, tend to dominate discussion.[16] In Centralia, for example, the federal Office of Surface Mining and the state's Department of Environmental Resources were the agencies designated to be in charge of the mine fire situation. Representatives of these agencies would attend public meetings and continually be called upon to answer questions of health and safety which went far beyond their technical expertise. When the officials would avoid answering such questions, many residents would fear that information was being withheld. At times, the work of technical officials was feared to be in direct opposition to what was best for community safety. Indeed, in both Centralia and Love Canal, abatement or reconstruction work on the disaster agent was itself seen by many as further endangering the health and safety of the residents.[17]

Reinforcing the government's difficulty in responding to victims of CTDs is the problem of defining victims. Studies by government and independent scientists are likely to produce incomplete or conflicting evidence concerning physical effects of the disaster agent. As shown, for example, in recent court decisions concerning Three Mile Island, psychological victimization has not yet been widely accepted as a basis for government action. Even in Love Canal, where a psychological health emergency was declared, its "victims" were not treated nearly as well financially by New York State as were those who were seen to be in physical danger.[18]

In addition, the governmental bureaucracy is not set up so as to deal efficiently with CTDs. Since there is confusion over whether or not a CTD should be seen as a "disaster" by the government, few communities victimized by a CTD are declared official disaster areas. This deprives them of access to the usual channels through which disaster aid is made available. Moreover, as with environmental policy in general, the bureaucracy which ends up dealing with CTDs is decentralized. This leads to problems concerning turf, responsibility and funding, causing delays which can adversely affect gaining control over the disaster agent as well as the safety of community residents. In Centralia, it is widely believed that on more than one occasion, governmental red tape prevented projects from being completed successfully which could have controlled the mine fire. The decentralized bureaucracy also encourages the release of contradictory or conflicting information by governmental agencies, angering residents and leading many to wonder who if anyone is in charge of the situation.

Finally, there are the private social service agencies. Because CTD victims are less clearly "victims" in the usual sense, the Red Cross and other disaster relief agencies usually do not become involved. Instead, environmental and social activist groups are likely to enter CTD communities. More sensitive to viewing those affected by CTDs as "victims," these groups generally align themselves with the fledgling grassroots "victims" group, using this as the nucleus by which to attempt to organize the rest of the community. However, these groups tend to underestimate the degree of community conflict inherent in the situation and mistakenly think that the "victim" group is representative of the community at large. Seen by many as "outside agitators," these groups may exacerbate community conflict rather than unite community factions.

In short, both governmental agencies and private social service groups are seldom sensitive to the roles they play in heightening community conflict and social breakdown. Private agency activity tends to increase intra-community hostility, while slow, ineffectual and contradictory actions by the government increase uncertainty, anxiety, and the belief that no one is in control.

Knowledge and Information Use

With IINDs, information use can be seen as attempting to predict the time, location and/or severity of a disaster, or to deal with its aftermath. It has been commonly accepted that techniques for predicting earthquakes or the exact locations of tornados or hurricanes are inexact. The information and knowledge that is collected is passed on to the public by the media so that rational precautions can be taken. After the disaster, what happened is clear, as is what is needed to clean up and rebuild. Information is concerned with health and safety measures, the aid that is available, and how to receive it. The role of the media is primarily that of transferring factual information from governmental and social service agencies to the victim population.

With CTDs, the role and use of knowledge and information is very different. As with IINDs, techniques for predicting the effects or advance of the disaster agent are inexact. But unlike IINDs, technical knowledge is expected to be used not only to predict but to *control* or *abate* CTDs. In addition, given that CTDs last a relatively long time, there is more time for scientific studies and therefore, from the point of view of the public, less of an excuse for science not to decide exactly what is happening and how dangerous it is.

But given the nature of CTDs and our limited scientific knowledge, information on CTDs can be expected to be conflicting. Consequently, so is information over who should be labelled as a victim. As discussed above, this can lead some to believe the worst possible scenario and others to believe that the dangers are being exaggerated. By and large, since human interest stories about victims make good press, the media tend to support and thereby reinforce the worst possible scenario perspective.[19] Therefore, the media become involved not only in transferring factual information but in helping to define the reality of an ongoing situation. In so doing, they become allies of those whose view of reality they embrace and enemies of those with whose view of reality they disagree. Through its use and transmittal of information, then, the press, too, becomes an agent in producing increased social division.

The government also is caught in a difficult situation concerning the acquisition and transmission of information. Agencies must make difficult decisions about gathering and acting on technical information concerning the disaster agent and its dangers, about how much information should be passed on to the public, and about how and when the information should be transmitted. Of course, agencies have their own political agendas and at times manipulate information to achieve their own ends.[20] Even when that is not so, representatives of technical agencies usually do not recognize the social consequences which may flow from information gathering and use. In some cases, the mere gathering of technical information can heighten public concern.[21] Other times, researching the problem is seen as stalling by a public anxious for action.

The transmission of information also is fraught with difficulties. As mentioned above, due to the decentralized nature of the governmental structures which deal with CTDs, conflicting, contradictory or premature information is apt to be released to the public from time to time. This serves to increase uncertainty, apprehension and distrust of the government's motives and/or abilities. In order to avoid this situation, some agencies may (and do) decide to withhold information from the public. However, if the public discovers that information is being withheld (as often happens), the credibility of the government plummets still further, as it is assumed that there is something major to hide.[22] Overall, in terms of the release of information, it appears that the government is damned if it does and damned if it doesn't.

The receipt of information by residents of a CTD community also may be a "no win" situation. Assuming that the information is contradictory and not definitive and assuming the development of different threat beliefs by factions within the community, information that is made available will be sorted and used to support preestablished positions, rather than to provide a factual basis for rational decision-making. The provision of such information, then, often heightens conflict. Yet if information is withheld, people are deprived of the possibility of making decisions which may very much affect the health and safety of themselves and their families.

Blame

IINDs are seen to be acts of nature or of God but not of humans. Nobody expects humans to stop a tornado or to turn a hurricane around. It is accepted that humans do not have control of such situations.[23] Therefore, humans are not to blame.

This is not so with CTDs. Here, humans are instrumental in causing the disaster, and/or are expected to be able to control or abate it.[24] Yet time and again, in CTDs, it is apparent that we are dealing with a myth of controlability. Scientific techniques for decontaminating groundwater poisoned by toxic wastes, or cleaning radioactive land or stopping the advance of an underground mine fire are inexact at best. But in this age of technological miracles, many have expectations of science which are unrealistically high. When science fails, someone must be to blame. The question is who.

Surely there are some situations in which blame can be established clearly; in which greed, corruption, negligence, or incompetence caused a CTD to occur or prevented it from being dealt with effectively. Usually, however, things are not so clear cut. There are arguments over who is to blame and over who should be held responsible for the present bad situation. Of course, each side musters ammunition from the files of conflicting information, and once again, individuals are forced to take sides based on information which is at best incomplete. But what is insidious about CTDs is that even if nobody is truly at fault, the question of blame is built into the structure of the situation. By expecting science to control a CTD, its inability to do so automatically implies that blame must lie somewhere. The question of blame, then, becomes yet another point at which people in CTD communities tend to fight, not only with representatives of outside agencies but also among themselves.

It is interesting to note that on this point, IINDs and CTDs may be becoming more similar over time. Scientific strides are being made if not in the control, at least in the *prediction*, of IINDs. Science's increasing ability, for example, to predict the weather is sold to us every day on radio and television. But perhaps this is being oversold, or perhaps many of us jump to incorrect conclusions. Once again, our expectations of science tend to outrun reality. We may come to expect scientists to warn us of impending disasters when they do not possess the ability to do so. If we do that, then there arises the question of blame. An incident of flooding near Pittsburgh provides an example. Victims were furious with weathermen for not warning them of the impending danger. Meteorologists responded that they had no way of knowing where the storms would hit; indeed, the storms were so localized that while rains were causing the deadly flooding, a Pittsburgh Pirates baseball game continued uninterrupted only five miles away.

Pre-disaster Community Structures

Tornados and hurricanes are not especially class biased. By and large, IINDs are as likely to strike middle- and upper-class areas as they are to hit lower- and working-class neighborhoods. Due to a variety of factors, including poor housing quality, lack of insurance and lack of savings, the poor suffer most and have the hardest time recovering from IINDs. But rich and poor alike can be struck. This results in a levelling in social class position immediately following an IIND, which helps form a basis for the formation of a therapeutic community. After a time, of course, this levelling passes. But in the critical period right after an IIND strikes social classes have common problems and seek common solutions to the devastation.[25]

In contrast, CTDs are very class biased. They are much more likely to strike communities composed largely of working- or lower-class inhabitants.[26] These communities lack the political and economic power to ward off CTDs. Falling toward the middle of the rural-urban continuum, they possess neither the finances nor the bureaucratic structures with which to fight CTDs. They also lack experienced indigenous leadership able to organize, unite and lead the community. Love Canal was primarily a working-class area without experienced political leaders (although fortunately containing Lois Gibbs, a housewife, who despite tremendous odds was able to organize much of Love Canal and accomplish a great deal). Centralia was composed of working- and lower-class families and was without a tradition of community decision-making. Dependent first on absentee coal companies and then on government aid, indigenous leadership never developed in the town.[27] Both Love Canal and Centralia are good examples of the unsettling fact that CTDs are most likely to occur in communities least able to resist their social damages. Coupled with the lack of post-disaster levelling and the difficulties in defining the situation discussed above, this means that social divisions already in place before the CTD are likely to be exacerbated rather than minimized.[28]

Discussion

This chapter began by illustrating the fact that CTDs produce a different kind of suffering than do IINDs. It is a social victimization brought about by the breakdown of the social community and an increase in debilitating community conflict. We proposed that this social victimization is due largely to the nature of the disaster agent in a CTD and attempted to outline some of the ways in which this is so.

While scholars increasingly are recognizing that CTDs affect communities in ways very different from IINDs, they have had virtually no success in translating those insights into practical suggestions for helping victim communities. Let us consider briefly three examples.

Schwartz, White, and Hughes[29] recognize the adverse effects a technological disaster can have on rational human beings and note the difficulty in knowing what the dangers are because of inconclusive scientific evidence. They make a good case for the similarity of social process and response between environmental threat situations (where the danger is real) and hysterical contagion (where it is not real). However, they then imply that policy in such cases should rest on an objective determination of the plausibility of the environmental threat. Unfortunately, they themselves showed this to be impossible because of a lack of conclusive scientific evidence.

Baum, Fleming, and Singer[30] point out that, on the basis of studies of Three Mile Island, those who employed "emotional" coping styles and who internalized blame adjusted better to the situation than those who attempted to deal directly with the problem through "situational" coping. Implied here is the suggestion that the former kind of coping style be encouraged in such situations. While this may aid individual adjustment, it ignores totally the root causes of the situation and the fact that a *social* problem is involved. Certainly, determining the extent of danger posed by TMI (or other CTD situations) and working to alleviate whatever problems exist can be frustrating; the situation is difficult to change. But ignoring it may prove disastrous in the long run.

Finally, after a detailed and provocative attempt to consider how different kinds of disasters affect communities differently, Kliman, Kern, and Kliman offer suggestions for constructive intervention into disaster-stricken communities. With psychological adjustment of victims as their aim, they state their goals as facilitating expressions of distress and allowing the translation of passive experience into active mastery.[31] To accomplish the first goal, they argue that "natural groups" (voluntary associations) within the community be used as forums. For the second goal, involvement in activist groups is urged. However, they themselves apparently recognize that there are problems when applying this strategy to CTDs. They wrote:

"Our frustrating and saddening experience in consulting with the United Way agencies at Love Canal was that the murkiness and pessimism of the situation resulted in divisions among victims. . . . Effective community organization was nearly impossible in an atmosphere of hopelessness and misplaced conflict."[32]

We are not so presumptuous as to think that we can at this point develop a formula for helping CTD-ravaged communities. But we do think that the key to creating effective helping strategies is found in recognizing the socially divisive nature of the disaster agent. CTD communities are communities in conflict, in which different definitions of the situation become hardened into rigid sets of threat beliefs and opposing perceived interests. In Centralia, there was plenty of opportunity for expression of distress, but the main forum was not voluntary associations (of which there were very few) but public meetings. These meetings became the stage for displays of hostility, aggression, and verbal and even physical conflict. Those who attempted to actively master the situation through participation in activist groups found themselves not only fighting a mine fire and the government but also their friends and neighbors, resulting in extreme anxiety and stress. As mentioned above, the greatest stressor in Centralia turned out not to be the fire but the breakdown in the social community.

If that is the case, then helping strategies should focus directly on healing the social divisions in a CTD community. This is no easy task, and to our knowledge it has never been achieved. But, at least in theory, it is possible. This is because, by and large, the differences in interests *vis-à-vis* a CTD are illusory; they are subjective, rather than real.

Residents of CTD communities tend to have common desires. They want the community to remain intact if possible. If not, they want help relocating to a safe area. This is simple enough. However, the problem is that scientific evidence is inconclusive concerning how dangerous the disaster agent is and to whom. This is the basis for intra-community disagreements. And it must be recognized that this problem cannot be solved in its entirety. Yet we can offer some implications of our work for policy makers and implementers who wish to avert or minimize the effects of community social breakdown in CTD situations.

1. In a CTD, different sectors and subsystems of the community will experience very divergent levels of stress and social disruption. The more pronounced the differential impact of the disaster agent on the community, the more difficulty

residents will experience in agreeing upon a common definition of the problem, its extent and severity, and a collective course of action.

2. The first indigenous group to emerge in a CTD situation will most likely base its agenda on worst case interpretations of the problem. This creates problems for social agency personnel who might normally use this organization as a host group to gain access to the community. Given the divisive nature of a group so organized, unless the group is reoriented around a less severe interpretation of the crisis (a task that may not be possible), it would be wasted time attempting to use it as a host group.
3. Other groups will emerge in opposition to this first group. A "we" *versus* "them" dynamic will ensue, fostering a conflict that puts the basic consensus of the town in question. The severe social disorganization caused by the CTD is dysfunctional not only for the community but also for government and social service agencies responsible for responding to the crisis. The task of policy in this situation is to implement strategies for mitigating this conflict, for reversing this hostile dynamic.
4. Just as outside intervention is necessary to abate an aversive agent, it is also necessary to assist a town in resolving its social conflict. However, conventional models of social service response to communities in crisis are not likely to succeed in CTD situations. The community organizer(s) who undertakes this task must not make the mistake of identifying with one of the groups in town. Neutrality is the key. Strategies for remaining neutral while gaining *entrée* into the community would be very difficult, if not impossible, for community organizers associated with private social service agencies. It is likely that personnel from such government agencies as the Department of Community Affairs would have the best chance of being perceived as neutral by the competing factions. Or perhaps the creation of a community advocate at the state level (as some

have created consumer advocates) would be a possibility. The advocate would attempt to heal the divisions within the community by encouraging residents to work toward common interests; would act as liaison with government agencies and other involved parties; would actively seek all relevant information concerning the disaster agent and would acquire independent expert interpretations of this information; would avoid alignment with any group or faction within the community; and would look for and train indigenous leaders who may emerge and around whom the community can unite. Overall, the community advocate could be seen as a healer and a facilitator; as one who channels the community's energies into uniting around common interests and encourages the translation of those interests into action.

5. At the small group level, an effort should be made to create a committee whose membership consists of representatives of the opposing groups and others in town who have remained at the periphery of the conflict. This group should seek to become a model for community cooperation rather than another model of the conflict.
6. At the communal level, activities should be planned that permit everyone in town to participate, regardless of their beliefs about the dangers. Participation should take place in an atmosphere which fosters the sharing of ideas in working toward a common goal and in which hostility and personal recrimination are quelled if they arise.
7. At the extra-local governmental level, legislation should be drawn which clearly demarcates which agencies will have jurisdictional responsibility for CTDs and what the social policy should be which governs their work. The agencies involved should include people-oriented, not just technical, agencies. The policy should recognize the debilitating social and psychological effects of CTDs on communities and their members and be geared toward alleviating those effects swiftly and

efficiently. In addition, notwithstanding the problems associated with misinterpretation of information, mechanisms should be developed which allow the timely release to the public of all information concerning CTD situations. Moreover, communities should be given the resources to hire independent scientists to interpret the information which is collected and released. At the same time, increased attention should be paid to preventing the development of CTD situations in the first place. So long as our relationship with the environment is primarily one of exploitation, the number and seriousness of CTDs is bound to increase. The development of policies which prevent CTDs is surely better than having to heal the hurts once the damage has been done. At the same time, it is the hardest type of policy to implement, as it runs to the heart of our political and economic system.

8. In responding to CTDs which have occurred, it is essential to keep in mind that all factions feel victimized. The social hatred that emerges restructures the community, as each side sees the other as threatening their unity and goals. Ironically, before this process has proceeded very far, the town's residents have lost whatever bases they had for communal life, thus insuring the continuation of the conflict. With CTDs, the loss of community functions to feed on itself, increasing and intensifying the consequences of the loss. The primary goal of the community organizer should be the reestablishment of community, or, if need be, the creation of a new one.

References

1. See J. Stephen Kroll-Smith and Stephen R. Couch, *The Real Disaster Is Above Ground: A Mine Fire and Social Conflict.* Lexington, KY: University Press of Kentucky, 1989; Adeline G. Levine *Love Canal: Science, Politics and People,* Lexington, MA: Lexington Books, 1982; Martha R. Fowlkes and Patricia Y. Miller, "Love Canal: The Social Construction of Disaster." Final report

for Federal Emergency Management Agency, RR-1, 1982; and Lois Gibbs *Love Canal: My Story,* Albany: State University of New York Press, 1982.

2. Fowlkes and Miller, op. cit., 66.
3. Ibid., 88.
4. Ibid., 80.
5. Ibid., 77.
6. Stephen R. Couch and J. Stephen Kroll-Smith, "The Chronic Technical Disaster: Toward a Social Scientific Perspective," *Social Science Quarterly* 66, 1985, 564–575.
7. Fowlkes and Miller, op. cit., 14–15.
8. Jodie Kliman, Rochelle Kern, and Ann Kliman, "Natural and Human-Made Disasters: Some Therapeutic and Epidemiological Implications for Crisis Intervention." In V. Rueveni, R.V. Speck, and J.L. Speck, eds. *Therapeutic Intervention.* New York: Human Science Press, 1982, pp. 273–274.
9. Ibid., 254–258.
10. Andrew Baum, Raymond Fleming, and Jerome E. Singer, "Coping with Victimization by Technological Disaster," *Journal of Social Issues* 39, 1983, p. 123.
11. Ibid., 120–122; R.J. Lifton and Eric Olson, "Death Imprint in Buffalo Creek." In H. Parad, H. Resnik, and L. Parad, eds. *Emergency and Disaster Management: A Mental Health Sourcebook,* Bowie, MD: Charles Press, 1976.
12. Kroll-Smith and Couch, op. cit.; see also J. Stephen Kroll-Smith and Stephen R. Couch, "The Chronic Technical Disaster, Small Town Conflict and the Social Construction of Threat Beliefs." In Edward J. Miller and Robert P. Wolensky, eds. *The Small City and Regional Community.* Stevens Point, WI: Foundation Press, 1987, pp. 262–269.
13. Steven P. Schwartz, Paul E. White, and Robert G. Hughes, "Environmental Threats, Communities, and Hysteria," *Journal of Public Health Policy* 6, 1985, 63–68.
14. Robert P. Gephart, Jr., "Making Sense of Organizationally Based Environmental Disasters." *Journal of Management* 10, 1984, 205–225.
15. Kliman, Kern, and Kliman, op. cit., 260–261.
16. J. Stephen Kroll-Smith and Stephen R. Couch, "A Chronic Technical Disaster and the Irrelevance of Religious Meaning: The Case of Centralia, PA," *Journal for the Scientific Study of Religion* 26, 1987, 25–37.
17. Fowlkes and Miller, op. cit., 13.
18. Ibid., 20.
19. Ibid., 7–8; Schwartz, White, and Hughes, op. cit., 69–70.

20. Gephart, op. cit.; Kliman, Kern, and Kliman, op. cit., 264–265.
21. Fowlkes and Miller, op. cit., 7–8.
22. Schwartz, White, and Hughes, op. cit., 70.
23. Baum, Fleming, and Singer, op. cit., 120–122; Lifton and Olson, op. cit.
24. Andrew Baum, Raymond Fleming and Laura M. Davidson, "Natural Disaster and Technological Catastrophe," *Environment and Behavior* 15, 1983, 351–352.
25. Kliman, Kern, and Kliman, op. cit., 274–275.
26. Couch and Kroll-Smith, op. cit.
27. Kroll-Smith and Couch, 1989, op. cit.; Barbara Knox Homrighaus, Stephen R. Couch and J. Stephen Kroll-Smith, "Building a Town but Preventing a Community: A Social History of Centralia, PA." In Lance E. Metz, ed. *Proceedings of the Canal History and Technology Symposium*, vol. 4. Easton, PA: Center for Canal History and Technology, pp. 69-91.
28. Fowlkes and Miller, op. cit., 23–24; Kliman, Kern, and Kliman, op. cit., 267.
29. Schwartz, White, and Hughes, op. cit.
30. Baum, Fleming, and Singer, op. cit.
31. Kliman, Kern, and Kliman, op. cit., 277–278.
32. Ibid., 267.

14

Monitoring the Quality of Life of Disaster Victims: A Prototype System

Knowlton W. Johnson, Ph.D.

Gerald Hutchins, Ph.D.

Jim Phifer
Urban Studies Center
University of Louisville

Victims who have been touched by natural or man-made disasters have been the subject of considerable study in recent years, but there is still little evidence that this research has been beneficial to disaster victims. As a result, this chapter proposes a prototype disaster impact monitoring system (DIMS) that would generate information on a continuous basis which can be used by emergency managers to mitigate the short-term and long-term effects of disasters.

The conceptual discussion of the DIMS focuses on victims' quality of life as it might be affected by disaster stressors and environmental factors. In addition, implementation aspects of the model, including data collection, storage, and retrieval are discussed, with attention given to the results of a national survey of federal and state emergency agencies.

Analysis and reporting features of the model are also discussed. The highlight of the chapter is the concluding discussion of a paradigm which presents the prototype DIMS in its entirety.

This research was supported in part by Grant No. MH40411 from the National Institute of Mental Health.

In recent years publication and dissemination of information about the "well being" of victims of natural disasters and man made hazards have increased significantly. Studies have been presented on the immediate and long-term psychological effects of disasters (Adams and Adams, 1984; Green, 1982; Norris, 1986); long-term health effects (Logue et al., 1981); and the economic impact of disasters (Hall and Landreth, 1975). Further, there are federal- and state-supported information diffusion centers (e.g., the Natural Hazards Research and Applications Information Center at the University of Colorado and the Central United States Earthquake Consortium Information Center at Murray State University), which promulgate information intended to assist citizens in responding to and recovering from natural and man-made hazards.

Unfortunately, there is no evidence available to indicate that this "knowledge expansion" has a major impact on decisions about policy or programming to restore and/or maintain disaster victims' quality of life. In fact, federal agency support is being cut back due to reduced funding of victim relief programs sponsored by the National Institute of Mental Health through its Center of Emergency Mental Health Studies. Additionally, the Federal Emergency Management Agency (FEMA) has proposed federal declaration guidelines that will reduce the proportion of federal aid for this purpose to states in the future.

While technical information like research studies, victim service descriptions, and training manuals is informative and potentially useful at the local level, we need to know what type of disaster information might make a "significant difference" in federal and state level decisions to provide assistance to disaster victims in both the short and long run. This question is central to the purpose of this chapter, which is to present a prototype of a system for collecting, storing and diffusing statistical information to a variety of audiences on an ongoing basis. The assumption is that "continuous information" about disaster activity within a state will be more useful to government officials than "one-time information" vis-à-vis study results, manuals, etc. In other fields, like criminal justice, monitoring systems have been developed and implemented to provide statistical data on a routine basis (Johnson, 1983). To date, however, there is no information system in place in the United States to monitor either the immediate or the long-term effects of disasters.

How can a disaster-impact monitoring system help restore and/or maintain the quality of life of victims after a traumatic event has occurred? Foremost, producing data and documentation on the immediate effects, and potential long-term consequences, of a disaster is paramount for states when making application for a federal declaration, as well as in applying for other types of assistance, e.g., assistance from the Department of Agriculture. In addition, clear and significant facts should be produced about the response to and recovery from disasters if this need is to compete successfully with other needs within the state. Finally, an ongoing system to monitor the impact of disaster victims needs the assistance of a multitude of local and state agencies and it possibly may require a local volunteer network to supply the data for the system. A positive side effect of maintaining the database could be increased interagency cooperation in responding to those recovering from disasters.

With these potential benefits of a disaster-impact monitoring system (DIMS) in mind, we present a discussion of the planning and preliminary work of a project being considered for the state of Kentucky. The report being presented has been prepared with the assistance of personnel from the Division of Disaster and Emergency Services of Kentucky. The idea of a prototype disaster impact monitoring system stemmed from a much smaller systems development project for Kentucky, which is currently being funded by the Center of Emergency Mental Health Studies. We plan to seek additional funding to develop and implement the prototype system presented today.

First, we present the results of a survey of disaster data management practices in the United States. These findings provided planning information on the activities of other states in collecting, analyzing and storing disaster and quality of life indicator data. Second, a prototype disaster-monitoring system is described which discusses the stages and components of each stage. Finally, in the conclusion we discuss ways to enhance the development and implementation of the DIMS.

Disaster Data Management Practices in the U.S.A.

One source of valuable information in the development of our impact monitoring system has been a survey of the data management practices in other areas of the United States. The sample for this survey consisted of the ten regional offices of the Federal Emergency Management Agency (FEMA) and the agencies responsible for disaster/emergency impact assessment within fifteen states (California, Colorado, Connecticut, Florida, Georgia, Illinois, Kentucky, Maryland, Massachusetts, Mississippi, New York, Pennsylvania, South Dakota, Texas, and Washington), which varied in terms of population, geographic location, disaster frequency, and disaster type. These fifteen states were recommended by the various FEMA regional offices because they are more progressive than others in regard to collection and use of disaster data.

The data were obtained through telephone interviews with the individuals responsible for coordinating the disaster damage assessment procedures at the state or regional level. At the regional level, the survey addressed data collection procedures (i.e., measures obtained, definition of criteria, forms used), personnel composition and training; data storage and analysis methods, and whether there were qualitative differences in data management practices among states within the region. At the state level, the survey elicited information on collection procedures, personnel composition and training, data storage and analysis, and data utilization and dissemination. At both the state and regional levels, the respondents were asked if they were aware of any existing system which monitored the impact of disasters on social indicators.

One objective of the survey was to assess the type of data collected at the state and regional levels. In general, the primary concern of the state disaster assessment teams was to determine whether the disaster impact exceeded the state's response capability and, accordingly, whether federal assistance should be requested. Consequently, the initial survey at the state level evaluated the number of casualties (dead, injured, evacuated, or sheltered) and damage to dwellings, businesses, hospitals, agriculture, dams and levees, public buildings, roads and bridges. In some states an estimate was made of more indirect effects such as interference with employment, commerce, or access to health care. If the state evaluators determined that the disaster was of sufficient magnitude to warrant federal assistance, then FEMA was requested to conduct a survey, either individually or in conjunction with local and state personnel. The FEMA surveys are the primary source of data for consideration for a presidential disaster declaration. Only in the event of a major disaster might any additional information be collected by the state regarding more long-term impacts such as social, economic, health and environmental consequences.

Following the occurrence of an event such as a hurricane, tornado, flood, earthquake, volcanic eruption, snowstorm, fire, or explosion state disaster management officials initiate damage assessment procedures in order to determine whether the event exceeds the state's response capabilities and to provide information on the event to the governor of the state. In most states, the inspectors conducting the assessment are experts from various state agencies (e.g., Highway

Department, State Engineers Office, Department of Natural Resources, Housing Department) who then report to disaster management officials. These inspectors are usually experts in a given area and receive only brief training regarding the forms and evaluation criteria used by the state. In a small number of states, the evaluations are conducted by disaster management personnel who are trained to do all types of damage assessment. Other data are obtained from the American Red Cross, Small Business Administration, state police, local government officials, local business and commerce associations, the Census Bureau and the state's department of social services. Those states with a high frequency of disasters may have a permanent staff of inspectors, whereas those states with a low disaster frequency may train new personnel only upon the occurrence of a disaster.

Another purpose of the survey was to determine how disaster impact data were stored and analyzed. In most states, the data are stored on microcomputers using word processing or spreadsheet software. In the remaining states, the data are stored on paper. Generally, very little data analysis is conducted. Since the main purpose of collecting data at the state level is to provide the information to the governor which is necessary for a request for federal assistance, only summary measures are calculated.

With regard to the dissemination and utilization of the data, the destination of this information largely depends on whether or not a federal disaster declaration is obtained. If federal assistance is not sought or obtained, this information is presented to the governor; to federal agencies such as the Small Business Administration and the Department of Agriculture; to various state agencies responsible for rectifying damage, such as the temporary housing program, State Engineers Office, State Department of Natural Resources, State Highway Department, etc., and to other private organizations like the American Red Cross. If a federal declaration is requested, the data are made available to the President and to FEMA. If a declaration is obtained, then the data are made available to various federal agencies, depending on the nature of the damage. These agencies include the Corps of Engineers, Federal Highway Administration, Bureau of Reclamation, Soil Conservation Service, and the Environmental Protection Agency.

A final objective of the survey was to determine whether a disaster impact monitoring system was in use anywhere in the United States. A survey of the federal and regional offices of FEMA, fifteen state disaster management offices, the Emergency Management Institute, and relevant scientific journals indicated that such a system was not currently in use. Although there have been numerous post hoc studies of the socioeconomic impact of major disasters such as hurricanes and earthquakes, there does not appear to be a system in operation which monitors impact on an ongoing basis.

A Prototype DIMS for Kentucky

The disaster-impact monitoring system (DIMS) presented in this chapter is being proposed for the Division of Disaster and Emergency Services of Kentucky as a prototype model. Our discussion of the national survey results has served as a guide for the model design. Among other things, this survey raises the issue regarding the definition of a disaster. According to Quarantelli (1985), various definitions have been posed in recent years. For purposes of our discussion, we view a disaster as a physical agent whose impact is substantial enough to result in disruption of social life, and the demand for action exceeds the governmental response capabilities. This definition was selected because it takes into consideration the physical, economic and social elements of an actual event, and it highlights the imbalance between demand for services and the governmental response capability. That is, in order for an event to be classified as a disaster, it must have created a discernible physical and social impact and there must be evidence that the demand for services in response to the impact is greater than the government ability to respond. As will be shown later, demand and capability elements of the definition expand the data requirements of a monitoring system, thereby providing additional information on the impact of an event.

Overview of the DIMS Model

Figure 14.1 presents an overview of the DIMS Model. The model is designed as a four-stage process that characterizes the logical sequence of the developmental activities: database specification, data collection, data storage and retrieval, and data analysis and reporting.

A number of characteristics of the data specification stage need to be highlighted. Foremost, we wanted the data requirements to be couched in a conceptual framework with cause-effect attributes (Land, 1975). In addition, the data should be quantifiable, organized in a time series, and aggregated and disaggregated according to some relevant variable in a social system (Land, 1971; Kisiel, 1974). Further, while subjective measures have a number of advantages, we based the DIMS on objective indicators because objective measures are viewed as more policy relevant, less intrusive upon victims' privacy and more practical for a statewide system (Stevens, 1984; Wright, 1985). In selecting the

Figure 14.1
DIMS Prototype Model

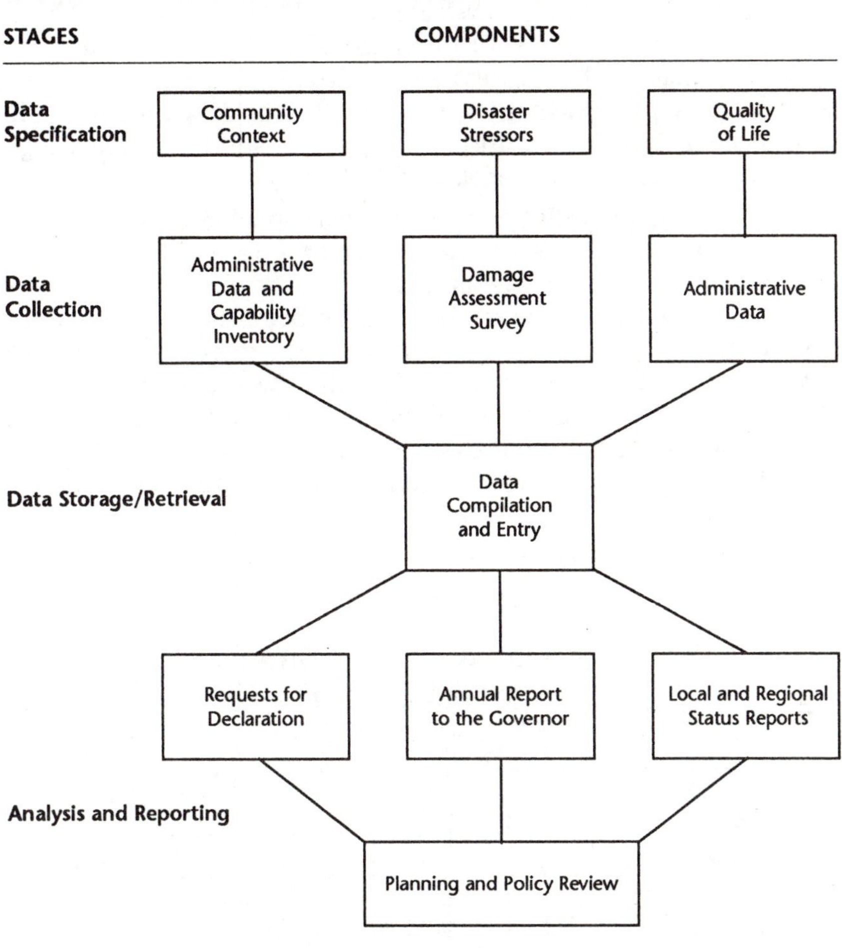

specific objective measures, we also took into consideration sensitivity of the measure (Headey et al., 1984) and the extent to which the data were available for the 120 Kentucky counties (Urban Studies Center, 1981). The final characteristic of our system concerned its inclusion of multiple measures for particular indicators, as has been recommended by Sullivan and Feldman (1979).

The data collection for the system is characterized by a strategy which optimizes the collection of accurate data without overtaxing personnel of the state's disaster and emergency services. The data storage and retrieval development would also allow flexibility and provide the capacity to access information in a timely manner for multiple users.

Analysis and reporting requirements for the system would emphasize compatibility of data with the needs of multiple users. Havelock (1969) and Glaser (1983) discuss the importance of this characteristic. Johnson (1980) found that the compatibility of data with multiple users' needs influenced the use of program evaluation results in a large network of criminal justice agencies in Maryland.

The information collected and analyzed should also relate directly to the specific needs, such as fulfilling reporting requirements, and bookkeeping and accounting functions of the host agency (Wilcox et al., 1976). Additionally, the results should provide direction to service delivery changes (Johnson, 1985). Finally, the results should point to general trends and should isolate differential effects of events. Headey et al. (1984) discuss an analytical procedure that establishes cause-effect relationships using panel data, and Joreskog and Sorbom (1984) have developed LISREL VI, a computerized statistical package for conducting such an analysis.

Figure 14.2

A Conceptual Framework for a Disaster-Impact Monitoring System

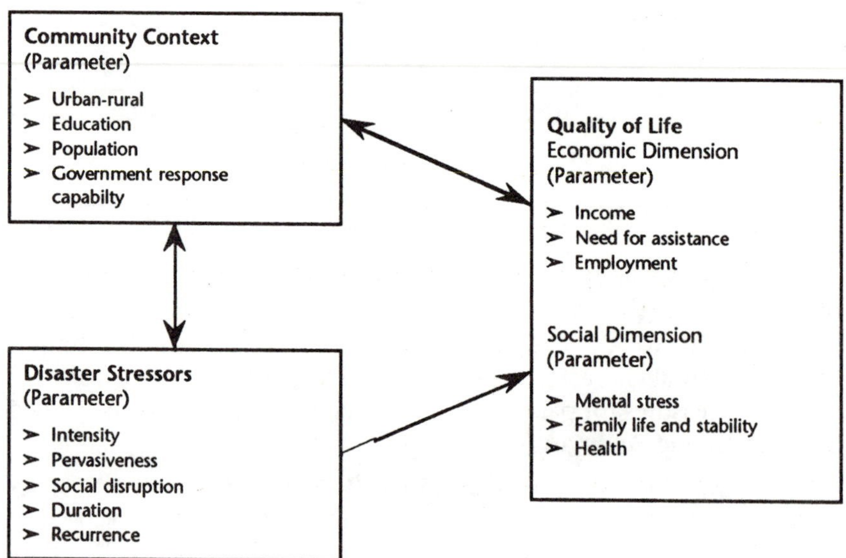

The specifics of each of the stages of the DIMS and their components are presented below.

Database Specification Stage

The database consists of three components: (1) community context, (2) disaster stressors, and (3) quality of life indicators. Each component is parameterized along a number of dimensions, each of which is measured by multiple indicators. Figure 14.2 below presents the database components, and their parameters. A discussion of these parameters and illustrations measures for specific indicators follows.

The design of the prototype model was based on relationships assumed to exist among the components of the database. Once the monitoring system is implemented, we can test these relationships empirically. Until then, it will be useful to examine our assumptions and describe the model on a conceptual basis. The first assumption implicit in our work is that, in the absence of a hazardous event, the quality of life which exists in one time period is drawn from the quality of life and the community context of previous time periods. The second assumption is that when a hazardous event occurs in one time period, it continues to affect the quality of life in subsequent periods. The third assumption is that governmental action relative to the event can change the way it affects the quality of life. The details of each database component are discussed in separate sections.

Community Context

The lack of social theory leaves the analyst without a guide to separate the important from the unimportant in describing communities. Hazardous events happen within a community context which affect the impact the event has on life within the community. The community context is categorized by four parameters of the DIMS model: (1) urban-rural, (2) education, (3) population, and (4) governmental response capability. The selection of these parameters was based on an evaluation of how likely they were to affect the impact of the event on the quality of life. The extent of their impact and illustrative measures are described below.

The urban-rural parameter describes the extent to which the community is set in an urban or a rural context. The concentration of population in urban settings naturally increases the number of people that an event of a given type and size is likely to affect. Population density and licensed vehicles per square mile are examples of indicators which measure this parameter.

Education describes the community context regarding the amount of knowledge embodied in its residents and the value placed on learning. The ability to plan for, deal with, and/or avoid hazardous events may be related to education. The high school dropout rate, the percentage of persons with a high school education, and the number of high school graduates entering college are illustrative indicators of education.

The population parameter identifies the kinds of special groups within the community who may be particularly vulnerable to a disaster. For example, persons over age sixty-five may have more difficulty dealing with the physical effects of a hazardous event. This parameter encompasses population change (new residents lack support networks) and the occupational distribution of employment (exposure to hazardous environments).

The governmental response capability reflects the ability of community resources to deal directly with the hazards constituting the event. It also reflects the level of services available within the community and plays a role in the declaration of the event as a disaster. Illustrative indicators include net property value and tax revenue per capita.

Disaster Stressors

Quarantelli (1985) challenges disaster researchers to be more rigorous in defining and characterizing disasters. Indeed, the basic concepts for studying disasters have not been adequately developed. The case study approach frequently used to study disasters emphasizes the unique aspects of the event. As a result, there has been little integration, and the parameters of the event are underdeveloped. Five parameters relating to hazardous events characterize the data specification for our system: (1) intensity, (2) pervasiveness, (3) social disruption, (4) duration, and (5) recurrence. This list is not exhaustive but it covers a broad portion of the key data. Nearly all of the characteristics discussed by Quarantelli can fit into these dimensions, although Quarantelli's perspective on them may differ somewhat. These five parameters are discussed below.

The intensity of the event refers to the degree of destruction. Some indicators of this parameter would include homes damaged or destroyed and bridges destroyed. Presently, data for these indicators are collected as part of the preliminary damage assessment.

The pervasiveness of the event refers to the degree that the event is widespread. This parameter addresses the extent to which the whole community is affected and the extent to which the event affects multiple communities. As damage from an event becomes more widespread, the perception of personal loss takes on relative properties which may alter psychological effects. Illustrative indicators include the percentage of the population affected, total damage relative to property value, and the number of other communities affected. These measures, combined with the intensity parameter, indicate the magnitude of the event.

Social disruption refers to the extent that the event alters normal living patterns and disturbs social networks. The indicators are an ad hoc list of items similar to those which Quarantelli (1985) discussed as social centrality. They include the impediment to critical public services, the effect on nonprofit institutions, the number of deaths relative to the size of the community, and the geographic centrality of the event.

The duration of the event measures the length of time the emergency persists. Relying on administrative data makes the operationalization of this measure more difficult than may be apparent. The crisis may end long before the threat is removed.

The actual or potential recurrence of a hazardous event changes its effect on the community. Where the potential for recurrence is strong, additional emotional strain may result. Yet actual recurrence may lead to acceptance of the threat, particularly if little or no direct involvement or results. Example indicators include prior occurrence, repeated threat, and hazard mitigation activity.

Quality of Life

The clear distinction in the literature between economic and social aspects of the quality of life is maintained within DIMS. The indicators of the economic parameters attempt to measure the stock of financial resources within the community and the relative size of subpopulations which have limited access to those resources. The assumption made is that money is the predominant feature upon which United States culture is based. Cultural values do not translate directly into financial cost, but wealth expands the range of values in which one can participate. The economic indicators are parameterized as (1) income, (2) need for assistance, and (3) employment. Some of the ways disasters affect indicators of these parameters are discussed below.

Income indicators are related to the level of financial resources available to the general population within the community. These resources generally control the extent to which people share in the valued goods of the community. Higher income results in greater options for the individual to select things of value and to participate in whatever the community/society defines as "the good life." Relative income measures reflect status within the community. In addition, hazardous events usually create unexpected costs for people and income measures reflect the capability (or lack of it) to absorb these costs.

The need for assistance, as a parameter of the economic dimension of the quality of life, measures the size of subpopulations who have limited access to values within the community. The relative size of these subpopulations describes not only the relative magnitude of the group but also identifies disparities in the distribution of income. These disparities indicate the limited extent to which the community has achieved a balanced distribution of income—one of the presumed ideals of our culture. Illustrative indicators would include Medicaid eligibility and AFDC recipients.

The employment parameter measures the primary means of receiving income. Unemployment is one indicator of this parameter. Keeping in mind that this indicator is based on the number of people who are looking for work, unemployment viewed can be as a measure of dissatisfaction with access to societal values. The greater the unemployment, the lower the economic aspects of the quality of life.

The social aspects of the quality of life are parameterized as (1) mental stress, (2) family structure and stability, and (3) general health. These parameters attempt to measure participation in or separation from "the good life."

Freedom from mental stress is an ideal within our culture. At the individual level, this parameter may be described as ranging from experiencing no mental stress to having a mental breakdown. Objective measures commonly available approach this concept from the mental stress or breakdown end of this dimension. Illustrative indicators include admissions of residents to psychiatric facilities and incidence of highway accidents. Such indicators are estimates of the number of people suffering a breakdown or disruption of normal mental functioning. Another group of indicators (suicides, rapes, murders, and assaults) indicate not only major mental stress but also high stress among the victims of such actions. The rate of incidence of victimization by theft is a further indicator of level of mental stress.

Strong cultural traditions make family life and stability a parameter of the social aspect of the quality of life. During the past generation, this tradition has been strongly challenged by the emphasis upon individual, personal fulfillment. This emphasis has been accompanied statistically by increasing numbers of single-parent families, increasing primary individual households (persons living alone), and fewer people per household (Koebel, 1982, 1985). However, the family is still the predominant type of household, and research indicates that persons living alone and persons in single-parent families are less satisfied with life (Schulte, Brockway, and Murrell, 1978; Schulte and Murrell, 1980). Example indicators of family life and stability include marriage dissolutions, single-parent families, as well as the percent of family-type households. The fewer the marriage dissolutions, the fewer the single-parent families, and the greater the family-type households, the higher the indicator for a community's quality of life.

Health is one of the more frequently used parameters for the quality of life. Illness is equated with low quality of life and wellness with "the good life." Illustrative indicators are the number of hospital admissions by county of residence, number of work-related injuries, and overall mortality rate (Urban Studies Center, 1981). Hazardous events can have both direct and indirect effects on these indicators. The direct effects are fairly obvious although not necessarily guaranteed. The indirect effects operate through various reductions in available social resources and increased levels of stress.

Data Collection Stage

The DIMS utilizes three types of data: (1) state administrative data, (2) the damage assessment survey data, and (3) the government capability inventory data. These data components are discussed below with reference to the source of the data, the method of collection and the personnel requirements.

The administrative data used in the DIMS would be obtained from published reports which are in the public domain. Economic indicators may be obtained from reports of various state agencies. For instance, per capita income is available in the Housing Reports for Kentucky, published by the Urban Research Institute. The number of persons eligible for Medicaid is published by the Bureau for Social Insurance of the Kentucky Department for Human Resources. Unemployment rates are supplied by the Bureau for Manpower Services of the Kentucky Department for Human Resources. Other economic indicators (e.g., cost of living, public assistance eligibles, AFDC eligibles, food stamp eligibles) are similarly available in published reports. State and county level data on social indicators are also available in published reports. For example, the numbers of hospital and psychiatric admissions are available from the Health Data Branch of the Bureau for Health Services, Kentucky Department for Human Resources. The number of single-parent families is published in the Housing Reports for Kentucky. Other social indicators (e.g., suicide rate, arrest statistics, crime statistics) are also published in the public domain.

The disaster damage data is collected through a damage assessment survey conducted by the Kentucky Disaster and Emergency Services. This survey, implemented immediately after a disaster, assesses human casualties as well as damage to dwellings, businesses, medical services, agriculture, dams and levees, public buildings, and roads and bridges. This survey generally consists of visual inspection of the disaster area by trained personnel from an automobile, boat, or other vehicle. Damage is rated according to established criteria and recorded on survey forms.

Another category of data in the DIMS, the government resource inventory, consists of a listing of the state resources/capabilities which are likely to be committed to coping with specific emergency conditions. This inventory may include information (e.g., number/type of equipment, number of personnel) on medical services (e.g., hospitals, clinics), emergency rescue squads, police and fire departments, state National Guard (e.g., troops/equipment available for rescue missions, armories available for shelter), and the state Highway Department (e.g., snow removal equipment and personnel). This information is available from the individual services and from state agencies (e.g., medical service data is available from the Cabinet for Human Resources). This government resource inventory may also include data pertaining to the financial status of local governments (e.g., required participation thresholds, tax revenue per capita). These data are also available in published reports such as municipal and county yearbooks, state Department of Revenue.

The method of data collection and the type of personnel required are also keys to the DIMS. On the basis of our national survey of data collection procedures, it appears that the most efficient method of evaluating disaster damage is to utilize experts in specific fields from other state agencies. For example, engineers from the state Highway Department are used to assess road damage. This method avoids the need for training individuals to assess more than one type of damage. Since these state employees are already proficient in a given area, they need only to be provided with the evaluation criteria and appropriate forms at the time of the disaster. With regard to the administrative data, given that this data is publicly available, it may be collected by volunteer staff (e.g., older adult volunteers) and updated at regular intervals. The government resource inventory may be collected in a similar manner, with volunteer staff contacting various state agencies and services to obtain counts of available equipment and personnel. For those types of data which may not be collected by volunteer staff and require staff time of other agencies, an effort would be made to develop data-recording forms which allow the staff to extract and record the required data in an efficient manner.

Data Storage and Retrieval Stage

The systems design for the DIMS model remains highly tentative until a thorough review and acceptance of the prototype has been made. At that point a full-scale systems analysis will be done to develop the necessary technical specifications. The fourteen regional field offices of the Kentucky Department of Disaster and Emergency Services each have an IBM-PC/AT computer system. To remain compatible with this hardware, the system would reside on an IBM-PC/AT located at the Kentucky Disaster Operations Center. IBM-compatible hardware offering special features will be evaluated in the full-scale systems analysis. The software would be developed using the UCSD-P system Pascal. The development tools available in this system maximize the portability of the resulting software. Thus, the software would not be locked into one hardware configuration.

The system would be designed for full-screen interactive data entry and update. All data will be entered on an availability basis. This ensures that the data are as up to date as possible, avoids delays waiting for the data to be complete, and makes the system more flexible in changing the data elements. The capability inventory and damage assessment data would be entered on a site-by-site basis with network linked and geocoded identifiers.

Data retrieval can include update and display functions, report summaries, and data sharing with regional offices. Three types of summary reports might be developed: (1) declaration request formats, (2) annual reports for the governor, and (3) event status summaries for local and regional offices. The reporting capabilities should include customized geographic aggregation and multiyear comparisons.

Analysis and Reporting Stage

Analysis and use of data from an information system is an "afterthought" in most organizations. To overcome this typical lack of forethought, the analysis and reporting stage of the DIMS emphasizes the production of statistical information which is compatible with the needs of a multitude of user audiences. The Kentucky DIMS would be designed to produce information for use in (1) justifying federal declarations, (2) justifying state budget (3) keeping local and regional agencies informed, and (4) planning and/or modifying disaster response and recovery strategies.

The analysis of data for federal declaration justification would be descriptive, yielding summary statistics of the current (pre-event) conditions and the impact of past incidents similar to the immediate crisis. Where appropriate, the data should be standardized for making county comparisons. The assumption is that more accurate and extensive description of the impact of an event will assist the state in determining whether a federal declaration may be justified. If the state makes the decision to submit a declaration application, this information will assist in filing an accurate, thorough, and timely application.

A format for reporting summary results to the governor of Kentucky on an annual basis would also be developed to justify yearly state appropriation requests made by the Division of Disaster and Emergency Services. Additionally, data would be organized so that it could be retrieved for use by regional and county level disaster coordinators in making comparisons with other areas of the state. These results, which would be descriptive, should serve a social bookkeeping and accounting function for state and local governments.

Finally, results from a more detailed analysis could be useful in planning and policy review in the short term and in the long term. Analysis of the data relating to demand for services and governmental response capability should be particularly helpful for these purposes. Additionally, after the system has been in operation for several years, longitudinal data included in the system can be analyzed using powerful statistical techniques to uncover any cause-effect relationships. Since the conceptual framework for the system allows for the relationships between indicators of community context, disaster stressors, and quality of life to be modeled, such techniques as the LISREL computer program discussed above would be especially appropriate. The analysis might address such policy questions as: To what extent do disasters impact the social and economic well-being of the community? To what extent does the type of disaster impact the community? Under what varying conditions might different types of disasters impact the community? The answers to such questions may be of interest to policymakers in federal and state governments as well as to researchers in the academic community.

Conclusions

This chapter has presented an innovative disaster-impact monitoring system (DIMS) which was conceptualized as a four-stage process, with multiple components at every stage. The presentation highlights the ways in which an information system yield information which can be compatible with the needs of various types of users. While it is essential that the DIMS and its products be compatible with the users' needs, one should not overlook the importance of (1) the relationship between the developers of the system and its users, and (2) the capability of potential users to apply DIMS information in the decision-making process.

Patton (1978) has found that the "personnel factor" is an essential ingredient in getting evaluation results used. Johnson (1980) uncovered the fact that extensive involvement of and quality contact with potential users enhanced use of research results. Others, (Havelock, 1969; Dunn and Swierczak, 1977) have discussed the importance of collaboration between decision makers and researchers.

Where relationships are concerned, we contend that it is important to consider the nature of the relationship between the development team and the users of the information from the system throughout the development process. We advocate adopting an "outside/inside" team approach to developing the system. That is, throughout the various stages of the system development, the outside team members from the University of Louisville's Urban Research Institute and its Center for Hazards Research and Policy Development should work closely with designated personnel in the Division of Disaster and Emergency Services of Kentucky. The inside team members would, in consultation with others in the agency, decide what data should be maintained, determine how the data should be collected and stored, and select the appropriate format for reporting information. The university team members would serve as technicians to the project and provide advice and recommendations, where appropriate.

Decision makers' awareness and understanding of the disaster-impact monitoring system and the type of data it contains is also essential. In the early 1970s Horst et al. (1974) discuss the relationship between the users' basic understanding of how the system was developed, how it works, and the kind of results it can produce and their commitment to the maintenance and use of the products. Fairweather et al. (1974) and others have provided guidance regarding the best way to enhance understanding among users. This research has shown that two-way verbal exchange is the most effective method of transmitting results to users.

Since two-way transmission methods of communication have been found to be the most effective, it is important to institute a variety of modalities to train and assist users in interpreting and using DIMS-generated information. At a minimum workshops would be conducted about the system and how to use its products and assistance would be provided in data analysis and data interpretation. Maintaining the relationship with key users is also essential to utilization of the information.

In summary, if the data products of the system are perceived as compatible with users' needs if the developmental team establishes and maintains good relationships with potential users of the information and if potential users are trained to use the information, then the DIMS can make a significant difference in the quality of life of disaster victims living in Kentucky.

Bibliography

Adams, P., and R. Adams

1984 "Mount St. Helens Ashfall: Evidence for a Disaster Stress Reaction." *American Psychologist,* 39: 252–260.

Dunn, W.N., and F. Swierczak

1977 "Planned Organizational Change: Toward Grounded Theory." *Journal of Applied Behavioral Science,* 13: 135–157.

Fairweather, G.W., D.H. Sandler and L.G. Tornatzky

1974 *Creating Change in Mental Health Organizations.* Elmsford, NY: Pergamon.

Glaser, E.M., H.H. Abelson, and K.N. Garrison

1983 *Putting Knowledge to Use: Facilitating the Diffusion of Knowledge and the Implementation of Planned Change.* San Francisco: Jossey-Bass.

Green, B.L.

1982 "Conceptual and Methodological Issues in Assessing the Psychological Impact of Disaster." In B.J. Sowder, ed. *Disasters and Mental Health: Selected Contemporary Perspectives.* Rockville, MD: U.S. Department of Health and Human Services, pp. 179–195.

Hall, P.S., and P.W Landreth

1975 "Assessing Some Long Term Consequences of a Natural Disaster." *Mass Emergencies,* 1: 55–61.

Havelock, R.G.

1969 *Planning for Innovation Through Dissemination and Utilization of Knowledge.* Ann Arbor: University of Michigan, Institute of Social Research.

Headey, B., E. Holmstrom, and A. Wearing
1984 "The Impact of Life Events and Changes in Domain Satisfactions on Well-being." *Social Indicators Research,* 15: 203–227.

Horst, P., J.N. Nay, J.W. Scanton, and J.S. Wholey
1974 "Program Management and the Federal Evaluator." *Public Administrator Review,* July-August.

Johnson, Knowlton W.
1980 "Stimulating Evaluation Use by Integrating Academia and Practice." *Knowledge: Creation, Diffusion, Utilization,* 2: 237–262.
1983 "Combating Violence: Using Research in Planning for Change." In *Issues and Strategies in Confronting Violence in Alaska: Conference Proceedings.* Anchorage, AK: School of Justice, University of Alaska.
1985 "Research Influence in Decision Making to Control and Prevent Violence." *Knowledge: Creation, Diffusion, Utilization,* 7: 161–189.

Joreskog, K.G., and D. Sorbom
1984 *LISREL VI: Analysis of Linear Structural Relationships by the Methods of Maximum Likelihood.* Mooresville, IN: Scientific Software, Inc.

Kiesel, G.A.
1974 "Social Indicators and Their Use in City Government." Unpublished doctoral dissertation. School of Human Behavior, United States International University, San Diego, CA.

Koebel, T.C.
1982 *1981 Housing Report for Kentucky.* Louisville, KY: Urban Studies Center, University of Louisville.
1985 *1984 Housing Report for Kentucky.* Louisville, KY: Urban Studies Center, University of Louisville.

Land, K.C.
1971 "On the Definition of Social Indicators." *American Sociologist* 6: 322–325.
1975 "Social Indicator Models: An Overview." In K.C. Land and S. Spilerman, eds. *Social Indicator Models.* New York: Russell Sage Foundation, pp. 5–36.

Logue, James N., Holger Hansen, and Elmer Struening
1981 "Some Indications of the Long-Term Effects of a Natural Disaster." *Public Health Reports,* 96: 67–79.

Norris, Fran H.

1986 *Flood Exposure and Anxiety in Older Adults.* Paper presented at the meeting of the Second World Congress of Victimology, Orlando, FL.

Patton, M.Q.

1978 *Utilization-Focused Evaluation.* Beverly Hills, CA: Sage.

Quarantelli, E.L.

1985 "What Is Disaster? The Need for Clarification and Conceptualization in Research." In B.J. Sowder, ed. *Disasters and Mental Health: Selected Contemporary Perspectives.* Rockville, MD: U.S. Department of Health and Human Services, pp. 41–73.

Schulte, P.J., J.M. Brockway, and S.A. Murrell

1978 "Kentucky Elderly Needs Assessment Survey." Louisville, KY: Urban Studies Center, University of Louisville.

Schulte, P.J., and S.A. Murrell

1980 "The In-Home Survey." In *Kentucky's Social Service Needs Assessment.* Louisville, KY: Urban Studies Center, University of Louisville, pp. 1–50.

Stevens, J.B.

1984 "Objective Indicators, Personal Characteristics, and Satisfaction with Safety from Crime and Violence: An Interaction Model." *Social Indicators Research,* 14: 53–67.

Sullivan, J.L., and S. Feldman

1979 *Multiple Indicators: An Introduction.* Beverly Hills, CA: Sage.

Urban Studies Center

1981 *The Kentucky Health Status Information System: The Annual Report: A System.* Louisville, KY: Urban Studies Center, University of Louisville.

Wilcox, L.D., K.W. Wasson, F. Fear, G. Klonglan, and G. Beal

1976 "Toward a Methodology for Social Indicators in Rural Development: Base Report." Sociology Report 125. Ames, Iowa: Department of Sociology and Anthropology, Iowa State University.

Wright, S.J.

1985 "Health Satisfacation: A Detailed Test of the Multiple Descrepencies Theory Model." *Social Indicators Research,* 17: 299–313.

15

Discrimination Against Harijans and Dowry Deaths: Examples of Ongoing Victimization in India

Bhanuprasad Pandya
Indian Research Society for the Welfare of Backward Classes

This chapter examines in depth two major forms of victimization that have existed for centuries and still survive in contemporary India, notwithstanding its official status as a democracy: the discrimination against Harijans and the dowry deaths. The author presents the historical roots of both problems, analyzes their current forms and variations, and looks at some of the efforts that have been undertaken in recent times to correct the problems.

Victimization of Harijans and Dowry Deaths in India

One unique form of discrimination and victimization is prevalent in most parts of India. It is more pronounced in the north than in the south. It is neither based on race, religion, culture, nor complexion of the skin. It springs from antiquated notions of the divine origin of caste hierarchy in the Hindu society of India and the derisive and contemptuous treatment customarily meted out to the lowest rung of the social hierarchy by regarding them as "untouchables."

Poor Harijans are regarded as untouchables by the higher caste Hindus to such a degree that they have to live in separate settlements away from the main villages. This social discrimination does not end with segregation. It goes far beyond. The caste Hindus simply do not wish to have any social contacts with the Harijans. Any chance contact with a Harijan has to be atoned for by undergoing purification rites.

After the advent of independence, India opted for a democratic form of government. Democracy presupposes freedom of speech, freedom of expression, freedom of association and guarantees equality of opportunity to all citizens of the country. Accordingly, there has been a mass upsurge among the Harijans, what with the spread of education, improvement of living standards and, last but not least, realization of their inherent political power. As a natural consequence, Harijans have started competing with the caste Hindus for admission to educational institutions, for employment opportunities, for setting up new enterprises, etc. This brings them in acute emotional conflict with the caste Hindus, who have not been yet weaned away from their orthodox notions of untouchability, despite legislative measures and administrative inducements. As the caste Hindus are fairly entrenched in positions of power, they still manage to manipulate the government machinery in such a way as to thwart the legitimate aspirations of the Harijans.

There is a systematic conspiracy to keep the Harijans out of society and to continue to hold them in their century-old status of vassalage. Harijans are very often subjected to unmerited or excessive punishment by manipulation of the juristic and administrative machinery. If that does not silence the Harijans, the caste Hindus even resort to extra-legal, often cruel and barbarous actions to quell them. This phase of victimology is peculiar to India. It is unlike apartheid in South Africa or discrimination against blacks in the United States. The Harijans profess the same religion as the caste Hindus; they speak the same language; racially there is hardly any difference between the two, and yet they are singled out for inhuman treatment simply because the orthodox Hindu mind is unable to accept the new ideas of liberty, equality, and fraternity guaranteed by the Constitution of India.

Cases of lynching, murder, rape, arson and mass exodus of the oppressed Harijans are everyday occurrences in India. The government, no doubt, is working to cure these evils, but the roots of the disease have penetrated too deep for any superficial treatment.

One must realize that untouchability is not merely a notion based on superstition. It is a heritage which has come down from centuries of India's distinctive theories of social evolution. The concept of untouchability is such a complex and intriguing jumble of beliefs, customs, religion, and lifestyle of the caste Hindu society that it is difficult for a non-Hindu to understand its full implication. There are social, historical, ethnic, economic and anthropological ingredients to this peculiar and unique phenomenon.

Historical Background

Early Aryans were a pastoral community moving from one region to another in search of fodder and water for themselves and their cattle. There were distinct groups known as "tribes" localized in a particular tract of land in the vast hilly regions of central Asia, but there were no varnas or orders during this phase. When they came to the Indian subcontinent, they found that the climate and soil were suitable for agriculture. Gradually, they took to agriculture as a means of livelihood.

Transition from the pastoral to agricultural way of life lent greater stability to the community, and the erstwhile nomadic tribes settled down on the fertile plains of the Indo-Gangetic basin. The Aryans subjugated the local inhabitants as they forged ahead in their quest for new lands. The locals were allowed to stay, so that they could be employed as servants and menial assistants. Among the subjugated tribes, those that were powerful and organized were gradually absorbed into the Hindu fold, and a fourth varna of the "Sudras" emerged. The weakest ones among the conquered tribes were reduced to the position of serfs. They were not permitted to stay near the village community. Their settlements were on the periphery of the village and had such menial duties as scavenging and removal and flaying of the carcasses of dead animals. Since the nature of their work was repellent to the refined community, they were treated as Asprushyas or untouchables, the "Panchams." They were ordered about like slaves, treated with contempt, and regarded as harbingers of evil. The earliest reference to the stratification of society occurs in the Rigveda, where in the canto known as "Purush Sookta"(an allegorical description of the prevailing social order) the Brahmins are presented as the mouth of the Supreme Deity.

The Khshatriyas were the arms, the Vaishyas constituted the trunk of the deity, and the Sudras were the feet of the deity. Here, we see the beginning of the four varnas. Earlier, there were only three. To a critical student of ancient lore, the allegory does not imply any suggestion of caste hierarchy. At least, it was not intended as such in the beginning. However, as time passed, the four orders became fairly rigid conduits wherein the community moved from generation to generation. The interchangeability of vocations which was characteristic of the earlier society, the horizontal mobility, if we may call it so, was lost and a person born in a particular caste belonged to it right up to his death. His descendants likewise belonged to that caste. Functional or occupational division of society thus became rigid and unchangeable by reason of endogamy and heredity. A belief also emerged that a change of caste would entail divine wrath as the four "varnas," which had been ordained by the Supreme Deity, were sacrosanct and any attempt to change that would be sacrilege. The Brahmins, who enjoyed a monopoly of book learning and were naturally reluctant to give up their privileged position, invented myths glorifying the four varnas and linking a person's birth in a particular caste to his Karmas, both in his present and previous lives.

The doctrine of "Karma" and transmigration was a very clever device to prevent any kind of dissent, any protestant trends, or any challenge to the Brahmins' perpetual position of authority. There must have been rumblings of discontent among the less-privileged castes, but they were drowned in the cacophony of a superstitious and ritualistic society.

Influence of Buddhism and Jainism and Revival Under Shankracharya

The first break from Hindu orthodoxy occurred when Buddha started preaching a more rational and egalitarian social order. During the ascendance of Buddhism, the traditional Aryan philosophy and way of life did suffer a setback. Jainism also challenged the caste hierarchy and many basic assumptions of traditional Hindu thought.

Under the influence of Shankracharya, however, there was a revival of Hinduism in a more virulent form which placed Brahmins on a high pedestal, far above the rest of the community. For instance, Brahmins were forbidden to pass on their knowledge of the "Sastras" to a person who was not a twice born. This phase saw the ascendance of Brahmins in the Hindu society on a scale unheard of in the ancient Vedic times. There were, however, some Vaishnav saints who disagreed with the philosophy and teachings of Shankracharya. They preached fatherhood of God and brotherhood of man, for whom caste was only an identification label without any suggestion of intrinsic superiority.

Ramamuj, Ramanand, Guru Nanak, Kabir, Rohidas, Mirabai, and Vallabhacharya, among others, did make a sincere effort to democratize the Hindu society, but they could not make any appreciable dent on the traditional, convention-ridden ritualistic and superstitious Hindu society.

Challenge of Islam and Christianity

The first serious challenge to Hinduism came from Islam and Christianity. They were both monotheistic societies. They did not have anything bearing even remote resemblance to a caste system. Nor did they believe in the Hindu version of Karma and transmigration. They were better organized, more rational, more democratic and, at the same time, more dynamic religions. Hinduism continued to lose ground both politically and socially, as it could not present a united front against the inroads of Islam and Christianity by reason of its inherent dissensions and doctrinal weaknesses.

Nineteenth Century Reformers

Men like Dayanand, Ram Mohan Roy, and Vivekan could perceive the structural unsoundness of Hindu society and tried their own ways to make it broad-based but had little success. Matters, however, came to a head when, as a result of the Freedom movement, the British government was driven to consider the necessary constitutional set-up for and modus operandi of the transfer of power. At the Round Table Conference (RTC), representatives of leading political parties had been invited. Gandhiji also attended the conference. In the course of the second round of discussion at RTC II, the question of protection of the rights of minorities came up.

Freedom Movement and the Communal Award

As was to be expected the parties took up intransigent stands. A compromise formula could not be reached with the result that the matter was entrusted to Mr. Ramsay Macdonald, prime minister of the United Kingdom, for arbitration. After considering the various points of view, Mr. Macdonald gave his formula which came to be known as the "Communal Award" which interalia provided for separate constituencies for the minority groups.

Like the Muslims, the Scheduled Castes were to have their separate constituencies and separate electorate. Gandhiji was very much perturbed at this turn of events because with him it was a matter of conviction that the Scheduled Castes formed an integral part of the Hindu society and any attempt to drive a wedge between the Hindus and the Scheduled Castes would ultimately endanger the very existence of the Hindu society. Gandhiji was a devout believer in equality for all, and yet he knew that equality had been denied to the poor "Depressed Castes," "Harijans" as he called them. Relevant at this stage is Gandhiji's historic utterance wherein he condemned untouchability in unequivocal terms.

Gandhiji's Views on Untouchability

"I believe that if untouchability is really rooted out, it will not only purge Hinduism of a terrible blot but its repercussion will be worldwide. My fight against untouchability is a fight against the impure in humanity. . . . My fast, therefore, is based first of all on faith in my cause, faith in the Hindu community, faith in human nature itself, and faith even in the official world."

Gandhiji resolved to "fast unto death" in protest against the imposition of separate electorates for the depressed classes. The whole country was shaken to its foundations by Gandhiji's abrupt decision to stake his life for the sake of a cause so dear to his heart. After prolonged negotiations, anxious inquiries from all over the world, frantic appeals and mass prayers, the Hindu leadership realized the gravity of the occasion, and Dr. B.R. Ambedkar, who had been adamant in his plea for separate electorate for the depressed classes, decided to relent in order to save the life of the greatest man of India.

The Poona Pact of 1932

The historic Poona Pact of 24 September 1932 was signed by the top ranking leaders of the Hindu society. The salient provisions of the Poona Pact were

1. Reservation of seats of depressed classes (out of general electorate in the provincial legislatures).
2. Reservation of seats in the Central Legislature.
3. Reservations to stay for ten years in the first instance.
4. No disabilities on the ground of being a member of depressed classes in regard to election or appointment to public office.
5. Adequate grants to be earmarked for providing educational facilities.

The agreement popularly known as the Poona Pact of 1932 was the Magna Carta for depressed classes.

Importance of the Historical Background

One only has to recall the anti-reservation riots of 1980–1981 and 1985, which shook Gujarat to its foundations, to appreciate the importance of the historical background of the problem of untouchability. In the absence of a correct understanding of the historical background, the rising generations are apt to misjudge the special provisions for Scheduled Castes and Scheduled Tribes as acts of charity. By reserving certain seats for the Scheduled Castes and Scheduled Tribes in the Legislatures, in educational institutions and in the services, society is obliging them. It is their right. It is nothing but the implementation of the solemn pledge taken by leaders of the Hindu society more than fifty years ago to save the life of Gandhiji, the Messiah of the new born "Indian Nation."

Untouchability After Independence

The provisions of the Poona Pact came to be incorporated in the Government of India Act of 1935 and later, in the Constitution of India as drafted by the Constituent Assembly of India under the guidance and inspiration of Dr. B.R. Ambedkar. Article 17 of the Constitution states: "Untouchability is abolished and its practice in any form is forbidden. The enforcement of any disability arising out of untouchability shall be an offence punishable in accordance with law."

The states have framed their own acts to stamp out untouchability. In Gujarat, there is the Removal of Untouchability Act of 1955 and the Civic Rights Acts, which inter alia prescribe penal provisions for the practice of untouchability in any form.

Legislation Not Enough

If legislation by itself could bring about a social reform, there would be no child marriages, no offenses against public morals, no cases of dowry deaths, and likewise no instances of the practice of untouchability. But experience shows that mere legislation is not enough to usher in social reform. Change comes from the spontaneous realization on the part of the community that it must do away with certain evil customs and to abjure from unsocial practices. It is a sad reflection on the efficiency of the enforcement machinery when, even after four decades of independence, the situation is very much where it had been for centuries before.

In spite of the vaunted claims of progress and amelioration, the Scheduled Castes, the erstwhile untouchables, are in many regions still subject to the same disabilities as they were before independence. While there has been an appreciable change in the attitude of the urban population because of the inevitability of closer collaboration between the caste Hindus and the Scheduled Castes, the countryside still remains blissfully ignorant of the changing philosophy and outlook on life.

Untouchability Still Exists

One can still see the caste Hindu women obligingly filling pails of water brought by Harijan women because the latter cannot draw water from the village well in spite of the sign announcing that the well is open to all and sundry. During the Community Project era many wells were constructed from the project funds on the condition that they could be opened to the Harijans as well. Project Officers invariably affixed stone tablets stating this on the wells constructed from project funds. Today, the tablets are still there making hideous grimaces at the credulity of the bureaucrats who blink at realities and prefer to live in a world of make–believe. Hardly a day passes when there is no incident of Harijan baiting. In Gandhiji's Gujarat, there have been instances of mass exodus of Harijans because of the brutal harassment and incessant bullying they must endure in the villages.

Observations Made by Commissioner of Scheduled Castes and Scheduled Tribes

One has only to refer to the latest available report of the Commissioner of Scheduled Castes and Scheduled Tribes to see that a wide gap exists between our aims and present day realities. Comments on the shortfalls in the matters of amelioration of the lot of Scheduled Castes are:

a) Harijans are still being ousted from agricultural lands legitimately held by them. The local authorities simply stand by and look on as this flagrant deprivation goes on day in and day out under their very noses.

b) The Chamars and Bhangis still have to carry on their unwelcome and disgusting work under the most inhuman conditions. There still has been no improvement in the matter of giving them improved tools and better working conditions.

c) Untouchability is still practiced on an extensive scale in spite of the fairly stringent provisions of the Removal of Untouchability Act of 1955. In spite of the Commissioner's specific recommendation, no legal aid is given to victims of untouchability.

d) The benefit of vocational training is still not made available to Scheduled Caste candidates.

e) Considerable leeway still has to be made in the

matter of extending educational facilities to the Scheduled Caste children. There are very few boarding schools for Scheduled Caste boys and girls.

f) Government effort in the matter of prevention of untouchability in public places is minimal. There are special enforcement units at Gandhinagar, Rajkot and Vadodara. But looking to the size of the problem, the size of the enforcement machinery is disproportionately small.

I have tried to present in a nutshell the salient aspects of the evil of untouchability as it persists today. Untouchability in my opinion, still exists in spite of tall claims about its eradication. Harijans are still, by and large, excluded from the private and cooperative sectors in the matter of employment. Even in the field of small trades, poor Harijans have no opportunity to make any appreciable progress because of the caste stigma attached to them. For example, a Harijan milkman, a Harijan tea-stand owner or, a vendor of snacks cannot possibly sell his product to non-Harijans.

Illusion of Success

After some 40 years of independence, the seven Five-Year Plans, and a plethora of social welfare measures, there has been some success in creating an illusion of prosperity among the backward classes, the Scheduled Castes especially. There are indeed a handful of Harijan employees in the Government Departments, particularly on the lower rungs of the administrative ladder. The upper rungs by and large are still beyond the reach of the Harijan employees. True, the literacy rate has gone up. Some of the Harijan youth also have been able to reach the university stage of education, but their percentage is minute when compared to the total Scheduled Caste population as will be evident from the following table:

Table 15.1

Literacy Among the Scheduled Castes (per 10,000)

	Rural		Urban	
	Male	Female	Male	Female
Illiterate	690	907	551	848
Literate	133	42	160	56
Primacy	165	51	274	95
Matriculate	3	—	14	1

The percentage of dropouts among the Scheduled Castes at the primary and secondary school stages is simply staggering. How can we account for the high percentage of dropouts except by referring to the grinding poverty which still infects Harijan households and which still compels them to remove their school-going children from their classes and put them in the field to earn supplementary income?

If one turns to the highly technical branches of education, one finds that in spite of various measures the fact remains that many of the seats reserved for Scheduled Caste and Scheduled Tribe candidates still remain unutilized. The only explanation for this phenomenon is that the benefits of our welfare programs still have not percolated to the lower strata of the Scheduled Caste community.

The Bureaucratization of the Civil Rights Movement

To Gandhiji, Harijan uplift was his life's mission. He even created a cadre of honest and dedicated social workers to carry the program all over the country. With the martyrdom of Gandhiji, his lofty spiritual approach, his prominent moral tone, and his indefatigable effort were lost forever. Gandhiji had a legion of political successors but very few talented followers to carry forward the removal of untouchability by bringing about a change of heart on the part of the Hindu caste.

Gandhiji's political heirs thought they would carry on Gandhiji's mission with the help of their social and economic programs to be implemented by their formidable ranks of bureaucrats. They proved right to some extent. We have witnessed innumerable social welfare schemes which have been pushed to the remotest villages with all the thoroughness and efficiency of salaried employees whose performance is judged quantitatively with the help of job charts and statistical returns. They have done a marvelous job in terms of physical targets. But very unfortunately, none of them has ever shown some of the emotional and spiritual zeal which formed all Gandhiji's action.

Thus, the altruistic, humanitarian and spiritual approach has been forgotten. In consequence, the caste Hindus have virtually lost all interest in these programs. On the other hand, there is an increasing awareness on the part of the younger generations of Harijans who have become conscious of their constitutional rights and also of their political clout. They are intensifying their demand for pro-rata representation in all cadres of government and semi-government institutions.

They want their share of educational facilities, easy access to advanced technical education, and their quota of seats in universities and in the public services. Not surprisingly, the caste Hindu students and employees seem to feel that the Harijans have already snatched more than their share of benefits, that they are being pressed into service even by relaxing educational standards and age restrictions with the result that overall efficiency of the administrative machinery supposedly has registered a downward trend. They are backed by other caste Hindus who see in reservations of any kind a potential threat to the privileged positions they have held so far.

These perceptions have lead to the anti-reservation, anti-Harijan agitations of 1980–1981 and 1985. The unfortunate sequence of those events regrettably confirms the apprehension of many that Gandhiji's philosophy and his ethical and humanistic approach to problems facing India are heading towards extinction.

Dowry Deaths in India

Another persistent and troubling example of victimization in Indian society is the evil custom of the bridegroom demanding a price in consideration of his acceptance of a particular girl as his bride. The bridegroom gets in marriage not only a bride but also a sizeable ransom from the bride's parents in the form of her trousseau containing jewelry, ornaments, household articles and sometimes a generous amount in hard cash, too, for the favor of accepting her as his bride in preference to other aspiring young women.

The origin of the dowry system is shrouded in mystery. There are some revealing verses in Hindu scriptures, like the Vedas, which suggest that when a girl was given in marriage her parents were to give some household articles in order to enable the newlyweds to set up a decent household. As the ancient Aryan community was by and large agricultural, the Vedic Mantras envisage a gift of agricultural implements such as a yoke for the oxen, a pestle for thrashing the corn, or a broom to sweep the house. These articles were of everyday household use, and the purpose was to enable the newly married couple to set up an independent household.

In the course of time, as the occupations of people became diversified, a symbolic donation of toy-sized yoke, pestle, and other items became part of the marriage ritual which survives till this day.

As time passed, the demographic ratio of males and females must have changed. It is conceivable that at some stage in history, the females exceeded the males, with the result that polygamy came into vogue.

Later, people realized the pitfalls of a polygamous society and switched back to a monogamous society, with an ideally contented and functional pair who tried to emulate the Ram-Sita model of idyllic marital life. This once again must have created a sharp rivalry among the prospective brides to claim a promising young man as a mentor and guardian for the rest of their lives. This competition introduced the concept of premium, a pay-off for closing the deal with the prospective bridegroom. Added to this was the inherent human weakness for lucre. If the father of a bridegroom was sure that he could get any number of girls for the asking, there was nothing to prevent him from placing a price on his son's head.

The evil of dowry became aggravated as a result of the undisguised anxiety of brides' parents to secure prosperous young men for their daughters to ensure a secure life for them. Eligible bridegrooms and their parents saw in the marriage of their son a golden opportunity to bolster up their own financial position by stipulating a heavy dowry and taking unfair advantage of the girls' parents.

The vicious custom of a dowry developed over the centuries, creating economic disparities on the one hand and contaminating the institution of marriage on the other.

The lot of parents with a large number of girls is simply pathetic, as they are worried about getting suitable alliances for their daughters as well as exhausting their financial resources by shelling out their life's savings to propitiate the dowry hunters each time a daughter is married.

Partly owing to difficulties of getting suitable matches for the girls and partly due to mistaken notions of family honor, people began to regard the arrival of a daughter as a family calamity and the custom of girl infanticide developed among certain caste groups where the evil of dowry was most rampant. Vigilance and enforcement of the penal law have succeeded in curbing the evil of infanticide to some extent, but the evil of dowry exists despite the enactment of a law prohibiting it in any form.

With the impact of modern ideas, the dowry scenario has changed slightly but the evil persists nevertheless. Of course, there are some redeeming features today. A large number of social service groups are ready to help if their help is sought. A network of press reporters and voluntary institutions who would never miss an opportunity to get a good story. These factors do act as deterrents to a certain extent, and they keep the dowry phenomenon from mushrooming to alarming proportions.

It is a well-known fact that in India cases of accidental deaths due to burning are far more frequent among females than males. The chief reason is that females have to look after the household chores, including cooking. Females have to handle and manage fire day in and day out. With the development of modern kitchen appliances, fire making has become at once easy and risky if proper precautions are not taken. On the other hand, the dress materials of females have become lighter, more fragile, fluffy and inflammable compared with the coarse cotton fabrics of past generations. This partially explains the alarming increase in the number of accidental deaths by burning.

Any unusual death (other than due to illness or old age) can be either suicide, accident or murder. In the cases surveyed by us, the official cause of death is either accident or suicide. Unless there is a pretty brisk investigation on the part of the police, it is fairly easy for a murder to be passed off as suicide or accidental death. Many dowry victims are liquidated, and then the in-laws go through the customary rituals, as if the departed soul had been ever so dear to them and that they are infinitely grief stricken by the calamity. One notices such charades day in and day out in the small circle of one's own friends and acquaintances.

It is true that the amended section 498 of the Indian Penal Code has complicated the situation for the bride liquidators to some extent. Now, it is easy for the blood relatives of the liquidated bride to set the legal machinery in motion by voicing skepticism about the cause of death as notified and by recounting some previous history of harassment.

This, however, does not act as a deterrent because the murderers in disguise know full well that criminal law requires convincing proof and a link between the act constituting the offense, its perpetrators, and those masterminding the operation. Such link is difficult to establish when the victim is dead and her remains have been cremated quickly as required by custom and ritual.

Part II

Prevention and Treatment

Introduction to Part II

Victimization and the involvement of the victim with the justice system create many problems and difficulties for victims for which they generally have little or no remedy. The consequences of the crime can be psychological, medical, financial, practical and affect personal relations, family life, ability to function at work and productivity, and the general outlook towards society. Trauma, fear, lost income, medical expenditures, short- and long-term medical problems and disabilities also affect many victims.

When victims become involved with the justice, medical, and social assistance systems, they do so with certain expectations that are often not met. Other problems develop as well. Victims frequently are or feel exploited, inconvenienced, shabbily treated, at times even threatened, at a minimum ignored, and faced with considerable financial expenditures. Involvement with the justice system for them means a considerable commitment of time and resources and having to absorb substantial losses. There are transportation expenses, child care expenses, lost income, the threat or real possibility of losing one's job, missed opportunities and added burdens to one's daily schedule because of the considerable amount of time that must be allocated to dealing with any bureaucracy.

On their part victims expect at least some information on the progress of the case, protection in situations when it is dangerous to cooperate with the system, some active role in the conduct of the case, and a satisfactory resolution of the matter, all of this within a reasonable amount of time. Most of all, victims want to prevent a reoccurrence of their victimization. Unfortunately, they are often disappointed on one or more counts.

Many programs with different goals, philosophies, allegiances, and approaches have been established during the last two decades in various countries and most notably in the United States to assist victims deal with the many problems they encounter in the aftermath of their victimization. Assessments of their usefulness, effectiveness, and legitimacy vary. Certainly, there are considerable disparities among victim programs and even controversy, at times, as to who their true client may be.

While the different types of victim assistance programs perform by and large a useful and needed function, comparable to medical intervention to repair the damage inflicted by an injury or illness, there is no question that they also represent a certain defeat of society. After all, the crime has been committed; the criminal has been able to carry out his plan, exert his dominance and impose his will; and now society, impotent to stop the criminal from prevailing, is helping the victim pick up the pieces and rebuild his life. In most cases, the victimizer goes undetected and unpunished.

In many ways, victim assistance programs face some of the same troubling questions and ethical dilemmas that confront other helping organizations. There are indeed reasons to question, for example, international assistance and relief efforts when no steps are taken to correct the underlying reasons why famine, civil strife, religious or ethnic conflicts, man-made disasters and other calamities take place. Not only is it valid, but is it correct to mobilize the community to alleviate the suffering of people, whatever the cause, and particularly when it is chronic and recurrent, without questioning the causes of what one is trying to correct? One could argue that this way one may even become a conspirator and collaborator of a repressive, exploitative or warmongering regime or of various oppressive ideologies by softening the impact of their actions and making it bearable, while at the same time not challenging the causes and the roots of the evil.

Gloria Steinem, a foremost feminist in the United States, is often quoted as saying: "We are swimming through a river of change. . . . We have spent the last decade standing over the river bank, rescuing women who are drowning. In the next decade, some of us have to go to the head of the river to keep women from falling in." This statement aptly summarizes the need to think not only of helping the victim but also, and foremost, of stopping the victimization.

The importance of prevention is finally being recognized. Just as in the medical field it has been learned that preventing instead of just curing illness should be the foremost goal of medicine and is the only way to improve a population's health on a more permanent basis, so we are learning that preventing victimization must at least go hand in hand with treatment.

Preventing victimization also reminds us of the role of the state as protector of the safety and well-being of its population. This role is basic to responsible government and constitutes the foundation for the introduction of policies and concrete measures to lessen the likelihood of victimization. Some legal experts in the United States even argue that there is a still unrecognized constitutional right to be free of victimization based on the Constitution's guarantee to the pursuit of happiness. This argument is further reinforced, proponents say, by the overall social contract theory which is at the foundation of the American state. It is also supported by the clear vision of the state as an organization providing public services which has characterized the American republic, as opposed to European thought, from the very beginning. There is no doubt that the present constitutional government is clearly based on the concept of the state as a public-service rendering organization.

This section of the book addresses both issues, prevention and treatment, striving to present a balanced view of how to respond comprehensively to victimization.

James T. Turner (chapter 16) bases his presentation on the fact that hostage incidents are an inherent risk of modern life. The challenge is to understand what steps one can take to enhance the likelihood that one will survive. Turner describes those vital steps and offers important insights, gleaming from both his work and that of the FBI.

Part of the burden imposed on women by the ever-present threat of rape consists of the decisions they must make in choosing strategies for coping with that threat. **Lita Furby, Baruch Fischhoff,** and **Marcia Morgan** (chapter 17) report on their study which examined in depth the initial phase in that decision-making process, namely, how women perceive the set of possible rape prevention options. Those results are discussed in terms of the burden that this decision making imposes on women, the locus of responsibility for preventing rape, and people's implicit theories of the causes and effective deterrents of rape.

Sarah M. Rieth (chapter 18) argues that the linear and feminist approach to the treatment of adult survivors of sexual abuse is that of perpetrator and victim and that this therapeutic approach has been found to perpetuate the client's self-concept as a victim. As an alternative, she maintains that a systems approach provides a complement to the linear approach and enables the client to move from victim to survivor status. Her chapter introduces clinicians to this theoretical framework and discusses issues and treatment goals for members of a homogeneous, ongoing psychotherapeutic group for adult survivors of sexual abuse. Group design and process are discussed and clinical material is presented.

Sondra Gardner and **Jane Timmons-Mitchell** (chapter 19) report on a clinical investigation undertaken to assess the merits of providing a structured group intervention for black single mothers in violent families to help them learn non-abusive ways of relating to their children. Group effectiveness was assessed by measuring the parents' perception of their children, the children's perceptions of themselves, and the parents' perception of family relationships before and after the group was conducted, and at follow-up. The results indicate positive and promising changes.

Heinz Leymann and **Jan Lindell** (chapter 20) examine social support after armed robbery in the workplace. They interviewed 221 bank employees who were victims of holdups. The analysis of the data indicates that the most important groups providing social support were primary groups such as relatives, friends, and colleagues at work. The authors speculate that the possible reason for this is that people with whom the victim had previous supportive relationships were also those who could act most supportive. The victims reported negative experiences when meeting with journalists, another finding to be added to the existing evidence of media insensitivity and unethical behavior when dealing with victims of crimes and disasters. Another relevant finding of this Swedish study is that there were considerable differences between the genders in receiving social support.

Leila Dane (chapter 21) covers issues related to effective assistance to hostage families. She identifies family members as indirect victims of crime and draws comparisons and contrasts with current victimological literature. She sees three issues as requiring immediate attention in such a situation: the effect of hostage taking on sources of income, the primary importance of ego-syntonic social involvement especially in terms of its relationship to the dysfunction of denial in long term stress, and the need to monitor coping. According to Dr. Dane, effective therapeutic interventions are those that use crisis techniques and informal counseling by individuals trained to minimize "second wound" effect and that attend to sequence of effect in this type of situation. As in the preceding chapter, major precipitants of anxiety and depression are identified as news coverage and stressed relations with others. The role of victim assistance programs in working with hostage families is also addressed.

16

Preparing Individuals at Risk for Victimization as Hostages

James T. Turner, Ph.D.
The Clark Center
Memorial Medical Center
Savannah, Georgia

A knife-wielding man commandeers your Delta Air Lines jumbo jet as it lands and holds the 232 persons aboard hostage. Officials do not know if he has made any demands. . . . A gunman takes a priest, a secretary and two students hostage in a high school. The seven-and-a-half-hour ordeal begins. The gunman demands that the President resign and turn the country over to him. . . . A gunman enters a convenience store and begins a robbery. A silent alarm alerts the police. He takes you and your toddler hostage demanding that the police allow him to escape with the money.

Hostage incidents are an inherent risk of modern life. It may be a terrorist, a criminal in the process of committing a crime (robbing a 7-Eleven or a bank), or an estranged lover/ spouse who takes you hostage. The challenge is to understand what steps you can take to enhance the likelihood that you will survive. The steps are gleamed from both my own work and that of the FBI. These steps have been taught to health care staff, bank tellers, public service workers, and corporate executives. This may be one of the most important lessons you can learn. You are guided on how to act, what to say, and what not to do. These easy guidelines can make the difference between life and death.

This presentation focuses at the primary level of intervention with victims, i.e., preparing them before such incidents occur. The first part of this presentation will acquaint you with the most likely types of hostage takers and their unique psychologies. Some specific issues in coping with them at different stages of the incidents will be discussed. A general series of survival guidelines and their rationale will then be explored.

Preparing Individuals at Risk for Victimization as Hostages

As you stand in line at the bank to deposit your paycheck, two men enter and the quiet routine of the bank is destroyed by the clatter of gunfire. As clouds of plaster and glass settle around you and the other stunned patrons, a heavily armed gunman calls out, "The party has just begun." The party ends 36 hours later in a blaze of gunfire as the police assault the bank. With stun grenades and flashbangs going off, you wonder if you will survive.

Hostage dramas are played out in America almost on a daily basis. While we may hear a lot about the terrorist hostage drama in France, the dramas in our own backyard have become so commonplace that they often are not even front page news. There is virtually no place where you are immune from becoming a hostage—on an airplane, in your home, at the store, in the hospital, or at the bank. And a common tread throughout these incidents is that the hostage becomes an integral player in the play. The degree of skill with which you play the part will mean the difference between life and death. Studies by Tom Strentz and others in the Federal Bureau of Investigation show clearly that individuals who have some preparation are not only more likely to survive but also to have fewer problems after the incident is over.

Multinational hostage taking and airplane hijackings have made the traveler at increased risk. Hostages chosen by terrorists tend to be innocent, unarmed and untrained individuals. In domestic hostage taking, it is much more likely that either you are involved with the individual, work in an institutional setting or business, or you are just a happenstance bystander. For example, seldom are the terrorists angry with the airline companies or particular individuals on the airplane; they use the aircraft as a vehicle to acquire a large number of people in a contained environment.

Since each of us is a target for terror of one kind or another, it makes sense to explore what preparations we might make to prepare ourselves for the possibility of being taken hostage. This kind of education is no more alarmist than having a smoke alarm in your house or seatbelts in your car. It doesn't mean you continually worry about being taken hostage, but it does mean that should this event happen at some future time you may remember some of the ideas given here and save your own life or someone else's. These guidelines will help you recover from the stress of such an incident and minimize the impact of post-traumatic stress syndrome on your life.

For those who work in institutional settings that deal with the public, it is very important to become more aware of each individual's level of upset. Many hostage incidents in institutional settings occur because individuals feel wronged and feel that no one will listen to them. If you increase this feeling by treating them like a piece of furniture or trying to shuffle them off like a piece of paper, you may one day be taken hostage. A sincere effort to help people will defuse many of these individuals. They will leave your office feeling like someone has listened. They have not been forced to take a hostage to get someone to listen to them. In Chicago, a man who requested action on a traffic ticket pulled a toy gun and took two attorneys hostage in a judge's chambers. Associate Judge Carl Cipolla said he was in his chambers with the attorneys discussing an unrelated matter when a man walked in and said, "I have this here traffic ticket." Cipolla told the man that he could not hear the case and told him to come back for an afternoon court call. The man then replied, "I don't have to do anything," and reached into the pocket of his suit coat. The judge ran out a back door of the chambers as the man pulled a handgun. One of the attorneys, Michael Fall, described the gun as "a very credible toy gun, especially when you're looking down the barrel" (Associated Press, 1985a).

Sometimes these incidents are caused by individuals who are mentally ill and are acting out a delusional fantasy. In Ohio, a major demand of a hostage taker was that all white people vacate the earth within twenty-four hours. In Arizona, a psychotic man held the staff of a television station hostage because he wanted his story of the six stolen books, which Johnny Cash knew about, aired along with his of warning of future events. In yet other cases, the demands have been that the moon be turned off, that all the people in California go to the sea and wash, or five million pounds of birdseed be distributed. These people, even though clearly mentally ill, are dangerous.

As a hostage, you will go through four stages during the incident (Strentz, 1984):

Alarm
Crisis
Accommodation
Resolution

Alarm. You will pass in one breath from being an everyday person into a victim whose life hangs in the balance. Your world is turned around and fear may be overwhelming. The situation may seem dream-like. "This can't be happening" to me is often heard from hostages. The first reaction is probably the one of denial. Panic occurs only when the chances of a favorable outcome are perceived to diminish rapidly. You may also come to fear the police more than the hostage taker. "They were the enemy. If only they had given him what he wanted it would all be over. I was afraid they would come in here with guns blazing," a thirty-year-old bank employee stated, looking back on the incident.

Crisis. The relationship patterns established during this period sets the stage for maximizing your survival. Continuing to perform routine activities may provide some relief. A paranoid schizophrenic took a Southeast law enforcement agency site. The siege lasted several hours. During this siege, the switchboard operator remained at her station and handled calls as she had been trained. She found refuge and comfort in the familiar, nonthreatening routine. She felt this had helped her stay in control, and, on follow-up, she appeared to have survived the event with the least trauma. Three areas may cause you problems—feelings of isolation, claustrophobia, and a distorted sense of time. Each of these is a normal reaction and does not indicate the imminent loss of your mind.

Accommodation. This is the most tranquil time in the incident. One of three patterns will emerge depending on the type of hostage taker you are dealing with. The criminal will be bargaining with the authorities. He is trying to strike a deal which will gain him freedom. A give and take attitude on the part of the police may develop. They may give the impression that for releasing the hostages, he will be allowed to go free. A vehicle, or the offer of one, is often a ploy to convince him that he will go free. The offer of movement may also be an attempt to get him into a situation where the police can use force while minimizing the risk to you.

The emotionally disturbed hostage taker will talk with great emotion and skill about the problem that drove him to this desperate act. Often the desire to be heard and to feel that someone in authority cares is at the core of even delusional demands. It may become very apparent to you that he wants to talk, not escape. After he has had his say to his satisfaction, he will begin to work out the process for surrender or begin on a death ritual. Problems may arise in two areas: the first is irrational demands for media coverage, such as national or international coverage of their views: the second difficulty occurs when they lose hope and begin to demand that police kill them (which happens in a significant percentage of these cases).

Terrorists may identify and separate the hostages. They may review passports and engage in political education of the hostages to convince them of the justness of their cause and that their actions have been forced upon them by the authorities. These individuals may become more reasonable as the incident goes on and looks for face-saving ways to end the hostage siege rather than clinging rigidly to their often unrealistic and symbolic initial demands.

The loss of a time sense becomes prominent in this phase. You may feel that hours seem like days. Fatigue and boredom work to reduce your control. The Stockholm Syndrome may begin to develop. The Stockholm Syndrome as defined by Tom Strentz, special agent for the Federal Bureau of Investigation, concerns

> the positive feelings of the captives toward their captor(s) that are accompanied by negative feelings toward the police. These feelings are frequently reciprocated by the captor(s). To achieve a successful resolution of a hostage situation, law enforcement must encourage and tolerate the first two phases so as to induce the third and thus preserve the lives of all participants. (Strentz, 1979)

This process, which may lead you to feel grateful to the hostage taker for not taking your life, appears to be an unconscious one. Some hostages have even reported trying to resist these feelings. After the incident you may feel angry with yourself for feeling grateful to this person who put you through such an ordeal. The hostage may even begin to actively assist the hostage taker as in the Patty Hearst case or the original case in Sweden where the hostages got on the telephone and attacked the prime minister for his unjust treatment of the hostage taker. The outside authorities seem to become the enemy. If only they would give him what he wanted, it would all be over.

This syndrome has a productive aspect in that the positive feeling expressed by the hostage may be reciprocated. It makes you more of a human being, and it is difficult even for terrorists to shoot human beings. It is much easier to shoot a caricature or a stereotype. A moving account of this is presented by Gerard Vaders, a newspaper editor in his fifties, who was held on a train by the South Moluccans, December 1975:

> On the second night they tied me again to be a living shield and left me in that position for seven hours. The one who was most psychopathic kept telling me "your time has come. Say your prayers." They had selected me for the

> third execution. In the morning when I knew I was going to be executed, I asked to talk to Prins (another hostage) to give him a message to take to my family. I want to explain my family situation. My foster child, whose parents had been killed, did not get along too well with my wife, and I had at that time a crisis in my marriage just behind me. . . . There were other things too. Somewhere I had the feeling that I had failed as a human being. I explained all this and the terrorist insisted on listening. (Ochberg, 1977: 151)

When Vaders advised his captors he was finished, the South Moluccans said, "No, someone else goes first."

The transition from a faceless symbol of the "enemy" to a human being had saved Vaders' life. The next person selected for execution the South Moluccans didn't know and made sure they didn't get to know. Vader describes his subjective feelings of the syndrome:

> And you had to fight a certain feeling of compassion for the Moluccans. I know this is not natural, but in some way they come over human. They gave us cigarettes. They gave us blankets. But we also realize that they were killers. You try to suppress that in your consciousness. And I knew I was suppressing that. I also knew that they were victims, too. In the long run they would be as much victims as we. Even more. You saw their morale crumbling. You experienced the disintegration of their personalities. The growing despair. Things dripping through their fingers. You couldn't help but feel a certain pity. For people at the beginning with egos like gods—impregnable, invincible—they end up small, desperate, feeling that all was in vain. (Ochberg, 1977: 166)

During this period of accommodation, other hostages have gained strength by exploiting a perceived weakness of their captor. This can be very dangerous. The Marines in Tehran quickly learned that threats to immediately execute them were only bluffs. They began to tell the captors to go ahead, that they wanted to be shot. They harassed their captors as they had been harassed in boot camp. This perceived control on their part improved morale and allowed them to survive captivity without the Stockholm Syndrome. Let me reemphasize however, that such actions are to be taken with extreme caution in hostage incidents.

Resolution. During the final stage you may begin to feel exhausted. This may lead to feelings of desperation and fantasies of flight. Your energy levels will have begun to run out with the ups and downs of the situation. Release may be complicated by danger and fears of immediate death if an assault is necessary. You may have mixed feelings toward the hostage taker. One of the best descriptions of the personal ambivalence is offered by a stewardess on TWA 355:

> After it was over and we were safe I recognized that they (the subjects) had put me through hell and had caused my parents and fiance a great trauma. Yet, I was alive. I was alive because they had let me live. You know only a few people, if any, who hold your life in their hands and then give it back to you. After it was over, we were safe and they were in handcuffs, I walked over to them and kissed each one and said, "Thank you for giving me my life back." I know how foolish it sounds, but that is how I felt. (Strentz, 1976)

You may feel hostility toward those who rescue you. The rescuing force not only did not share in the trauma in the barricaded place, they, in fact, are often assumed to have caused the suffering by not cooperating with the hostage taker.

How to Survive

Some general guidelines will help you survive each phase. A general guideline that applies throughout the incident is never to lose hope. John had taken his estranged wife and two children hostages in the home. Police had surrounded the home after being called by neighbors who heard a gunshot. John was trying to hold on to his wife in a last ditch attempt. He felt if he could keep her from moving out with the child he could convince her to try again. A reconstruction from police listening devices indicates that Joan kept initially insisting that this was only making things worse, but as the incident continued, she began to sob and cry that there was no hope. She knew either the police were going to kill him or he would hurt her. John became more and more depressed. He too gave up hope not only for holding onto his family but of getting out of the hostage situation either alive or without going to jail. All his plans had gone astray. Not only had this desperate attempt to prove his love driven his wife further away but now he might not get to see his children grow up. In the midst of this depression his clouded thinking process could show only one way out—death. In death they would all be united. He proceeded to shoot his wife and two children. He then fired on the police so they would kill him. The loss of hope by the hostage increased the depression of the hostage taker. So keep hope alive. No matter how bleak the outlook, becoming desperate will only increase the likelihood of victimization. Positive mental attitudes may give the courage to both you and your hostage taker to find a way out of the predicament.

The first five minutes are extremely dangerous. Try to calm the hostage taker. He is desperate and more anxious than the victims. A bank patron held hostage described how the rifle the terrorist was holding shook visibly, and she feared that he would accidentally shoot her as his hand shook. She worked to avoid upsetting him more. She modeled calm behavior—breathing deeply and talking slowly—encouraging him to take his time and think it through.

Keep a low profile. The thing you don't want to do is make yourself stand out in a group of hostages. Those with politically strong views who make them known early, may find themselves the first ones out the door—dead. If you are someone important, keep it to yourself. If you're not, don't try to be. Keeping a low profile requires you to watch what others are doing and blend in. Being overly compliant with the hostage taker can cause you to be seen as weak. As hostage takers take their anger out on the mighty, they also tend to be disgusted with the weak.

In London in early 1980 an articulate Khomeini supporter, Abbas Lavaasani, was held hostage in the Iranian embassy. His captors were less articulate Arabs from Khuzestan, and they could not counter his arguments. They took exception to what they perceived as his arrogance. Lavaasani was shot while tied to a railing and his body thrown from the embassy on the sixth day (Stentz, 1985).

Try to rest. Some hostages report sleeping during as much as 90% of the incident. This helps you to be rested and to control your frustration. Your hostage taker will become more short tempered as he goes without sleep. If you become short tempered as well, you are setting the stage for a confrontation that you will lose. If you are able to sleep, back yourself against the wall so that you face your hostage taker even when asleep. Again, it is more difficult to shoot someone facing you than someone with their back to you.

If you are sick, say so. Or if you require special medicine, ask for it. Hostage takers don't like sick hostages. They want to kill you when they are ready. They do not like having hostages die on them. In numerous cases they have released individuals after they were sure they had the illness they claimed. Negotiators are always able to send in medications if you need them. Some caution is in order. If you try to fake an illness, they may make you take medicine that is sent in and that could be hazardous if you don't need it.

Escape attempts should be evaluated with extreme caution. If you feel that your chances of escape are very high, go. Otherwise, be aware that a failed escape attempt may lead to reprisals. Also realize that your successful attempt may lead to punishment for other hostages. In New York, a prisoner held five hospital staff hostage (Dunlap, 1982). Over the 40-plus hour ordeal three were able to make their escape. However, with each escape the hostage taker became more violent and more directly threatening to the remaining hostages. A nurse in Texas (Ferman, 1982) describes her feelings of being the last hostage; the others had at first been traded and the last two slipped away. While she was happy for the others, she felt a sense of isolation and desertion. She began to know that she would die. In Kentucky a self described heroin addict and murderer held two teenagers hostage for thirty hours. Dennis Lucas was shot to death shortly after one hostage escaped and police decided the escape had led to a deteriorating situation (Associated Press, 1985b).

Be observant and prepared to talk over the telephone. Negotiators will ask that you be allowed on the telephone and will try to gain important information. In one case, even though the hostage knew nothing about guns, she was able to read the label off the ammunition box during the conversation to the police (Turner, 1985, 1988). They were able to confirm that the hostage taker was armed with a .357 Magnum, a very lethal weapon.

Rescues. Much has been made about rescue attempts in hostage situations. First, they are a small minority of the cases. In most cases a professionally trained negotiator, with your help, will be able to talk the hostage taker out. At times, less than 15 percent of the cases, it becomes necessary for the TACT (Tactical Action Control Team) to mount an assault. This usually happens when the negotiator feels all is going bad or when the hostage taker begins preparing to kill hostages. If a hostage is killed during the takeover, it may not elicit an assault but if he begins to seriously threaten someone after negotiations have stabilized, an assault becomes very likely. If a rescue comes expect noise and lights. The assault force will use something called flashbangs or stun grenades. These are not hand grenades. They will not kill you. The purpose is to try and use bright lights and loud noise to momentarily stun you as a deer is frozen by the headlights of your car. Also, the loud noise will lead the hostage taker to orient to the noise rather than to you. These few seconds the assault team gains may well spell the difference between your being killed by the hostage taker and their killing the hostage taker before you are killed. Try not to panic and run. The best action is to hit the floor and stay there. Put your hand either behind your head or flat on the floor. Don't get up until you are told to and raise your hands before standing.

You can survive being taken hostage. A number of hostages have indicated that there was a positive side to the experience. They felt they had been dramatically reminded of the relativity of life. They had reassessed what they felt was important and had redirected their lives toward those values. Even the worst of experiences can provide an opportunity to meet a challenge and grow.

Bibliography

Associated Press

1985a "Chicago Man Uses Toy Gun to Take Hostages." December 13.

1985b "Police Kill Gunman, Free Teen Hostages." December 31.

Dunlap, D.W.

1982 "Gunman Frees Last of Five Hostage and Surrenders." *New York Times*, December 31.

Ferman, D.

1982 "Nurse Recalls JPS Ordeal." *Short Horn*, September 22.

Ochberg, F.

1977 "The Victims of Terrorism: Psychiatric Considerations." *Terrorism*, l: 147–168.

Strentz, T.

1976 Interview with Ms. Kathy Robinson, Stewardess on TWA 355, New York City, September 20.

1979 "The Stockholm Syndrome: Law Enforcement Policy and Ego Defenses of the Hostage." *The Law Enforcement Bulletin*, April.

1984 "Preparing the Person with High Potential For Victimization as a Hostage." In J. Turner, ed. *Violence in the Medical Care Setting*. Rockville, MD: Aspen Press, pp. 183–208.

1985 "A Hostage Psychological Survival Guide." Unpublished manuscript, FBI Academy.

Turner, J.

1985 *Understanding and Managing Hostage Incidents in Health Care.* Savannah, GA: LifeStyle Management Association.

1988 *Handbook of Hospital Security and Safety*. Rockville, MD: Aspen Publishers, Inc.

17

Preventing Rape: How People Perceive the Options for Assault Prevention

Lita Furby
Baruch Fischhoff
Marcia Morgan
Eugene Research Institute, Oregon

Part of the burden imposed on women by the ever-present threat of rape consists of the decisions they must make in choosing strategies for coping with that threat. This study examines in depth the initial phase in that decision-making process, namely, how women perceive the set of possible rape prevention options. The study also examines how men and how sexual assault experts perceive the options and what they infer to be women's perceptions. Three groups of women, one group of men, and one group of sexual assault experts completed an open-ended questionnaire on rape prevention strategies. Results were coded and categorized according to a previously developed typology which distinguishes (a) the *stage* of an assault at which a strategy is directed (preventing assaults from occurring, preparing to react to an assault, or defending oneself during an assault), (b) the *level* of action involved (individual or societal), and (c) the *intended effect* of the strategy, in terms of how it is expected to prevent rape. This article presents both the general results for people's overall repertoire of strategies, along with a detailed analysis of strategies designed to prevent rape assaults from occurring. A companion article (Furby, Fischhoff, and Morgan, 1986) presents the

Support for this work has been provided by the NIMH Center for the Prevention and Control of Rape under Grant No. MH40481-02. We thank Mark Layman, Nancy Collins, and Cecelia Hagen for their invaluable assistance.

detailed results for thwarting an assault once it is underway. Results are discussed in terms of the burden that this decision making imposes on women, the locus of responsibility for preventing rape, and people's implicit theories of the causes (and effective deterrents) of rape.

The threat of rape is an ever-present stress in women's lives. Women's choice of strategies for coping with that threat should depend upon a variety of factors, including what they perceive to be the risks of rape, the effectiveness of rape prevention strategies, and the "side effects" of implementing those strategies (e.g., restrictions on nighttime social activities). The more accurate these perceptions are, the better able women will be to choose the best strategies for their particular situations. To help women with this task, various investigators have begun to study the effectiveness of rape prevention strategies (see Furby and Fischhoff, in press, for a review). Unfortunately, such research requires considerable resources and is extremely difficult. Even if the pace of research were to increase substantially, it is questionable whether accurate estimates would ever be available for all strategies and all situations. A woman's choice of strategy will, therefore, always remain something of a gamble, as she tries to select those measures that will give her the most protection with the fewest negative side effects.

A theoretical basis for identifying good gambles may be found in the theory of decision making under uncertainty (e.g., Edwards and von Winterfeldt, 1986; Fischhoff, Lichtenstein, Slovic, Derby, and Keeney, 1981; Raiffa, 1968). At its simplest level, decision theory specifies the following steps: (a) identify the set of possible strategies or "options"; (b) characterize the set of significant consequences that may follow from these options in terms of their desirability (or "utility"); (c) assess the likelihood of those consequences occurring; (d) combine all the above considerations according to a "decision rule" in order to choose the most attractive option.

Within this framework, there is no one universally best decision outcome. The optimal choice depends upon what options particular decision makers consider feasible, how they evaluate the different possible consequences, what likelihoods they assign to those consequences, and what decision rule they use. Thus, the application of decision theory would not produce unqualified advice regarding what all women should do to avoid rape—unless, of course, all women viewed their situation in the same way. One way to help women with their decision making, without imposing someone else's perspective, is to help them execute the steps of this process more adequately.

Providing such help is the domain of behavioral decision theory (Fischhoff, Svenson, and Slovic, 1987; Slovic, Lichtenstein, and Fischhoff, 1988). Research here begins by describing how people intuitively perform these tasks, followed by an attempt to build on their strengths and compensate for weaknesses. As part of a larger project using these techniques to examine how women perceive and choose rape prevention strategies, the present study examines in depth the initial phase in the decision-making process, namely, how women perceive the repertoire of possible strategies.

A decision involves a choice among options. Even when the decision is to do what one has always done or what one has been told to do, there is at least implicit rejection of other possible alternatives. As a result, the quality of a woman's decision about rape prevention strategies is bounded by the number and appropriateness of the options she considers. The process would be incomplete, for example, if she considered only strategies involving individual action (e.g., lock home doors and windows), to the exclusion of ones involving social action (e.g., change attitudes toward women and sexuality)—unless a woman *a priori* believed that all social strategies are ineffective or inappropriate. Knowing what options women already consider provides a basis for knowing what additional options might profitably be brought to their attention, for determining which options require studies of their effectiveness, and for understanding the shaping factors in this aspect of women's social reality.

A secondary focus of this study is how men perceive the options for reducing women's risk of rape. Since those individuals who perpetrate rape are male, men (even those who have never raped) may know something women do not know about possible rape prevention options. Comparing men's responses with those of women should also indicate to what extent men are aware of the burden women bear in trying to prevent rape.

Finally, this study examines how sexual assault experts perceive rape prevention options. Differences between expert and lay perceptions should suggest differences between the realities they experience. Since experts are in the business of giving advice to women, knowing where lay perceptions diverge from those of experts is essential to identifying significant options overlooked by either group and for designing effective communications between them.

Method

Data Collection

Respondents

An open-ended questionnaire was administered to five groups of volunteer respondents: (a) 43 women recruited through a university newspaper advertisement; (b) 44 women belonging to support groups for parents of young children, recruited at their regularly scheduled meetings; (c) 45 middle-aged university alumnae, recruited by mail solicitation; (d) 44 men recruited through the same university newspaper advertisement; and (e) 43 sexual assault experts (37 females and 6 males) working primarily in criminal justice, victim assistance, or private consulting, and recruited by mail solicitation. The first four groups resided in or around a medium-sized university and logging city with a tiny ethnic minority population. The sexual assault experts were located throughout the country.

The advertisement recruiting the two university groups requested subjects for "experiments in judgment and decision making." When candidates phoned to reserve a place, the women were assigned, without their knowledge, to a group that was entirely female. When they arrived for the experiment, these women were informed of its focus and allowed to answer questionnaires on a different topic (included in the same packet) if they preferred. All chose to complete the rape questionnaires. Thus, whatever self-selection pressures shaped their initial decisions to volunteer were not compounded by reticence to address these issues. The men were assigned to a group that included both men and women; men received the rape questionnaire whereas women received questionnaires on other topics (accomplished surreptitiously, so that respondents were unaware of the difference).

Members of the other three groups were informed of the questionnaire topic when initially approached to participate. They were asked to complete the questionnaire at their convenience (prior to a specified deadline) and to return it by mail. Thirty four percent of the middle-aged alumnae and 46 percent of the experts (both groups recruited by mail) returned completed questionnaires. Approximately 80 percent of the young mothers (recruited in person) returned completed questionnaires. It is unclear how the nature of the topic affected participation decisions, but returned questionnaires indicated high levels of involvement by those who participated.

The three female groups were selected to differ in age, income level, and living situation. The differences between their responses should suggest how those aspects of life experience affect women's thinking

Table 17.1

Summary of Female Groups' Characteristics

	College students (N=43)	Lower-income young mothers (N=44)	Higher-income middle-aged women (N=45)
Age			
Mean	22.6	28.1	48.8
Range	18-34	16-43	40-70
% with children	7%	100%	98%
Highest level of education achieved	93% some undergrad. college 5% some post-grad.	66% some undergrad. college 9% some post-grad.	40% some undergrad. college 60% some post-grad.
Income	No data collected	27% over $20,000/yr 48% under $15,000/yr	100% over $20,000/yr
Years of residence in county (mean)	5.0 years	11.0 years	32.6 years
Marital status	95% single	84% married	80% married
Occupation	84% students (the rest work)	32% work outside home (most of the rest are homemakers)	73% work outside home (the rest are homemakers)
Living situation	65% in dorms; co-ops; with friends 16% alone 12% w/ husband or male partner 5% w/ parents 2% w/ children only	91% w/ husband or male partner 5% w/ parents 2% w/ children only 2% w/ significant other	80% w/ husband or male partner 9% alone 9% w/ children only 2% w/ friends

about these issues. Table 17.1 presents demographic characteristics of the three female groups. The students were primarily unmarried undergraduates in their twenties; few were employed outside of school; most lived in dorms or apartments with friends. The higher-income women might be thought of as the same women 25 years later; most were married and lived with their husband or other male partner; almost all had children; almost three-quarters were working outside the home; all lived in households with incomes of $20,000 or more. The lower-income women were primarily in their twenties and thirties; all had children; most were married and lived with their husband or male partner; only a third worked outside the home; few had household incomes over $20,000 per year. The life experiences and circumstances of these groups would seem to be quite varied along dimensions that could produce differences in the perceptions of the risk of rape and strategies to prevent it.

The male respondents were similar to the female college students in most respects. They were very slightly older on average, slightly more likely to be married, and somewhat more likely to be working.

The experts had, on average, 10 years of experience in the field. Female experts described themselves as being primarily consultant/instructors or involved in community work and victim assistance. Three of the six male experts (and one woman) were primarily in offender treatment. Only one male and one female were primarily engaged in research.

Table 17.2 presents female respondents' reported rape experience, both personally and that of their close associates. Given the possibility of self-selection biases in our sample, these results cannot be taken as reflecting the prevalence of these events in the general population. However, they do show that a substantial minority of female respondents report first-hand experience with rape assault, and even more know friends and relatives who have been raped. In each case, these include substantial numbers of both stranger and acquaintance rapes. Thus, there is reason to think that rape is a significant and real consideration for these women.[1]

Table 17.2

Reported Rape Assault Experience of Respondents or Their Close Associates[1]

	Females		
	College Students	Lower-income young mothers	Higher-income middle-aged women
OWN EXPERIENCE			
Number of respondents assaulted[2]	14 (33%)	17 (39%)	11 (24%)
by stranger	5 (12%)	9 (21%)	2 (4%)
by known person	13 (30%)	13 (30%)	9 (20%)
KNOWLEDGE OF FRIENDS/RELATIVES' EXPERIENCE			
Number of respondents who know of at least one friend or relative who has been assaulted	30 (70%)	29 (66%)	20 (44%)
by stranger	26 (61%)	22 (50%)	12 (27%)
by known person	16 (37%)	21 (48%)	9 (20%)

[1] Responses to: (a) Have you ever been the victim of a rape or an attempted rape by a stranger [someone you know]? (b) How many of your close acquaintances (personal friends or relatives) can you think of who have been the victim of a rape or an attempted rape by a stranger [someone they know]?

[2] Some respondents had been raped by both a stranger and a person known to them.

Questionnaires

The questions analyzed here asked respondents to list as many rape prevention measures as they could. The first half of the questionnaire focused on strategies for preventing rape assaults from occurring; the second half asked about strategies for stopping an assault once it is under way. Each half began with questions specific to the individual (i.e., "We would like to know what things you personally do, or have done to reduce the chances of being raped") and then proceeded to more general questions (i.e., "We are also interested in rape prevention measures that you do not use yourself but which might be appropriate for someone else"). Once respondents exhausted the store of strategies that came to mind spontaneously, they were presented various prompts. One prompt stressed societal measures (i.e., "We would like you to think about measures that are not individual actions, but rather are things that can be done by groups of individuals or by society as a whole to reduce the chances of women being raped"). Others focused on actions by individuals in specific situations (e.g., "A woman and man are riding an elevator in a downtown office building"). For the male and expert groups, questions about individual strategies were reworded slightly to ask what they think a woman typically does or could do to reduce her risk of being raped (rather than what they personally do). Table 17.3 presents the full text of the questions.

Data Analysis

Fischhoff, Furby, and Morgan (1986) describe the procedure for coding strategies and present a comprehensive list of strategies derived from applying that procedure to these questionnaires and to the popular literature on rape prevention. In general, the coding system maintains relatively fine distinctions among strategies, in order to respect any differences that may affect women's usage decisions. For example, "do not walk downtown" and "do not walk downtown at night" appear as separate strategies. Further research may show that some of the strategies that appear separately in our canonical list are distinguished neither in women's minds nor in their ability to prevent rape. However, retaining their separate identities for the present maintains the option for further empirical clarification (albeit at the price of maintaining a somewhat cumbersome list and including nonexclusive entries).

These generic 1,140 strategies were categorized according to the typology in Table 17.4. In it, each strategy is expressed in terms of a "strategy grammar" of the form "Doing *action* X in order to achieve *intended effect* Y [which is believed to deter rape]." In this view, a strategy

Table 17.3

Rape Prevention Questions[1]

PART I

All of the questions in this part concern *rape prevention measures,* that is, ways of reducing the chances that a rape attempt will ever occur. They do *not* concern ways of dealing with a rape attack once it has begun—Part II will focus on that issue. Please remember this distinction when answering the questions below.

RAPE PREVENTION—MEASURES

A. Most women take some measures to minimize the chances of being raped. These measures range from everyday habits to things done only in special situations. They include steps that are taken deliberately after much thought, and steps that are taken routinely almost without thinking.

We would like to know what things *you personally* do, or have done to reduce the chances of being raped. We are interested in as complete a list as possible, so please take your time, and number each of your answers as you go. (If you feel that you do not take any special steps to reduce your chances of being raped, please indicate that.)

B. We are also interested in rape prevention measures that you do not use yourself but which might be appropriate for someone else. Here, think about things that you have considered doing but choose not to do, things that you have considered doing but have not yet done, things that you have heard other people talk about doing, and things that you have read about. Again, we are interested in as complete a list as possible.

C. Are there any other measures that you think can help reduce women's risk of being raped?

D1. Please read the following brief description of a situation in which a woman could be sexually assaulted. Does it remind you of any *additional* rape prevention measures that you have not already listed in any of the questions above? If so, please list them in the space provided below.

A woman and man are riding an elevator in a downtown office building.

D2. Now consider this next situation. If it calls to mind any further measures one might take to reduce the chances of being raped, please list them below.

A man comes to the door saying he is a representative of the gas company and needs to check the furnace.

D3. Now consider this situation. If it calls to mind any further measures one might take to reduce the chances of being raped, please list them below.

A woman who is home alone for the evening is visited by a male friend. He begins physically forcing himself on her.

E. Finally, we would like you to think about measures that are not individual actions, but rather are things that can be done by groups of individuals or by society as a whole to reduce the chances of women being raped. You may have listed some of these already. Please list here any additional societal measures that come to mind. Think of things that you've been involved in, things that you've heard about others being involved in, and things that you just think would be a good idea.

PART II

Now we would like you to think about ways of dealing with a rape attack *once it starts to occur.* Unlike Part I which dealt with preventing assaults from ever getting started, all of the

---

[1] Questions are presented here first as they were worded for female respondents (with answer space omitted). Male and expert variations appear in the last section of the table.

questions in this part concern the ways a woman can deal with an attack *once it begins*. Please keep this in mind when answering the questions below.

SELF-DEFENSE—MEASURES

R. Imagine that *you personally* are the victim of a rape attempt. Think about what you might do in such a situation. That is what kinds of things do you think you would do to try to keep from being raped and to stop the assault? We are interested in as complete a list as possible, so please take your time and try to think of all the various things you think you would do in case of a rape attack. If you think that some self-defense measures depend on the situation, feel free to indicate those specific conditions in your responses. (If you would not try to stop the assault, exactly what would you do—how would you describe your way of dealing with the situation?)

S. We are also interested in things that you wouldn't do yourself but which might be appropriate for someone else when confronted with a rape attack. Here, think about things that you might consider doing but probably wouldn't actually do, things that you have heard other people talk about doing, or things that you have read about. Again, we are interested in as complete a list as possible.

T. Is there anything else you can think of that a woman might do in dealing with a rape attempt? Think especially about things that might not necessarily stop the rape, but which a woman would do for other reasons.

U1. Please read the following brief description of a situation in which a man attempts to rape a woman. Does it remind you of any *additional* resistance measures that you have not already listed above, that is, anything else that might be done to stop the rape from being completed? If so, please list them in the space provided.

A woman living alone awakens to hear someone breaking into her bedroom window. She wishes there were a man in the house she could call to for protection.

U2. Now consider this next rape attempt situation. If it calls to mind any *further* measures a woman might take to protect herself, please list them below.

A woman is accosted on the sidewalk and is forced into a nearby car. As she struggles and resists, the attacker tells concerned passers-by that "we're just having a family disagreement."

Z3. Finally, after having thought about the threat of rape during the course of answering this questionnaire, do you have anything else to add with respect to what can be done to reduce or eliminate this problem in our society?

The following questions were worded slightly differently for the *male and expert groups*.

A. We would like to know what things you think women typically do to reduce the chances of being raped. We are interested in as complete a list as possible, so please take your time, and number each of your answers as you go.

B. We are also interested in any additional rape prevention measures that you think women could take but that few, if any of them, actually do. Here, think especially about things women may be reluctant to do, things whose effectiveness they may underestimate, and things they may not even be aware of. Again, we are interested in as complete a list as possible.

R. Imagine that a woman is the victim of a rape attempt. Think about what she might typically do in such a situation. That is, what kinds of things do you think a woman normally would do to try to stop the assault? If you think that some self-defense measures depend on the situation, feel free to indicate those specific conditions in your responses. Also, include ways of dealing with the attack that are not necessarily designed to stop the assault but still reflect some women's ways of handling the situation. We are interested in as complete a list as possible, so please take your time and try to think of all the various things women normally would do in case of a rape attack.

S. We are also interested in things that you think women could do but that few, if any of them, actually do. Here, think about things that women may be reluctant to do, things whose effectiveness they may underestimate, and things they may not even be aware of. Again, we are interested in as complete a list as possible.

may be ineffective either because it fails to produce the intended effect or because that effect does not deter rape assaults. Of course, a strategy may have more than one possible intended effect; our categorizing procedures placed each strategy according to what was judged to be its primary intended effect. The typology further distinguishes (a) the *stage* of an assault at which a strategy is directed: preventing an assault from occurring, preparing to react to an assault, or defending oneself during an assault, and (b) the *level* of action involved: individual or societal. Fischhoff, Furby, and Morgan (1986) describe the rationale and application of this scheme in greater detail.

Results and Discussion

Organization

The following discussion of results initially considers people's overall repertoire of rape prevention strategies by examining the number and types of strategies mentioned by respondents in all parts of the questionnaire. The remainder of this article then considers the specific strategies that people think women use to keep rape assaults from being initiated. A companion article (Furby, Fischhoff, and Morgan, 1986) examines the specific strategies that people think women use to thwart an assault (where the intent is rape) once it has commenced.

The questions that described specific situations to respondents (D1, D2, D3, U1, and U2 in Table 17.3) were intended to investigate the effects of such memory prompts on strategy production. Unless otherwise indicated, the responses to these questions are considered only in the section devoted specifically to that topic.

Overall Analyses

Total Mentions

The first column of Table 17.5 presents the total number of different rape prevention strategies mentioned by respondents in each group over all of the general (i.e., non-prompted) questions. In each case, the number of strategies is strikingly large. The pooled knowledge of any one of the relatively homogeneous female groups includes more than 300 different measures. This is a daunting number of options to consider. The lower-income young mothers produced slightly more strategies than the other two female groups. It may be that lower-income women are exposed not only to a greater risk of rape (McDermott, 1979) but also to a wider variety of risky situations (e.g., taking public transportation at night), making them familiar with a larger repertoire of strategies.

The three female groups combined mentioned a total of 569 different strategies, an even more overwhelming option array. In it, there was moderate overlap among the strategies raised by each of these different populations. Approximately one-quarter of the strategies mentioned by each group were not mentioned at all by the other two groups, suggesting that the differences in their life experiences and circumstances made them familiar with somewhat different strategies.

Females as a group mentioned only slightly fewer strategies than did experts. However, there were three times as many respondents in the female group, and each of the three subgroups of females (which were the same size as the expert group) mentioned considerably fewer strategies than did the experts. One possible interpretation is that lay women and experts are equally well informed about the rape prevention strategies appropriate to any particular living situation; however, experts deal with a broader set of situations than do the women in any one of these groups.

Perhaps surprisingly, the males produced about as many strategies as the comparable group of females. This suggests that the pooled knowledge of this relatively homogeneous group of males regarding rape prevention is almost as broad as that of a comparable group of females.

Mean Number of Strategies

Table 17.5 also presents the mean number of strategies mentioned per respondent, separately for the three stages of assault at which a strategy can be directed (see Table 17.4 typology). On average, females produced somewhat more strategies than did males, with the difference most pronounced for Stage I, preventing assaults from occurring. Given the similar diversity of strategies produced by these two college groups, this difference in individual strategy production may reflect either a difference in the degree to which each groups' pooled knowledge is shared by its members or simply a difference in effort (males averaging about 22 different strategies for the three stages combined, females about 26). By contrast, the average expert produced almost twice as many strategies, with the difference again being greatest for Stage I. Although experts' pooled knowledge of different strategy options was only slightly greater than that of females, either the experts' group knowledge is more widely shared among its members or they are simply willing to work harder (averaging almost 50 strategies for the three stages combined).

Table 17.4

Rape Prevention Strategy Typology[1] *(with verbatim examples from respondents, preceded by hyphen)*

I. Prevent Assault from Ever Occurring

A. Societal Action

1. Reduce visibility of women to potential assailant (measures intended to prevent him from ever seeing a woman or knowing of her existence)
2. Reduce accessibility of women to potential assailant (measures intended to maintain a physical barrier or distance between woman and assailant, given that he knows of her existence)
   —provide safehouses
   —law forbidding hitchhiking
3. Increase women's perceived ability to cope with potential assailant if assault were to take place
   —set up dog escort services
   —publicize that there are rape resistance study groups and self-defense courses for women (so rapists will know)
4. Increase perceived chances of outside intervention if assault were to take place
   —put emergency sounding devices on every block
   —set up neighborhood watch programs
5. Increase perceived chances of punishment if assault were to take place
   —make laws against marital rape
   —encourage your community to set up a rape crisis center
6. Reduce men's propensity to rape
   —have complete psychological rehabilitation for rapists
   —therapy for men who are lacking in self-confidence
7. Increase women's ability to implement prevention measures successfully
   —public school education programs for females on rape prevention
   —post notices on bulletin boards and in newspapers of rape prevention clinics
8. Alter societal beliefs and attitudes that promote rape
   —portray rape as a violent crime, not as a crime of passion
   —change attitude that sex is a commodity
9. Alter structural characteristics of society that promote rape
   —eliminate poverty
   —full employment in the country

B. Individual Action

1. Reduce visibility of women to potential assailant
   —avoid dangerous neighborhoods
   —do not hang around bus terminals
2. Reduce accessibility of women to potential assailant
   —do not hitchhike
   —move to a place with a doorman
3. Increase perceived ability to cope with assailant if assault were to take place
   —when approached by a stranger, make direct eye contact
   —when entering house, let dog in first to scare person
4. Increase perceived chances of outside intervention if assault were to take place
   —do not drive alone

---

[1] Adapted from Fischhoff, Furby, and Morgan (1986).

—fake presence of others

5. Increase perceived chances of punishment if assault were to take place
   —wear identifying armband to designate membership in rape prevention group
   —report known rapists/press charges
6. Reduce potential assailant's propensity to rape
   —don't wear tight or revealing clothes
   —women should be available for proper relationships and willing to go on dates
7. Manage yourself in ways that increase ability to implement prevention measures successfully
   —get educated about high risk situations
   —notice other people's behavior
8. Contribute to societal action
   —be involved in political action
   —encourage setting up or participate in rape crisis center

II. Prepare for Reacting to an Assault

A. Societal Action

1. Increase women's ability to cope with assailant in the event of an assault
   —inform women about common elements in rape assaults
   —whistles, batons, and other defensive weapons provided by police departments
2. Increase chances of outside intervention in the event of an assault
   —set up escort services
   —public transportation buses should run later in the evening

B. Individual Action

1. Increase ability to cope with assailant in the event of an assault
   —own a dog
   —learn self-defense
2. Increase chances of outside intervention in the event of an assault
   —install burglar alarm system
   —carry noisemaker

III. Defend Yourself During an Assault

(A. Societal Action—not applicable)

B. Individual Action

1. Manage yourself in ways that maximize your ability to implement self-defense measures successfully
   —do not faint or pass out
   —assess attacker's personality
2. Reduce/minimize assailant's propensity to rape
   —do crude, unfeminine things
   —make him see you as a human
3. Increase perceived ability to cope with assailant
   —make it known you have a weapon
   —clear verbal resistance
4. Increase perceived chances of outside intervention
   —fake arrival of others
5. Increase actual chances of outside intervention
   —yell "fire"
   —summon nearest male
6. Increase perceived chances of punishment
   —state you will press charges against attacker
7. Establish distance or barrier between self and assailant
   —get out of house
   —run away
8. Physically impede or incapacitate assailant
   —incapacitate him with drugs or alcohol
   —kick

Intended Effects

Table 17.6 shows the percentage of respondents mentioning at least one strategy for each intended effect in the strategy typology of Table 17.4. The three columns on the left contrast the females, males, and experts. The three on the right contrast the three groups of females.

Females. Six societal action categories are relatively widely known, being mentioned by at least one-third of the women. The most widely mentioned societal category is a rather general one that actually places the ultimate responsibility for preventing rape on individuals: increasing women's ability to implement prevention measures successfully (e.g., public awareness and educational programs). Two other frequently mentioned categories have as their intended effects eliminating men's basic motivation to rape: altering societal beliefs and attitudes that promote rape (e.g., sexist and sex-role attitudes) and reducing men's propensity to rape (e.g., rehabilitation for rapists). The other three most widely mentioned societal categories assume that at least some men will want to rape. Their intended effect is to convince a potential rapist that the expected payoff of a rape assault is low: increasing the perceived chances of punishment for rapists, increasing the perceived chances of outside intervention (e.g., escort services, police patrols), and

Table 17.5

Number of Different Strategies Mentioned

		Mean per Respondent		
Respondent Group	Group Total	I Prevent assault from ever occurring	II Prepare for reacting to assault	III Defend yourself during an assault
Females	569	13.56	3.95	8.83
College students	325	13.51	4.00	8.93
Lower-income young mothers	374	13.47	3.80	7.93
Higher-income middle-aged women	311	13.70	4.07	9.66
Males	307	10.20*	3.27	8.68
Experts	607	26.49**	5.88**	15.21**

* = significantly different from mean for females in the same column at p<.05
** = p<.001.

increasing the perceived ability of women to cope with an assailant (e.g., teach females to be more assertive/confident).

More individual action than societal action categories are relatively widely mentioned (12 of the former compared to 6 of the latter were mentioned by at least one-third of the women). Since one of the questions asked specifically about societal strategies, this difference cannot be interpreted as reflecting what comes to mind spontaneously when the general topic of rape prevention strategies is mentioned, but rather must reflect an actual difference in the numbers of societal and individual strategies known to these respondents. Of course, the emphasis on individual actions reflects, in part, the impossibility of societal action to thwart most assaults once they have commenced—a woman is usually on her own at that point. In this sense, societal actions are only applicable to Stages I and II. However, the relatively greater emphasis on individual strategies compared to societal ones is consistent with the general crime prevention literature showing that urban residents report using many more individual than societal crime prevention measures (Warren, Harlow, and Rosentraub, 1982; Warren, Rosentraub, and Harlow, 1984).

The six most widely known individual action categories were each mentioned by at least 80 percent of the women, and all implicitly assume that at least some men will want to rape. Of them, four focus on how a woman deals with an actual assault: increasing her ability to cope with the assailant, physically impeding or incapacitating the assailant, reducing the assailant's propensity to rape, and obtaining outside intervention. The other two are designed to prevent an assault from ever occurring: increasing the perceived chances of outside intervention and reducing the accessibility of a woman to a potential assailant (i.e., maintaining a barrier or distance between them).

Differences among the three female groups were remarkably few, with most of them distinguishing the college students from the other two groups. Societal strategies designed to convince a potential rapist that the woman could thwart an assault were more widely known among college students, whereas individual strategies designed to reduce a woman's visibility or accessibility and those designed to increase the chances of outside intervention in the event of an assault were less widely known among this group.

Males and Experts. The categories widely known to men were remarkably similar to those widely known to women. Results for experts, on the other hand, were often rather different. All in all, experts are aware of strategies that include a wider variety of intended effects. One notable feature of their results is their greater awareness of societal

Table 17.6

Percent of Respondents Who Mentioned Each Category

All Females	Males	Experts		Females: College students	Females: Lower-income young mothers	Females: Higher-income middle-aged women
			I. Prevent assault from ever occurring **A. Societal Action**			
0	0	0	1. Reduce visibility of women to potential assailant (measures intended to prevent him from ever seeing the woman or knowing of her existence)	0	0	0
11	14	12	2. Reduce accessibility of women to potential assailant (measures intended to maintain a physical barrier or distance between the woman and assailant, given that he knows of her existence)	9	14	11
32	32	44	3. Increase women's perceived ability to cope with potential assailant if assault were to take place	51	25	20**
39	45	35	4. Increase perceived chances of outside intervention if assault were to take place	58	41	18**
52	57	58	5. Increase perceived chances of punishment if assault were to take place	56	52	49
**45	36	81	6. Reduce men's propensity to rape	53	41	40
62	48	63	7. Increase women's ability to implement prevention measures successfully	70	59	58

Note: A difference of approximately 20% between any two percentages is significant at p<.05, and a difference of approximately 30% is significant at p<.01 (precise values vary with the absolute percentages). For comparisons involving All Females combined (N = 132), somewhat smaller differences are signficant.

** = at least one group difference of 30% or more.

* = at least one group difference of 20–29%.

Table 17.6 (continued)

**47	48	91	8. Alter societal beliefs and attitudes that promote rape	56	41	44
*8	7	28	9. Alter structural characteristics of society that promote rape	12	7	4
			B. Individual Action			
*48	48	70	1. Reduce visibility of the woman to potential assailant	33	59	51*
**85	48	95	2. Reduce accessibility of the woman to potential assailant	67	89	98**
*56	48	70	3. Increase perceived ability to cope with assailant if assault were to take place	67	50	51
96	98	84	4. Increase perceived chances of outside intervention if assault were to take place	100	98	91
*28	32	51	5. Increase perceived chances of punishment if assault were to take place	37	27	20
29	32	40	6. Reduce potential assailant's propensity to rape	37	20	29
60**	48	91	7. Manage yourself in ways that increase ability to implement prevention measures successfully	65	57	58
8**	5	53	8. Contribute to societal action	7	11	7
			II. Prepare for reacting to an assault			
			A. Societal Action			
23	20	28	1. Increase women's ability to cope with assailant in the event of an assault	21	27	22
5	9	9	2. Increase chances of outside intervention in the event of an assault	2	5	7
			B. Individual Action			
98	95	88	1. Increase women's ability to cope with assailant in the event of an assault	98	100	96
43	36	53	2. Increase chances of outside intervention in the event of an assault	25	48	56**

Table 17.6 (continued)

			III. Defend yourself during an assault **(A. Societal Action—not applicable)** **B. Individual Action**			
**32	52	79	1. Manage yourself in ways that maximize ability to implement self-defense measures successfully	42	30	24
90	84	91	2. Reduce/minimize assailant's propensity to rape	93	95	82
**28	36	70	3. Increase perceived ability to cope with assailant	37	23	24
16	14	28	4. Increase perceived chances of outside intervention	9	20	18
84	89	91	5. Increase actual chances of outside intervention	84	80	89
2	2	5	6. Increase perceived chances of punishment	2	0	4
**60	55	77	7. Establish distance or barrier between self and assailant	65	73	42**
97	100	98	8. Physically impede or incapacitate assailant	93	98	100

steps designed to eliminate men's basic motivation to rape (reducing men's propensity to rape, altering beliefs and attitudes that promote rape, and altering structural aspects of society that promote rape). They also showed much more awareness of individual actions that women can take that contribute to societal rape prevention efforts.

Individual Strategies

Table 17.6 dealt with general possibilities for rape prevention at all stages. Table 17.7 narrows the focus from categories to particular strategies, from possibilities to perceived actualities (in the sense of strategies that women are believed actually to undertake), and from all stages of rape prevention to preventing assaults from being initiated. Specifically, Table 17.7 lists the strategies mentioned by at least 20 percent of any of the respondent groups in response to questions about what women do to prevent assaults from occurring.

One striking feature of this list is that almost all of these strategies assume that the assailant is a stranger (with two possible exceptions being, "Learn self-defense" and "Do not go to or be in secluded spots with a male"). This is remarkable, given that approximately half of rape assaults are committed by acquaintances (U.S. Dept. of Justice, 1985), and the fact that more than twice as many female respondents reported being assaulted by acquaintances as reported being assaulted by strangers (Table 17.2). Apparently neither lay women and men nor experts recognize the relatively high frequency of acquaintance rape, or if they do, they see women as doing relatively little to protect themselves against it.

A second striking feature of Table 17.7 is the preponderance of strategies directed at rape assaults taking place out of doors. The only exceptions are keeping one's home locked and, perhaps, learning self-defense and owning a dog. Given that at least a third of reported rapes occur inside the home or some other building (U.S. Dept. of Justice, 1985), this result suggests that either people underestimate the risk of rape indoors or they know of relatively few things that women do to protect themselves against rape indoors.

Females. A third striking feature of the results is that, for female respondents, the five specific strategies most frequently mentioned in response to questions about what women do to prevent assaults from occurring are actually Stage II strategies. That is, they are not strategies that prevent an assault from being initiated (Stage I) but rather ones that prepare a woman to react once an assault commences. All in all, however, these women mentioned less than half as many Stage II as Stage I strategies (see Table 17.8, column 1). Thus, strategies designed to prepare for reacting to an assault are fewer in number but seem to be especially salient for women, even when they are asked specifically for strategies designed to prevent assaults from occurring.

Males. Relative to these females, males mentioned on the average about half as many things that women do to prevent rape assaults from occurring (Table 17.8), even though as a group they were aware of a similarly long list of possibilities (above). In addition to this general tendency to see women as doing fewer things, fewer men than women mentioned most of the specific strategies. Aside from the Stage II strategies, this was particularly true for strategies intended to reduce a woman's accessibility. In summary form, this can be seen in the lower portion of Table 17.8, where only 15 percent of all strategies mentioned by men fell into this latter category, compared with 28 percent of those mentioned by women. Particular examples can be seen in men's failure to mention various locking activities. Perhaps they overlook the details of women's self-protection rituals; perhaps they are unaware of how specifically those behaviors are directed at preventing rape (as opposed to other crimes). The only strategy mentioned by substantially more men than women is one designed to secure outside intervention—staying in well-lit areas.

Table 17.7

What People Think Women Do To Prevent Rape Assaults From Occurring[1]

CATEGORY[2] Stage-Level-Intended Effect	STRATEGY	Percent who mentioned strategy (rank order in parentheses)[3] RESPONDENT GROUP Females	Males	Experts
II-i-increase ability to cope$_a$	CARRY SPRAY CHEMICAL, LIKE MACE	63.6	29.5 (3)	30.2 (6/7)
II-i-increase ability to cope$_a$	LEARN SELF-DEFENSE	56.1	34.1 (1/2)	46.5 (2)
II-i-increase ability to cope$_a$	GET/OWN/BE WITH DOG FOR PROTECTION(FOR WARNING, ATTACK, ETC.)	43.2	18.2 (8/9)	23.3 (12/15)
II-i-increase ability to cope$_a$	CARRY KEYS IN YOUR HAND WHEN GOING TO YOUR CAR OR HOME	31.8	2.3 (42/92)	18.6 (21/23)
II-i-increase ability to cope$_a$	HAVE/CARRY SOMETHING TO USE AS A WEAPON	31.1	13.6 (11/13)	25.6 (11)
I-i-outside intervention$_p$	DO NOT WALK ALONE AT NIGHT/ IN THE DARK	31.1	27.3 (4/5)	14.0 (26/31)
I-i-reduce accessibility	LOCK DOORS IN YOUR HOME	30.3	11.4 (14/16)	48.8 (1)
I-i-increase ability to cope$_p$	APPEAR CONFIDENT (LOOK AGGRESSIVE, STRONG, AND ALERT)	27.3	22.7 (6/7)	27.9 (8/10)
I-i-outside intervention$_p$	DO NOT GO OUT (BE OUT) ALONE AT NIGHT	25.0	18.2 (8/9)	32.6 (4/5)
II-i-outside intervention$_p$	CARRY WHISTLE (BUT NOT AROUND THE NECK)	24.2	11.4 (14/16)	11.6 (32/36)

[1] Strategies mentioned by at least 20% in one or more groups, to questions A and B (females) or A (males & experts). A difference between the females and either of the other two groups of approximatelly 20% is significant at $p<.01$.

[2] Stage codes: I = prevent assault from occurring; II = prepare for reacting to an assault; III = defend yourself during an assault. Action level codes: s = societal action; i = individual action. Intended effect subscripts: p = perceived; a = actual. See Fischhoff, Furby, and Morgan (1986) for a fuller description of the category system.

[3] Tied ranks are indicated by giving the range of ranks that are tied (e.g., 42/92 means that there were 51 strategies all mentioned with the same frequency and thus tied for the 42nd through 92nd slots).

[4] Ordering shifts to frequency of citation by experts.

[5] Ordering shifts to frequency of citation by men.

Table 17.7 (continued)

I-i-reduce accessibility	LOCK CAR DOORS	23.5	4.5 (23/41)	30.2 (6/7)
I-i-reduce accessibility	LOCK YOUR CAR DOORS WHEN YOU ARE IN THE CAR	22.0	0	2.3 (141/286)
I-i-reduce accessibility	ALWAYS CHECK REAR SEAT AND FLOOR OF CAR FOR INTRUDERS BEFORE ENTERING IT.	21.2	0	27.9 (8/10)
I-i-manage self	BE AWARE OF YOUR SURROUNDINGS	20.5	4.5 (23/41)	23.3 (12/15)
I-i-outside intervention$_p$	TAKE POPULATED ROUTES. AVOID ISOLATED,DARK NON-POPULATED ALLEYS, PARKS, BUSHES, DOORWAYS, VACANT LOTS, AND DARK PARKING AREAS	20.5	22.7 (6/7)	16.3 (24/25)[4]
I-i-outside intervention$_p$	GO OUT WITH FRIEND OR TWO FOR PROTECTION	19.7 (16)	27.3 (4/5)	37.2 (3)
I-i-reduce accessibility	LOCK ALL WINDOWS	9.1 (29.32)	2.3 (42/92)	32.6 (4/5)
I-i-reduce accessibility	DO NOT HITCHHIKE	3.8 (60/69)	0	27.9 (8/10)
I-i-reduce visibility	AVOID AREAS THAT ARE DANGEROUS OR MAKE YOU FEEL UNSAFE	12.1 (23/24)	13.6 (11/13)	23.3 (12/15)
I-i-reduce accessibility	NEVER PICK UP HITCHIKERS (ESPECIALLY MALE)	11.4 (25/26)	2.3 (42/92)	23.3 (12/15)
I-i-reduce accessibility	ONLY LET PEOPLE YOU KNOW VERY WELL IN YOUR HOME	9.1 (29/32)	0	20.9 (16/20)
I-i-outside intervention$_p$	DO NOT GO TO OR BE IN SECLUDED SPOTS WITH A MALE, ESPECIALLY WITH SOMEONE YOU DO NOT KNOW WELL, MAKES YOU FEEL UNCOMFORTABLE, OR DO NOT TRUST (INCLUDING YOUR HOME)	6.8 (42/44)	2.3 (42/92)	20.9 (16/20)
I-i-reduce accessibility	INSTALL OR MAKE SURE THERE ARE SPECIAL LOCKS OR BARS ON THE WINDOWS	3.8 (60/69)	0	20.9 (16/20)
I-i-reduce accessibility	INSTALL OR MAKE SURE THERE ARE SPECIAL LOCKS OR BARS ON THE DOORS	3.8 (60/69)	2.3 (42/92)	20.9 (16/20)
I-i-manage self	DO NOT TRUST OR TALK TO STRANGERS (E.G., ON THE STREET, WHEN ALONE, IN PUBLIC)	12.1 (23/24)	11.4 (14/16)	20.9[5] (16/20)
I-i-outside intervention$_p$	WALK/TAKE WELL-LIT AREAS (AT NIGHT)	14.4 (20/21)	34.1 (1/2)	4.7 (70/105)

Experts. On the average, experts mentioned considerably more strategies than did females, suggesting that they think women do more than women actually do do to prevent rape assaults from occurring. Overall (Table 17.8), a somewhat higher proportion of the strategies that experts attributed to women involved reducing accessibility; a somewhat lower portion pertained to increasing perceived or actual ability to cope with the assailant.

Given the experts' generally higher strategy production rate, any cases in Table 17.7 where considerably fewer experts mentioned a particular strategy are notable. Aside from several Stage II strategies, there was only one such instance: locking car doors when you are in the car. It is not readily apparent why this particular strategy is less widely known among experts than among lay women.

What Women Say They Themselves Do

Although the males and experts were asked only about others' behavior, the females provided both strategies that they used (question A, Table 17.3) and strategies that they believed other women (but not themselves) use (question B, Table 17.3). Table 17.9 presents the most common specific strategies that women report using personally to prevent rape assaults from occurring. Here, a variety of categories are salient, and preparation for reacting to assault does not dominate as it did in Table 17.7. Table 17.10 clarifies this discrepancy. It shows the most frequently mentioned specific strategies that women think others use but they themselves do not use. All consist of Stage II strategies, and four of the top five strategies in Table 17.7 appear here. Thus, the apparent emphasis on preparation for reacting to an assault derives mostly from these strategies that at least some women explicitly decide not to use (insofar as they are aware of them but do not use them). Only a small number of women say they actually do these things themselves.

On average, the number of things that women think that others do but which they do not was half as large as the number of things they do themselves to prevent rape (means = 3.99, 7.93). The apparent rejection of these strategies may simply reflect a denial (conscious or unconscious) of the personal threat of assault (and thus of the need to take concrete preventive measures). The most frequently rejected strategies (Table 17.10), may simply require greater expenditures of money (to buy spray chemicals, a dog, a gun) or time (to take a self-defense course, to care for a dog) than many women are willing to make. In the case of "learning self-defense," it may also be that many women may feel inadequate to implement physical resistance (even if they were to receive instruction): Riger and Gordon (1981) found that 63 percent of their three-city sample of women thought they were less competent physically than both the average man *and* the average woman.

There were few differences among the three female groups with respect to specific strategies that they themselves use. The most notable (greater than 20 percent) were that college students mentioned appearing confident more frequently than did the other two groups, whereas the latter more often mentioned several home- and car-locking strategies.

By comparing the results of Table 17.9 (what women say they personally do to prevent rape assaults from occurring) with those for males in Table 17.7 (what males think women do), it can be seen that considerably fewer females say they learn self-defense, walk in well-lit areas at night, and carry spray chemicals than men think women do these things. The first and last of these are Stage II strategies, which are known also to a much larger number of women than actually use them. In contrast, males seem particularly unaware of strategies women use to reduce accessibility when using a car. At the level of intended effects (Table 17.8), a larger percentage of the strategies that men think women use are designed to increase outside intervention (compared to what women say they do), whereas a smaller percentage are intended to reduce accessibility. Either women are not aware of the degree to which they depend on the help of others (particularly men) to protect them, or men exaggerate this dependence.

In comparison with what women say they do (Table 17.9), experts are more likely to mention learning self-defense, carrying spray chemicals, and having/carrying a weapon (i.e., to prepare for coping with an assault). Many more experts are aware of these Stage II strategies than are women; fewer women actually use them. At the level of intended effects, however, experts' perceptions of the types of strategies women undertake are quite similar to what women say they do (Table 17.8).

Table 17.11 shows the specific strategies mentioned most frequently by males or by experts as measures that women could but do not generally take to prevent rape assaults from occurring. Males emphasize strategies intended to increase a woman's ability to cope with an assault. Remarkably, five of the six most frequently male-advised strategies are also those most frequently mentioned by women as things they know other women do but they do not do themselves (Table 17.10). Thus, these men advise women to use Stage II strategies that many women apparently consider but decide not to use. Experts advise strategies designed to increase both perceived and actual ability to cope with an assailant, and to improve managing oneself. In contrast to the males, experts advise only two strategies that are things many women consider but chose not to do.

Table 17.8

Number and Distribution by Category of Strategies People Think Individual Women Use to Prevent Rape Assaults from Occurring[1]

	Means Females	Males	Experts	What women say they do
Overall	11.61	5.75**	14.75***	7.93
Stage[2]				
Prevent assault from ever occurring	7.77	4.20	11.33	6.61
Prepare for reacting to an assault	3.34	1.41	3.00	1.15
		Distribution by Category		
Intended Effect[3]				
Reduce accessibility of the woman to potential assailant	28%	15%	34%	34%
Increase perceived or actual ability to cope with assailant[4]	32%	31%	21%	27%
Increase perceived or actual chances of outside intervention[4]	26%	36%	22%	22%
Reduce visibility of the woman to potential assailant	5%	6%	8%	6%
Manage yourself to better implement prevention strategy	5%	6%	10%	6%
Reduce potential assailant's propensity to rape	3%	5%	3%	4%
Contribute to social action	0%	0%	1%	0%
Increase perceived chances of punishment	0%	0%	0%	0%

[1] Responses to questions A & B (females) or question A (males and experts), Table 17.3.

[2] A small number of Stage III strategies (those designed to defend yourself during an assault) were mentioned. They are omitted from these category analyses (but are included in the overall total accounting).

[3] Stages I and II combined.

[4] Although our typology distinguishes between *perceived* and *actual* ability to cope (or, chances of outside intervention), many strategies that do one also do the other, making the assignment of a given strategy to one category or the other often problematic. Thus, for the purpose of this analysis, the two types of categories were combined.

** = significantly different from females at p<.01

*** = p<.001

Situational Prompts

After the general questions regarding strategies for preventing rape assaults from occurring (questions A, B, and C in Table 17.3), respondents were asked whether three specific situations (questions D1, D2, and D3), reminded them of any additional rape prevention strategies. The situations were fairly common occurrences: a woman riding in an elevator; a utility representative coming to the door; a male friend visiting when a woman is home alone.

The effect of these prompts on strategy production was considerable. The female respondents produced an additional 75 strategies, the males 63, and the experts 69. The most frequent of these included: do not enter elevator alone with a strange man; when in an elevator, stand near the controls; check salesman/repairman's identification before letting him in your house; let only people who you know very well in your home ; tell a male friend to leave you alone. Several of these were mentioned by more than half of the respondents, suggesting that they are by no means obscure or little known strategies. Thus, even when people are encouraged to take their time and to think of as many measures as possible for preventing rape assaults from occurring, there are apparently quite a few strategies that require the cues of a specific situation to be recalled.

Conclusion

The threat of rape imposes an enormous burden on women. One aspect of that burden is defined by the ways in which women's efforts at self-protection limit their freedom and foster a docile, dependent role (e.g., Brownmiller, 1975; Griffin, 1981; Riger and Gordon, 1981). A second aspect is the attention and energy that women must devote to deciding which of the enormous array of prevention options to implement. Just enumerating the possibilities is daunting, not to mention thinking about how to implement them, following public discussion of their relative effectiveness, and pondering their possible side effects.

Even women themselves seem to be unaware of the size of this burden. When asked to produce rape prevention strategies, the average woman in our study was able to list only a small portion of the things that other women drawn from the same population report doing to prevent rape. The large number of additional strategies elicited by the mention of relatively common situations suggests that our respondents were unable to bring to mind spontaneously even many strategies that they themselves routinely consider. Not surprisingly, men are even less aware of women's decision burden, mentioning on the average only

Table 17.9

What Women Say They Do to Prevent Rape Assaults from Occurring[1]

CATEGORY[2] Stage-Level-Intended Effect	STRATEGY	Percent Who Mentioned Strategy
II-i-increase ability to cope$_a$	CARRY KEYS IN YOUR HAND WHEN GOING TO YOUR CAR OR HOME	30.3
I-i-outside intervention$_p$	DO NOT WALK ALONE AT NIGHT/ IN THE DARK	27.3
I-i-reduce accessibility	LOCK DOORS IN YOUR HOME	27.3
I-i-increase ability to cope$_p$	APPEAR CONFIDENT (LOOK AGGRESSIVE, STRONG, AND ALERT)	25.8
I-i-reduce accessibility	LOCK CAR DOORS	22.7
I-i-reduce accessibility	LOCK YOUR CAR DOORS WHEN YOU ARE IN THE CAR	22.0
I-i-outside intervention$_p$	DO NOT GO OUT (BE OUT) ALONE AT NIGHT	22.0
I-i-manage self	BE AWARE OF YOUR SURROUNDINGS	20.5
I-i-outside intervention$_p$	TAKE POPULATED ROUTES; AVOID ISOLATED, DARK NON-POPULATED ALLEYS, PARKS, BUSHES, DOORWAYS, VACANT LOTS, AND DARK PARKING AREAS	20.5

[1] Strategies mentioned by at least 10% of females (N=132) in answer to question A.

[2] Stage codes: I = prevent assault from occurring; II = prepare for reacting to an assault; III = defend yourself during an assault. Action level codes: s = societal action; i = individual action. Intended effect subscripts: p = perceived; a = actual. See Fischhoff, Furby, and Morgan (1986) for a fuller description of the category system.

half as many prevention strategies when asked what women do to prevent rape (although men as a group seem to know just as wide a range of strategies as do women).

Rape prevention strategies include both (a) measures designed to keep rape assaults from being initiated, and (b) measures designed to thwart an assault (where the intent is rape) once it commences. For a woman, there may be considerable practical and psychological differences between keeping assaults from occurring and interrupting them

Table 17.9 (continued)

CATEGORY Stage-Level-Intended Effect	STRATEGY	percent who mentioned strategy
I-i-reduce accessibility	ALWAYS CHECK REAR SEAT AND FLOOR OF CAR FOR INTRUDERS BEFORE ENTERING IT	18.9
I-i-outside intervention$_p$	PARK IN WELL-LIGHTED AREAS AND CLOSE TO YOUR DESTINATION	15.9
I-i-increase ability to cope$_p$	WALK BRISKLY AND AT A STEADY PACE	15.2
I-i-outside intervention$_p$	WALK/TAKE WELL-LIT AREAS (AT NIGHT)	14.4
I-i-outside intervention$_p$	GO OUT WITH FRIEND OR TWO FOR PROTECTION	14.4
I-i-reduce accessibility	LOCK YOUR HOUSE DOORS WHEN YOU ARE HOME ALONE AT NIGHT	13.6
II-i-increase ability to cope$_a$	GET/OWN/BE WITH DOG FOR PROTECTION (FOR WARNING, ATTACK, ETC.)	12.9
I-i-outside intervention$_p$	DO NOT GO OUT ALONE IN ISOLATED PLACES (ESPECIALLY AT NIGHT)	12.9
II-i-increase ability to cope$_a$	LEARN SELF-DEFENSE	12.1
II-i-increase ability to cope$_a$	CARRY SPRAY CHEMICAL, LIKE MACE	10.6
I-i-reduce visibility	AVOID AREAS THAT ARE DANGEROUS OR MAKE YOU FEEL UNSAFE	10.6
I-i-reduce accessibility	CHECK WHO IS AT YOUR FRONT DOOR BEFORE OPENING IT	10.6
I-i-reduce accessibility	NEVER PICK UP HITCHHIKERS (ESPECIALLY MALE)	10.6

once initiated. Achieving the former keeps her in what may seem to be a safer world (the degree of safety depending on whether rape assaults have been eliminated entirely or a woman simply succeeds in preventing them from happening to her). Achieving the latter means having to confront direct threats to her person, although knowing how to fend them off might contribute to an ultimate sense of security (Cohn, Kidder, and Harvey, 1979). Women produced roughly equal numbers of strategies aimed at preventing assaults from occurring (Stage I in our typology) and strategies aimed at thwarting assaults once they are intiated (Stages II and III), suggesting that both are important parts of women's psychological reality. However, when women were asked specifically about preventing rape assaults from occurring, the most frequently mentioned strategies consisted of preparations for defending oneself once an assault commences. Thus, dealing with an actual assault seems to have overwhelming salience when women think about rape prevention. Remarkably, however, these Stage II strategies were most frequently mentioned as things that women would not do themselves but that they believe at least some other women would do. It may be that even though the image of an actual assault may come to mind when the topic of rape is mentioned, women defend themselves psychologically against the thought of such a negative event by imagining women other than themselves dealing with the assault. Alternatively, they may feel that other women could deal with an actual assault more competently

Table 17.10

What Women Think Others Do that They Do Not Do to Prevent Rape Assaults from Occurring[1]

CATEGORY Stage-Level-Intended Effect	**STRATEGY**	Percent who said they do not use this strategy but other women do	Percent of women who said they use this strategy[2]
II-i-increase ability to cope	CARRY SPRAY CHEMICAL, LIKE MACE	55.3	10.6
II-i-increase ability to cope$_a$	LEARN SELF-DEFENSE	47.0	12.1
II-i-increase ability to cope$_a$	GET/OWN/BE WITH DOG FOR PROTECTION (FOR WARNING, ATTACK, ETC.)	34.8	12.9
II-i-increase ability to cope$_a$	HAVE/CARRY SOMETHING TO USE AS A WEAPON	27.3	6.1
II-i-outside intervention$_a$	CARRY WHISTLE (BUT NOT AROUND THE NECK)	18.2	6.8
II-i-increase ability to cope$_a$	HAVE/CARRY A GUN FOR PROTECTION	14.4	3.0

[1] Strategies mentioned by at least 10% of female respondents in answer to question B, Table 17.3.

[2] Strategies mentioned in response to Question A, Table 17.3.

than they could. If so, this is another form of psychological damage that rape causes, even among women who have not been raped.

Although it is men who perpetrate rape, strategies that place the responsibility for preventing rape on men are noticeably absent. Moreover, there are about three times as many strategies that place the responsibility for rape prevention on an individual as there are strategies that place it on society, and it is almost always women who must bear that individual burden. Indeed, even many of the societal strategies consist of measures that help women to protect themselves (e.g., educational programs for women regarding rape prevention), leaving the ultimate responsibility for preventing rape with individual women. Furthermore, only 8% of women say that they contribute to societal strategies. Perhaps they consider them to be ineffective; perhaps they see them as effective but as someone else's responsibility.

Looking at rape prevention strategies in terms of their intended effects helps to reveal people's implicit theories of what causes rape, what motivates rapists, and who is responsible for rape prevention. For example, lay women and men showed moderately widespread knowledge of strategies that are aimed at eliminating men's basic motivation to rape, suggesting that at least some of them believe that it might be possible to achieve this goal. Such strategies were much more widely known among sexual assault experts than among laypeople, suggesting perhaps a more widespread belief among experts in the possibility of eliminating men's desire to rape. On the other hand, the apparent recognition that most people do not believe it is possible to eliminate the desire to rape is reflected in the three intended effects believed to be most widely used to prevent rape assaults from occurring (those that target the woman's accessibility, outside intervention, and the woman's capability of dealing with the assailant), all of which assume that at least some men will want to rape (and must be impeded or dissuaded from doing so).

Ignorance of strategies aimed at preventing acquaintance rape suggests that women erroneously assume that rapists are likely to be strangers to their victims. It may also reflect the paucity of strategies that women find viable for preventing acquaintance rape, given the negative consequences such strategies might have on their social lives. Men's relative emphasis on strategies focusing on outside intervention may reflect a feeling that women alone cannot defend themselves or should not be forced to do; in either case, that emphasis highlights yet another way that women must be dependent on men. All respondents' emphasis on reducing only individual women's vulnerability suggests either the general individualistic bias of our society (Furby, 1979) or a lack of faith in societal strategies to solve this particular problem.

Table 17.11

What People Think Women could but Rarely Do to Prevent Rape Assaults From Occurring

CATEGORY[1] Stage-Level-Intended Effect	**STRATEGY**	Percent who said women could but do not use this strategy	Percent of women who said they use this strategy
MALES			
II-i-increase ability to cope with assailant$_a$	LEARN SELF-DEFENSE	25.0	12.1
II-i-increase ability to cope with assailant$_a$	HAVE/CARRY SOMETHING TO USE AS A WEAPON	22.7	6.1
II-i-increase ability to cope with assailant$_a$	CARRY SPRAY CHEMICAL, LIKE MACE	15.9	10.6
II-i-increase ability to cope with assailant$_a$	GET/OWN/BE WITH DOG FOR PROTECTION (FOR WARNING, ATTACK, ETC.)	13.6	12.9
I-i-outside intervention$_p$	DO NOT WALK ALONE AT NIGHT/IN THE DARK	13.6	27.3
II-i-increase ability to cope with assailant$_a$	HAVE/CARRY A GUN FOR PROTECTION	11.4	3.0
EXPERTS			
II-i-increase ability to cope with assailant$_a$	LEARN SELF-DEFENSE	34.9	12.1
II-i-increase ability to cope with assailant$_a$	TAKE ASSERTIVENESS TRAINING/PRACTICE BEING ASSERTIVE	25.6	0.8
I-i-manage self	TRUST FEELINGS AND INSTINCTS (E.G., IF HOUSE DOES NOT "SEEM RIGHT" LEAVE)	23.3	2.3

[1] Stage codes: I = prevent assault from occurring; II = prepare for reacting to an assault; III = defend yourself during an assault. Action level codes: s = societal action; i = individual action. Intended effect subscripts: p = perceived; a = actual. See Fischhoff, Furby, and Morgan (1986) for a fuller description of the category system.

Strategies mentioned by at least 10% of male respondents to question B, Table 17.3.

Strategies mentioned by at least 10% of sexual assault experts to question B, Table 17.3.

Table 17.11 (continued)

CATEGORY Stage-Level-Intended Effect	STRATEGY	Percent who said women could but do not use this strategy	Percent of women who said they use this strategy
I II-i-increase ability to cope with assailant$_a$	PRACTICE MENTALLY OR REHEARSE WHAT YOU WOULD DO IN CASE OF AN ATTACK (REACTIONS, WHERE TO RUN TO, WHERE TO GET AID, ETC.)	18.6	4.5
II-i-increase ability to cope with assailant$_p$	APPEAR CONFIDENT (LOOK AGGRESSIVE, STRONG, AND ALERT)	18.6	25.8
I-i-increase ability to cope with assailant$_a$	WEAR CLOTHING THAT ALLOWS YOU TO MOVE EASILY AND QUICKLY, WEAR THAT SHOES YOU CAN RUN IN	14.0	6.1
I-i-manage self	GET EDUCATED ABOUT HIGH RISK SITUATIONS/BE MORE KNOWLEDGEABLE ABOUT RAPE	14.0	0.0
II-i-increase ability to cope with assailant$_p$	CONFRONT MEN WHO ARE TRYING TO GET SOMETHING FROM YOU OR ACTING INAPPROPRIATELY	11.6	0
II-i-increase ability to cope with assailant$_a$	BE PHYSICALLY FIT	11.6	1.5
II-i-increase ability to cope with assailant$_a$	HAVE/CARRY SOMETHING TO USE AS A WEAPON	11.6	6.1
I-i-manage self	BE AWARE THAT PEOPLE YOU KNOW COULD RAPE YOU (E.G., ACQUAINTANCE, RELATIVE, DATE, ETC.)	11.6	0.8
I-i-manage self	BE AWARE OF YOUR SURROUNDINGS	11.6	20.5
I-i-manage self	DO NOT TRUST OR TALK TO STRANGERS (E.G., ON THE STREET, WHEN ALONE, IN PUBLIC)	11.6	9.1

Reference

1. One interesting observation is that more women in each group reported being raped by acquaintances, whereas more had heard about others being raped by strangers. Apparently, there is greater reluctance to talk about acquaintance rapes. One possible result is that women may underestimate the risks of acquaintance rapes.

Bibliography

Brownmiller, Susan
1975 *Against Our Will: Men, Women and Rape.* New York: Simon & Schuster.

Cohn, Ellen S., Louise H. Kidder, and Joan Harvey
1979 "Crime prevention vs. victimization prevention: The psychology of two different reactions." *Victimology,* 3: 285–296.

Edwards, Ward, and Detlof von Winterfeldt
1986 *Decision Analysis and Behavioral Research.* New York: Cambridge University Press.

Fischhoff, Baruch, Sarah Lichtenstein, Paul Slovic, Steven L. Derby, and Ralph L. Keeney
1981 *Acceptable Risk.* New York: Cambridge University Press.

Fischhoff, Baruch, Lita Furby, and Marcia K. Morgan
1986 *Rape Prevention: A Typology and List of Strategies.* ERI Technical Report 86-1. Eugene, OR: Eugene Research Institute.

Fischhoff, Baruch, Ola Svenson, and Paul Slovic
1987 "Active Responses to Environmental Hazards." In D. Stokols and I. Altman, eds. *Handbook of Environmental Psychology.* New York: Wiley.

Furby, Lita
1979 "The Individualistic Bias in Studies of Locus of Control." In A.R. Buss, ed. *Psychology in Social Context.* New York: Irvington Publishers.

Furby, Lita, Baruch Fischhoff, and Marcia K. Morgan
1986 *Preventing Rape: How People Perceive the Options. II: Defending Oneself During an Assault.* ERI Technical Report 86-6. Eugene, OR: Eugene Research Institute.

Furby, Lita, and Baruch Fischhoff

Forthcoming "Rape Self-defense Strategies: A Review of Their Effectiveness." *Victimology*.

Griffin, Susan

1981 "The All-American Crime." In M. Vetterling-Braggin, F. A. Elliston, and J. English, eds. *Feminism and Philosophy*. Totowa, NJ: Littlefield, Adams & Co. (First published in *Ramparts*, September 1971, 26–35.)

McDermott, M.J.

1979 *Rape Victimization in 26 American Cities. National Crime Survey Victimization and Attitude Data*. Analytic Report SD-VAD-6. Washington, DC: U.S. Dept. of Justice.

Raiffa, H.

1968 *Decision Analysis*. Reading, MA: Addison-Wesley.

Riger, Stephanie, and Margaret Gordon

1981 "The Fear of Rape: A Study in Social Control." *Journal of Social Issues* 37: 71–92.

Slovic, Paul, Sarah Lichtenstein, and Baruch Fischhoff

1988 "Decision Making." In R.C. Atkinson, R.J. Herrnstein, G. Lindzey, and R.D. Luce, eds. *Stevens' Handbook of Experimental Psychology*. Second Edition. New York: Wiley.

U.S. Department of Justice

1985 *The Crime of Rape*. Bureau of Justice Statistics Report NCJ-96777. Washington, DC: Author.

Warren, R., K.S. Harlow, and M.S. Rosentraub

1982 "Citizen Participation in the Production of Services: Methodological and Policy Issues in Coproduction Research." *The Southwestern Review*, 2: 42–55.

Warren, R., M.S. Rosentraub, and K.S. Harlow

1984 "Coproduction, Equity and the Distribution of Safety. *Urban Affairs Quarterly*, 19: 447–464.

18

A New Model for the Treatment of Adult Survivors of Sexual Abuse

Sarah M. Rieth
Church Mission of Help
Buffalo, New York

The linear and feminist approach to the treatment of adult survivors of sexual abuse is that of perpetrator/victim. This therapeutic approach has been found to perpetuate the client's self-concept as a victim. It is crucial that the therapeutic community not replicate with the client her experience in her family of origin. A systems approach provides a complement to the linear approach and enables the client to move from victim to survivor status. This chapter introduces clinicians to this theoretical framework and discusses issues and treatment goals for members of a homogeneous, ongoing psychotherapeutic group for adult survivors of sexual abuse. Group design and process are discussed and clinical material is presented. This chapter also includes a discussion of flashbacks and an approach to their treatment.

Don't tell
He said
Carry this alone

The world will end
If you let them know
Don't tell

So the silence echoes
Through long years
Crying to be broken

But no one hears
What can't be spoken
Don't tell

The silence runs deeper
Burying the secret
The pain

Where it can't be touched
By a caring question
Don't tell

Broken silences
Like mirrors splinter
Cutting deeply

Healing comes
But scars remain
Forever telling.[1]

Recent media attention to the issue of child sexual abuse has enabled many adults[2] who experienced sexual abuse in childhood to disobey their abusers by talking about what happened to them. This chapter will begin with a theoretical framework for treating adult survivors of sexual abuse. This chapter will be followed by a discussion of the clinical implications and practice for a homogeneous, ongoing psychotherapeutic group for adult survivors of sexual abuse. Clinical case material will be cited.

In my clinical practice with adult survivors of sexual abuse, I have observed that the role of victim is deeply embedded within these women's psyches. Supportive and empathic psychotherapy is, after a period of time, incomplete and may even be counterproductive in enabling clients to make the inner shift from "victim" to "survivor" (Deighton and McPeek, 1985). If she is unable to make this shift she is likely to feel victimized throughout the various arenas of her life, even when no overt victimization is taking place. We cannot underestimate the power previous sexual abuse has in enabling a person to relive the abuse from the past. This happens by means of transference, projections, flashbacks and other dissociative experiences, and by the person getting herself set up into new abusive relationships. Significant contributions have been made by A.H. Green, M.D. (1978, 1985) in illuminating the compulsive and repetitive process of attempting to master the childhood trauma by repeating and reenacting it in adulthood.

Therapeutic Framework

The classical view of the dynamics of sexual abuse is a linear one: there is a perpetrator and there is a victim. This perspective is enhanced by the traditional feminist view of the woman who was innocent and thus "in the right" and of the man who was "in the wrong." She was helpless and he was sick. In addition, the feminist perspective historically has implied that to suggest that the woman has played a part in the abusive dynamic is to be part of the oppressive patriarchal structure of society and to be sexist.

The sexual harassment, exploitation and abuse of women do have roots in and exacerbate the profound sexism in our society (Bussert, 1986). Sexual abuse is a process of victimization through the abuse of a perpetrator's power and urge to control. Yet as a feminist psychotherapist I have found that to support only this viewpoint with a client is too often to support her remaining a victim for life. It enables her to remain stuck with her rage at the perpetrator and at the colluding parent. This cannot offer the client a healing transformation and mastery of the original trauma. At its worst the perpetrator/victim model facilitates uncritical empathy which engulfs the client. It may also allow for unempathic blame which distances or extrudes the client and/or members of her family of origin. Further, it allows the clinician to collude with the family system by being iatrogenic; that is, it keeps the victim in the victim role and mentality. Finally, in terms of the traditional triangle of persecutor-victim-rescuer, this perpetrator/victim model sets the therapist up to destroy the therapeutic relationship by rushing in as a rescuer and ending up as another persecutor in the client's life. It cannot be overemphasized that for the mental health system and individual clinicians to be of help to survivors of sexual abuse we must not replicate the family system of the client.

A systems approach to work with survivors of sexual abuse enhances our understanding of the trauma of the abuse and its sequelae throughout the client's life. It serves as an additional, complementary, and balancing perspective along with the previously described approach.

A systems view of sexual abuse considers that incest is a system-maintaining symptom in a matrix of dysfunctional relational patterns. Inappropriate sexual behaviors on the part of a parent or significant adult towards a child or on the part of an older sibling towards a younger sibling are symptoms which reduce tension in the family by maintaining homeostasis. The symptoms are regulators of closeness and distance within the family.

The crucial addition to our understanding which the systems approach contributes is that each family member has a part to play in the family drama. For example, it is true that in father/ or stepfather/ daughter sexual abuse the mother often knows consciously or unconsciously about the abuse. Her knowing that her daughter is being sexually abused and her not stopping the abuse colludes with the perpetrator and gives tacit permission for the problem to continue. Often the mother colludes with the problem out of helplessness, lack of job skills, fear of abuse towards herself, and even out of relief that the man is "off her case" for a while. In addition, she may not be empowered to act on behalf of her child because she may have repressed or not adequately have worked through her own history of abuse. The father's role of acting out towards his daughter meets his needs for power and control. His behavior may also meet his needs for intimacy, albeit in an inappropriate manner. Some daughters describe fathers as having been tender as well as rough, coercive and violent. If, for example, he is a substance abuser, his wife may refuse to have anything to do with him sexually. He then reaches out in the only way he thinks he knows. If he is a substance abuser the sexual abuse further distorts the family dynamics in which denial, projection, and splitting defenses are already strong (Black, 1981; Barnard, 1984a and 1984b). If he himself was abused as a child, he will consider his own behavior as normal and warranted. Meanwhile, the daughter is afraid and confused. Sometimes what the father does feels good but she knows that something is not right because he threatens to hurt her, her family or her pet if she tells. So she does not tell. She may decide that what he does to her is better than getting beaten the way he beats her mother. She may get favors or money for what she and her father do; and at times it meets her needs to feel special.

For clinicians to be part of the solution and not part of the problem there is a need for appreciating both linear (perpetrator/victim) thinking and systems thinking. In no way does this mean that we blame the victim. She is in an untenable situation of violence and the persons she should be able to rely on to help her in her distress are part of the problem. In addition, it is likely that the mother serves as no positive model of assertiveness for her. But too often a client either puts all of the blame on her father or mother or introjects all of the blame herself. A transforming of blame into responsibility and a reapportioning of responsibility among the three central figures is crucial for a healthy outcome of the therapy. For the client to own her own part in what happened to her is the truth that sets her free to move beyond life experienced as a victim.

Ongoing Issues for Survivors of Sexual Abuse and Implications for Treatment Goals

There is a constellation of ongoing issues for adult survivors of sexual abuse. The following includes the most crucial issues:

Trust; self-esteem; boundaries; control; intimacy/isolation; indebtedness; asexuality/promiscuity; impaired relationships with persons of both sexes; guilt, shame, and neurotic (inappropriate) guilt; "don't talk"; "don't feel" (Black, 1981); self-destructive behaviors; grief and; spiritual problems. Keeping these issues in mind, the following goals have been established for group treatment:

1. To develop criteria to discern whom she will risk trusting and talking about what is really happening in her life.
2. To discover her own victim behaviors and patterns.
3. To move in her self-concept and behavior from helpless victim to empowered survivor. Achieving this goal necessarily involves mourning for the loss of her childhood and the loss of the family she needed and wanted.
4. To experience how the defenses of isolation, projection, splitting and transference maintain her victim status.
5. To come to understand how she got singled out as a victim in her family of origin.
6. To attempt to stop the intergenerational abusive patterns of behavior by knowing the abuser introjected within herself and by differentiating from the family of origin.
7. To achieve more functional relationships with self, God, others, and members of her family of origin.
8. To become empowered by developing a new and expanded repertoire of skills to use when she feels threatened, helpless or powerless, in order not to repeat the cycle of participating in her own victimization.

Criteria for Selection of Group Members

A no-charge screening interview is offered to women who have been referred to the group. This enables the therapist to assess the woman's suitability and readiness for the group, and it enables the woman to sense if the chemistry is right for her to work with the therapist.

The most important criterion for a potential group member to possess is that the sexual abuse is a real issue for her. A woman in her forties was interviewed, having come reluctantly after having been referred by her primary therapist. She had been sexually abused by two brothers and was in the midst of physical and emotional abuse by her alcoholic husband. Her distress was real, but she had no emotional sense that her past and her present are related. She was referred back to the primary therapist with the understanding that, when the timing was right, she could join the group.

Timing is crucial for a member to benefit from the group experience. It is preferable for this group that a woman not be in the immediate crisis of her first remembering[3] or first talking about the sexual abuse. She will be much more able both to give and to receive in the group once she has had some individual therapy related to the sexual abuse. She will already have risked breaking the family secret by talking about the abuse. She will have developed a degree, however small, of competence by doing what she thought she could never do. With one such experience under her belt she will be more ready to try to do the even more difficult thing of talking about the abuse in a group (a new family).

It is the expectation that a member will remain in individual therapy while she is in the group. This is to provide the strongest possible network of support for her as she confronts extremely sensitive and volatile material. In addition, the telling of and the working through of the actual memories of the abuse is best done within the privacy and protection of the individual session. This protects the client from feeling overexposed and humiliated by sharing these memories in a group setting.

A member makes a minimum twelve-session commitment when she joins this ongoing group. The shortest length of stay in the group has been 21 sessions; the longest length of stay is 150 sessions; the average length of stay in the group is about 100 sessions. She also agrees that the group therapist and her primary therapist be allowed to communicate with each other as may be necessary for her best interest. Her willingness to be evaluated for medication, if necessary, is assessed at the screening interview. If there is a primary diagnosis of substance abuse, she may join the group only if she is both abstinent and receiving concurrent treatment for the substance abuse.

Finally, the ego strength of the woman is assessed in the screening interview. Psychotic clients are not appropriate members for this group. Because many women with a diagnosis of Borderline Personality Disorder were sexually abused in their childhoods, extra care must be taken to assess the ego strength and history of acting-out behaviors with these clients. The primary therapist is invaluable in assisting the group therapist with this assessment; the strength and resilience of the client's relationship with the primary therapist can be a good predictor of her ability to gain from and contribute to the group.

How the Group Is Run

The group is currently led by one therapist[4] for two-hour sessions once a week. The optimal number of group members at any one time is four. A maximum number of members is five. This is because the needs of the client are so deep and often her ability to get those needs met is so impaired that a larger group mitigates against depth work.

A variety of formats has been used for group process. The group members have taken part in the selection of the process they want. This has given each member the opportunity to have input into how things will go for her, to have her point of view considered and taken seriously, and to participate in a group-made decision. It is likely that she experienced none of these in her first group, her family.

The type of format the group needs and is able to use reflects the developmental stage of the individuals and of the group. At one phase in the group's life the members found that an open format was what they wanted but that its lack of structure and lack of clarity about boundaries were too threatening for them. Their passivity was reinforced by experiencing another threatening situation in which boundaries were not clear to them. This passivity, in addition to the problem members have in trusting, worked against the cohesion process in the group. To resolve this difficulty, they experimented with choosing topics for discussion, such as "How we feel about our mothers." This structure worked for some members at some times, but more often than not the topic was not pertinent to where members were emotionally on a given evening.

The process which that constellation of individuals chose and developed reflected their developmental needs for clear structure. At the beginning of each session they would ask for the amount of time they wanted for themselves for that night. From there negotiations took place, if necessary, in order to adhere to the two-hour time frame. This gave the members the opportunity to practice identifying what they wanted and needed and then going ahead and asking for it. One member would volunteer to be the time-keeper for the evening; her role was to monitor the time and to let members know when they have five minutes left and when their time is up. This, too, was therapeutic in teaching about boundaries, an issue around which there is much ambivalence.

At other stages in the life of this group other constellations of members have opted for and utilized an open process effectively. How a member utilizes the process itself is a therapeutic issue; for example, her feelings about taking up time and space and her feelings about asking the "family" for help are fertile ground for working through the sexual abuse issues.

In general, how a client uses her time in group is up to her. The focus is on working through present recapitulations of the past. The therapist and other group members help her by identifying her victim behaviors, exploring the gains she achieves through her victim role, and helping her to work through the projections and transferences which surface within the group. The goal is directed at finding new endings for the old story being repeated in the present.

Case Histories

Case #1

Dawn[5] became increasingly withdrawn and passive after Betty left the group and a new member joined. She did not want to interact with anyone in the group. The group members encouraged and confronted Dawn about her behavior, and over the course of many weeks they explored the meaning of Dawn's behavior. In doing this, the group gained the experience of working through things together as a family. Dawn continued to remain withdrawn in group until she ran into Betty in a shopping mall. This encounter surfaced Dawn's unmourned grief at Betty's leaving. This served as an entryway into her doing the mourning she never did when her father left the family when she was five.

Dawn was then able to express her anger at the therapist for bringing in a new group member, which for her was a recapitulation of mother bringing in her stepfather/abuser immediately after father moved out. At that time her mother had told her, "This is your new father and I want you to like him and make it work out." When Dawn was able to make the connection between her past and the present she was freed to interact with all of the group members for who they are as individuals.

The newest member of the group ceased to wear her stepfather's face for Dawn. In addition, Dawn saw her isolation and passivity as part of her own victim pattern. The next time new members entered the group, Dawn took significant initiative and leadership in including the new members and in facilitating the group's cohesion process.

Once Dawn began to want to participate in the group again, she was demanding and impulsive. Because feelings of deprivation had surfaced during her mourning of her losses, she was unable to tolerate having, for example, only the thirty minutes she asked for in the group. One night when Cynthia asked for and received an hour in which to work, Dawn's frustration was especially high. Yet Cynthia's work touched on many of Dawn's own issues of betrayal and trust. Dawn was surprised to find that she benefited from the work another member had done. She began to see and to trust that getting her needs met is a process, not an event.

Case #2

Cynthia broke Pam's confidence to a third party known to both of them outside of the group. When Pam confronted Cynthia with her anger at the betrayal of her confidence, Cynthia, a social work student, was unable to see that what she did was wrong or to own any responsibility for hurting Pam. She saw her own behavior as positive: she was open, honest, sharing, and not keeping secrets.

Since trust within the group had been broken, there could be no further work until this issue was sufficiently worked through and trust could be restored. Cynthia was unable to own up to the destructive aspects of her behavior until she was able to see herself unconsciously attempting to master the family trauma of denial by having to keep the abuse secretive. She did not want to re-experience the bondage she felt in her family of origin where she could not talk about what was really happening. As the group talked about what was really happening in the present, Cynthia began to be able to differentiate between confidentiality as freely honoring another's privacy, and secrecy as binding her under the threat of punishment or destruction. She was able to apologize for what she did and to begin to acknowledge her own ability to victimize.

Case #3

Judy was enraged with the group therapist for not protecting her from another group member's expression of anger. The therapist saw three goals for this situation: one, to receive and appreciate Judy's feelings while also gently helping her to explore what would empower her in the situation; two, to explore Judy's projection: she, too, is abusive with her anger; and three, to explore the transferential nature of her rage at the therapist: "Why didn't mother protect me from what my father and my brother did to me?" No amount of venting of her anger seemed to help her, and she was unable and unwilling to allow the group and the therapist to be with her in an exploration of her feelings. An important complication was that at this time Judy's male therapist at another agency began to tell Judy that she was not getting her needs met in group. Judy was once again caught between "mother" and "father," and she resolved this by once again going with her "father." In her final session Judy accused the therapist of allowing her to remain in danger many times. Since she had not previously expressed this, she ended up recapitulating her past experience of not telling her mother and letting herself feel abused.

Case #4

Nancy had been hospitalized for 2 $^{1}/_{2}$ years when she was an infant. Although Nancy had glimpses of memories of the hospital and its personnel, her parents denied that Nancy had any such hospitalization. She was certain that she was crazy, especially after her parents denied the sexual abuse Nancy experienced. Nancy was certain that the group would not believe her either, and she was so afraid of rejection that she remained passive in the group. She was able to tolerate talking about what made it difficult to talk in group, and the breakthrough for her came when she told about the way she was treated by her parents about the hospitalization. She was confused because she found the group to be safe and the group members to be taking her seriously. Nancy talked openly about her fear, confusion and delight about this new experience. She discovered the criteria she will use to know if she can trust another person and her own sense and experience of things: first, is this person I am with consistent with me over time? And, second, are this person's actions congruent with her/his words?

Flashbacks

Many people who experienced the trauma of childhood sexual abuse display symptoms which meet the criteria for Post-Traumatic Stress Disorder (PTSD) in the *Diagnostic and Statistical Manual of Mental Disorders* (American Psychiatric Association, 1987). Goodwin (1985) and Green (1985) have illuminated the field with their studies of abused children who exhibit the symptoms of PTSD. Flashbacks are one of the symptoms which sexually abused children carry into adulthood.

Flashbacks are non-psychotic, dissociative episodes in which a person actually relives the abuse as it happened in the past. She has no sense that she is here now, that she is safe, or that she has a therapist or other solid object who is for her and with whom she can talk about what is happening to her. In these ways flashbacks are very different from memories. The client is temporarily disabled by this PTSD symptom.

Flashbacks do not occur capriciously, although it seems to be so to the client. Rather than a flashback happening "from out of the blue," it usually occurs in response to some stimulus in the present environment. The feeling she presents in the flashback, be it the feeling of powerlessness, terror, frustration, rage, or of having been abused, or of not having been heard, is present in some live way at the time of the flashback. She may not actually be being abused at the time, but the feelings from her earlier experiences come to intrude upon her, overwhelm her, and flash her back to the previous abuse. She is likely to be unaware of the connection between what she is feeling in the flashback and what is precipitating that feeling in the present environment.

This group for survivors of sexual abuse has met with success in working with clients having flashbacks. The method is to help the client to talk about the feeling presented in the flashback. Then, rather than heightening the flashback (Schultz, 1984: 409–461), the goal is to discover how the feeling in the flashback is present now. From there we work through the "now" experience by discerning what is different now from back then, what would help her to feel safe and grounded now, and what would be empowering for her to do now. Working through flashbacks as they are happening in group teaches clients how to cope with flashbacks and how to bring themselves through the flashbacks. Clients have felt less victimized and more in control of their lives when they have been able to use this "formula" as a means of self-help and empowerment. A second benefit is that all members gain when one member works through a flashback; there is comfort and strength in knowing that others also experience this phenomenon and that the symptom does not necessarily mean that the client is "crazy."[6]

Evaluation of Results

Feedback from the women who have participated in the group has been positive. They have found that the group environment has provided an atmosphere of both support and challenge which has enabled them to break through old and unsuccessful patterns to a new and stronger sense of self. Data is congruent with that of Deighton and McPeek (1985), in that there is a "marked decrease in suicidal ideation, suicidal attempts, and depressive episodes."

Members have become more self-contained, less reactive and more able to act from within themselves. There is an increased sense of control over one's life because of the improved self-esteem, the ability to deal with and set boundaries, and the knowledge of skills and choices which are available to them as they move actively into life.

Relationships outside the group are improved. As an MSW candidate began to deal with her own issues of being a victim/survivor, she was able to develop a therapeutic relationship with her client in a locked forensic mental health ward. A member of a religious community has taken initiative to develop intervention strategies with abusing families in her parish. A daughter of two alcoholics achieved sobriety while in the group and maintained sobriety since she left the group; she is comfortable differentiating herself from her family of origin in this way. A newly married woman was able to confront both parents with the prior sexual abuse and to give their part in the problem back to them. This freed her to enjoy a more fulfilling emotional and sexual relationship with her husband. A less distorted sense of blame and the ability to talk about what is real have enabled group members to live more authentically and abundantly.

Summary

This group for adult survivors of sexual abuse was developed in response to the needs clients presented as the media began to draw greater attention to the problem of sexual abuse. Members have found the group to have been instrumental in their finding new life for themselves beyond the childhood trauma. "Healing comes but scars remain forever telling." Members of the group have found healing, and the scars now tell a new ending to the old story.

References

1. This poem was written by Suzette J. Reuss.
2. In the six years this group has been running to date, twenty-one female survivors of sexual abuse have been part of the group; thus this chapter will refer to women only. However, it must be appreciated that significant numbers of adult men were sexually abused in childhood and are also in need of treatment to resolve their difficulties resulting from the childhood abuse.
3. One group member was fifty-four before she consciously remembered that she had been sexually abused. This is not

uncommon; the survivor of sexual abuse has survived in part because of her ability to repress and dissociate.

4. A second group is being offered, co-led by a male and a female therapist. While it is still early in the life of this group, initial soft data indicates that the addition of the male co-therapist has enhanced the group members' opportunity to work through transferences and projections.
5. All names of group members have been changed.
6. Group members who have been able to work through flashbacks and whose healing process has progressed to the point that they are able to give more to others have volunteered to be trained to do telephone counseling to help others work through flashbacks and to provide support to other survivors who are in crisis. This hotline project, which is now sponsored by Church Mission of Help in Buffalo, New York, will be the subject of a forthcoming article by this author.

Bibliography

American Psychiatric Association

1987 *Diagnostic and Statistical Manual of Mental Disorder.* 3rd Edition, Revised. Washington: American Psychiatric Association.

Barnard, Charles P.

1984a "Alcoholism and Incest Part I: Similar Traits, Common Dynamics." *Focus on Family and Chemical Dependency*, Jan./Feb.: 27–29.

1984b "Alcoholism and Incest Part II: Issues in Treatment." *Focus on Family and Chemical Dependency*, Mar./Apr.: 29–32.

Black, Claudia

1981 *It Will Never Happen to Me.* Denver: M.A.C.

Bussert, Joy M.K.

1986 *Battered Women: From a Theology of Suffering to an Ethic of Empowerment.* Kutztown.

Cook, David R.

1984 "A Systemic Treatment Approach to Wife Battering." *Journal of Marital and Family Therapy*, 10, No. 1: 83–93.

Courtois, Christine

1988 *Healing the Incest Wound.* New York: W.W. Norton.

Deighton, Joan, and Phil McPeek

1985 "Group Treatment: Adult Victims of Childhood Sexual Abuse." *Social Casework: The Journal of Contemporary Social Work,* Sept.: 403–410.

Fortune, Marie Marshall

1983 *Sexual Violence: The Unmentionable Sin.* New York: Pilgrim.

1987 *Keeping the Faith.* New York: Harper & Row.

Goodwin, Jean

1985 "Post-traumatic Symptoms in Incest Victims." In S. Eth and R. Pynoos, eds. *Post-Traumatic Stress Disorder in Children.* Washington: American Psychiatric Press, Inc., pp. 157–168.

Green, A.H.

1978 "Psychiatric Treatment of Abused Children." *Journal of the American Academy of Child Psychiatry,* 17: 356–371.

1985 "Children Traumatized by Physical Abuse." In S. Eth and R. Pynoos, eds. *Post-Traumatic Stress Disorder in Children.* Washington: American Psychiatric Press, Inc., pp. 135–154.

Kepner, James I.

1988 *The Healing Tasks in the Therapy of Adult Survivors of Childhood Abuse: A Clinicians' Guide.* Cleveland Hts., OH: unpublished.

Khan, M. Masud R.

1963 "The Concept of Cumulative Trauma." *The Psychoanalytic Study of the Child,* 18: 286–306.

Schultz, Stephen J.

1984 *Family Systems Therapy: An Integration.* New York: Aronson.

Yassen, Janet, and Lois Glass

1984 "Sexual Assault Survivors Groups: A Feminist Practice Perspective." *Social Work,* May/June: 252–257.

19

Facilitating Capable Parenting Among Black Single Mothers in Violent Families

Sondra Gardner, Ph.D.
Biodyne Ohio, Inc.

and

Jane Timmons-Mitchell, Ph.D.
Case Western Reserve University School of Medicine

The present clinical investigation was undertaken to assess the merits of providing structured group intervention for black single mothers in violent families to help them learn non-abusive ways of relating to their children. Group effectiveness was assessed by measuring the parents' perceptions of their children, the children's perception of themselves, and their parents' perception of family relationships before and after the group was conducted and at follow-up two months later. The results indicate that, when compared with the normative samples for the measures used, changes in the direction of more positive parent perceptions of their children as well as of their family relationships were found. Children's perceptions of their own feeling states tended to conform more closely to the mean levels expected for children of similar ages.

The administrative support of Fannie Johnson-Baxter, Murtis-Taylor Center, and the assistance of Dianne Blabolil, Marguerite Randolph, Pam Senders, and Jill Weissberg, students affiliated with Beech Brook, in interviewing is gratefully acknowledged.

Facilitating Capable Parenting Among Black Single Mothers in Violent Families

Rationale

Family violence is a problem which has far-reaching effects on family members. Gelles' social exchange theory (1982) posits that people abuse others because they can: the cost of abusing is not great enough to prevent the violent behavior. The present investigation focuses on a distinguishing feature among violent families: that the abusive person may be subtly empowered by the rest of the family members to be abusive. In order to stop empowering oneself or others to be violent in family interactions, parents need to see themselves as capable and competent rather than helpless. In Gelles' terms, the cost for abusive behavior within the family system must be increased.

Battered women are at risk to become physically abusive to their children primarily because of feeling powerless to challenge abusive patterns of relating (Walker, 1981). Clinical application of attributional theory (Forsterling, 1986) to violent families suggests that both battered women and their children may view themselves as incapable of structuring relationships in other, nonabusive ways. Cognitive behavioral theory explains these perceptions in terms of learned helplessness resulting from externally imposed outcomes that may be unpredictable. Battered women, like other abusive parents, may feel as though they have very little to say about what happens to them, reacting instead to circumstances orchestrated by others (Goldstein, et al., 1985).

The effects of violent patterns of family interaction can be seen in the higher incidence of aggression in freeplay situations demonstrated by children who have been abused compared to those that have not (Barahal, et al., 1981). Where physical fighting exists between parents, children exhibit higher rates of parent-directed aggressive acts (Reid, et al., 1981). Burgess and Conger (1978) found higher rates of aggression among members of abusive families than among members of nonabusive families. These findings may indicate that children living in abusive families perceive violence as part of the normative family experience.

Current research indicates that parent training can significantly modify child abusive responses of parents by teaching child management skills. Skills training that facilitates the development and reinforcement of alternative nonabusive and noncoercive tools for dealing with children has been effectively utilized by parents who have been abusive (Sandler, et al., Wolfe, et al., 1981; Patterson, 1986). The importance of teaching interpersonal skills to parents engaged in conjugal violence in order to change the family structure that incorporates violence as an accepted mode of interaction has also been emphasized (Reid, et al., 1981).

The present clinical investigation was undertaken in order to test the effectiveness of a particular structured group intervention designed to facilitate both the development of non-coercive parenting skills and competent self-attributions among parents from violent families.

Glenn and his associates (Glenn, 1983; Glenn and Wagner, n.d.; Glenn and Warner, 1984) have developed a multi-faceted parent training program which addresses the dysfunctional interactions among members of coercive family systems. The attributional aspects of the coercive interactions as well as parenting and interpersonal skill deficits are addressed. To modify inappropriate attributions, abusive and coercive ways of thinking are identified in a non-threatening way through generalization (i.e., discussion of common forms of verbal abuse of children). Sandler, VanDercar, and Milhoan (1977) have emphasized the sensitivity of coercive parents to their own incompetence. The incompetent self-attribution of the coercive parent is addressed indirectly by teaching the parents to teach their children that they are capable people who can make significant contributions to things greater than themselves and that they have control over the choices they make. The common deficits that both the child and the parent manifest in the coercive family system (Barahal, et al., 1981) are addressed simultaneously in Glenn's program.

In addition to modifying attributions about both the self and the child through perceptual change, the program teaches parenting and interpersonal skills in the areas of commmunication, negotiation, and discipline. Teaching parents to set rules and consequences in non-confrontive ways trains parents to discipline through induction. The child, encouraged to focus on his behavior rather than on the parental response to the behavior (Gibbs and Schnell, 1985), develops a sense that he or she can influence what happens to him or her. It was expected that as parents applied these perceptions and skills to interactions with their children that their self-attributions would also become more positive.

Method

Subjects were drawn from the July-August 1985 Children's Clinic caseload at a mental health center serving a predominantly inner city black population. The total number of families available for group participation was 98, of which, according to the director of the clinic, 95 families' issues involved family violence. Nineteen cases were referred to the group. Seven mothers agreed to attend the group. Six mothers attended one group session or more, and 5 were available for follow-up. All of the mothers who attended the group sessions were battered women parenting children who had witnessed family violence. The children were aged 8 to 14 years. Measures administered to the parents who participated in the group and to their identified patient children prior to the beginning of the sessions, following the last group session, and two months after the conclusion of the group included the Moos Family Environment Scale (subscales measuring family Cohesion and family Conflict); the Externalizing Dimension of the Achenbach Child Behavior Checklist (assesses extent of overtly acted out behaviors) and the Aggressiveness subscale (measures aggressive behavior); and the Structured Pediatric Psychosocial Interview Factor Scores for Feeling (measures felt level of distress), Relating (measures how the child views relating to others), Thinking (measures concerns about own capabilities), and Impetuosity (measures level of agitated behavior). All of these measures are normed and have been standardized for use with children ages 6 to 16 years. The Moos FES and the CBCL are paper and pencil ratings which parents completed about their child and about their family interaction patterns. The SPPI was administered to each child individually. These measures were used to assess (a) the parent's perception of the child's behavioral difficulties (CBCL), (b) the child's perception of himself (SPPI), and (c) the parent's perception of the quality of family relationships (FES).

Intervention

The structured group program titled *Developing Capable Young People* (Glenn, 1983; Glenn and Wagner, n.d.) was presented in seven weekly two-hour sessions. The intervention uses 30 minute audiotapes to give permission to the parents to acknowledge the abusive aspects of their parenting; to enhance parent perceptions of the self and child as competent and capable of self-control; and to teach new parenting skills in the areas of age-appropriate responsibility, judgment, communication, negotiation, and structuring rules and consequences in ways that facilitate autonomous development. In addition to the audiotapes, group discussion, group exercises, and structured role play encourage practice and reinforcement of new skills in the group interaction. Homework tasks are assigned to facilitate integration of the new skills into daily activities. The program is replicable since the published materials contain clear guidelines about how to structure presentations.

Table 19.1

Means of Standard Scores for Parent Ratings

Achenbach Child Behavior Checklist (CBCL)			
	Pre	Post	Follow-Up
Externalizing Dimension	73	66*	65*
Aggressiveness Subscale	78	65*	67*
Moos Family Environment Scale (FES)			
	Pre	Post	Follow-Up
Cohesion Subscale	41	59*	54*
Conflict Subscale	59	46	56

* p < .05 that these scores are not different from the pre-test score

Results

The primary findings of the present study indicate that (1) parents' perceptions of their children's behavior as measured by the CBCL moved from the abnormal to the normal ranges and (2) parents' sense of family cohesion as measured by the Moos FES increased during and after participation in the group. The results of pre-group, post-group, and two month follow-up administration of the CBCL, FES, and SPPI for the five subjects are presented in tables 19.1 and 19.2. A difference was said to exist if any pair of means differed by more than twice the standard error of measurement for the test as reported in the test manuals (Achenbach and Edelbrock, 1983; Moos and Moos, 1981; Webb and Van Devere, 1985). On the CBCL Externalizing Dimension and Aggressiveness Subscale, differences were found between the initial scores and the post-group and follow-up administrations (see Table 19.1). However, the post-group and follow-up scores were not different from each other. Initially, the Externalizing Dimension score and the Aggressiveness scaled score were in the abnormal range (above the 98th percentile), but dropped into the normal range for scores on subsequent testing. Table 19.1 also shows that the Cohesion score on the Moos FES changed significantly at both post-test and follow-up compared to initial ratings; however, there was not a significant change in perceived Conflict associated with family interaction. The results from the SPPI (see Table 19.2) show that the deviation from the mean for the Feeling Factor Score declined from 2.6 scaled score points at initial assessment to 0.6 scaled score points at follow-up. Since this overall difference is more than twice the standard error of measurement for this scale, it is probable that there is a difference between the initial and the follow-up scores.

Discussion

The purpose of the present clinical investigation was to assess the merits of conducting a structured group experience for battered women to help them learn non-abusive ways of relating to their children. The group intervention addressed interpersonal relational and parenting skills by providing exercises designed to teach parents how to teach their children that they are capable people. In order to assess the effectiveness of the group, parents' perceptions of their child, the child's perception of him or herself, and the parent's perception of the family relationships were measured. The results indicate that, when compared with the normative samples for the measures used, changes in the directions expected were found. Parents were able to see their children as less aggressive and as having fewer behavioral difficulties. Children were able to see themselves as more closely allied with other children of similar age in terms of experiencing emotional distress. Although parents did not tend to see Conflict in the family as being significantly reduced, they did see their family interactions as more Cohesive.

The women who attended the group represented a highly selected group which may have contributed to the positive changes reported. Despite the fact that these women are members of a group disenfranchised by reason of race (black), marital status (single parent), and economic status (poor), all but one were employed. All had sought therapy on behalf of their children and themselves, and all had been able to separate from the abusive partner. Walker (1981) discusses the special strength of women who are able to leave abusive relationships despite social and economic obstacles. It is possible that the women who attended the group were primed to utilize the intervention offered,

Table 19.2

Deviation from Factor Score Means on Child Measure (SPPI)

Achenbach Child Behavior Checklist (CBCL)	Pre	Post	Follow-Up
Feeling Factor Score	2.6*	2.1	0.6*
Relating Factor Score	1.8*	2.0	1.4
Achenbach Child Behavior Checklist (CBCL)			
Thinking Factor Score	1.4	1.2	1.0
Impetuosity Factor Score	1.4	1.6	1.6

* $p < .05$ that these scores are not different from each other

since they had already taken steps to modify the abusive family system. All of the women attending the group had been involved in therapy prior to and during the group intervention.

Despite involvement in traditional family therapy, all of the women continued to view their children as abnormally aggressive, and their family interactions as less than cohesive at the time of the pre-test. The children viewed themselves as more distressed than did the normative sample. Despite similar caseloads and the pervasive issue of family violence in most of their cases, therapists differed in the number of cases referred for the group intervention. This finding suggests that therapists, in some cases, may not be receptive toward employing structured group interventions with abusive families, which may affect the delivery of service to members of abusive family systems.

Directions for further clinical investigation include the addition of two control groups drawn from the clinic population: an unstructured support group to test the benefits of decreasing isolation without offering specific skills training and families who are in child and family treatment but not group treatment to test the relative effectiveness of these two modalities in decreasing patterns of intrafamilial violence.

Bibliography

Achenbach, Thomas M., and Craig Edelbrock

1983 *Manual for the Child Behavior Checklist and Revised Child Behavior Profile.* Burlington, VT: University of Vermont.

Barahal, Robert M., Jill Waterman, and Harold P. Martin

1981 "The Social Cognitive Development of Abused Children." *Journal of Consulting and Clinical Psychology* 49: 508–516.

Burgess, R. L., and Rand D. Conger

1978 "Family Interaction in Abusive, Neglectful, and Normal Families." *Child Development* 49: 1163–1173.

Forsterling, Friedrich

1986 "Attributional Concepts in Clinical Psychology." *American Psychologist* 41: 275–285.

Gelles, Richard J.

1982 "An Exchange/Social Control Approach to Understanding Intrafamily Violence." *Behavior Therapist* 5: 5–8.

Gibbs, John C., and Steven V. Schnell
1985 "Moral Development vs. Socialization: a Critique." *American Psychologist* 40: 1071–1080.

Glenn, H. Stephen
1983 *Developing Capable Young People* (audiotapes). Humansphere, P.O. Box 1566, Hurst, TX 76053.

Glenn, H. Stephen, and Brenda J. Wagner
n.d. "Developing Capable Young People Instructors Manual." Unpublished manuscript.

Glenn, H. Stephen, and J. W. Warner
1984 *Developing Capable Young People.* Hurst, Texas: Humansphere.

Goldstein, Arnold P., Harold Keller, and Diane Erne
1985 *Changing the Abusive Parent.* Champaign, IL: Research Press.

Moos, Rudolph H., and Bernice S. Moos
1981 Family Environment Scale Manual. Palo Alto, CA: Consulting Psychologists Press.

Patterson, Gerald R.
1986 "Performance Models for Antisocial Boys." *American Psychologist* 41: 432–444.

Reid, John B., Paul S. Taplin, and Rudy Lorber
1981 "A Social Interactional Approach to the Treatment of Abusive Families." In R. B. Stuart, ed., *Violent Behavior: Social Learning Approaches to Prediction, Management and Treatment.* New York: Brunner/Mazel, pp 83–101.

Sandler, Jack, Candy VanDercar, and Mariann Milhoan
1978 "Training Child Abusers in the Use of Positive Reinforcement Practices." *Behavior Research and Theory* 16: 169–175.

Walker, Lenore E.
1981 "A Feminist Perspective on Domestic Violence." In R. B. Stuart, ed., *Violent Behavior: Social Learning Approaches to Prediction, Management, and Treatment.* New York: Brunner/Mazel, pp 102–115.

Webb, Thomas E., and Chris A. Van Devere
1985 *Structured Pediatric Psychosocial Interview.* Akron, Ohio: Fourier.

Wolfe, David A., and Jach Sandler
1981 "Training Abusive Parents in Effective Child Management." *Behavior Modification* 5: 320–335.

Wolfe, David A., Jack Sandler, and Keith Kaufman
1981 "A Competency-based Training Program for Child Abusers." *Journal of Consulting and Clinical Psychology* 49: 633–640.

20

Social Support After Armed Robbery in the Workplace

Heinz Leymann
University of Umea

Jan Lindell
Research Foundation for Occupational Safety
Sweden

A total of 221 bank employees who were holdup victims were interviewed. Besides other topics, the interview focused on their receiving support from 15 different groups of people, including relatives, co-workers, authorities, different agencies, etc. The analysis of the data indicates that the most important groups providing social support were primary groups such as relatives, friends, and co-workers. The possible reason is that people with whom the victim had previous supportive relationships were also those who could be most supportive. Negative experiences were reported when meeting journalists and other curiosity seekers. There was considerable difference between the sexes in receiving social support. Women, particularly young ones, have the social competence needed to activate social support in their social network. Men do not seem to possess the same level of social competence.

On reviewing the literature on reactions to stress, one finds that in recent years there has been an increasing number of reports on the significance of social support (Cohen and Syme, 1985). More and more frequently researchers conclude that social support is one of the most

---

The division of responsibilities between the authors of this study was as follows: Heinz Leymann was responsible for the general planning and implementation of the study and the interpretation of the findings, while Jan Lindell was responsible for the statistical methodology and design.

important factors, if not *the* most important factor, when it comes to limiting the duration of stress effects or even preventing them, provided that they have not resulted in physical injury.

Research on social support has most often dealt with health outcomes regarding patterns of life events (Cobbs, 1979) or elderly people (Blazer, 1982). Research on stress traceable to organizational conditions in the workplace has produced a number of interesting findings. Here social support is regarded as a buffer function (Dean and Lin, 1977) in the face of pressing work situations, especially the combination of "heavy demands and little scope for control" by the employee in question. Significant statistical differences with regard to high blood pressure and myocardial infarction have been found (Karasek et al., 1981; Johnson, 1986).

On the other hand, the number of published studies on social support and its effect in connection with acts of violence seems to be very small as we actually did not find any after having searched in the files. Considering the social support given by co-workers, close friends, and members of the family in this context, our study is one of the first on this subject.

The Definition of Social Support

The term social support does not only refer to an overt supportive and empathic behavior. Social psychologists like House (1981) do include in social support different kinds of behavior from other people which might help a subject (in our research a victim) to overcome his or her obstacles:

- *emotional support* (esteem, affect, trust, concern, listening);
- *appraisal support* (affirmation, feedback, social comparison);
- *informational support* (advice, suggestion, directives, information);
- *instrumental support* (aid in kind, money, labor, time, modifying the environment).

In our research where we wanted to find out what kind of social support might be the one which helped best in an emotionally very disturbing situation, this definition along a functional line was somewhat troublesome. We wanted to know something about the difference between social contacts which felt good emotionally and gave comfort (e.g., a hug from a co-worker) and those social contacts which, after a victimization, were accepted as necessary and neutral/formal (such as an interrogation by the police).

This might be an oversimplified view, however. Johnson (1986) used the term "social support" in his study of a Swedish population. In this data base, regarding the Swedish survey of living conditions, social support meant a work-related social situation measured using a scale consisting of five dichotomous items: Respondents were asked whether they (1) could talk to co-workers during breaks, (2) could leave work to talk with co-workers, (3) could interact with co-workers as part of work, (4) met often with co-workers outside work, (5) and when they last paid a visit to a co-worker.

Johnson gave a very broad definition to social support, namely the opportunity to meet at all (which also is the case in Blazer's above-mentioned study of elderly people). Studies of this kind carried out by Johnson and others show the extreme importance of the mere access to other people to interact with. Johnson showed significant differences in cardiovascular diseases according to whether his measurement showed the existence of these contacts (less disease) or their non–existence (more disease).

One can of course criticize the numerous possibilities of definitions hidden behind the term "social support." Research in this area showed that the mere existence of social contact can result in supportive effects. Therefore, in our investigation, we looked for social support which did not necessarily mean empathic support. We used the social-psychological definition of social support and asked if the victim had had social contacts after the robbery (yes or no) and if he or she regarded the contact of being neutral emotionally helpful (supportive) or distressing (nonsupportive).

The Original Study

The present study is based on analyses of data from subjects who participated in a previous wider research program aimed at investigating psychological effects of violence at the workplace: namely which stressful experiences can bank employees encounter after their branch has been robbed? The interviews were carried out in February 1983. An analysis of the recall rates for groups of individuals (grouped according to the amount of time that had elapsed between the robbery and the interview) indicated that the memories of the individuals did not show any significant differences (Leymann, 1988b). The reason for this may be that the robbery was a significant event in the lives of the victims and the mental images were etched in their memories. The results of that study have been published in a number of reports. Leymann (1984) has given a detailed account of the study, its design and execution, as well as a presentation of the descriptive statistics.

Aim of the Present Analysis

In this report, we shall give an account of the subjective experience of social support received by victims of violence. We shall not deal in this report with the issue as to whether or not this support was beneficial to the subsequent state of health of the individuals. This point will be elucidated in a forthcoming article. Thus our questions are

(1) Do groups of people around the victim have criteria which separates them from each other according to their function in society?
(2) If people suffer from extreme life stresses, which groups of people in their environment do they feel will give them a certain kind of social support?
(3) How did the victims feel about the social contacts which they received?
(4) Are there differences to be observed regarding the former question and according to different groups of victims (such as sex, age, marital status, etc)?

Subjects and Methods

Subjects

Two hundred twenty-one bank employees from 3 large banks in the Greater Stockholm area and a bank in Jönköping were interviewed. This population comprised all of the employees involved in the 87 robberies committed over a period of 4 years at branches of these banks in these regions. The original population consisted of 230 persons. The drop-out total of 9 employees consisted of 4 persons who had moved to other towns, 3 who questioned the purpose of the study and refused to take part in it, 1individual whose responses referred to the wrong robbery, and 1 who was afraid that the interview might stir up unpleasant memories.

Methods

The data was collected by means of interviews using set questions and multiple-choice answers. In all cases the answers consisted of self-assessments and the victims' own observations. The questions pertinent for this report were as follows: Were you contacted or aided by (or did you seek consultation yourself with) any of the following persons in connection with or some time after the robbery? How did you experience this contact? Did you feel supported? Was it a formal, neutral contact? Or did you feel negative about the contact? Thus, the multiple choice consisted of 14 categories of possible individuals to contact or to be contacted by after the robbery. It also consisted questions about 3 types of contacts which the receiver evaluated differently. A few general follow-up questions were asked concerning the victims' feelings about having had or not having had such contacts after the holdup.

Statistical Analyses

Frequencies were calculated. Four separate factor analyses were performed for each type of contact or non-contact respectively.

Results

Frequency Distribution

The contact frequencies are shown in Table 20.1. The most frequent contacts were with supervisors, co-workers, police patrolmen (those arriving first at the scene of the crime), the interrogating police officer, family and friends. Contacts with the office supervisor, co-workers, family, and friends were generally considered to be positive, while those with the police were generally perceived as being formal. Negative contacts most frequently involved journalists and bank customers.

Results of the Factor Analyses

One way to obtain additional information about relationships and response tendencies is to use factor analysis. This shows the extent to which different groups of individuals were mentioned together with regard to the social contacts. Such findings can also be interpreted in terms of the significance of the different groups for the victims of the robbery. In these four factor analyses, the groups of individuals were largely referable to the same six factors, which are presented in Table 20.2.

Office supervisors, co-workers, friends and family were mentioned most frequently together by the victims when indicating the contacts they had had. Thus the tendency is that those who mentioned contact with co-workers *also* had contact with their family or friends. A more careful analysis of the nature of these contacts shows which groups of individuals were more or less important for the victims.

The Nature of the Contacts

Formal (neutral) contacts. Different groups of individuals were found to form factor groups. The analyses of the 4 forms of contact and non-contact deviated only marginally from the overall distribution in Table 20.2 in that the bank authorities ranked here as the second factor group

Table 20.1

Types of contact had by the 221 bank robbery victims with different persons in immediated connection with or after the robbery

Type of contact in connection with/after robbery

	Persons contacted	Yes, a formal contact (%)	Yes, supportive (%)	Yes, but negative experience (%)	No contact occurred (%)
1.	Senior executives	36.7	23.5	5.0	34.8
2.	Office supervisor	21.1	57.3	1.5	20.1
3.	Co-Workers	21.7	64.3	1.8	12.2
4.	Personnel Officer	13.6	6.8	2.7	76.9
5.	Chief Security officer	28.1	27.6	3.6	40.7
6.	Auditor	31.2	17.2	8.1	43.4
7.	Psychologist, soc. worker	1.8	3.2	0.5	94.6
8.	Physician, nurse	13.1	19.5	4.5	62.9
9.	Police patrolman	66.5	11.3	5.4	16.7
10.	Police technical expert	72.4	3.6	2.7	21.3
11.	Interrogating officer	69.2	11.8	8.1	10.9
12.	Law court staff	8.6	0.5	3.6	87.3
13.	Family, friends	13.1	72.9	3.2	10.9
14.	Bank customers	27.6	14.9	29.0	28.5
15.	Journalists	10.9	0.5	12.2	76.5
16.	Others	2.3	4.1	1.8	91.9

Table 20.2

Fifteen groups of individuals giving social support, broken down according to 6 factors

Factor group	Group of individuals and the number designating it in Table 20.1		Group characteristic
1	2	Supervisor	Primary groups
	3	Co-workers	
	13	Family, friends	
2	9	Police patrolmen	Public authorities
	10	Police technical experts	
	11	Interrogating public officer	
3	4	Personnel officer	Professional providers of aid
	7	Psychologist	
	8	Physician, nurse	
4	1	Senior executive	Company authorities
	5	Chief security officer	
5	6	Company auditor	Judicial functions
	12	Law court personnel	
6	14	bank customers	Curiosity-seeking bothersome
	15	Journalists	

ahead of the public authorities. The two groups of individuals accounting for the largest amount of variance (13 percent and 12.3 percent respectively) were (1) primary groups (co-workers, supervisor, family and friends), and (2) bank authorities (senior executives, personnel administrators, chief security officer and auditors). The third factor group was comprised of the public authorities (police patrolmen, scene-of-crime investigators and the interrogating police officer).

Supportive contacts. Here the breakdown of the groups of individuals is exactly the same as for the total distribution (see Table 20.2). The primary groups accounted for 15.8 percent, the public authorities for 11.3 percent and the professionals for 8.7 percent of the variance. Journalists and customers contributed least to supportive contacts after the robberies.

Negative contacts. These factor groups deviate completely from the pattern seen in the other groupings. The results are ambiguous; the groups of individuals do not fall into factor groups that can be interpreted in terms of uniform functions in relation to the victims. Cronbach's ala (1955) also yields poor reliability values. We interpret this lack of clarity not as a negation of a positively experienced contact (i.e., that the contact is *either* positive *or* negative) but rather as a sign that an intervening variable is involved. A contact is probably felt to be negative not only with regard to a particular group of individuals but also to what these individuals did or did not do in connection with specific events that occurred at the time of the particular robbery. Some statements in the interviews (see below) indicate, for instance, that a general state of discontent with the bank may cause contacts with it to be generally perceived as negative.

No contacts. Table 20.1 shows that the robbery victims generally had more or less extensive contacts with the different groups of individuals. The pattern of assignment to factor groups in the non-contact analysis follows that of the formal and supportive contacts relatively well. The primary groups account for 16.3 percent of the variance, the company authorities for 10.9, percent and the professionals for 9.1 percent.

Groups of Individuals Giving Support

Primary groups consist of the individuals with whom the victims have already established emotional contacts: they know each other, know what to expect from each other, they have (in many cases) a confidential relationship (or know that they do not have one and can therefore eliminate the contact in certain emergencies). It is only natural that individuals in these particular groups are best suited to give emotional social support.

Public authorities are important after the robbery since they can help to reduce the immediate fear that the robber may strike again, which is a relatively frequent source of anxiety (Leymann, 1984). The function of individuals in this group is to deal with the culprit. It is important that they arrive quickly at the scene of crime, that they work effectively, and that they catch the robber. The social support here is of an entirely different nature. It posits a respectful demeanor toward the robbery victims.

Professional providers of aid cannot give the same type of social support to the victims as the primary group can. The social support that these individuals can give is professional understanding. The victim also expects to have it confirmed that he/she has not suffered psychological damage—or at least that the processional knows how to treat it. Here the professionals have a very important function which we do not believe they are aware of. One frequently see these individuals competing with the family to show who can give the best emotional support. Much too frequently they increase the anxiety of the victims with exaggerated pronouncements concerning the degree of psychological damage which, in their opinion, the victims can expect in the future. They would probably be able to provide an entirely different kind of support if they became aware of this and concentrated on the social role they have vis-à-vis the victim of violence in this context, that is, to reduce anxiety by means of adequate information.

Company authorities are placed in an impossible situation by the robbery victims and their union representatives. Emotional support is expected from them. They are expected to show sympathy and to "stand up" for the victims. At the same time, it is not usual for company executives to be criticized by the robbery victims when they tried to show their sympathy by, for instance, sending flowers or treating the victim to refreshments. The fact of the matter is that the company authorities seldom have a chance to give emotional support. They and the victims generally have no previous emotional relationship to fall back on. Awkward attempts are then likely to be experienced as being—awkward. The role of the company authorities in this connection should be a different one: they can support the employees by preparing routines to be followed in such emergencies; they can see to it that the work stations are equipped with modern safety devices and that more reliable work routines are introduced (e.g., routines resulting in the keeping of minimal amounts of cash by the tellers); they can work out reserve routines to be used when a robbery occurs so that the victims can get immediate relief through temporary reorganization of the work; and perhaps most important, the executives could see to it that the employees get good training in all these routines as well as education in, for example, general knowledge in psychosomatic reactions in order to interpret correctly their own body reactions during and after the holdup. In this way it would be possible to take into consideration the high level of stress that afflicts most employees directly after a robbery and for at least 24 hours thereafter (Leymann, 1988b; Leymann, 1985).

Juridical functions. In the light of the criticisms that were voiced, great improvements can be made here. Above all, the *modus operandi* should be attuned to the attitudes of present-day society which, since the 1950s, has been characterized by much more democratic forms of social intercourse than those that existed in the older authoritarian society. It would appear that a considerable amount of the old authoritarian spirit has been preserved in the *modus operandi* of the judiciary.

Today the company auditor already has a different role to play in connection with robberies than he did just 10 to 15 years ago. At that time it was quite possible (executives told me that this doesn't happen any more!) that he would give the victim a piercing look and ask whether he/she had not taken money out of the till himself/herself!

Curiosity-seekers and bothersome individuals. These terms refer to customers who importune the victims with their curiosity. This complaint applies to journalists to an even greater extent. We are unable to see what these groups might be able to contribute in terms of social support for the victims.

There is, however, another problem that has not been included until now in the public debate about bank and post office robberies. The general public (i.e., customers in the bank or post office) can get involved in the robberies. It was formerly thought that rarely would robbers strike when customers were present. But this is incorrect. The general public is involved to about the same extent as bank and post office personnel: the number of customers who have experienced bank or post office robberies is approximately the same as that of the employees working there. Leymann and Andersson (1985) have shown that the customers involved in these robberies also have resultant psychological problems, although not as severe and persistent. These individuals have clearly expressed the desire that bank management and personnel show an interest in them. They would like to meet the staff and get the frightening experience "off their chest" by talking to them. These individuals, then, are needed for social support. But the bank employees do not agree, however. They do not make it possible to enter their group and regard these customers as troublesome.

Table 20.3

Calculated alpha values (Cronbach's alpha) for the factor groups with regard to the 4 forms of contact (only values ≥ 0.40 are indicated)

Factor group	Had contact: Formal	Had contact: Supportive	Had contact: Negative	Had no contact
1. Primary groups	.69	.67	—	.57
2. Public authorities	.40	.49	.46	—
OVERALL	.42	.54	—	.61

Reliability

In order to assess the appropriateness of the summations of values based on each of the six factors in the four forms of contacts and non-contacts, a homogeneity value (Cronbach's alpha) was calculated. The reliability is acceptable if alpha is greater than approximately 0.60 and is good above 0.80. Table 20.3 shows values above 0.40 which have some informative value.

Differences in Forms of Contact Between Different Groups of Victims

Up to this point the analysis applied to all robbery victims as if they were a homogeneous group. By no means, however, do "robbery victims" constitute a homogeneous group of individuals. Differences must of course be expected with regard to different background or personal variables. We looked at some differences of this nature between individuals: sex, age, brutality of the robbery, whether the victim had been robbed before, whether the victim had been involved in ongoing conflicts at home or on the job before or after the robbery, the degree of life stress in general at the time in question. The method of analysis used was a simple analysis of variance.

Sex. Women had fewer formal contacts on the whole than men ($p=.002$). They experienced contacts with the primary groups as being supportive more often than men ($p<.000$) and also with all the different groups of individuals as a whole ($p=.005$). The police contacted male victims more frequently than female victims ($p=.06$).

Women reported more frequently than men that they had received social support which they had experienced as being positive. Men reported less frequently than women that they had had *no* contact with others in connection with the robbery (neither a contact that was *offered* them nor that they *sought* themselves). Men also reported more often than women that they had experienced the contacts as formal ($p=.002$). With regard to these differences between the sexes, we would suggest three possible explanations:

(a) The men themselves choose *not* to establish contact or they choose formal/neutral contacts over other forms;

(b) they are offered emotionally supportive contact by society to a lesser extent than women and if support is offered, it is of a formal/neutral nature;

(c) a combination of these alternative explanations is also possible: men receive and are offered emo-

> tionally supportive contacts less often than women, so they do not seek such contacts—either because they know that they are difficult to obtain for men or because they have never learned to seek them.

Age. The oldest and youngest men in the population had formal contacts with the primary groups most frequently (p=.05). On the whole, considering all groups of individuals, the three youngest groups of males experienced these contacts as being negative most frequently (p=.06). The oldest and the youngest women had formal contacts with public authorities most frequently (p=.06).

Marital status. An interesting difference was found between males and females living alone. We saw that, on the average, men had more contacts of the formal/neutral type with regard to all the different groups of individuals contacting or contacted than women. We also found that single men had more of these contacts than married or cohabiting men. There was no similar difference between the women with different marital statuses. The situation proved to be the opposite with regard to the average number of contacts with all groups experienced as being supportive. Here we found that women generally had more contacts of this type than men. Moreover, single women had more such contacts than married or cohabiting women, while single men had an even smaller number of such contacts than married or cohabiting men. This is illustrated in Figure 20. If we compare these variations with the total number of contacts these different groups of men and women had, our data indicate that men and women had equivalent numbers of contacts (of different types) and that single men and women had insignificantly fewer contacts. The difference lies, then, in the type of contact that occurred. These findings present new questions: Did the single men actually *have more* formal/neutral contacts or did they have the tendency to classify the contacts they have as "formal/neutral"? And, conversely: Did the single women actually *have more* supportive contacts or did they have the tendency to classify the contacts they have as "supportive"? Or, stated as a general question: Are the differences between the single men and women due to differences in coping styles or to differences in their social perception?

Degree of brutality of the robbery. As a general rule, the degree of brutality of the robbery has nothing to do with the manner in which the formal contacts function in the primary groups. In the case of women, the more frightening the robbery was, the more forceful was the intervention of the company's professional providers of aid. This applies, however, only to the women who experienced this contact as being supportive (p=.04). In the case of the men, the more brutal the robbery, the more supportive contact there was with the primary groups (p=.01) as well as with all groups as a whole (p=.07). It can be assumed that the reason for these patterns may be that after witnessing a more frightening robbery, the victims themselves more actively sought close contacts with other people in whom they had confidence. Furthermore, in the case of both men (p = .05) and women (p = .03) it was found that the more brutal the robbery, the greater was the tendency to experience contacts *in general* as being negative. It is possible that this reaction is the negation of the preceding one, i.e., if a robbery was brutal and the victims wanted to be left alone with their anxiety or stress, they did not establish contacts themselves and the ones they had were perceived as being bothersome. We have no conclusive data to corroborate such an assumption, however.

No previous experience of robbery. Thirty-three percent of the robbed employees had experienced a robbery before. The men who had not experienced a robbery before tended to respond to contacts negatively (p = .06). This observation might possibly be explained by an earlier finding (Leymann, 1988b): men, more frequently than women, vent their feelings of stress after a robbery in the form of anger, although this was the case for only a *very small* group of men. The situation was different with women: the professional providers of aid intervened more often in a manner that the women who had never experienced a robbery before perceived as being supportive (p =. 05).

Life events occurring before the robbery. We found a significant deviation with regard to the number of contacts. Individuals who had experienced a large number of stressful life events *before* the robbery and also witnessed robberies of the more brutal type, had more social contacts after the robbery than those experiencing a less brutal one.

Life events occurring after the robbery. Stressful life events that occurred *after* the robbery produced no significant effects at all. A possible interpretation is that social support must be given *in connection and in relationship with* specific stress-producing events in such a manner that the victim will look for and recognize a connection himself (for example, as in this study, social support in connection with robberies). Presumably, social support must include explicit *communication* concerning the stress-producing event. Social support which is only potentially *available* in the victim's environment but which is not explicitly directed at a stress-producing event obviously does not give relief to the victim either, since there is no communication regarding the cognitive and social problems that are brought to the fore by, for instance, a robbery. If this suggested interpretation is correct, our conclusion would be that general life events have no bearing on the social support recorded here because the focus of this support was of an entirely different nature. It was on the robbery and not on any other stressful event. Thus, the social support recorded here had no spinoff effect on possibly timely life events.

Problems in human relations before and after the robbery. Sixty-six of the 219 robbery victims had problems in human relations at home or at work before the robbery, and 65 had such problems after the robbery. Of the groups of individuals listed in Table 20.2, only the professionals showed a statistically significant difference in the number of contacts. This applies to the formal/neutral contacts ($p<.000$). The subjects who had had problems with human relations before the robbery had more contacts of this type.

No significant difference was ascertainable with regards to the victims who had had problems with human relations after the robbery. There are probably logical reasons for this finding. If a person has problems with human relations and becomes a victim of a robbery, he/she has the chance to avail himself/herself of the offers of social support with connection with the robbery. It is more difficult to obtain social support with regard to problems in human relations occurring after the robbery because there is no "ready-made reason" for seeking supportive contacts. Information obtained from bank personnel officers indicate that robbery victims who had had different types of problems on and off the job were inclined to take advantage of the robbery situation and seek consultation about them. As one of the personnel officers put it: "They then had a more socially acceptable reason to approach me."

What Opinions Did the Employees Hold Regarding Social Contacts?

At the time when the participants completed our questionnaire, they were asked a number of open-answer questions in order to obtain some ideas about different aspects of their experiences as victims.

These questions were (1) Did you miss any particular types of contact, and, if so, which ones? (2) Describe your general reaction to having been supported by those who cared for you. (3) Describe your general reactions to *not* having been supported. (4) Are you disappointed, on the whole, with the action of (a) executives or the personnel department and/or (b) authorities after the robbery? (5) How did you react to the handling of the robbery by the mass media and their action in this connection?

Comments on the action of company management after the robbery. In response to the question as to whether they had missed any particular form of contact, 62 percent of the robbery victims stated that they had *not* done so. The following comments were made by the remaining victims who had missed such contact:

"Headquarters should have contacted us some time after the robbery."—"I would have liked to have talked to somebody in the personnel department who didn't just molly coddle and pity you, but could give objective answers."—"I would have liked to have had contact with a lawyer during the trial."—"A psychologist or physician should have come immediately."—"I am very surprised that headquarters did not get in touch. You would have thought that they would have been interested in knowing how we had managed."—"I would have liked to have had contact with a bank management representative."—"They don't get involved enough. They should have called up and expressed their concern more."—"They should stand up for you doing the trial and not turn their backs on you."—"The personnel manager showed no understanding. The only thing he could think of doing was to hand out flowers."—"The personnel manager's 10-minute visit was of no value."—"They could have shown a little sympathy. Given you a present, flowers or treated you to dinner."—"I don't know what they should have done. But they should have done something."

Comments on the action of the authorities after the robbery. Nearly 1 out of every 3 victims did not know whether the police had caught the culprit. Those who knew that he or she had or had not been caught had found it out in different ways: through the police, through the mass media or by hearsay. Since some of the victims had symptoms of anxiety in the sense that they believed that the robber would strike again, it would have, of course, been beneficial if the victims had been informed of the results of the work of the police as a matter of routine.

Twenty-seven percent of the robbery victims were obliged to witness in the presence of the robber or identify him at the police headquarters. Seventy-nine precent of these witnesses felt that this was a very unpleasant experience: "The police headquarters are so large. Nobody cared about you. Nobody asked me how I felt. I felt worse than during the robbery itself."—"I was scared to death and was not able to point out the robber with certainty."—"The robber got to know who I was. My name and address were read out. I felt exposed."—"I sat in a little waiting room about 4 or 5 feet from the robber."—"The police made terrible demands on me and my memory"—"The robber stared at me the whole time. It was unpleasant to see him and live through it all again."—"The robber's lawyer was aggressive."—"There were a lot of policemen in the court room. The robbers were handcuffed. Their leader stared at me the whole time when his lawyer cross-examined me. Heard that he had threatened witnesses before."

It is probably a normal reaction for law-abiding citizens to find it unpleasant to come into contact with the judicial agencies of society. Many of the robbery victims did not even know what takes place during a trial. The fact that the summons was written in a bureaucratic language and also threatened action against the person summoned in case he/she failed to appear was disturbing.

One-third of the victims were disappointed, on the whole, with the action of the public authorities after the robbery: "The emergency operator or the police called to check whether it was false alarm. In the meantime, the robbers were able to escape."—"I was summoned to appear the day after my wedding and had big difficulties to get that changed."—"There was little or no information from the police about how their work was progressing."—"The court's planning was poor. I was summoned and had to wait a whole day there, but still I didn't get in to witness."—"The police pressed me with their questions and didn't trust my statements."—"The chief examining officer was condescending."—"The robber's lawyer was impudent during the trial."

There was a large number of such statements. Most of them refer to the fact that the witness was disappointed in the slow work of the police in the investigation, that the witness was not informed as to whether the robber has been caught, that officials were rude, that the judiciary threatens witnesses and that so little respect is shown for the witness and his/her integrity.

Discussion

Sources of Error

Before drawing any conclusions from the present study, we want to focus on possible *sources of error*. Some of our findings are new within the research area focusing on social support. Thus, we found that different kinds of individuals, because of the differences in their occupational status, might have different support to offer the victims. After having shown this, one might say that the fact is an obvious one. But is that so? How many therapists would accept the notion that a victim can feel much more comfortable with a couple of co-workers than with an empathic therapist?

So far we cannot be too sure regarding this finding. The reason is that the concept of social support does not discriminate very well between its functions for a certain person (emotional, appraisal, informational or instrumental support) and the psychological effect this might have on the person in question (feeling supported, feeling helped).

But even if there may be one source of error here, we think we have contributed to the field by being able to point this out in our study. Thus, a development of the concept of social support should include , for example, a differentiation of the emotional responses of victims to social contacts: supportive social contact, neutral social contact and (which is, so far we can judge, not even mentioned in the literature) hostile social contact (as shown in Leymann [1986, 1988a] who investigated types of hostile behavior at the workplace).

Another source of error may be that persons with varied occupational status emerge on the scene at different points in time. As a result of this, the victim might evaluate and experience different persons as more or less disturbing or more or less helpful not because of what they might represent to the victim but by the fact that the victim at different points in time after the robbery can or cannot cope with certain types of social communication.

This is hypothetically not too difficult to explain. Using the same data as for the present study, Leymann (1985) shows that during the period immediately after the robbery, including the next 24 hours, all bank employees reported more stress symptoms than at any other time. These stress symptoms are of a certain kind, usually difficulties in concentration, despondency, listlessness, enervation, weeping, restlessness, aggressiveness. It might be that the victim wants to retreat to somewhere he or she can rest, surrounded by other people with whom he or she already has built long-lasting and mentally well-functioning social contacts while other people, such as police officers, auditors from the bank's head office or customers, are experienced as being disturbing people. This might change relatively quickly perhaps after one or some more days.

What needs to be stressed as a *finding* is the tendency shown in the study that a definition of social support not only has to focus on the *social function* which a certain social contact has (House, 1981) but also on the fact that these social functions possibly cannot be provided regardless of the individual giving social support. Social function thus has to be viewed as something belonging to a person because of his or her occupational or social position. Thus, it might not be worthwhile for a senior bank executive from the head office to rush to the scene of the crime in order to give empathetic emotional support, thereby competing with co-workers with whom the victim has had a very good relationship for a long time.

It is important to realize that a human being seems to need to be surrounded by a social network providing different kinds of social support as mentioned by House (1981) who points out that social support from co-workers, relatives, and friends seems to be the more important one.

Comments

One of the questions which Swedish company health service centers discuss is how to help employees who become involved in a holdup. Since one of the main aims for the original study (Leymann, 1984) was to improve this work, the outcome of the present study should be of great interest to professionals in these service centers.

As the data indicate, employees caught up in a robbery sometimes had great expectations about the help that they would receive from professionals and from the head office staff. How should these groups of individuals act when a holdup is reported from one of the bank's branches? The present study encourages a continued discussion utilizing as a point of departure some of the points of views expressed below. An interesting point in this analysis is that the factor groups do not sort the groups of individuals randomly. Implicit significances can be gleaned from the structures which then appear.

Conclusions

What, then, were the answers to the questions asked at the beginning of our report?

1. *Do groups of people around the victim have criteria which separates them from each other?* The answer is "Yes, we can find different groups of people." As mentioned in our discussion, these groups of individuals (see also Table 20.2) cluster together in a way which explains their occupational or social role towards the victim with reference to the victimization. The reliability of this finding is not very high probably because the 221 respondents were divided into 24 factor groups (6 occupational groups and 4 groups of contact and non-contact). Nevertheless there is a high level of consistency between the ranking of these groups according to their different types of contacts with the victims as shown earlier in the factor analysis.

2. *Which groups of people give what kinds of social support to the victims*? In our discussion we stated that these different occupational groups play different roles in the social network around the victim, and we propose to bear this in mind in future research into this role division. It is probably the case, especially in occupational settings, that a victim of violence cannot expect all kinds of social support from only one

group of individuals (see, for instance, some of the complaints which victims had during the interview). One result of this study then is this very concept, even if relevant data cannot yet be collected to prove it statistically.

3. *How did the victims feel about these social contacts*? Taking into account the number of respondents (namely 221) and the number of groups of people in the social network (namely 15, see Table 20.1) it was not possible to divide the number of victim reactions into a larger variation than we did (see column headings in Table 20.1). Adding their answers to our open questions, one can say that the victims seldom had ill-feelings about social contacts with two exceptions: journalists chasing them for sensational stories (see also Leymann et al., 1985) and customers in a never-ending line disturbing them with questions about the robbery or even with irritating jokes about it. We suspect that those victims who expressed the most serious complaints about contacts were in a situation where a number of problems, emerging in addition to the holdup, were irritating enough as to disturb these contacts.

4. *Differences according to the victim's sex, age, marital status, etc.* A number of differences emerged. Women had fewer formal but more supporting contacts than men in their surrounding. The data provided no explanatory clues for this finding. It is probable that social role differences between the sexes may play a part in this. Also regarding *age* we found that the youngest and oldest men and women showed significant differences in some aspects as to whether contacts were received formally. *Married* women had more supporting contacts than men. Unmarried women and men had more formal contacts than women and married men. Differences were also shown regarding the *brutality of the robbery*, whether the person had had *previous experiences of robberies* or *life events before the robbery*. Also victims who had *problems in human relations* before and after the robbery showed differences in experiencing different types of social contacts from different groups of individuals. These differences were discussed in detail earlier in this chapter.

Bibliography

Blazer, D.

1982 "Social Support and Mortality in an Elderly Community Population." *American Journal of Epidemiology,* 115: 684–694.

Cobbs, S.

1979 "Social Support and Health Through the Life Course." In N.W. Riley, ed. *Aging from Birth to Death.* Boulder, CO: Westview Press.

Cohen, S., and L. Syme, eds.

1985 *Social Support and Health.* New York: Academic Press..

Chronbach, L.J., and P.E. Meehl

1955 "Construct Validity in Psychological Test." *Psychological Bulletin* 52: 281–312.

Dean, A., and N. Lin

1977 "The Stress Buffering Role of Social Support." *Journal of Nervous and Mental Disease,* 165: 403–417.

House, J.

1981 *Work Stress and Social Support.* Reading, MA: Addison-Wesley.

Johnson, J.V.

1986 *The Impact of Workplace Social Support, Job Demands and Work Control Upon Cardiovascular Disease in Sweden.* Stockholm University, Dept of Psychology. Report, p. 1.

Karasek, R.A., D. Baker, F. Marxer, A. Ahlbom, and T. Theorell

1981 "Job Decision Latitude, Job Demands and Cardiovascular Disease: A Prospective Study of Swedish Men." *American Journal of Public Health,* 71: 694–705.

Leymann, H., and P. Andersson

1985 *Bankkunder och bankrån.* Stockholm: Arbetarskyddsstyrelsen. Undersökningsrapport 1985, p. 37.

Leymann, H., E. Svensson, D. Grunditz, and C. Enström

1985 *Att exploatera psykiska chocker—En överblick över studier kring massmedias rapportering.* Uppsala Universitet. Disaster Studies No. 19.

Leymann, H.

1984 *Psykiska reaktioner hos banktjänstemen efter bankrån. Del 2: Frekvenser.* Stockholm: Arbetarskyddsstyrelsen. Undersökningsrapport, p. 11.

1985 "Somatic and Psychological Symptoms after the Experience of Life Threatening Events: A Profile Analysis." *Victimology: An International Journal,* 10(1–4): 512–538.

1986 *Vuxenmobbning—Om psykiskt våld i arbetslivet.* Lund: Studentlitteratur.

1988a *Ingen annan utväg—Om utslagning och självmord efter psykiskt våld i arbetslivet.* Stockholm: Wahlström & Widstrand.

1988b "Stress Reactions after Bank Robberies: Psychological and Psychosomatic Reaction Patterns after Different Points in Time." *Stress and Work,* 2(2): 123–132.

21

Counseling Hostage Families: What We Have Learned from the Iran Hostage Experience

Leila Dane
Institute for Victims of Terrorism
McLean, Virginia

This chapter, drawn from a study of the Iran hostage wives' coping process, covers issues related to effective assistance to hostage families. It identifies family members as indirect victims of crime and draws comparisons and contrasts with current victimological literature. Three issues commanding immediate attention are the effect of hostage taking on sources of income, the primary importance of ego-syntonic social involvement especially in terms of its relationship to the dysfunction of denial in long-term stress and the need to monitor coping.

Effective therapeutic interventions use crisis techniques and informal counseling by individuals trained to minimize "second wound" effect and to attend to sequence of effect in this type of situation. Major precipitants of anxiety and depression are identified as news coverage and stressed relations with others.

The role of victim assistance programs in working with hostage families is also addressed.

Hostage family members are a growing population of indirect victims of crime whose demographics are so varied that commonality is found only in terms of shared personal and situational needs. They come from all walks of life, varied skills and educational backgrounds, ages, nationalities. Though some are related to a hostage who is politically aware and involved, others are related to a person who was simply in the wrong place at the wrong time. Whereas some family members may seek more media attention than the hostage situation is getting, others want no press attention whatsoever. Because this type of crisis is on the increase, it is incumbent on the helping professionals to become acquainted with hostage family needs and appropriate interventions to serve them. This chapter is based on research findings drawn from structured interviews with fourteen of the Iran hostage wives and from the Bugen-Hawkins Coping Response Profile (1981) noting differences in their everyday coping before and after the hostage taking (Dane, 1984). The research design focused uniquely on the hostage wives for statistical purity; however, these women reported that the effects discussed below were frequently found among parents, siblings and children alike.

Situational Factors Commanding Immediate Attention

There are three factors that warrant immediate attention: economic viability, or family sources of income; the need to affiliate, to be surrounded, connected; and the dysfunction of denial or the need to self-monitor and self-regulate, to assess and adjust one's coping skills in crisis. These factors warrant ongoing attention, too, but if they are addressed in the first few weeks of hostage taking, the stress experienced by the family members tends to be decidedly lower.

Economic well-being has been identified as a significant personal mediator in the victimology literature (Gottfredson et al., 1984). The hostage is often the sole producer of family income. If he or she was self-employed, the family members must either find work or turn to the extended family, or both. If the employer is industry or government, it may be possible for the family to receive a paycheck. But chances are that it is very time consuming to activate this change, and other efforts to cope with the situation cause the bills to pile up. It is important to pay immediate attention to the hostage family's financial situation.

The buffering effects of social support are also well documented in the victimology literature (Gottfredson et al., 1984). Research on the Iran hostage wives showed expressed commonality of need to be that of affiliation (Schachter, 1959) rather than support. One of the fourteen women interviewed was adamant that giving support to others was a very effective way of coping for her. She had no social needs beyond that; she felt it immediately and responded to it immediately. Avoiding isolation is thus of primary importance, especially in view of its effect on denial.

The interrelationship of denial and stress has gained considerable attention in recent years (Breznitz, 1983). The process of denial is best explained by the concept of a feedback loop which determines how much threatening information is registered before the individual becomes anxious and blocks off further exposure to threat until the anxiety wears off (Spence, 1983). It has become clear that in long-term crisis situations denial is dysfunctional (Lazarus, 1983). The changes in coping patterns resulting from the hostage taking are consistent with this literature. At the .05 level of significance there was a notable decrease in the use of denial and notable increases in the use of problem solving and of social support (Dane, 1984). When a certain type of stress must be addressed on an ongoing basis, denial can no longer maintain morale and minimize distress. Continued use of this coping response prevents ultimate mastery over the stressful situation. Although denial can have a certain positive value in the very early stages of coping, it cannot maintain this value if the individual's resources cannot address the situation in a more problem-focused way.

One of the women interviewed gave a clear example of this relationship in response to the question "What helped you most to survive the ordeal?" She stated: "In the beginning, I felt totally helpless, and I slept. When I could do things, then I felt better. Worrying must have been going on inside, but I was not conscious of it. Sleep was like dead. I got active when the State Department and FLAG asked me to do things. The activities were not self initiated" (Dane, 1984). The point made here is that the hostage family member must quickly learn to self-assess, to monitor his or her coping ability, and he or she may need considerable help in arriving at that point.

Therapeutic Interventions

The same resistance to professional intervention noted in the victimology literature (Symonds, 1980) exists to some degree among hostage family members. The mere fact of receiving attention from helping professionals raises anxiety. They are well aware of the human situation they are in and yet they easily feel scrutinized for evidence of pathology, as opposed to feeling relieved by recognition of an empathic outreach. Most of the pre-release contacts Iran hostage family members had with helping professionals were generated by the professionals themselves. Apparently, they were unaware of the effect of their style of presentation. The "second wound" effect often sets in, and the result can be anger reaction or obsessing over the severity of stress reactions the individual may have experienced. An effective therapeutic approach must follow the principles of crisis intervention. It must be information based and client centered. The coping response scale mentioned earlier shows a post-hostage-taking decrease in the use of Life Review. One can interpret that an individual's adaptive resources are too taxed to permit the reflectiveness necessary for reconstructive therapy.

Effective focus is on the individual's needs at the time of the counseling session. Media attention to hostage family members is often immediate, persistent and unrelenting. Individuals who have never been exposed to this kind of attention need help in defining the difference between personal matters that can become public information and those that must remain private affairs. They also need help in defending their right to privacy by establishing when and how they will be available to the press. If these limits of self-disclosure are not established early in the adjustment process, the hostage family member runs the risk of being disturbed at all hours of the night and of feeling exploited by the press.

Because denial cannot operate as a long-term coping mechanism, another primary need is the development of hope on some level. As Breznitz (1983) points out, the combination of no hope and no denial leaves an individual "psychologically defenseless." It is relevant to note that the one woman interviewed who had no hope of her husband's release experienced more stress-related symptoms than the norm. This woman eventually resolved her dilemma by getting back in touch with her childhood feelings of self-sufficiency; she is now divorced and very comfortable with her new life (Dane, 1984). Hope can be expressed actively through individual and group self-help efforts or passively through religious involvement or meditation. There is no need to alter an individual's activity patterns to help him or her develop hope.

Another need that deserves attention by those counseling hostage family members is that of social support or meaningful social involvement. The feelings of vulnerability can be so strong that effective social support is not always experienced from expected sources. Depressive reactions can be obviated by suggesting alternative sources of support and exploring the individual's possible resistances against reaching in that direction. Many of the Iran hostage wives were surprised by the support they received from the wives of Vietnam soldiers still missing in action, because their experiences of helplessness, solitude and an unpredictable future were similar. Some Iran hostage wives did not choose to identify themselves with that group because to do so would trigger anxiety-producing fantasies of what life would be like if the hostage did not return. Fear of the unknown was the most frequently reported pre-release stressor among the hostage wives (Figley, 1981).

Major Precipitants of Anxiety/ Depression

The traumatic stress symptoms of anxiety and depression are also experienced by hostage family members. Interview responses revealed that mood swings were frequently described by the Iran hostage wives as "an emotional roller coaster." At times the intensity of the experience was so acute that no amount of support from others was adequate; some women needed solitude to give vent to their emotions and soothe themselves. The major precipitant of anxiety and depression was news and the lack of news. A brief report announced over the radio or TV would raise hopes of a resolution to the crisis or trigger a full-blown fear reaction that the hostage would be put to death or that he was incapable of surviving his experience. Helplessness and lack of control over the political situation led to often futile quests for further, more complete information from the State Department and/or the media. At these times of high stress, turning to their informal sources of support, such as extended family members or their organized and unorganized self-help networks only made them aware of their stressed relations with others. This awareness was of itself a major precipitant of anxiety and depression. The vicious cycle would complete itself, and there was nothing to do but accept the mood swings, keep learning to self-monitor, and explore ways of curbing the extremes of their emotions.

The Role of Victim Assistance Programs in Working with Hostage Families

This is a small population of victims when compared to victims of other crimes. Services appropriate to their needs are not costly to provide, if there is pre-planning. Much of the work is performed by volunteers and self-help groups.

The first step is to establish a national network of identified volunteers who have survived this type of crisis, who understand the sources of these intense emotions, who serve as role models. These men and women would be ex-hostages and their family members, or family members of prisoners of war missing in action, or ex-political prisoners. They would be screened for adequate communication skills and minimally trained to avoid the kinds of judgment calls and value-laden interpretations that provoke a secondary wound effect. As the victim assistance coordinator learns of a hostage taking and acquires names and addresses of family members, he/she can identify the volunteer whose geographic situation is closest to the family. The volunteer should be approached by phone and by fax machine or the designated alternative means of communication that assures a prompt receipt of pertinent information in writing. The volunteer should establish contact with the family as soon as possible. This contact is most effective when it is maintained at least once a week until well after the hostage situation is resolved. Whatever model of volunteer counseling an administration develops, the value is in the support of consistent informal counseling, in the knowledge base of facilities and opportunities available, and in the familiarity with the sequence of effects of this long-term stress situation.

The sequence of effects of this specific type of situation merits a counselor's attention for two reasons: the danger in addressing post-release issues too early and the personal growth value of the experience. In the case of the Iran hostages, formalized professional attempts were made to prepare the families for the possibility that the hostages would show extreme signs of stress on their return. These group meetings, based on the principles of stress inoculation (Janis, 1983), took place well before the release was finalized and in most instances without the backup of ongoing counseling. The resulting effect among the majority of the families was disbelief and even hostility towards the helping professionals (Dane, 1984). This researcher's interpretation is that anxiety related to whether or not the hostage would be released was very high. It was taxing to address that issue with full attention. Post-release issues precipitated emotional overload and thus the defensive mechanism of denial. Personal growth due to the experience was interpreted from post-hoc self-assessment of coping. All fourteen hostage wives considered that they coped well; eleven spoke of increased self-esteem, sense of competence, self-awareness in terms of their strengths and their limits. Although the positive interpretation may be influenced by the fact that their husbands were released, it is their understanding that the growth was a part of the 444-day process whatever the outcome would have been.

The victim assistance coordinator can encourage the establishment of an organized hostage family members' self-help group whose officers have defined functions. One must give structure to the group in terms of objectives, long- and short-term goals, tasks and priorities. One must educate the members to the principles of group process that will emerge and how they tie in with the personal growth phenomenon mentioned above. One must emphasize the value of such a group, demonstrating for example, that managers of hotels and airlines are very willing to offer extremely reduced fares to members of a defined victim group organized in this manner when their travel is related in any way to their victim situation.

Depending on the size of the hostage family group, the victim assistance coordinator can encourage the group to start a newsletter. If the group members are passive, as can be the case early on, the coordinator can organize the first issue, eliciting articles and photos, establishing cohesiveness. Topics would be recent efforts to free the hostages, articles on federal regulations and actions concerning hostages and their families, and contributions from current and former hostage family members. The purpose of the newsletter would be threefold. It would define and maintain a viable support network and forum of communication. It would meet the need for a steady supply to the family members of reliable hostage-related information. And it would provide a means of informing the family members of the most effective ways to cope with their long-term stress situation.

Bibliography

Breznitz, Shlomo, ed.
1983 *The Denial of Stress*. New York: International Universities Press.

Bugen, Larry A., and Raymond C. Hawkins
1981 "The Coping Assessment Battery: Theoretical and Empirical Foundations." Presented to the annual meeting of the American Psychological Association, Los Angeles.

Dane, Leila F.
1984 "The Iran Hostage Wives: Long Term Crisis Coping." *Dissertation presented to Florida Institute of Technology.*

Figley, Charles R.
1981 *Survey of the Ex-Hostage Families Results*. West Lafayette, IN: Purdue Research Institute.

Gottfredson, Gary, Martin Reiser, and C. Richard Tsegaye-Spates
1984 "Psychological Help for Victims of Crime and Violence." In Arnold S. Kahn, ed. *Victims of Crime and Violence: Final Report of the American Psychological Association Task Force. Washington, DC: American Psychological Association.*

Janis, Irving Lester
1983 "Preventing Pathogenic Denial by Means of Stress Inoculation." In S. Breznitz, ed. *The Denial of Stress*. New York: International Universities Press, pp. 35–76.

Lazarus, Richard S.

1983 "The Costs and Benefits of Denial." In S. Breznitz, ed. *The Denial of Stress*, New York: International Universities Press, pp. 1–30.

Schachter, S.

1959 *The Psychology of Affiliation*. Stanford, CA: Stanford University Press.

Spence, Donald P.

1983 "The Paradox of Denial." In S. Breznitz, ed. *The Denial of Stress*. New York: International Universities Press, pp. 103–123.

Symonds, Martin

1980 "Acute Responses of Victims to Terror." *Evaluation and Change*. Minneapolis: Special NIH Publication.

Part III

Public Policy

Introduction to Part III

In the late 1960s, the Violence or Eisenhower Commission established by President Johnson in the wake of the assassination of Senator Kennedy, concluded that "the United States was the clear leader among modern stable democratic nations in its rates of homicide, assault, rape, and robbery" (National Commission: xv). The National Advisory Commission on Civil Disorders or Kerner Commission reviewed riots in 23 cities during 1967. The assassinations of Robert Kennedy and Martin Luther King, Jr., and the attempts on the lives of Gerald Ford and Ronald Reagan maintained a long tradition of political violence.

More than twenty years later, crimes like murder, assault, rape, and robbery have increased to epidemic proportions. The most recent *Report to the Nation on Crime and Justice* (1989) states that the chance of being a violent crime victim in the United States is greater than being hurt in a traffic accident and that five-sixths of Americans will be victims of a violent crime during their lives. Minorities are disproportionately affected as both victims and offenders. For example, 1 in 30 black males will be a homicide victim compared to 1 in 179 white males. Increasing crime rates are also being experienced by other Western industrialized countries.

Just as troublesome as the trend over time is the fact that the level of criminal activity in the United States is dramatically higher when compared to that of other industrialized and democratic countries. The fact that more than 1.5 percent of the U.S. adult population is under some form of correctional sanction should also raise serious concern. Some experts point out that, when it comes to crime, the United States more and more looks like some Third World countries racked by endemic violence.

Regardless and beyond actual crime rates, fear of crime has not diminished since the 1960s. Fear and perception are important indicators because they affect our lives and actions. In particular, the elderly—a growing segment in the populations of Western nations—are very afraid of crime, even though data indicate that they are actually victimized less frequently than other age groups and, particularly, youth. Most offenders and most victims are young and males.

Violent crime is so complex that no single explanation can account for all its manifestations and for all the assortments of victims and offenders. There is also considerable controversy as to what policies constitute the appropriate response to these enduring realities.

In this regard, a distinguishing feature of the 1980s is that it was the decade during which a serious start was finally undertaken toward acknowledging victims of crime as central characters in the criminal event, deserving concern, compassion, and respect. Research has played a major role in this rethinking and reformulating of public policies about victims of crime.

Actually, in the United States, concern for victims of crime has stemmed from two major philosophical and political orientations which are quite divergent in their reasoning and goals and which came to champion the victim's rights from different and at times even opposite directions: the women's movement for which this quest fit into an overall architecture of women's rights, and the conservative "crime control" movement for which the victim constitutes an effective political symbol and a rallying point for a variety of grievances, dissatisfactions, and political agenda (Viano, 1983).

Emilio C. Viano in chapter 22 examines the development of the victim rights movement in the United States within the framework of the history of the United States Constitution and Bill of Rights. He also refers to the recently adopted United Nations Resolution 40/34. The struggles, successes, and setbacks of the movement are highlighted.

Particular attention is paid to the passage and implementation of federal legislation on victim compensation and to recent developments in restitution, mediation, and reconciliation. The pitfalls of the emphasis on individual rights—a powerful cultural and political force in the U.S.—are analyzed. In its conclusion, the chapter calls for the adoption of an approach that stresses unity and cooperation as vital steps for the survival and success of the victim rights movement.

An excellent example of an innovative approach to criminal justice that takes the victim into account is victim-offender mediation and reconciliation which has grown considerably during the 1980s. The majority of the programs are operated by private organizations working with the courts. The vast majority of cases represent non-violent property-related offenses. The best model of victim-offender mediation is the Victim-Offender Reconciliation Program (VORP).

Mark Umbreit in chapter 23 examines the basic theory of victim-offender mediation and reconciliation in the context of its possible relevance to mediating violent victim-offender conflict. After reviewing current theory and practice, he fleshes out implications for modifying the current VORP model and also presents preliminary guidelines for practice. While recognizing the need for additional research and experimentation, Umbreit concludes that the process of victim-offender mediation and reconciliation holds a great deal of potential for addressing the emotional needs of some people involved in violent crimes as well.

Tim Newburn considers in chapter 24 the process of criminal compensation in Great Britain. This covers both compensation paid by the offender and by the state (the former called "restitution" and the second "compensation" in the United States and elsewhere). More particularly, the chapter looks at those groups of victims that are eligible for compensation under the two systems and considers what proportions of the eligible populations receive compensation.

Newburn argues that not only are large numbers of victims excluded by "threshold criteria" used by both systems but that other factors ensure that both state compensation and court-ordered compensation from the offender are not paid to all those who are eligible. The reasons for this are explored and the implications for both systems discussed.

In chapter 25 **Heinz Leymann** and **Kurt Baneryd** describe the development of victimological research in Sweden which has been spurred by developments in the area of work legislation. This, in turn, has resulted in regulations on how the risk of violence should be prepared for and treated at the workplace. Company health service centers and trade union safety delegates—the two most important entities charged with the implementation of the Work Environment Act in Sweden—then follow up these regulations with practical procedures.

Research has been stimulated by the increasingly intensive demands for more information about victimization in people's working lives. Three examples are given of how regulations relate to the Work Environment Act and how they are implemented in daily routines at the workplace. Recent developments in Sweden are also discussed. The current focus is on increased information on the situation of victims. The role of the mass media and of court procedures in secondary victimization are mentioned as areas of increasing interest for research and intervention.

Jacquelien Soetenhorst presents in chapter 26 the results of a study in comparative law concerning the revision of the criminal code in the areas of pornography and sexual violence in Denmark, Sweden, and the Netherlands from 1960 to 1985. She shows how during this period the political climate changed at first in the direction of liberalization and later—from the second half of the seventies—in the opposite direction. The women's rights movement played a role in this latter change. The aim of this study is to enhance our insight into what politicians meant by the revision of the penal code. Was it meant to express shared values (symbolic) or was it primarily meant to help solve a social problem (instrumental)? If the latter was the case, what is the influence of research on the decision-making process?

Parliamentary documents in Denmark, Sweden, and the Netherlands were systematically analyzed for the arguments used by the different participants to back the proposed revisions of the legislation on pornography and sexual violence. The analysis revealed that political demands determined the outcome of the revisions. Thus, the symbolic meaning dominates the more instrumental notions. Soetenhorst also found that the significance of research results was subordinate to the need to reach political deals. This decision-making practice on the part of the legislator increases the discrepancy between the expectations of the general public and the effects of the revisions in reality. The author concludes with recommendations for the legislator in order to narrow this gap and thus enhance the credibility of the political system.

Bibliography

National Commission on the Causes and Prevention of Violence

1969 *To Establish Justice, To Insure Domestic Tranquillity, Final Report.* Washington, DC: U.S. Government Printing Office.

U.S. Department of Justice, Bureau of Justice Statistics

1989 *Report to the Nation on Crime and Justice.* Washington, DC: U.S. Government Printing Office. Second Edition.

Viano, Emilio

1983 "Violence, Victimization, and Social Change: A Socio-Cultural and Public Policy Analysis." *Victimology: An International Journal,* 8 (3–4): 54–79.

22

The Recognition and Implementation of Victims' Rights in the United States: Developments and Achievements

Emilio C. Viano
School of Public Affairs,
The American University
and
Victimology: An International Journal

This chapter examines the development of the victims' rights movement in the United States within the framework of the history of the United States Constitution and Bill of Rights. It also refers to the recently adopted United Nations Resolution 40/34. The struggles, successes and setbacks of the movement are highlighted. Particular attention is paid to the passage and implementation of federal legislation on victim compensation and to recent developments in restitution, mediation, and reconciliation. The pitfalls of the emphasis on individual rights, a powerful cultural and political force in the United States, are analyzed. An example used is the current controversy between anti-pornography and anti–censorship feminists. In its conclusion the chapter calls for the adoption of an approach that stresses unity and cooperation as a vital step for the survival and success of the victim rights movement.

The United Nations Resolution 40/34 and the accompanying Declaration of Basic Principles of Justice for Victims of Crime and Abuse of Power adopted by the General Assembly on November 29, 1985, represent an important milestone in the development of a more equitable, balanced, and just approach to the treatment of the victim in the criminal justice process. They represent another important contribution of the twentieth century to the expansion and protection of human rights. As Bassiouni (1986: 15) aptly states: "This expansion can be attributed to an ever-increasing sharing of fundamental values and expectations among nations. As a result, the world community now acknowledges the need to protect the individual from a variety of human depredations."

When it adopted the Declaration, the General Assembly underlined the need to introduce national and international measures to obtain the universal and actual recognition of, and respect for, the rights of victims of crime and of abuse of power.

Obviously, different countries and areas of the world have responded differently to the call of the United Nations. This variety of responses reflects varying social, economic, cultural, financial, and legal systems and circumstances.

Since the early 1970s in the United States there has been a concerted effort to bring about the recognition of the rights and needs of victims of crime and to provide them with various types of services deemed useful and appropriate. This process has considerably intensified in the 1980s. While it is difficult to measure at this point in time the extent of the impact that the U.N. Declaration has had on it, there is no doubt that it provided added credibility, urgency, and importance to the efforts of those working on behalf of the victims.

The Rights Movement in the United States

Victims of crime have attracted increasing attention in recent years in the United States. The reasons behind this movement are many and complex. One reason often mentioned, for example, is the concern about the continuous escalation of the rates of violent crime in the country and about the concomitant amount of victimization. Violent crime in America, at this time mostly connected with drug trafficking, is indeed touching more and more homes in the country.

However, at this time when the country has just finished celebrating the bicentennials of the Constitution and of the Bill of Rights, it is quite fitting that this contemporary concern be examined and understood within a constitutional framework.

If one were to ask what the Constitution of the United States really means, most people would probably answer: rights. The right to free speech, the right against incriminating oneself, the right to privacy, and many others that may or may not actually exist under the Constitution's explicit language. In the context of American history and culture, "rights" is a powerful symbol leading to action and struggle. This is particularly true now in this age of individualism and thus, naturally, of individual rights.

Actually, the Bill of Rights, as the Constitution's first ten amendments are called, was not part of the original document signed in Philadelphia on September 17, 1787. It was not adopted by Congress until 1789 under pressure from several states' legislatures. However, it remained virtually dormant for more than a century. Between 1789 and 1925, the Supreme Court used the Bill of Rights to outlaw government acts in only 15 cases. During the entire nineteenth century, only nine cases were decided under this rubric.

It was only after the Civil War with the enactment of the 14th Amendment guaranteeing rights of citizenship and equal protection of the law to all races and forbidding states to deprive "any person of life, liberty and property without due process of law" that a substantial change took place. Still, it was not until 1925 that the Supreme Court began to interpret that due process guarantee as encompassing most provisions of the Bill of Rights. The doctrine of "incorporation" with its far-reaching effects had been created with momentous consequences to unfold.

Another important development was the determined campaign by the National Association for the Advancement of Colored People (NAACP) and similar groups to see that post–Civil War civil rights guarantees were effectively enforced. A major victory, *Brown v. Board of Education*, was achieved in 1954. It signified not only the end of legal segregation in the United States but also the beginning of a concerted effort on the part of key justices to use constitutional law to tackle widespread social ills and address individual grievances.

It is against this background that one must place and understand the campaigns to gain more rights and achieve full equality in recent times by a variety of groups with different grievances that were inspired, motivated, and emboldened by the success of blacks. There is no doubt that the idea of equality, once officially recognized and declared, acquired an unstoppable life of its own and aroused the attention and interest of disparate groups feeling neglected, abused, ignored, and downtrodden.

During the last two decades in particular, the thirst and hunger for equality in American society have appeared to be almost insatiable and universal. Everyone has or claims to have rights: the accused defendant, the landlord, the tenant, the divorced father, the divorced mother, the surrogate mother, the adopting mother, the welfare parent, the fired employee, the employee passed over for promotion in order to redress past discrimination, the prison inmate, the homeless, the stranded airline passenger, and even proxies for animals used in medical experiments or raised industrially under severe confinement and living conditions.

The Victim's Rights Movement: Its Struggle and Success

One of the groups that have emerged in recent years seeking recognition and respect has been the victims' rights "movement." Disparate elements and forces have and still are campaigning for victims' rights.

The women's movement did much to emphasize the plight of rape victims in the legal process and to bring out into the open the difficult and controversial issue of domestic violence. Concerned physicians, nurses, and social workers championed the cause of the abused and neglected child. Parents of Murdered Children and Compassionate Friends worked to increase society's awareness and recognition of the problems encountered by homicide survivors. Mothers Against Drunk Driving (MADD) and Students Against Drunk Driving (SADD) have campaigned for the enactment of stricter laws and more severe sanctions against people arrested for driving while intoxicated. Other organizations, like the Society's League Against Molesters (SLAM) and the National Center for Missing Children, work for the needs and rights of abused, molested, abducted, and missing children and for the passage of stronger laws and sanctions against the perpetrators.

The success of these groups concerned with particular crimes and crime victims has served to highlight the general importance of "victims" as an effective political symbol and as a rallying point for a variety of grievances, dissatisfactions, and political agendas (Viano, 1983a and b). The early 1980s saw several expressions of this political awareness and recognition: the establishment of a Victims of Crime Task Force (1980) (subsequently, Presidential Commission of Victims of Crime) and of the Family Violence Task Force (1984) and the passage at the federal level of the Victims and Witness Protection Act of 1982, of the Victims of Crime Act of 1984 and of the Justice Assistance Act also of 1984. At the state level, the approval by the California voters of the widely publicized Victim's Bill of Rights or Proposition 8 (1982) amending the state constitution; the adoption of a similar constitutional amendment by the overwhelming majority of Florida voters in 1988;

and the enactment by twenty-eight states of similar bills of rights represented similar developments. For example, the Florida constitutional amendment gives victims the right to be notified, be present, and be heard at all steps of the case in the criminal justice system.

The rapid advances of the victim's movement can also be measured by the fact that, for example, in 1975 only ten states provided victim compensation, but ten years later forty states and the District of Columbia had such statutes. In the mid-1970s only three states allocated funds for domestic violence shelters; in the 1980s forty-nine states do so. Quite a few states now also fund victim/witness assistance programs, which was rare just a few years ago. Victim impact statements have also been enacted in many jurisdictions, although unfortunately the U.S. Supreme Court on June 13, 1989, in *South Carolina v. Gathers* reaffirmed the 1987 *Booth v. Maryland* ruling that banned their use, at least in death penalty cases. Thirty-five states now also allow some form of victim participation at sentencing.

We will now examine in some detail the implementation of at least one of these central pieces of legislation in light of the U.N. Declaration. This case study will be instructive in highlighting the pivotal role that the federal government plays in the introduction of legislation as a tool for social change while the states maintain considerable autonomy in the actual delivery of services. It is also important because it addresses the issue of financial support for victim programs, a crucial indicator of society's commitment to redressing the plight of the victim.

Implementation of Federal Legislation on Victim Compensation

The central element of the Victims of Crime Act of 1984 was the establishment of the Crime Victims Fund to be used to support state compensation and assistance programs for victims of state and federal crimes. The state crime victim compensation programs receive grants from the Fund according to a formula based upon the level of their compensation awards (which vary from state to state). In order to receive this financial support, the state compensation programs must cover medical expenses, including mental health counseling and wage loss attributable to physical injury and funeral expenses; it must promote victim cooperation with law enforcement; it must offer benefits to non-residents and victims of federal crimes on the same basis as state residents and may not use the grant to substitute for otherwise available state compensation funds.

Funding: It is important to note that the Crime Victims Fund is made up entirely of revenues from federal criminals like fines, penalty assessments, and appearance bond forfeitures. Law-abiding taxpayers are not contributing to it. The Victims of Crime Act also established special penalty assessments that are levied in addition to fines against persons and corporations and deposited into the Fund. It also introduced the so-called "Son of Sam" provision whereby a defendant's financial gains from the sale of literary rights and other profits derived from the crime may be claimed by victims or deposited into the Fund. The amount collected is steadily increasing: $68.3 million in 1985; $62.5 million in 1986; $77.4 million in 1987 (Office for Victims of Crime, 1988: 8). Interesting and important aspects of this approach are that, first, it directly links the size of the root cause of the problem to be addressed to the generation of the revenues needed to alleviate its impact and even to solve it and, second, that in this way, it provides a stable and certain source of income for funding and budgeting purposes.

Criteria for Funding: The victim assistance grants are distributed on a population basis. The base grant is $100,000. When it comes to victim assistance, priority must be given to programs serving victims of sexual assault, spouse abuse, and child abuse. Victim assistance sub-grants can be awarded to public or non-profit agencies that operate programs that use volunteers, coordinate victim services in the community, and assist victims in applying for compensation.

The Act is essentially meant to provide a financial incentive for states to develop and offer a complete range of comprehensive victim assistance and compensation programs serving all victims of crime. It supplements and encourages state support for existing programs and makes it possible for the states to address unmet needs by expanding programs that already exist or by establishing new programs.

The funds provided by the federal government must be used almost exclusively to directly assist victims. No funds may be used to cover state administrative expenses. Also, the intent of the Act is that, as much as possible, programs that already exist be utilized. In other words, the Act does not want to encourage the establishment of a separate network of services, unless absolutely necessary. It wants to encourage and support the utilization of services already in place.

Relative autonomy of the states: As one can readily see, the states have the primary responsibility to decide what types of programs best address their specific needs and to implement them accordingly. Federal requirements are few and relatively light. Regional, cultural, socio-economic, and other differences can influence and determine which types of services various states are going to offer.

One of the major reasons why the Victims of Crime Act of 1984 is examined in some detail here is that it may provide a good model when it comes to the possible establishment of an international, U.N. administered fund for compensation to victims of crime. The relationship between the U.S. federal government and the different states can be instructive when thinking of the relationship between the U.N. and member countries.

Actual disbursements: During the first two years of the program, some $51,000,000 was provided from the Crime Victims Fund for disbursement to the states to compensate victims of crime. Influenced by the Fund, the number and the amount of crime victim compensation awards increased dramatically. A comparison of 28 states shows that the number of awards doubled between 1985 (21,590) and 1986 (44,850) while awards climbed from $49,495,178 to $89,499,346 (Justice Dept., 1988: 21, 24).

Long-term impact: The impact that the Victims of Crime Fund has had on the establishment and viability of compensation and victim assistance programs in the United States can also be seen in the following outcomes:

- ➢ all states, except Nevada, that have a victim compensation program now compensate non-resident and federal victims as well
- ➢ compensation for mental health services as well as medical expenses is presently almost universal
- ➢ there has been an increase in the range and level of benefits—a fact that is particularly meaningful to victims that are poor
- ➢ the use of fines, penalties, and bond forfeitures to finance the cost of compensation awards has increased on the part of the states
- ➢ statewide coverage makes compensation available regardless of where the victimization takes place
- ➢ victims have better access to compensation thanks to the improved communications and sharing of information among victim programs
- ➢ there are signs that cooperation between police and victims has increased since the victims perceive the system in a more positive light (Justice Dept., 1988: 37–38).

Restitution: Bringing Disparate Interests Together

Quite often, the interests of the victim and those of the offender are contrasted as if they are at the opposite ends of a continuum; as if they are part of a zero-sum equation so that one's gain is the other's loss; as if they are antithetical and inimical. This perception and assessment are often used to dismiss victim-oriented approaches and to oppose proposals that address the needs of victims.

To illustrate the point that such an understanding of victim rights and assistance is incorrect, one could wisely use restitution. It constitutes an excellent example of convergent interests. While many, including victim advocates and academics, often assume that victims are principally interested in the loftier goals of justice and retribution, it may very well be that, particularly in the case of property crimes, their preponderant interests are recovery and financial reparation.

Most offenders, given the choice between jail and probation, most probably prefer probation and restitution. (Restitution has been used most frequently as condition of probation.) The state, faced with prison overcrowding and mounting expenses, also welcomes this arrangement as a practical and cheaper disposition of the case. Thus, the interest of all parties involved in the criminal process is apparently well served.

Along with compensation, the U.N. Declaration dedicates considerable attention to restitution as an important "sentencing option." Restitution generally calls for return of property or for damages, if it is not possible to return it; compensation for harm suffered; and restoration of rights in cases of violation of international criminal law, human rights violations, and other abuses of power where it is necessary to restore the injured party back to the legal status in which he or she was before the transgression happened.

Reflecting this approach, in the United States, for example, the Federal Victim and Witness Protection Act provides that the judge at sentencing "may" order restitution and "shall" state his or her reasons "on the record" for not doing so [18 U.S.C. §3579a(2) (1982)]. The California Victim's Bill of Rights goes even further, stating that "restitution shall be ordered . . . in every case, regardless of the sentence or disposition imposed . . . unless compelling and extraordinary reasons exist to the contrary" [Cal. Const. art. I, §28(b); also Cal. Penal Code §1191.1 (West Supp., 1985)]. Restitution and mediated agreements are now widely used as a sentencing option in the United States.

For example, a *victim-offender mediation* program in Minneapolis-St. Paul, Minnesota, confirms previous experience regarding the feasibility of implementing a victim-offender mediation program. The program primarily serves victims of juvenile burglary and their offenders. In the first two years, 165 offenders participated. There were a total of 162 victims, of whom 54 percent (87) decided to meet their offenders. One hundred twenty-eight agreements were negotiated involving 99 offenders and 84 victims: 44 percent called for monetary restitution; 17 percent for personal service restitution; 6 percent for both; 10 percent for community service restitution; 2 percent for both community service and monetary restitution; 20 percent for apologies only; and 2 percent had other requirements (Galaway, 1989).

Victims who experienced monetary loss experienced a mean loss of $745, including amounts reimbursed by insurance companies; offenders who negotiated monetary restitution obligations had a mean obligation of $247. Seventy-nine percent (101) of the agreements were successfully closed.

Another promising example of mediation programs are the various *Victim-Offender Reconciliation Programs* (VORP) that involve victims and offenders particularly in the United States and Canada. Originally begun in Ontario, Canada, the VORP idea was first operationalized in Elkhart, Indiana, and then vigorously diffused in the United States by the "Prisoner and Community Together" (PACT) organizations, the Mennonite Central Committee, several churches, and private foundations.

VORP represents a creative alternative to the traditional means of sentencing (e.g., incarceration) and dealing with criminal offenders that are available to judges and probation officers. The most important feature of VORP are the meetings arranged between offenders and victims which allow for negotiations, reconciliation, and restitution to take place and be agreed upon. The agreement reached at the meeting is articulated and recorded in a contract between the two parties which is then transmitted along with a written report to the criminal justice or community agency that first sent the case to VORP, for approval and follow-up. The cases referred to VORP are mostly property offenses, with burglary and theft at the top of the list. VORP has also been experimentally extended in some jurisdictions to violent offenses, like assault, armed robbery, and negligent homicide (Umbreit, 1985).

The benefits offered by VORP are substantial. The victim is provided a safe setting for meeting face to face with the victimizer in the presence of a well trained counselor. During the meeting, the victim has the opportunity to vent the feelings and emotions experienced in the aftermath of the crime, to ask questions of the perpetrator that may help resolve the fundamental question every victim asks, "Why me?," and to negotiate some way of receiving restitution.

The VORP meeting provides the offender with an opportunity to face the victim; realize the impact that the crime has had beyond the material value of what was taken; take responsibility for the crime; help the victim solve some of the feelings and conflicts generated by the crime by answering questions and providing insight into the dynamics and the actual carrying out of the offense; and ask for the victim's forgiveness. A clear benefit for the offender is avoiding serving time in a prison or jail with its dehumanizing and destructive effects, including the creation of a new set of victims, the spouse and family of the convict.

The community also derives substantial benefits from the VORP. They range from the practical ones, like some relief of prison overcrowding and of the cost of building and operating correctional institutions, to the more diffuse ones, like establishing a working model for the nonviolent resolution of conflict and experiencing the cathartic impact of reconciliation between people in conflict. VORP also stresses personal responsibility and accountability, the importance of facing up to one's mistakes, and the practical and spiritual benefits to be derived from forgiving and giving someone else another chance.

These experiences show that implementing a victim-offender mediation program is feasible. These programs provide victims with opportunities to participate in the criminal and juvenile justice process; serve important correctional goals; impact recidivism equally or more than other penal measures; furnish a reasonable alternative to the problem of prison and jail overcrowding; and generally receive remarkable support from the victims and the public. The results of the Minneapolis-St. Paul program, of the various VORP, and of other similar programs throughout the United States show that victim-offender mediation should be systematically implemented as the preferred response to at least property victimizations by offenders.

Restitution is especially meaningful and important because it reestablishes the original manner in which disputes and crimes were resolved between parties before the state gradually acquired total control over the disposition of crimes, preempting the actual victim from any active role or input into decision-making. Restitution is a powerful statement about the impact that crime has on a real, live person; about the needs and rightful expectations of the victim to be taken directly and personally into consideration; about the relationship that exists, uncomfortable as it may be, between the offender and the victim; and about the salutary effect that being faced with the concrete responsibility of making payments to someone out of one's earnings can have on the offender. Thus, restitution provides a genuine mechanism through which the victim is recognized as the legitimate aggrieved party whose needs must be taken into account by society and by the offender. That those needs are serious and important is underlined by the fact that neglecting them by not making restitution may lead to the convict then being imprisoned.

It is true that, at times, unfortunately, probation and restitution may work more to the advantage of the offender than of the victim. Few offenders, except in some white-collar crime cases, have the skills, the earning power, and the employment opportunities needed to meaningfully make restitution. At the same time, the state is reluctant to revoke probation because of non-payment when there may not be enough prison beds for more serious offenders. No doubt, there are victims whose expectations were raised by a restitution order only to see them dashed by the realities of life and the shortcomings of the system.

When the criminal cannot provide financial restitution and also when the perpetrator may never be found, the state then has the ultimate responsibility to pay compensation, at least in the most serious cases of injury and damages. Realistically, it may not be possible to ask the state to make good on relatively trivial harms. When it comes to property damages, another alternative is for the state to subsidize insurance plans covering them, particularly in high crime areas. While the political, social, and financial situation of a country will ultimately influence which solution is adopted, the important point is to formally recognize and support the principles of restitution and compensation.

Restitution does indeed offer an excellent opportunity to satisfy different needs and interests. The fact that at times it is an attractive but empty promise alerts us to the tensions and complexities of attempting to reconcile disparate interests in criminal justice. It also reminds us of the need to carefully think through new approaches and solutions.

One example of this is the difficulty that conservatives encounter when they insist that offenders be required to make restitution while at the same time they also demand increased and mandatory prison terms. The incongruence and the paradox here are transparent, to say nothing of how long the victim would have to wait before finally receiving any payments. The tension here is between making amends (restitution) and punishment (imprisonment). Realistically, one cannot have them both as the proponents of the crime control approach demand.

Rights and Fights: The Dilemmas and Pitfalls of a Litigious Society

How we define and address victimization in the political context of any country is subject to distortion and selective perception. There is no doubt that culture, value orientations, and political agendas lead us to overlook forms of victimization that do not fit into our daily experience; that do not affect us directly and immediately; that challenge our assumptions, beliefs, and complacency; and that require a higher level of social consciousness and political sophistication.

For example, the typical approach to victimization focuses on the individual victim and on the individual offender, a one-on-one perspective and unit of analysis that reflects only a portion of reality. It is essential that we widen our horizons and begin examining more of the victimization at the hand of the state, of institutions, and of power structures. While most of the current victimological work falls along traditional lines of inquiry, focusing on individual-to-individual relationships, it is time that we begin looking at the more diffuse and subtle—but by no means less important—relationships of power and oppression.

There is an urgent need to devote more attention to the recurrent instances of genocide, displacement, exploitation, and persecution of select groups at the hand of other, more powerful ones; the various forms of patriarchalism and colonialism; the misuse of psychiatric labels and facilities to suppress dissent and stifle opposition or unorthodox, innovative behavior; the acceptance and support of certain belief systems to justify oppression, discrimination, and their various manifestations like ageism, sexism, and racism; the orchestration of disinformation and other cover-up activities to manipulate public opinion and justify reaching political ends of questionable value with violence and war; decrying terrorist activities of certain groups while supporting those of others whose political agendas may be more germane or palatable. . . . It is important not to become mired in atomized thinking, researching, and theorizing although the emphasis on individual rights acts like a powerful magnet, tempting one to do exactly that.

Another danger of addressing the problems of victims by emphasizing their rights is that, sooner or later, the proliferation of rights causes problems and conflicts among those claiming them. The United States, for example, has been called one of the most litigious societies in the world. This is actually to be expected not so much because of some basic flaw in the American character but rather because of the nature of our view of where we stand vis-à-vis each other. A society composed of individuals with a considerable number of rights which are still being discovered and expanded cannot help but be litigious.

The effect of discovering, recognizing, and asserting a growing number of rights for certain groups in the general population cannot avoid pitting innocent groups against each other in a high-stakes, zero-sum game. A current example of this is the ongoing battle over affirmative action, the concept of preferential hirings, promotions, and places in professional schools for minority-group members and, sometimes, women. Thus, minority group members and women, wanting jobs and promotions, wrestle them from white men who have never indulged in discrimination themselves but who are asked to pay for past misdeeds of others.

Ironically, the outcome may not be what the victims really want. There is actually little information about this. Most victim studies have focused on sociological questions—who is likely to become a victim, what are the incidence and patterns of victimization, what are the services being offered to victims. Consequently, while we assume many things about crime victims, our beliefs, convictions, and conclusions may not reflect the reality of what it means to be a victim.

Similarly, programs for victim assistance reflect the views of society or of a particular group (liberal, feminist, conservative, etc.) as to the nature of victims and of the needs they are considered or allowed to have. Thus, for example, the assumption is that victims welcome and seek an adversarial procedure in the resolution of their case. "Rights" again are paramount in this process. But what if, particularly in the case of minor or property offenses, victims preferred mediation, dispute resolution, and even some form of reconciliation? Ultimately, the assumption that we know what the victim wants robs the victim of the dignity and control over his or her life that victim assistance is supposedly attempting to provide.

While we celebrate the bicentennial of the Constitution and of the enactment of the Bill of Rights within the rich and multi-cultural context of contemporary American society, we should be mindful not only of the achievements and of the promise that those venerable documents entail but also of the pitfalls, divisiveness, and backlash that a "rights" approach to life and human relations may generate.

The Anti-Pornography versus the Anti-Censorship Debate

An example of the conflicts that can be generated is the current controversy on pornography which has brought together the strangest bedfellows and estranged people one would expect to find united.

Two major camps have traditionally been involved in the acrimonious debate over pornography: the conservative right arguing that obscene material incites immorality and the liberal left which fought for its protection as a form of free speech. In the 1970s, a new argument emerged articulated and presented by radical feminists. It saw pornography as neither sexual permissiveness nor free speech but as an effective instrument for the repression of women. It was said, for example, that "pornography is the theory, rape the practice." The depiction of sexual violence was deemed harmful to women because it incited violence against them and also because it strengthened a social order in which men dominate women.

Initially, the anti-pornography position dominated as a given in feminist academia. Today, that view is challenged by other feminists as being simplistic and also politically unwise. What is criticized the most is the anti-pornography depiction of all men as violent and of all women as victims (Viano, 1985: 746–747). On the contrary, some critics say, pornography "empowers" women because it challenges and disturbs traditional and legal notions of sexuality and morality which are predicated on the exploitation and submission of women.

Thus, in 1984, several feminists—many of whom were well established feminist scholars—founded the Feminist Anti-Censorship Task Force (FACT) to organize opposition to legislation and ordinances introduced in some localities by the anti-pornography feminists. They objected on the grounds, first of all, that the connection between pornography and harm to women had not been established firmly and clearly enough to justify its ban under the First Amendment. Secondly, they argued that those legislative proposals violated the guarantee of equal protection under the law provided by the 14th Amendment because they reaffirmed and strengthened gender-based classifications and sexist stereotypes of women as vulnerable, fragile, and exploitable.

In 1986, U.S. Surgeon General C. Everett Koop issued a report that summarized current knowledge and research on the subject. The report stated that prolonged exposure to pornography can affect values and attitudes toward sex and that violent pornography leads to increased acceptance to coercion in sexual relations and, at least in laboratory experiments, punitive behavior toward women. However, the report also pointed out that the relation between attitudes and actual behavior is unclear, particularly in the case of pornography that is non-violent but at the same time degrading toward women.

Thus, at this time there is considerable disagreement on this topic with the anti-pornography feminists finding themselves in the same camp as pro-life, pro-family, crime control, law and order conservatives, hardly positions they are comfortable or supportive of. At the same time, the anti-censorship feminists find themselves working alongside conservative libertarians, anarchists of various persuasions, supporters and apologists for the pornography business, and sexist users of it. The rift between the two groups is actually increasing, particularly as the anti-pornography feeling is growing.

The issue is far from settled and it represents a vivid example of the complexity, divisiveness, and passion that different interpretations of "rights" can engender even among people who share basic beliefs, values, and agendas. It also shows the difficulty and disagreements encountered when trying to establish if there is victimization and of what kind.

The Webster Supreme Court Decision and Its Implications.

The controversy raging in the United States about abortion is another example of the dilemmas and dangers posed to our society by the exclusive and obsessive fight over the "rights" of the fetus supported by the pro-life groups versus those of the pregnant woman championed by the pro-choice groups. The Supreme Court's decision in *Webster v. Reproductive Health Services* handed down in July 1989 symbolizes these dangers well and is prodromal of a societal backlash against individual rights. In fact, it goes far beyond the issues of abortion and privacy to call into question the entire legal construct of implied "fundamental rights" built by the court over the last several decades. Thus, it impacts large areas of individual decision-making that will sooner or later find their way into the court's calendar. *Webster* highlights a basic conflict that exists in democratic societies: the desire and need to protect certain rights and to protect democratic decision-making. While people want both, it is not always possible to have them both at the same time. Since rights are recognized in order to protect the interests of what could be a minority of the citizenry—and the Bill of Rights is the classic expression of this concern—then it is entirely conceivable that, at least during a certain period in time, the wishes of the majority, democratically expressed through properly enacted legislation, are violating those rights.

The idea behind the doctrine of implied fundamental rights was to increase and strengthen the set of interests that could not be touched or unsettled by democratic decision-making, particularly in the case of "transient" majorities.

Webster appears to support legislative superiority in the area of abortion and to open the door for such legislative dominance in other areas of individual choice as well which presently are believed to be well protected as implied fundamental rights. Consequently, it dramatically alters the parameters of the conflict between our coexisting interests in both the protection of basic human rights and the utilization of the democratic process to further the interests and the convictions of the majority.

Webster and other Supreme Court decisions of the late 1980s that appear to curtail the civil rights of minorities and of employees give a powerful signal that the legal climate favoring the discovery and emphasis on rights of the individual which has characterized our society during the last thirty years may be giving way to one emphasizing and supporting instead the interests of the community and of the state. The "anything goes" era of individual affirmation and expression which has spawned several important movements, including the one on victims' rights, may be coming to an end with mostly negative repercussions for the efforts to advance the legal rights of victims.

In light of the coming changes in the interpretation of the U.S. Constitution that these Supreme Court actions foretell, it is clear that divisiveness in the victim assistance field will have very negative outcomes since it leads to fragmented efforts, fierce competition for scarce and uncertain funding, and lack of cooperation in serving victims. Budget deficits and reductions mean a shrinking pool of financial resources to support victim assistance programs. This in turn often pits victim services agencies against each other, exacerbates their ideological conflicts, and lessens their chances for cooperation.

Just as in the economic and international trade arenas we have realized that cooperation and pooling of resources are the key to survival and success, as opposed to our traditional emphasis on individualism and competition, so in social life we may have to pause and re-evaluate whether or not the current adversarial approach to affirm the victim's place in the criminal process or in other domains is the wise and fruitful course to follow in the long term for both the victims and the organizations serving them. For example, the U.N. Declaration wisely stresses the themes of "informal mechanisms for the resolution of disputes," restitution, compensation, services, and assistance.

Unity, cooperation and a realistic approach that does not eschew compromise when needed are crucial to the success of the victim rights movement. Otherwise, in the end, the increased recognition of the plight of victims of crime will be more rhetoric than reality.

Conclusion

The victim movement holds great promise as a force for genuine change in every society's attitudes and patterns of caring for its members and as an opportunity to stand up to crime in a positive and preventative way. It is to be hoped that it will be able to gain true momentum, avoid theoretical and programmatic pitfalls, and attain its full potential as one of the major social and legal movements in our contemporary constitutional and social history. Most of all, it is to be hoped that the U.N. Declaration will provide the impetus, unity, and underpinning needed at the international level to sustain the victim rights' movement in its crucial quest while also guiding it in the right direction to a successful conclusion.

Bibliography

Austern, David
1987 *The Crime Victim's Handbook*. New York: Penguin.

Bassiouni, M. Cherif
1986 *International Criminal Law. Crimes Vol. 1.* Ardsley-on-Hudson, NY: Transnational Publishers.

Bienen, Leigh
1983 "Rape Reform Legislation in the United States: A Look at Some Practical Effects." *Victimology,* 8 (1–2): 139–151.

Elias, Robert
1983 "The Symbolic Politics of Victim Compensation." *Victimology,* 8 (1–2): 213–224.

Galaway, Burt
1989 "Victim-Offender Mediation as the Preferred Response to Property Offenses." In Emilio Viano. *Crime and Its Victims: International Research & Public Policy.*Washington, DC: Hemisphere Publ. Co., pp. 101–111.

Henderson, Lynne
1985 "The Wrongs of Victim's Rights." *Stanford Law Review,* 37: 936–1021.

Justice Department
1988 *Report to Congress, 1988*. Washington, DC: U.S. Government Printing Office.

Office for Victims of Crime
1988 "Implementation of Federal Legislation to Aid Victims of Crime in the United States of America." Paper presented at the Fourth World Congress of Victimology, Bologna, Italy, 1988.

Task Force on Victims of Crime

1982 *Final Report.* Washington, DC: U.S. Government Printing Office.

Taub, Nadine

1983 "Adult Domestic Violence: The Law's Response." *Victimology*, 8 (1–2): 152–171.

Umbreit, Mark

1985 *Crime and Reconciliation.* Nashville: Abingdon Press.

Viano, Emilio

1983a "Victimology: The Development of a New Perspective." *Victimology*, 8 (1-2): 17–30.

1983b "Violence, Victimization, and Social Change: A Socio-Cultural and Public Policy Analysis." *Victimology*, 8 (3–4): 54–79.

1985 "Theoretical Issues and Practical Concerns for Future Research in Victimology." *Victimology*, 10 (1985): 736–750.

23

Victim-Offender Mediation with Violent Offenders: Implications for Modification of the VORP Model

Mark S. Umbreit, Ph.D.
Director of Research and Training
Center for Victim-Offender Mediation
Minnesota Citizens Council of Crime and Justice

The practice of victim-offender mediation and reconciliation has grown enormously during the past decade. The majority of programs are operated by private organizations working with the courts, and the vast majority of cases represent non-violent property-related offenses. The most well-developed model of victim offender mediation is the VORP model (Victim-Offender Reconciliation Program). This chapter examines the basic theory of victim-offender mediation and reconciliation in the context of its possible relevance to mediating violent victim offender conflict. After reviewing current theory and practice, implications for modifying the current VORP model are identified and preliminary guidelines for practice are presented. While recognizing the need for additional research and experimentation, the author concludes that the process of victim-offender mediation and reconciliation holds a great deal of potential for addressing the emotional needs of some people involved in violent crimes.

One of the more controversial and unusual justice reforms to emerge over the past decade is seen in the nationwide development of Victim-Offender Reconciliation Programs (VORP). Having initially begun in Kitchener, Ontario, in the mid-1970s and first developed in the United States in 1978, victim-offender mediation and reconciliation programs are now known to be operating or developing in nearly 100 communities across the country (Umbreit, 1988a, 1986a; Gehm, 1986). More than thirty programs have developed in Canada and new project's are being established in several European countries. Through the process of bringing crime victims and their specific offenders face to face in the presence of a trained mediator, a forum is provided for the expression of feelings, answering of questions and negotiating of restitution. There appear to be a number of benefits resulting from the VORP process, for victims, offenders and the larger community.

While there are many dimensions of the victim-offender reconciliation process that could be further examined, including a review of recent research, the specific intent of this chapter, however, is to provide a critical examination of the underlying theory of the VORP model as it relates to its actual implementation in the field. This analysis will focus upon the issue of the model's potential relevance to violent crimes, rather than exclusively non-violent offenses. It will be based upon the concept of grounded theory; the importance of social theory being rooted in emperical real life data that is understandable to both researchers and laymen alike (Glazer and Strauss, 1967).

In order to proceed with this critical analysis of the VORP concept, it will first be necessary to briefly present the basic theory and model of victim-offender reconciliation. The primary research question, as well as methodology, will then be identified. Finally, after presenting specific findings, a number of implications for the theory and practice of victim-offender reconciliation will be offered.

Current VORP Theory and Model

Overview

The victim-offender reconciliation process involves bringing offenders who are referred by the court (most oftentimes burglars and thieves) face to face with their victims in the presence of a trained mediator (Umbreit, 1986b, 1986c, 1985; Zehr, 1980; Zehr et al., 1983). Following an initial screening by staff, each case is assigned to either a staff or volunteer mediator. The mediator separately contacts the victim and offender in order to discuss the offense, explain the program and invite their participation. If both agree, the mediator schedules and facilitates a meeting.

During this encounter, victims have the rare opportunity to confront their specific offender and receive answers to many lingering questions they have such as "Why me?," "How did you get into my house?," "Were you planning on coming back?" Victims are able to express some of their feelings of frustration, if not anger. In a similar vein, offenders are given the equally rare opportunity to both begin to understand the more human dimension of their criminal behavior and to portray a more human side to their character, including the possibility of expressing remorse. In addition, offenders who participate in mediation may avoid a harsher punishment, such as incarceration.

Following a discussion of the facts and feelings related to the criminal act, the mediator assists both the victim and offender in negotiating a mutually acceptable restitution agreement. The program remains in contact with the victim and offender until fulfillment of the contract is verified. Follow-up victim offender meetings may be scheduled in certain cases when deemed appropriate.

The primary goal of these Victim-Offender Reconciliation Programs is to facilitate conflict resolution between the parties involved by first allowing time to address informational and emotional needs, then permitting a more practical discussion of determining a mutually agreeable restitution obligation (i.e., money, work for the victim, work for the victim's choice of a charity, etc.). Part of the theory of this intervention is that through face-to-face communication, in the presence of a trained mediator, the conflict can be humanized, tension reduced and stereotypes of each other reduced. The mediation process is believed to result in a more satisfactory experience of justice for both the victim and offender.

Most often, the victims and offenders involved in the program had no prior relationship. Rather than a primary emphasis upon restitution collection, the Victim-Offender Reconciliation Program (VORP) first emphasizes the need to address the emotional and informational needs of both parties through the process of face-to-face mediation, with restitution representing an important additional goal, a symbol of "reconciliation." VORP is not meant to be an offender rehabilitation program. Nor is it only a victim assistance program. Rather, it is designed to address the needs of both victims and offenders in a manner which personalizes the process of justice by facilitating the empowerment of both parties to resolve the conflict at a community level. The early success of the initial program in Kitchener, Ontario, in the mid-1970s quickly led to replication of the program in other parts of Canada.

The first replication of the Victim-Offender Reconciliation Program (VORP) model in the United States occurred in 1978 in the northern Indiana community of Elkhart, through the leadership of Mennonite church representatives, a local judge, several probation staff, as well as a local community corrections organization called PACT (Prisoner and Community Together). Within several years, this new project in Elkhart, Indiana, began receiving nationwide and international attention from the criminal justice community. In response to the growing number of requests for information about the program, as well as technical assistance and training resources, the PACT organization established a national Victim-Offender Reconciliation Resource Center. The theoretical and descriptive literature available on victim-offender reconciliation draws heavily upon the PACT experience in both pioneering the first program in the United States and providing technical assistance to local agencies in more than twenty states who have replicated the model. Published by PACT in 1983, *THE VORP BOOK* (Zehr et al.) became the primary technical resource for this new movement.

Value Base

As one of the initial developers of the Victim-Offender Reconciliation Program in Elkhart, Zehr (1980, 1985) provides a theoretical and value base for the concept. He begins by pointing out the strong religious value base, premised upon a Biblical perspective that views crime as a rupture, a wound in the health of the community which needs to be healed. Zehr states that from this perspective, the emphasis is upon re-establishing right relationships through reparation rather than retribution. This must involve addressing the underlying feelings of frustration and anger caused by crime. VORP is to serve as an alternative conflict resolution process for the courts in order to strengthen offender accountability, provide assistance to victims and divert some convicted offenders from costly incarceration. The importance of a new program concept such as VORP in providing some relief, however small, to the extensive overcrowding in jails and prisons is specifically addressed in an article entitled "Victim-Offender Reconciliation: An Incarceration Substitute?" (Zehr and Umbreit, 1983).

In a subsequent publication, Zehr (1983) clarifies the basic goal and justification of VORP by stating that despite many important sub-goals (i.e., offender rehabilitation, victim restitution, alternative to incarceration) the primary goal of reconciliation remains. Recognizing the unusualness of such a goal within the criminal justice system and the difficulty of precisely defining such a goal, he goes on to state that however it is defined it must mean the first priority is upon the relational aspects of crime. Attitudes, feelings and needs of both victim and offender must be taken seriously. Restitution is important but should not be the only purpose of the victim-offender meeting.

Major Elements of Model

The major theoretical elements of the victim-offender reconciliation model can be summarized by the following statements: 1. Crime should be viewed as relational, as a conflict among people rather than primarily an offense against the state. 2. Response to crime should be restorative rather than retributive. 3. Response to crime should address the needs of both victims and offenders, allowing for expression of feelings and opportunities for healing of emotional "wounds." 4. Victims and offenders should be empowered to work out the conflict between them and to directly participate in the justice process. 5. Reconciliation of victim-offender conflict leads to greater understanding of each other, the events that occurred and a more humanistic understanding of crime and its impact. 6. Reconciliation of victim-offender conflict leads to a reduction in the stereotypes that both victims and offenders hold toward each other. 7. The negotiation and completion of restitution (either monetary or non-monetary) by the offender to the victim is an important symbol of reconciliation. 8. Since restitution is an integral part of the victim-offender reconciliation process, non-violent property offenses committed by either juveniles or adults are the most appropriate cases. 9. The process of mediation involving a neutral third party with no coercive power is integral to the victim-offender reconciliation process. 10. The process of victim-offender reconciliation works best when administered by private community-based agencies, including the use of trained volunteers, rather than public justice system agencies in which probation officers, police or other public agents serve as mediators.

Limitations of Current VORP Model

As the Victim-Offender Reconciliation Program model has developed over the past decade, both practice experience and preliminary research has found a number of important benefits for both victims and offenders. The research by Coates and Gehm (1985) represented the most thorough assessment of the model. Its findings included a high level of satisfaction with the process, a perception of fairness related to VORP as a criminal justice penalty, a high degree of actual restitution payment, and a perception that meeting each other was beneficial for both the victim and offender. This research also found that some victims were critical of the lack of follow-up involved in specific cases. Subsequent research by Umbreit (1988a, b) found a very high level of victim satisfaction with the victim-offender mediation process and a perception of fairness among victims that was grounded in a concern that their offenders get help through some type of treatment program, as well as the victim receiving restitution. On the other hand, an earlier and less rigorous evaluation of VORP in Canada conducted by Dittenhoffer and Ericson (1983) was more critical of the model. Focusing primarily upon the systemic impact of VORP, they concluded that the program did not serve as an actual alternative to incarceration, as its initial developers intended. While still recognizing the potential for VORP to address important victim needs, including the possibility of conflict resolution with the offender, Dittenhoffer and Ericson concluded that the VORP projects they assessed tended to be preoccupied with the issue of restitution, rather than "reconciliation," despite rhetoric to the contrary.

After reviewing the theoretical base of the current VORP model, as well as some important research findings, several important questions emerge related to both theoretical contradictions and programatic inconsistencies.

1. If crime is viewed as relational and the importance of addressing the emotional needs of both victims and offenders is so central to the model, why does VORP focus nearly exclusively upon non-violent property offenses in which the emotional trauma experienced by victims is not as great as in crimes of violence?
2. If the model operates from a restorative rather than a retributive paradigm of justice (Zehr, 1985), why is VORP so closely linked to the concept of restitution which for many represents a policy of retribution and punishment, particularly in the context of the current national ideology related to criminal punishment as evidenced by the Reagan administration's support for restitution as part of its commitment to get tough with criminals?
3. Even with the nearly exclusive focus upon non-violent property crimes, if the VORP model is so deeply committed to viewing crime as relational and reconciliation as the primary goal of the

process, why is only one meeting lasting an average of one hour, with rare exceptions, conducted between the victim and offender, rather than scheduling one or more follow-up meetings? Is it realistic to think that "reconciliation" will occur in such a brief single encounter?

4. To what extent is the very goal of the model, that of reconciliation, more an ideological and symbolic value statement of its originators, rather than a grounded and realistic goal that has a clear meaning to those victims and offenders participating in VORP?

Research Question

The purpose of this chapter is to examine the question of whether or not the VORP model is appropriate for victims and offenders involved in crimes of violence, contrary to the initial design of the model. If the model is found to be relevant to violent crimes, an attempt to identify preliminary implications for practice will be made. Particular emphasis will be placed upon trying to understand the meanings of the concepts of reconciliation, fairness and justice through the eyes of victims who have been involved in the VORP intervention. While it would be desirable to also assess these concerns from the perspective of the offender, limited resources will not allow such an analysis at this time.

With the growing nationwide concern to meet the needs of victims, particularly those hurt by crimes of violence, the importance of examining the relevance of the VORP model with violent offenses is heightened. Within the field of both VORP and the larger mediation movement this truly represents the "cutting edge," as evidenced by the fact that nearly all mediation programs do not consider violent criminal behavior to be appropriate for the mediation intervention. How much of this analysis is based upon well grounded experience and consumer input, rather than a conservative and bureaucratic ideology committed to avoiding controversy and maintaining funding, is yet to be determined.

Methodology

In examining the issue of the relevance of the VORP model to crimes of violence, the methodology consisted of several elements.

1. Review of the VORP practice experience of the author in typical VORP cases (i.e., burglary).
2. Review of periodic informal, and often unsolicited, conversations with crime victims and criminal justice professionals during the course of providing VORP training or presentations in more than thirty states.
3. Review of four audio taped and transcribed interviews with victims of violent crime who were involved in a VORP meeting through the program operated by the Genesee County Sheriff's Department in upstate New York. These were conducted on February 11 and 12, 1985, and included the offenses of negligent homicide, armed robbery, criminal endangerment, and rape/child molesting. None of this data has been reviewed or written about until now.
4. Review of the experience of the author as a co-mediator in a sniper shooting case in which the two victims were nearly killed, in upstate New York, as part of the Genesee County Sheriff's Department program. This occurred in the summer of 1986.
5. Review of structured interviews with two victims of residential burglary in Hennepin County, Minnesota, who were randomly selected from a larger pool of 21 victims of residential burglary involved in the VORP project operated by the Minnesota Citizens Council on Crime and Justice.

Findings

When the VORP concept was initially pioneered in Kitchener and later replicated in numerous communities of both Canada and the United States, it was assumed that this type of intervention was primarily meant for cases involving non-violent property offenses. The fact that the VORP process included negotiation of mutually acceptable restitution essentially ruled out consideration of more violent offenses where there was not any clear restitution obligation present. Certain levels of violent crime, such as robbery or even assault, which might also involve some possible property loss to the victim have been included occasionally in VORP programs, although they represent a very rare referral type. And yet, even during the earlier years of VORP development in the United States, there have been periodic statements by a small number of victims of very violent crime which suggested the relevance of VORP for such cases.

For example, after seeing the VORP project in Elkhart, Indiana, highlighted on the NBC "Today Show" in an interview with Phil Donohue, a rape victim called the VORP program to ask if there was any chance of helping her. She had apparently been victimized several years prior to that time and had an intense need to confront the person who victimized her. Other supportive people in her life discouraged this, and yet when she saw VORP highlighted on national television, she thought the program could be of assistance. Staff in the VORP project did find the offender in the Indiana State Prison but did not proceed any further with the case. Too much time had elapsed from the point at which the offense occurred. The offender was now pre-occupied with his own feelings of isolation and bitterness related to his prison experience.

Again during the course of a television interview in Chicago, a similar dynamic occurred. VORP was being highlighted along with the Illinois Chapter of Parents of Murdered Children on a local television station. During the course of sharing information about each program just prior to the taping of the show, the leaders of Parents of Murdered Children in Illinois indicated that they could see some real benefits from being able to confront the individual who they believed killed their son. As with so many homicides, there was an ongoing friendship between their son and the person who killed him and as parents they had many questions related to what led up to the killing. Needless to say, this came as a very real shock to the VORP representative (the author) who had never even considered the possibility that victims experiencing the very painful and traumatic loss of a loved one might find assistance in bringing closure to their pain through direct confrontation with the person responsible for the death. On several other occasions, it has been brought to the attention of this author by victims of violent offenses such as child abuse, incest, and negligent homicide that confrontation with the offender, in the presence of a trained mediator, was perceived as likely to be very helpful to these individuals during their healing process as they attempted to bring a more healthy closure to the pain and trauma they experienced.

Two of the earliest programs providing victim-offender mediation and reconciliation services with very serious violent offenses are both operated by public sector organizations. The Oklahoma Department of Corrections Post-Conviction Mediation Program periodically works with victims of violent crime, although the vast majority of their cases are non-violent property offenses. As mentioned previously in this chapter, the Genesee County Sheriff's Department in upstate New York focuses exclusively upon violent felony offenses. Specific cases they have worked with have included incest/rape, attempted manslaughter, negligent homicide, armed robbery, and criminal recklessness involving a sniper shooting of several individuals. As a result of personal interviews with four of these victims, as well as briefer interviews with the two sniper victims, it became very clear that the victim offender reconciliation process was quite helpful to all of these individuals, except one of the sniper victims. The victim-offender reconciliation process allowed them to get answers to questions they had about the offense and to gain a greater sense of emotional closure to the trauma they experienced. Comments from several victims are illustrative. After having nearly been stabbed during the armed robbery of a gas station, the victim (the attendant) stated "after meeting them (the two offenders), I found that they weren't really hard individuals and I found out they were younger people too. . . . If these guys go to prison . . . they would definitely be messed up, and the next time they probably would kill the guy if they ever robbed a gas station again." The mother of a five year old girl who was raped by the mother's thirteen year old brother initially was so angry that "I wanted to shoot him, kill him." After participating in a victim offender reconciliation conference, she claimed her anger was far less and she was now able to be in the presence of her brother during family gatherings without completely losing control. One victim who lost her husband from a drunk driver who was convicted of negligent homicide stated "it was only at that point at which I confronted the man who killed my husband that I was able to move beyond the bitterness within my heart to a greater sense of peace."

During the summer of 1985, the program in Genesee County, New York, mediated the first known sniper shooting case to be referred to a program providing victim-offender reconciliation services. First, the normal VORP process of bringing the two victims, who were shot and nearly killed, face to face with the young offender, who pulled a rifle out and began shooting across the main street in a small rural community, was conducted. After a break for lunch, a second meeting was held with all of these individuals plus seven community representatives consisting of a minister from a church near where the shooting occurred, a former judge, a housewife involved in promoting drug abuse programs, the investigating police officer at the time of the shooting, a realtor, and a local attorney. This very violent offense had received banner headlines in all of the local newspapers and frightened the entire community. Therefore, it was believed that the direct involvement of a number of community representatives was important in terms of working toward some level of reconciliation between the community at large and the offender. In addition, because of the complexity of the case, the risk involved in utilizing mediation in such a setting and the uncertainty of involving a number of community representatives with the victims and offenders, a decision was made by the Genesee County Sheriff's Department to request assistance in co-mediating the case. The Sheriff's Department contacted the National Victim-Offender Reconciliation Resource Center of the PACT Institute of Justice in Indiana, which had helped with the initial development of the program.

Despite a significant amount of tension and stiffness initially, the two mediation sessions appeared to go very well. The two victims were able to get answers to a number of questions they had, particularly if they had been shot because of a dispute with a girl friend that both the victims and the offender knew. The offender eventually admitted that "the girl" was part of what led to the shooting but not entirely. He was depressed, had attempted suicide several times before, was high on both alcohol and drugs, and claimed he had no rememberance of the shooting. He had no recollection of the fact that after shooting at and hitting the two victims he shot himself in the head with the rifle. Both victims indicated they were glad to finally get this issue cleared up. While one victim did not believe the story about not remembering the shooting, the other victim mentioned his own problems with drugs and it was very possible that he (the offender) had a blackout of this event. This same victim told the offender toward the end of the first meeting that while he could never forget what had been done to him, having been shot a quarter of an inch from his heart, he could forgive the offender. The other victim still harbored a great deal of resentment and anger. At best, the mediation process appeared to take the edge off of his anger according to his statements. Community members present expressed a high level of satisfaction with their direct involvement with such a controversial and violent case in which they felt their entire community had been victimized. The offender expressed his satisfaction, as did both victims, with being able to confront each other and sort out some of the issues all were facing.

On March 10, 1986, structured interviews were conducted with two randomly selected victim units (families) who participated in the VORP project in the Minneapolis/St. Paul area of Minnesota. Both interviews were audiotaped. They yielded some helpful information about perceptions of fairness, meaning of reconciliation and potential relevance of VORP with more violent offenses. Both cases involved juveniles who committed residential burglary. Participation in the victim-offender reconciliation process was reported as being beneficial by both victims.

Curiosity about how the offense occurred, who committed it, why their home was selected, as well as a concern to let the offenders know there was a human dimension, a family involved, not just an empty house, were all motivating factors for the victims agreeing to participate.

One couple who was victimized felt the process was fair because the offender, who had a mental health problem, was able to be handled in a way that did not worsen his condition. They did not even require restitution. Instead, they were most satisfied with having had the chance to find out what was happening to the offender and to be directly involved in part of the justice process. Commitment of their offender to an institution was not viewed as appropriate. For them, VORP was a fair penalty and their understanding of fairness was centered around the direct personal accountability of the offender to them and the information they learned. Particularly since they had met the offender before, since he had played with their son, these victims found the VORP process to facilitate reconciliation among all present, including the mother of the offender. Statements such as "it made us feel better about each other" and "we left on a good note" as well as the fact that the offender apologized suggest their understanding of reconciliation. When asked about what they thought about the possible relevance of VORP in a more violent offense, such as if their son had been assaulted by the offender and hurt, the idea of face-to-face mediation among people who knew each other and were involved in some violent act did seem appropriate, depending on the circumstances.

The other victim expressed her sense that VORP was a fair penalty in the context of the requirement that the offender complete restitution. Rather than paying back money, the victim in this case required the offender to complete several days of work around her home and yard. In addition to the restitution obligation, this victim also seemed to feel the process was fair because it allowed her to get answers to questions she had, it scared the offender a bit by having to personally confront her, and it gave him an opportunity to correct the wrong he committed. While this victim had no prior relationship with the young offender, she did feel that reconciliation occurred. When asked about her understanding of reconciliation, she emphasized the restitution obligation as a way of restoring her loss and the sense of closure she felt about the event. In reference to the possible use of VORP in more violent offenses, this victim also felt in some cases it might be quite appropriate, particularly those involving drunk drivers.

In summary, during the course of the last several years there has been a small but growing amount of evidence, grounded in the statements of victims of violent crimes and the limited practice experience of applying mediation in such cases, that face-to-face contact between victims and offenders may be appropriate in certain cases involving violent criminal behavior. While the Victim-Offender Reconciliation Program model was explicitly designed for application in non-violent property crimes involving a restitution obligation, the findings reported in this chapter would suggest that the VORP model is equally, if not more so, appropriate in selected crimes of violence. Drawing upon the most fundamental element of the model, that of promoting reconciliation and healing within a context of viewing crime as relational, serious consideration should be given to significantly modifying the initial VORP model to include a new initiative in making the service available to some victims and offenders involved in violent crime. This new initiative should include the development of appropriate training materials for practitioners in the field.

Implications for Practice

Particularly since the application of mediation with victims and offenders involved in violent criminal behavior is at such an early and experimental stage of development, the most that can be offered at this time are preliminary implications for practice. While this assessment of the VORP model certainly suggests that the concept of providing opportunities for reconciliation through a face-to-face meeting of certain victims and offenders may be even more appropriate in the context of violent criminal behavior, it also recognizes that a great deal of caution must be exercised in modifying the initial model. It is particularly worth noting three specific concerns as one begins to look at the issue of applying the VORP model with violent offenses.

1. Extreme sensitivity must be exercised in working with victims of violent crime, including a recognition of the different rhythm in which people deal with their feelings. At no point should a victim of a violent crime (or even a non-violent crime) be forced, coerced or outright manipulated into the mediation process with the offender. To do so would place the program in the victimizer role and would violate the basic integrity of the model. Nor must a victim be placed in the position of feeling they "should" be reconciled with the offender. Whatever level of reconciliation that might occur, if any, must be genuine.
2. Sensitivity should be exercised as to when victims involved in crimes of violence should even be

approached about the opportunity to confront the offender in a mediation process. Actual experience in Genesee County would suggest that several months must elapse, after normal support systems begin to fade, before suggesting the possibility of VORP.

3. Victims and offenders involved in crimes of violence are likely to be in need of more extended casework services than the more typical VORP case. Therefore, it will be important for mediators to either directly offer additional supportive services or, more preferably, to assist the victim or offender in securing needed services.

As one moves from the presentation of basic principles to actual guidelines for the practice of mediation through VORP with victims and offenders involved in violent crimes, the task becomes more difficult. The following chart should be understood as an initial and rather modest attempt to begin identifying critical practice guidelines.

	Current VORP Model	Modified VORP Model
Goal:	Reconciliation	Reconciliation
Symbol of Reconciliation:	Restitution Usually	Reparation Usually
Mediator:	Volunteer	Professional
Co-Mediator:	Rarely	Frequently
Training:	12–15 hours	40–60 hours
Preliminary Victim Mtg:	1	3 or more
Preliminary Offender Mtg:	1	3 or more
Joint Victim Offender Mtg.	1	2 or more when Appropriate
Average Time Per Case:	3–4 hours	15–20 hours
Referral Source	Primarily Probation	Prosecutor or Victim Asst. Prgm.

Far more research and experimentation are necessary before the above modified VORP model should be widely practiced among victims and offenders involved in violent crimes. Certainly the experience of the Oklahoma Department of Corrections in applying mediation with violent offenses needs to be thoroughly examined as well as continuing to review the practice of mediation with a much smaller caseload of violent offenses in Genesse County. Yet, it is hoped that the above initial guidelines provide a framework for further development of the VORP model as it attempts to cautiously adapt to the needs of crime victims and offenders involved in violent offenses.

Bibliography

Coates, Robert B., and John Gehm

1985 *Victim Meets Offender: An Evaluation of Victim-Offender Reconciliation Programs*: Valparaiso, IN: PACT Institute of Justice.

Dittenhoffer, Tony, and Richard Ericson

1983 "The Victim-Offender Reconciliation Program: A Message to Correctional Reformers." *University of Toronto Law Journal.*

Gehm, John

1986 *Victim-Offender Reconciliation and Mediation Program Directory.* Valparaiso, IN: PACT Institute of Justice.

Glaser, Barney G., and Anselm Strauss

1967 *The Discovery of Grounded Theory.* Chicago: Aldine.

Umbreit, Mark S.

1985 *Crime and Reconciliation: Creative Options for Victims and Offenders.* Nashville, TN: Abingdon Press.

1986a "Victim-Offender Mediation: A National Survey." *Federal Probation,* December.

1986b "Victim-Offender Mediation and Judicial Leadership." *Judicature,* 69(4): 202–204.

1986c *Victim-Offender Mediation: Conflict Resolution and Restitution.* Washington, DC: U.S. Department of Justice.

1988a "Mediation of Victim-Offender Conflict." *Journal of Dispute Resolution* (University of Missouri Law School, Columbia).

1988b *Victim Understanding of Fairness: Burglary Victims in Victim Offender Mediation.* Minneapolis, MN: Minnesota Citizens Council on Crime and Justice.

Zehr, Howard

1980 *Mediating the Victim-Offender Conflict.* Elkhart IN: Mennonite Central Committee Office on Criminal Justice.

Zehr, Howard

1985 *Retributive Justice, Restorative Justice.* Elkhart, IN: Mennonite Central Committee Office on Criminal Justice.

Zehr, Howard, and Mark Umbreit

1982 "Victim-Offender Reconciliation: An Incarceration Substitute?" *Federal Probation,* 46(4): 63–68.

Zehr, Howard, et al.

1983 *The VORP Book: An Organizational and Operations Manual.* Valparaiso, IN: National Victim-Offender Reconciliation Resource Center of the PACT Institute of Justice.

24

Victim Compensation by the Offender and the State

Tim Newburn
Home Office Research and Planning Unit

This chapter considers the process of criminal compensation in Britain, this covers both compensation paid by the offender and by the State. More particularly the author looks at those groups of victims that are eligible for compensation under the two systems, and considers what proportions of the eligible populations receive compensation. It is argued that not only are large numbers of victims excluded by what Miers (1984) calls the "threshold criteria"employed by both systems but other factors ensure that both State compensation and court-ordered compensation from the offender are not paid to all those who are eligible. The reasons for this are explored and the implications for both systems discussed.

The British Criminal Injuries Compensation Scheme

In Britain the State-funded compensation scheme is called the Criminal Injuries Compensation Board (CICB). It was one of the first compensation schemes of its kind and, typical of such programs, it is limited to those who have suffered criminal injury as a result of a crime of violence. The scheme, however, also includes those injured while apprehending or attempting to apprehend an offender.

The fact that applicants must have suffered injury as a result of a crime of violence is therefore the major threshold criterion employed by the CICB, other criminal offenses being excluded from consideration. The second barrier is that applications for compensation must be made within three years of the incident in which the injuries were sustained. A pilot survey conducted by the Home Office (Newburn, 1989), however, suggests that in practice almost all applications are made within one year. The scheme also operates a financial minimum. Originally

£50, this has risen recently to £550. The exclusion of injuries thought to be worth less than the financial minimum is justified on the grounds that the inclusion of such large extra numbers would bring the system to an effective standstill.

Applicants must also be deemed to have cooperated fully with the police. Non-cooperation may take several forms, any of which may result in compensation being witheld or reduced:

- refusing to give evidence;
- unnecessary delay in reporting the offense;
- failure to support the prosecution;
- failure to provide sufficient evidence, etc.

Finally, there is the most contentious of thresholds, the character and conduct clause. This threshold is only crossed by applicants who are viewed as deserving, and by implication therefore, as genuine victims. Here aspects of the applicants' character and conduct may be considered by the Board to make an award of compensation inappropriate from public funds. Reasons given include provocative conduct on the part of the applicant, sustaining injury while committing a crime, having a criminal record (though the pilot research suggests that it is only those who have previous convictions for crimes of violence who are as a group less likely to receive compensation from the Board), belonging to a terrorist or other similar organization, etc. Compensation may be withheld or reduced for any of these reasons.

The number of applications made to the CICB is largely determined therefore by the threshold criteria operated by the Board. Determining what is likely to be the eligible population for compensation from the scheme is difficult as there are no data which cover criminal injury, or more specifically, the frequency and relative seriousness of criminal injuries. Even if available, such data would still not take into account the differing ways in which victimization is experienced. Nevertheless, a crude estimate is possible. The approximate size of this population can be established by taking the gross number of notifiable offenses against the person, together with notifiable sexual offenses and offenses of aggravated burglary.

Using this figure and the most recent CICB statistics, the proportion of the eligible population making applications for compensation can be estimated. On this basis roughly a quarter of those eligible to do so make applications, but it is possible that the actual proportion may be higher. Many of those in the gross total of notifiable offenses will not have suffered serious injury (indeed a few will not have suffered any injury) and therefore would have been excluded by the lower limit. Again the proportion that would fall into a category of "serious injury" is difficult to judge.

The only data that are available that may help in this regard relate to the effects of crime on victims. Maguire and Corbett's work (1987) suggests that approximately one-third of victims may be classified as being "particularly affected" as a result of the incident in which they were injured. This is perhaps as close as one can get at the moment to an estimate of the proportion of those reporting injuries to the police that would be likely to qualify under the terms used by CICB. Dividing this revised figure by the number of new applications, the proportion making claims to CICB rises to a figure nearer 75%.

This would mean that at least one quarter of eligible victims do not even apply for compensation. There are several possible explanations for this shortfall. Research by Shapland et al. (1985) suggests that one of the major reasons is lack of knowledge of the possibility of compensation. Despite numerous and varied attempts by CICB to publicize the scheme, it would appear that a considerable proportion of victims of violent crime do not get to hear of this avenue that is open to them. This lack of knowledge has long been accepted as affecting the number of claims made to State-funded compensation schemes. Recent research conducted by the Home Office (Newburn, 1988) suggests that knowledge of compensation also plays a significant part in determining the number of awards made by the courts in England and Wales.

The Court-ordered Compensation System

Under the system of court-ordered compensation, money is paid by the offender to the court, and from there to the victim. (In the United States, this system is called "restitution.") There is a broader threshold whereby victims of a wider variety of offenses—those suffering loss, damage or injury—are eligible for consideration. However, in contrast to CICB, reporting the offense to the police is not sufficient. The threshold criteria in this system are different from those employed by CICB.

Firstly, the offense must be one for which an offender has just been convicted, or that was taken into consideration by the court. For the victim to obtain a compensation order from the court the offender must have been caught, prosecuted and convicted (many victims are thus automatically excluded). When an offender is sentenced to a term of custody, an order for compensation is rarely made, and thus again compensation is rarely obtained by victims in such cases. The offender must also have the means to pay compensation, the law stating that the amount of compensation ordered must be what the court considers appropriate having regard to the offender's means. Finally, compensation is payable in relation to injury, loss or damage due to an accident arising out of the presence of a motor vehicle on the road. The boundaries of the system are thus fairly clear.

The eligible population is also fairly easy to determine, for it consists of all those suffering injury, loss or damage (subject to a few limitations) in cases where the perpetrator comes before a magistrates' or Crown Court and is convicted. What proportion of these people actually receive compensation from the courts? Most of the literature on the use of compensation orders has pointed to their use being concentrated in certain areas. The general pattern is that offenses involving material loss result in compensation orders more frequently than cases in which there is physical injury. The proportions of the eligible population receiving compensation vary from almost three-quarters of criminal damage victims to under one-fifth of assault victims. The reasons for this have been explored in detail elsewhere (Newburn, 1987 and 1988), but essentially the disparity is caused by the fact that both magistrates and police officers—who are the major agents in this process—find it more difficult to assess quantum in cases involving bodily injury than those involving material loss.

The police are reluctant to become involved in a process that would put the onus on them for assessing injury and consequently do not encourage victims of assault to make claims in court for compensation. Research undertaken by the Home Office (Newburn, 1988) found that the presence of a request for compensation (and therefore by implication knowledge on the part of the applicant of the possibility of compensation) was one of the most significant factors affecting the likelihood of compensation being awarded. In the survey of magistrates' courts, 77% of the cases involved a claim for compensation, and of these 82% resulted in an order being made. Whereas, in those cases in which no request was made in court only 21% resulted in compensation being ordered. Thus, magistrates who are anyway generally unwilling to assess compensation for injury are rarely called upon to do so.

Lack of Fit between the Two Systems

It is clear therefore that the two compensation systems do not mesh; they cover predominantly different offenses, operate at different financial levels and have quite distinct threshold criteria. Even in the area of criminal injury there appears to be little correspondence between the court system and CICB. As it stands at the moment victims of crime can (within certain limitations) receive compensation up to a limit of £2,000 per offense from a magistrates' court. In practice, often because the claims are small but also because of the limited means of many offenders, the sums of money involved are generally far below the lower limit operated by CICB. On average victims of assault receive less than £100 compensation from the courts. Although theoretically compensation should cover injuries up to and over the minimum threshold at CICB, in practice there exists a considerable gulf between awards from the Board and awards from the court.

In an effort to standardize the awards made for injury, a tariff was produced by CICB for use in the courts. However, our research suggests that magistrates tend to feel that the tariff is too low and consequently do not use it. Indeed magistrates appear to be caught in a double-bind situation. On the one hand they express a desire to award sums larger than those suggested by CICB. However, without hard and fast rules as to what injuries are really worth, awards are frequently not made at all. On the other hand, magistrates also appear to feel that the majority of cases coming before the courts are too trivial to justify compensation. These two sets of views are not necessarily contradictory. Thus in cases involving what a magistrate perceives to be a relatively serious injury, they are often put off awarding compensation by the figures suggested in the tariff produced by CICB. However, the majority of assault cases which come before the magistrates involve injuries that are not particularly serious and given the fairly small sums suggested for more serious cases, are felt therefore not to be especially worthy of compensation at all. The long-term consequence of this lack of fit between the two systems has been to reinforce the situation where compensation for injury from the courts is a relatively infrequent occurrence.

Possible Solutions

Is there a solution to this problem of lack of fit between the two systems? There are several alternatives, all of which involve potential gains for victims, but all of which are costly. The first is simply to attempt to make the two systems of compensation for injury mesh more tightly. This would involve the construction of an overall tariff that could be operated by the courts and CICB, so that those injuries that were sufficiently serious to justify an award from the State would come within the range of the offender in court. To do this, however, the financial minimum at CICB would have to be lowered considerably in order not to leave a gap between the two systems as at present. Such a change would involve a large increase in the number of cases that would become eligible for consideration for compensation from CICB. The cost of such an alteration would be likely to be prohibitive.

A second option would involve the scrapping of court-based compensation for injury altogether and a reduction of the lower limit at CICB in order to incorporate all but the most minor injuries. The objections to such a proposal would include that used to justify the higher financial minimum now: that the system could not possibly cope with the extra burden. Other drawbacks would include the withdrawal of the possibility of compensation for injury from the offender which has both financial attractions (it is less for the State to pay) as well as being justified in terms of its particular effect as a punishment which links the offender (albeit tenuously) to the victim.

Perhaps the most attractive solution would use some of the characteristics of both of these options. Magistrates' court clerks and victims interviewed as part of the Home Office research were all in favor of compensation being taken from central funds, as is currently done with costs, and then recovered, or partly recovered, afterwards. This is not a new idea. The Hodgson Committee (1984) and other authors since, have recomended the establishment of a victim compensation fund. This, it is suggested, should use money from fines, proceeds of sale of forfeited property and confiscation orders, as well as money paid in by the offender. Compensation would be claimed from the fund by victims according to their needs, irrespective of the offenders' means and indeed independent of whether an offender had been apprehended. This would overcome the problems associated with the non-payment of compensation by offenders, difficulties experienced by victims who receive payments only in small and irregular instalments but would also dispense with the gap that currently exists between the system of compensation provided by the courts and that provided by CICB.

All of these possible alterations to the present systems of compensation have both positive and negative attributes. Perhaps the greatest stumbling block is the cost of such potential systems to the State. This in turn necessarily calls into question the efficacy of criminal compensation altogether. What is the money actually being spent on? There is little evidence that financial compensation has either any positive effects on those who are ordered to pay it or that it alleviates any of the major problems—be they material or emotional—faced by victims. Given the likely costs of any of the possible changes, it is clear that research into these areas should be high on the academic agenda.

Bibliography

Hodgson Committee

1984 *The Profits of Crime and Their Recovery*. London: HMSO.

Maguire, M., and C. Corbett

1987 *The Effects of Crime and the Work of Victims Support Schemes*. Aldershot, England: Gower.

Miers, D.

1984 "The Criminal Injuries Compensation Board." Paper prepared for the conference on "Victims, Restitution and Compensation in the Criminal Justice System." Cambridge.

Newburn, T.

1987 "Compensation for Injury in the Magistrates Courts." *Home Office Research Bulletin* No. 23. London: HMSO.

1988 "The Use and Enforcement of Compensation Orders in Magistrates' Courts." Home Office Research Study No. 102. London: HMSO.

1989 "The Settlement of Claims at the Criminal Injuries Compensation Board." Home Office Research Study No. 112. London: HMSO.

Samuels, A.

1984 "The Profits of Crime and Their Recovery." Justice of the Peace. August 25.

Shapland, J., J. Willmore, and P. Duff

1985 *Victims in the Criminal Justice System*. Aldershot, England: Gower.

25

Risks of Violence in the Workplace: Regulations and Their Implementation in Sweden

Heinz Leymann
Department of Psychiatry
University of Umea, Sweden

Kurt Baneryd
National Board of Occupational Safety and Health, Sweden

This chapter describes the development of victimological research in Sweden which has been spurred by developments in the area of work legislation. This, in turn, has resulted in regulations on how the risk of violence should be prepared for and treated at the workplace. Company health service centers and trade union safety delegates (the two most important entities charged with the implementation of the Work Environment Act in Sweden) then follow up these regulations with practical procedures. Research has been stimulated by the increasingly intensive demands for more information about victimization in people's working lives. Three examples are given of how regulations relate to the Work Environment Act and how they are implemented in daily routines at the workplace. Recent developments are discussed. The current focus is on increased information on the situation of victims. The role of the mass media and of court procedures in secondary victimization is mentioned as an area of increasing interest.

Background Information

The risk of violence at work is quite large in a number of occupations. From victimizing a bank employee at gunpoint in a bank robbery to beating up a social worker at the social service office or a nurse in the emergency room, the types of criminal assaults are widespread. In Sweden, during the last fifteen years, roughly 1,500 armed robberies have been carried out in banks and post offices—with some seven thousand employees being the victims. This means that one out of six or seven employees in these occupations is victimized.

During this period, two employees at post offices were shot to death. Recently, robberies at stores and shops with late closing hours have reportedly increased. Other victimized groups include taxi drivers, who are beaten up and robbed, and bus drivers on public transit lines (e.g., in Stockholm), who report more than one hundred cases per year in which they are victimized by violent passengers, mostly drunk. People who commit suicide by using underground trains as their weapon make train drivers the victims of "traumatic" experiences.

In a nationwide survey, Stymne (1981) listed 24 different occupations in which the risk of violence is part of the work environment and in which employees run the risk of extreme psychological stress.

Employees in Scandinavian countries have started demanding safer workplaces. In 1983, a desperate man set off an explosive device at a district courthouse in the south of Stockholm, blowing the whole place to pieces. Fortunately, no one was hurt. Department employees, some of whom developed severe anxiety, campaigned against the employer, stating that they would not return to the restored building unless they were guaranteed better security.

Another example of employee action is a recently founded association of employees in serious conflicts with their superiors at work most often because of having discussed moral issues with them like, for example, the defense of their own or others' civil rights. As a consequence, they have found themselves abused and victimized by psychological violence. Suicides have been reported.

The developing interest in victimological issues in the work environment parallels a similar, universal interest in victims of all kinds of violence in society.

The increased interest of Swedish labor unions in this matter is not at all farfetched. The Swedish Work Environment Act states that employees are entitled not only to physical security through prevention of work accidents, exposure to toxic substances, and so on, but also through prevention of psychological problems brought about by conditions or circumstances in their work environment. This law also stipulates that every workplace should have access to a health-care center either company owned or jointly owned by several small companies, thus guaranteeing its implementation.

In view of the risks of violence at some workplaces, labor unions set up workgroups. These well-organized groups pressured Swedish work-environment authorities into looking more seriously into the issues. The union activities produced good results:

a. The National Board of Occupational Safety and Health issued general recommendations and regulations.
b. Company health-care centers found ways to implement these recommendations.
c. The authorities also granted sufficient research funds for victimological studies.

Authority Regulations

Regulated areas include psychological and social aspects of the occupational environment in general, the risks of violence, and solitary work.

Psychological and Social Aspects of the Occupational Environment: The General Aspect

The basic principle enshrined by the Swedish Work Environment Act is that, in addition to being as free as possible from physical and mental hazards, work must also provide opportunity for involvement and job satisfaction. This is further described in general recommendations published by the Swedish National Board of Occupational Safety and Health, entitled *Psychological and Social Aspects of the Occupational Environment* (1980).

Job content has an important bearing on the job satisfaction of the individual. Job content is determined by machines and technical systems as well as by the disposition and organization of the work. Effort should thus be made already in the work planning and designing stages to consider how the person concerned might experience his or her work situation. Work should be designed so as to provide the employee with the opportunity to influence and vary the work pace and methods and to survey and verify the results of his or her labor.

Work should provide an opportunity to utilize knowledge and skills and, preferably, offer development and new experiences. A shift from monotonous working procedures toward greater independence and vocational responsibility is an essential means of increasing involvement in occupational safety and health measures.

Contact with fellow workers is important to most people. Human beings need to experience community and security; they need to feel appreciated at work. Opportunities of contact with one's fellow workers hinge to a great extent on the way in which work is organized. Methods of management and supervision do a great deal to influence the development of the interpersonal climate at a workplace.

There are various signs of unsatisfactory working conditions which must be addressed to prevent illness and to develop and improve the occupational environment. For example, employees in a certain department, occupational group, or shift may have a high rate of absenteeism because of illness, or may show other signs of stress or dissatisfaction. The main responsibility for observing signs of this kind lies with management and the safety organization. When such a situation arises, the working environment and conditions must be examined and discussed by management and the workers concerned. It is important for employees to participate in the transformation of their work situation.

These factors, once developed, serve more than their original goals. They also function as a healthy environment where social support is given when extreme situations of stress occur, i.e., violence in the workplace.

Risks of Violence

General recommendations concerning the risks of violence in the working environment have also been issued by the National Board of Occupational Safety and Health (1983). They are intended to provide a basis for efforts to improve the security of persons whose work involves exposure to the risk or threat of violence.

Situations can arise for example, when (1) work involves handling objects that are desirable to outsiders (bankers, jewelers); (2) the individual on the job is regarded as being invested with some kind of authority (police officers, guards); or (3) work is done in such a place or context that it entails a risk of confrontation with provocative or aggressive persons (bus drivers, subway attendants).

The general recommendations call for taking the risks of violence into account early in the planning of the workplace and in the organization of the work. In existing workplaces, risks should be charted and a practical program drawn up locally, for example, by the safety committee, to minimize the risks involved. The risk-prevention measures mentioned in the recommendations include work routines and organization, facilities and equipment, technical supervision and alarms, and safety routines and training. Personnel-care routines are recommended for persons subjected to violence or the threat of violence in the course of their work. Recording and reporting such incidents are also recommended.

Working Alone

An ordinance issued by the National Board of Occupational Safety and Health (1982) concerns the risks of working alone and lays down the general principles governing work done in physical or social isolation from other people. The term "physical isolation" refers to a situation in which contact with other people is only possible by telephone, radio, or some other technical means of communication. Social isolation implies that, although there are other people in the vicinity, one cannot count on their support and assistance in a critical situation. This applies, for example, to police duties and nursing.

The employee's opportunity to make contact with other people must be taken into consideration when solitary work is being planned and organized. Steps must be taken to organize solitary work as much as possible in such a way that a person working alone does not incur a greater risk of injury than would be the case if several persons did the work together. This regards not only the risk of violence but every possible risk situation, e.g., accidents.

If the work entails substantial accident risks, it must be organized in such a way that help would be rapidly forthcoming in an emergency. If acceptable safety cannot be attained by any other means, the work may not be done without a second person being present. If solitary work entails great mental stress, efforts must be made to give the employee an opportunity of direct contact with fellow employees or other people. Minors may not be given hazardous or strenuous solitary work, and it is the employer's duty to notify the safety delegate when such solitary work is arranged.

Implementation

The Swedish Work Environment Act is constructed to not only state how conditions should be but also to give directions for implementation. It gives employees and their union delegates the "right to know," which is quite important in order to press legal issues. Just to name one example, it states that every workplace with more than five employees must have a safety delegate elected by and from among the employees.

Companies large enough to have more than one safety delegate must elect a general safety delegate. Companies with more than fifty employees must have a safety committee on which the employees have one seat more than the employer who, however, is the chairman. Occupational safety and health planning and implementation is to be carried out by these committees.

The target, according to the law, is that every workplace be connected to a health-care center. For every 2,500 workers, these centers employ one physician, two nurses, and one safety engineer. In approximately one-third of all centers in the country there is also a psychologist on duty. This company health-care team is directed by the company's safety committee and not by the employer. This gives the employees quite a powerful ability to influence the implementation of the act. However, safety work is mainly carried out according to Swedish customs of more than fifty years, that is, through bargaining between the parties, and only rarely through open conflict.

This gives the company health-care center an important role in the practical implementation of safety regulations. However, the aim here is not to paint too nice a picture of working conditions in Sweden. The implementation of safety regulations has so far reached only a minority of employees at risk. Often ignored are those employed in small enterprises. As unions push on to bring about changes, this situation is expected to shift rapidly.

The following are some examples of health-care programs addressing the risk of victimization.

Example 1: The Swedish Foundation for Health, Occupation, and Safety for State Employees (SH)

This health-care service for government employees has branches all over the country with functions similar to those of company health service centers in the private sector. Its main office employs specialists in victimology who, with the authority's regulations as a platform, work out practical procedures for handling the risk of violence and victim situations at the workplace, especially those of government employees. Professions at risk are police officers (physical assaults), post office workers (robberies), train operators (suicide attempts on the tracks), sheriffs and prosecutors (physical assaults), and so on.

A special workgroup at the main office has developed a handbook and a training program to distribute information about victimology and how to handle certain situations. The documentation covers three areas.

Risk Prevention

Principal steps to prevent violence at the workplace are worked out. SH suggests starting with the following questions at every workplace: Is the work prone to the risk of violence or the threat of the use of violence? Have there been cases of violence at that workplace? Where at the workplace did it occur? In what circumstances and at what time during the day? How many employees work at the risky workplace, and how is their work organized? Is there a security plan, and what is it like? How soon after an attempt can help from the outside be expected? What information and training do employees have on handling these situations? What additional precautions have to be developed?

Risk prevention also covers equipping the physical plant (premises and furnishings) to increase the security—not, however, beyond the limit at which physical precautions increase the danger of injury to the employees. In other words, should a cashier workstation be made to look like an armed fortress, as this might increase the risk of hostage taking? Should alarms be installed instead?

Catastrophe Organization

A catastrophe organization should be set up at the workplace at risk to handle both the situation and run the main organizational functions. It is especially important that a personnel policy be chosen to guarantee the development of healthy work relations between employees of all ranks. The documentation points out that a built-in precaution would be the ability to gain the needed social support from fellow workers and supervisors. Social support is meant to be emotionally supportive, informative, self-confidence raising, and instrumental. This implies the development of democracy and equality at the workplace. Training should also cover the handling of upset people.

The Reactions of Victims and the Role of SH

The education of employees who risk violence at the workplace should cover how the body reacts under severe stress. This will prevent misjudging bodily stress symptoms. Information on crisis reactions should also be distributed. Professional staff at the various SH branches all over the country should be educated (if still necessary) on how to handle people in mental shock or crisis. Preventive measures that can be adopted at different points in time are discussed in the SH manual, covering from the acute situation to up to a year for more deeply shocked employees.

Example 2: The Banking Corporation

Suggestions for implementing safety law and regulations can now be found at many company health-care centers—at least, at those serving larger companies. This situation is exemplified by the banking corporation described here.

The company health-care center belonging to this bank employs three physicians, six nurses, one safety engineer, and four psychologists, covering all sorts of work-environment problems—not only the risk of violence. Besides this team and subordinated to bank management are three security officers.

As soon as a bank robbery is detected, while the nearest police station is alerted, the bank office is visited by members of the team to give initial psychological and social support and to get an overview of the situation. Are there employees who need immediate psychological help? Are there physical injuries to be taken care of? What type of catastrophe organization has to be chosen? Is there risk to prolonged anxiety for some employees?

Treatment is offered to the employees according to what they want and what is needed. Group or individual crisis support is offered. Employees in situations in which risk continues for an extended period and with deeper shock reactions receive special treatment.

Preventive work includes security education: instruction on how to minimize the risks of physical injuries and hostage taking; how to secretly sound the alarm that summons the police; how to systematically describe the robbers for purposes of identification; how bodily reactions feel under severe stress, and what the physiological reasons are; how to handle mental crises; how to give social support; and so on. The company's goal is for all employees to have this and/or additional training repeatedly. Incidentally, it must be noted that shootings and hostage-takings are very rare in Sweden.

Example 3: The Bus Line

Recently, one of the largest bus lines in Sweden developed an action program to offer support to bus drivers who were threatened or actually assaulted, attacked, or beaten up during their work hours. This bus line has a health-care center with two physicians, three nurses, two safety engineers, and five psychologists.

Training is mentioned as a preventive measure. Recognizing the need for it, a detailed training plan is developed. Those situations in which bus drivers run the greatest risk of being attacked are carefully described, and rules are given to prevent these situations. Certain work routines are changed to make the job safer.

External contacts that should be increased are determined, such as contact and exchange of experiences with police authorities and security companies. Contacts with the mass media are planned to prevent exaggerated reports which just might increase the risk of violence. Contacts with organizations where large numbers of people gather, such as football stadiums, youth centers, and so on are planned continuously, in order to communicate about special public events where certain precautions might be necessary (e.g., anticipating hostile behavior from drunken spectators at football games). The bus line also plans to keep statistics on violence toward bus drivers to gain detailed information about trends.

The reorganization of assistance protocols when violence has taken place shows a pattern similar to the one described for the banking company. Depending on the circumstances, the bus driver is invited to visit the health-center staff. Middle management is trained to give social support to harassed bus drivers and encourage them to seek professional help when necessary. In acute situations, employees are always given time to rest and recover. They also may take a day or so off, but supervisors are instructed to see to it that employees who live alone do not run the risk of being left completely alone at home while they are still in shock.

Recent Developments

Victimological research in Sweden is a good example of what is well understood in the scientific community but seldom talked about or even analyzed; that is, that social forces are pushing toward beginning to recognize employees' problems in their work environments. The current political situation in each country will determine how long this process will take. No doubt, it will at one point involve the national legislative body. The political situation may also allow the institution of procedures for gathering new information about these newly recognized problems in society.

This is exactly what has happened in Sweden. It was not long after the Swedish parliament in 1978 decided on the new Work Environment Act (including rules on psychosocial risks) that trade unions began to take action on behalf of their members running these risks. Some company health-care centers also took action. As a logical development, research was called for and research start-up funds were provided. Thus, Sweden and Norway—at the moment the only nations in the world with this kind of legislation—are developing new knowledge in the area of victimological research in work life with access to complete populations. This means that groups of people involved in disasters or crimes can now be researched utilizing survey research methodology. Also, groups of people who would never consider claiming victim status on their own (e.g., by not feeling shocked at all) can be reached through personnel departments and asked to cooperate.

As a consequence, in Sweden, employees, their trade unions, and employers are developing an increasing interest in victimization at the workplace and in its consequences. They want to know more. They want to understand the situation confronting the victim better and how to prepare the workplace better. Most of all, they want to know what can be done when the risk of violence becomes a reality. The fact that crime is increasing even in otherwise relatively peaceful areas, such as Scandinavia, is likely to increase this trend.

Much research remains to be made. By gaining better knowledge about the risks and facts of violence at the workplace, new problems in society become detected and become the subjects of further debate. One of them is the increasing consciousness about the role of the mass media in what has been called "secondary victimization." The commercially based structure of mass media corporations and the work environment of the journalist, influenced as it is by money and tough competition, stimulate reporting that is dangerous for the individual victim. Swedish newspapers specializing in work-environment issues have recently begun to focus on the internal work organization of the mass media. Every employed journalist has to compete with his colleagues for media space, resulting in a tendency to inflate events. A market-oriented specialist and not the individual journalist chooses the headlines. This means that there is a tendency to sidestep the truth to catch the interest of the audience and thus increase sales. Contact with the police in order to report a crime is very often handed over to a young journalist who, beside being inexperienced, is also eager to make a mark and thus is prone to exaggeration. These have now become serious issues for debate and action in Sweden.

Court procedures are also being questioned more and more. It has been observed all over the world that law-abiding citizens are, as witnesses, quite often mistreated by various agents of the government and by bureaucratic procedures. When this happens to witnesses in their roles as employees and union members, it increases their consciousness that these circumstances are detrimental to a satisfactory work environment. Some trade unions have already suggested changes in court procedures. Stronger demands can be expected if several trade unions coordinate their efforts.

Bibliography

National Board of Occupational Safety and Health

AFS

1980 *Psykiska och sociala aspekter på arbetsmiljön* (Psychological and Social Aspects to the Work Environment).

AFS

1982 *Ensamarbete* (Solitary Work).

AFS

1983 *Våldsrisker i arbetsmiljön* (The Risk of Violence at Workplaces).

Stymne, I.

1981:7 *Våldsrisker i arbetsmiljön.* Stockholm. Arbetarskyddsstyrelsen. Utbildningsrapport, p. 7.

26

Sexual Violence: A Challenge to the Legislator

Jacquelien Soetenhorst
Social Faculty, University of Amsterdam

This chapter presents the results of a study in comparative law concerning the revision of the criminal code (pornography and sexual violence) in Denmark, Sweden, and the Netherlands from 1960 to 1985. During this period the political climate changed at first in the direction of liberalization and later—from the second half of the seventies—in the opposite direction. The women's rights movement played a role in this latter change. The aim of the study is to enhance insight into what politicians meant by the revision of the criminal code. Was it meant to express shared values (symbolic) or was it primarily meant to help solve a social problem (instrumental)? If the latter is the case, what is the influence of research on the decision-making process?

Parliamentary documents in Denmark, Sweden, and the Netherlands were systematically analyzed for the arguments used by the different participants to back the proposed revision of legislation on pornography and sexual violence. The analysis revealed that political demands determined the outcome of the revision. Thus, the symbolic meaning dominates the more instrumental notions. The significance of Professional Social Inquiry (PSI) was subordinate to the need to reach political deals. This decision-making practice on the part of the legislator increases the discrepancy between the expectations of the general public and the effects of revision in reality. The study has resulted in recommendations for the legislator in order to narrow this gap and thus enhance the credibility of the political system.

Introduction

This chapter is based on the results of a study on the subject of sexual violence and the criminal law. The research consisted of an analysis of the arguments used by politicians as recorded in parliamentary documents during the revision of the criminal code on sexual offenses in Denmark, Sweden, and the Netherlands over the period 1960–1985. The study concentrated on pornography, serious sexual violence (rape and assault), and sexual abuse of children.

The reasons for embarking on this comparative study were twofold. First, there was a practical need for this type of information among Dutch politicians because this section of the criminal code had been under revision since 1971. The study was financed by the Ministry of Justice. Second, there is a long-term need to rationalize the lawmaking process. Lawmaking can be seen as a means of communicating with the public. Whenever an issue concerning a social problem is put on the political agenda, it is expected that instruments will be developed to help solve the problem. One of the instruments is the criminal law. This needs explanation to the public. Which reasoning is used?

Practical Politics

The revision of criminal legislation on sexual offenses in the Netherlands started in 1971, when an advisory committee was appointed. Progress was slow because of the lack of initiative and participation of the religious parties who form an essential block in Dutch politics. The advisory committee published its recommendation in 1976, and a draft bill was submitted in 1979 proposing some liberalization of pornography. The intervention of the women's liberation movement in 1981 halted this process and the draft bill was frozen. In 1983 the issue was the revision of legislation on pornography.

In the Scandinavian countries the criminal code was amended much faster because of a more tolerant attitude in sexual matters. In Denmark, for instance, written pornographic material became unrestricted in 1967, followed soon after by the decriminalization of pornographic pictures. When, at the end of the seventies, public opinion changed in the opposite direction—partly due to the interventions of women's rights groups—there was a certain pressure to criminalize sexual behavior. In Denmark, for instance, child pornography became a crime in 1980. In this case, for example, it would be useful for other legislators to know if the arguments in the Danish debate were based on the actual experience with their liberalized law. Was there, for instance, empirical material available on the effects of decriminalization that might underpin arguments for tackling the problem of child pornography by criminalizing it and therefore by formulating a new crime?

Unfortunately, the actual political process in Holland overtook the outcome of our study. In the summer of 1984 the draft bill on pornography was "defrosted" and rushed through parliament in 1985. This experience, however, was in line with one of the outcomes of our study: that the political decision-making process follows its own logic which is often incompatible with other lines of reasoning.

Theoretical Implications

The study places the revision of legislation on sexual crimes during the twentieth century in historical perspective. In this period not only did attitudes towards sexual relations fundamentally change, first in the direction of a uniform morality reflecting religious values and later in the direction of pluriformity but another predominant development occurred as well. It consisted of the role assigned to the state in contributing to the solution of social problems.

At the end of of the nineteenth century, when the Dutch criminal code was formulated, codification was mainly intended to limit the power of the state, by submitting state organs to the Rule of Law, with its principles of "due process" that emphasize the citizen's constitutional rights.

During the twentieth century, a growing number of tasks were assigned to the state in order to achieve social justice. One of these tasks was to protect the weak. Due to this development, the ability of the state and of state organs like the police to intervene in people's lives expanded considerably.

The function of the criminal code became threefold:

> First, to submit state organs to the principles of "due process"—the traditional function.
>
> Second, to express the values respected in society by criminalizing the rejected behavior.
>
> Third, to protect those who are, or might become, the victim of this rejected behavior.

Because these functions are difficult to reconcile, the criminal justice system operates within a permanent field of tension. Arguments derived from these different functions serve to legitimate its interventions. The "due process" principles—as expressed in criminal procedures to prove a case—may clash with the interests of the victim. The necessity to protect the weaker party in sexual relations, for example, makes it possible for state organs, like the police, to intervene in private affairs. This is not in accord with the ideology behind the "due process principles" to limit the power of the state. The "damage criterion" is a way of dealing with these difficult dilemmas. According to this criterion, behavior is only criminalized when it causes damage. Thus it is important to know when in relationships between the sexes effects of damage can be expected. To answer this difficult question, social research is necessary.

The debate on the revision of sexual offenses is influenced by the three trends mentioned in the diagram: the change in moral attitudes, the extension of the Welfare State, and the influence of the women's liberation movement. At the beginning of this century this movement was focused on the issue of prostitution which demonstrated the "double standard" of men in sexual affairs. Sexual violence became the issue in the seventies. The prevalence of these trends led to different lines of reasoning when it came to reformulating the criminal code.

By analyzing the arguments used by different participants during this process, one can unravel what the participants name as the function of the criminal law. Is its function to give expression to shared values or to solve problems, like violence in the family (instrumental function)? If the instrumental function has priority, what data are used to underpin the supposed damage caused by the rejected behavior and to support the supposed beneficial effects of criminalization?

Some Results of the Research

The material analyzed consisted of parliamentary documents and reports of advisory committees. The material was systematically examined using the following categories:

- Who placed the issue on the political agenda?
- Who participated in the debate (with special reference to the influence of the women's liberation movement)?
- What arguments were used to legitimate the use of the criminal code?
- Was attention paid to alternative ways of solving the problem?
- What was the impact of empirical data (Professional Social Inquiry)?

The results of this analysis are given separately for three main categories: pornography, rape and assault, and sexual abuse of minors and for each of the three countries included in the study. Only the more prominent findings will be discussed here.

Different Legal Cultures

Although the socio-cultural situation in Denmark and Sweden resembles that of the Netherlands in many respects, there is an important difference in legal culture between the three countries.

In Denmark the style is technical and pragmatic. The revision of criminal law related to sexual offenses was placed into the hands of a permanent committee of experts, chaired by a member of the High Court of Justice. The secretariat was in the hands of the Ministry of Justice. Thus, the priority option was of a juridical nature and was focused on the interests of the criminal justice system. The fact that in Denmark the period available for handling draft legislation is limited to one year encourages this restricted techno-juridical approach.

In Sweden the social sciences have a major say in the debate. Research experts are consulted intensely or participate as members of preparatory committees that are formed on an ad hoc basis.

The legal culture in the Netherlands reflects the traces of the corporate state. Whenever an issue of a moral nature is put on the political agenda, a committee is appointed representing the wide range of religious views. The dominating position of the judiciary on such a committee and the fact that the secretariat is handled by the Ministry of Justice guarantees however the dominance of the techno-juridical definition. In the balance of political power the religious block occupies a central position enabling it to delay the consideration of certain issues.

Apart from these differences, the procedures utilized by the three countries during the revision process display many similarities. Most remarkable is the personal role of the Minister of Justice in deviating from the line set forth by preparatory committees. His intervention is necessary in order to facilitate the draft bill's passage through parliament. In Sweden and Denmark, the Minister of Justice went a step further in liberalizing pornography than the preparatory committee had envisaged. In Holland the Minister of Justice changed the proposed regulation on sex for minors in the draft bill. Still this intervention was not enough to achieve sufficient public support for the proposal.

The Participants in the Debate

One of the main participants in the debate has already been mentioned, the Minister of Justice. Another important participant is the judiciary (including the public prosecutor's office). In all three countries the initiative to revise the pornography section came from the judiciary, supported by the Ministry of Justice. Thus, the impetus to change the law on pornography was not so much public opinion represented by the political parties as the apparatus which was faced with upholding an outdated law. Once the subject matter is on the political agenda, the influence of the different political visions becomes apparent. In the political debate three visions generally compete: socialist, liberal, and religious.

These visions can be discerned in all three countries, although the political constellation differs. Denmark and Holland have many small political parties, while Sweden has a few large blocks. The religious vision is a specialty of Holland. In the Scandinavian countries this faction of the political spectrum is to be found in the conservative/ traditionalist corner.

The material examined makes it clear that the liberal and socialist visions complement each other in stressing personal autonomy and rejecting a moralizing approach in the criminal code. This combination was dominant in the debate from 1965 until the mid-seventies. But the appeal on the state to protect the weak—as part of the socialist vision—serves as a bridge between the socialist and the more traditional/ religious vision. From the mid-seventies socialist politicians—who in particular formulated the claims of the women's liberation movement—stressed the possible damaging effects of morally rejected behavior. Thus, the balance of power switched from the principle of no state intervention (unless its necessity can be proved) to that of in principle intervention (unless there are strong arguments against it).

In all three countries the influence of the women's liberation movement on the switch in perception can be easily found.

The Legitimation of Criminalization

Traditionally the criminal code reflected the shared norms concerning sexual relations by defining what was deviant. Minors (under the age of sixteen) were denied sexual contact and activities, while for adults the norm was heterosexual contact within the context of marriage. In Holland for instance, rape within marriage is explictly excluded from criminalization. In the sixties it became apparent that these values were too strict. A great variety of lifestyles was then accepted. By that time the

Dutch slogan, "The state is not a guardian of morality" became applicable to the situation in Denmark and Sweden as well. The state and the criminal justice system had a role to play in regulating people's sex lives only if damage might be caused. The consensus in the debate at that time was to protect autonomous free citizens from unwanted and unnecessary state interference.

Thus from 1965 to 1975 the discussion centered on three issues:

- First, can damage be expected from the alleged behavior?
- Second, what is the effect of criminalization (instrumental function)?
- Third, should there be freedom of choice in sexual relations (i.e., the possibility of saying no, but also of saying yes, especially for minors)?

The burden of proof was laid on the shoulders of those who pleaded for criminalization. The demand for research data grew because the legislator had to be informed about the possibility of damage and the effects of criminalization. Thus, when considering the revision of legislation on pornography, the legislature could concentrate on those situations that might lead to involuntary confrontation with this type of material and to consequent damage. Cost/benefit calculations were necessary.

Criminal policy became an element of social policy. Especially in Sweden, alternatives, like education or socio-hygienic measures, were seen as part of the set of instruments which the government could use to contribute to solving a social problem. In this way the debate on pornography was placed in a broad perspective including the expected damaging effects of exposure to violence on television. This meant that criminal policy should include violence on television and not concentrate on printed pornography. As for sexual behavior between adults, the law had to be formulated in neutral terms. Even the necessity of maintaining a special section on sexual violence was questioned, on the grounds that this type of behavior was covered sufficiently by the section of violent crimes.

The possible damage done to minors constituted a special problem since it is difficult to decide. In 1971 Sweden financed an extensive research program among minors in order to get hold of the possible damaging effects of encounters with images of sex and violence on television and movies. The main conclusion was that repeated exposure to excessively violent scenes (not necessarily of a sexual nature) could have damaging effects. On the basis of these findings the preparatory committee drew up a draft bill that liberalized pornography but criminalized material of an "utterly dehumanizing nature." (The Minister of Justice deviated from this recommendation and proposed a complete decriminalization, a proposal that was passed by parliament in 1971.)

Sweden excels in the amount of time and funds invested in research. A report published in 1976 was also based on extensive research among minors on their attitudes on sex and their actual behavior. The proposals were quite revolutionary. One of them was to abolish the age limit of fifteen years because research data showed that minors were generally speaking sexually active before that age; the special crime of incest could be abolished as the genetic argument had been disproved; minors needed no extra protection against material of a sexual nature, for minors and adults repeated exposure with excessive violent scenes could have negative effects; educational measures were preferable, because of the damage done to the minor having to participate in a criminal case. This report also questioned the usefulness of long prison sentences and found the preventive effect of a long prison sentence small.

Before the proposals of the report could be converted into policy terms, the political climate changed. There was a greater support for criminalization and less interest in the cost/benefit argument supporting the liberalization of moral issues. The same switch in the legal-political climate appeared in Denmark and in the Netherlands whenever sexual offenses were placed on the political agenda.

What explanation can be given for this overall change in the approach to the legislation on sexual crimes? One possible explanation is the increased appeal on the part of the victims during the seventies to be protected by the criminal justice system. This is a claim that politicians cannot ignore. It also appears that the arguments for rationalizing the use of criminal law ignored strong emotional feelings inherent in the subject matter. Though public opinion polls still reflect a more liberal attitude of the public toward sexual behavior, there seems to be a discrepancy between the attitude expressed and the willingness to accept its consequences, like decriminalization.

Support of decriminalization might be interpreted as approving the behavior in question. An illustration of this emotional aspect can be found in Sweden where the proposal to decriminalize sexual relations between adult family members received great resistence. In Holland, however, this behavior never was criminalized. In Holland the proposal to restrict the intervention of criminal law in sexual relations of minors to situations of force received strong opposition from the public.

A further possible explanation is the necessity of the criminal justice system to uphold its pretensions. To demand that politicians admit their inability to solve a social problem like sexual violence is asking for the impossible. Thus, the legislator is always willing to respond to this appeal by criminalizing the rejected behavior.

In conclusion, during the last decade the pressure toward criminalization in order to protect the victims has increased. However, it has met two main obstacles. The first one consists of the need to uphold "due process" principles. A stronger orientation of the police and of the public prosecutor on the needs of the victim might lead to a weakening of the protection of the offender. A measure like "mandatory arrest" is known in the Danish code, but it is mainly used in minor cases of "drunken husbands." "The women often drop their complaint" was the remark of police officers during an interview session. This interview also showed that the change in procedural law, realized in 1981, forbidding the public prosecutor to question the victim on her previous sexual life, had no practical effects. The second barrier is a practical one—lack of funds. The implementation of a criminal norm costs money. The same could be said of the demand of victims to be better informed about procedures, to receive compensation for material and immaterial damages and to participate in the sentencing.

Alternative Ways of Solving the Problem

In the period of liberalization (1965–1975) some attention was given to socio-educational and socio-hygienic measures. In the debate on pornography no attention is given to administrative measures as a possible alternative. During the second period, 1975–1985, when the balance switched toward criminalization, the lack of creativity was even stronger. In Denmark, an innovative proposal introduced the possibility of giving the victim of rape the support of a state-paid lawyer. Recently, in Holland a remarkable development has taken place. Lawyers have encouraged victims of sexual violence to start a civil procedure, a much more precise and effective weapon than a criminal procedure in which the victim plays a minor role.

The Impact of Empirical Data

In Sweden legislators generally pay considerable attention to research findings. The Professional Social Inquiry has the tendency to broaden the problem definition and the scope of possible governmental measures. The results of research, for instance on the damaging effects of exposure to scenes of a violent nature, leave room for different interpretations. Thus, the results only find support when they underpin political arguments. In other words, research can never substitute for political decisions. On the other hand, politicians have the task to explain to the public the strength and limits of the instrument used to tackle a certain social problem. If they continue producing "make believe" solutions, in the long run the political system will lose credibility.

Recommendations for the Legislator

"We have to assume a quite radical distinction between the public realms of representations, significations and symbolic practices (word) and the operational realm of sanctions, institutions and practices (deeds). The first is not a theory of the second nor its 'ideational reflection,' but a 'separate realm of penal discourse'" (Cohen, 1985: 157). Stanley Cohen underlines in this quote the necessity to differentiate between the verbal act of legislation and the actual practice. Although the tacit assumption suggests a connection between these two forms of governmental action, in reality they belong to two different realms.

Verbal acts by the legislator can have a purely symbolic meaning. As Carson states: "Symbolic meanings are constructed in the course of reciprocal processes of interpretation which constitute an ongoing feature of legislative as of any other interaction" (Carson, 1974: 110).

Politicians are aware of this effect as the material we studied illustrates. The tactics of delay, the personal intervention of the Minister of Justice, the compromise type of formulations which leave room for different interpretations in order to convince the respective rank and file of their triumph are examples derived from the material studied. There is nothing wrong with this practice as long as it is presented as a merely symbolic activity. The value expressive function of the criminal code is vivid and real. However, the problem is that this type of legislation suggests that redefining the criminal code is the proper way of solving the social problem the norm refers to.

This instrumental function the criminal code is expected to fulfill is the consequence of the before mentioned causal connection between "words" (legislation) and "deeds" (implementation). Continuation of this kind of approach might lead to a growing distrust of the general public in the legislator and in the criminal justice system when they are unable to realize its stated aims.

The most important function of legislation, that of strengthening social cohesion in society, is in danger of disappearing. Lawmaking increasingly becomes a self-fulfilling ritual that has little to do with the real world. Instead of this ritualization, the lawmaking process should be used as a form of social learning for all those concerned with a social problem like sexual violence in the family. During this process the various participants acquire better insight into the problem itself and its relation to their life experience. It is crucial to break through the restricted techno-juridical approach to the problem.

Thus, the first lesson for the legislator is to place the problem in a broad frame of reference that includes a number of instruments for tackling the problem in question.

The second lesson is to strengthen communications between the executive apparatus (e.g., the police) and those who participate in the legislative process in order to reduce the expectations of the effects of criminalization to realistic proportions.

The third lesson is to extend the possibility of discussing different options which can be used in conjunction with or instead of criminalization. This type of discussion stimulates the development of solutions that are less costly and less dubious in their side effects. As long as no appeal is made to others to share responsibility in reducing antisocial behavior, the criminal solution will continue to be the priority option, regardless of its ineffectiveness.

A fourth lesson is directed at researchers. While the Professional Social Inquiry (PSI) does not have the authority to replace political decision-making (Cohen and Lindblom, 1979: 136), it certainly has the task to clarify the contents of the decisions to be made. Instead of strengthening the prejudices of a certain period, it should fulfill a critical function questioning the shared judgments and opening new perspectives for the handling of social problems that always exist. The challenge is to find humanistic and democratic ways of dealing with undesired life events like sexual violence.

Bibliography

Carson, W.G.

1974 "Symbolic and Instrumental Dimensions of Early Factory Legislation: A Case Study in the Social Origins of Criminal Law." In R. Hood. *Crime Criminology and Policy*. London: Free Press, pp. 107–137.

Cohen, S.

1985 *Visions of Social Control*. New York: Polity Press.

Cohen, D., and C.E. Lindblom

1979 "Solving Problems of Bureaucracy, Limits on Social Science." In C.H. Weiss and A.H. Barton. *Making Bureaucracies Work.* London: Sage Publications.

Habermas, J.

1982 *Theorie des kommunikativen Handelns.* Vols. 1 and 2. Frankfurt a. M.: Suhrkamp.

Hood, R. den

1974 *Crime, Criminology and Public Policy.* London: Free Press.

Weiss, C.H., and A.H. Barton

1979 *Making Bureaucracies Work.* London; Beverly Hills: Sage.

Contributors

Kurt Baneryd received a Ph.D. in educational psychology at the University of Gothenburg. Since 1976 he has been the director of the Social Division at the National Board of Occupational Safety and Health.

Susanne Chomicki has a degree in psychology from McMaster University, Hamilton, Ontario, and is presently a graduate student in social work at Wilfrid Laurier University in Waterloo, Ontario.

Stephen Robert Couch is Associate Professor of Sociology at the Schuylkill Campus of the Pennsylvania State University. He has written in a number of areas, including the social history of management and labor in nineteenth-century United States and the sociology of music and musical organizations. He is coauthor (with J. Stephen Kroll-Smith) of *The Real Disaster Is Above Ground: A Mine Fire and Social Conflict* (University Press of Kentucky, 1989) and is currently coediting (with J. Stephen Kroll-Smith) a collection of essays on collective responses to chronic technical disasters (*Communities At Risk*, Peter Lang Publishing, forthcoming 1990).

Mary E. Craig received her M.A. degree at Columbia University. She is currently a Ph.D. candidate in Clinical Psychology at the University of South Carolina. She has published in the areas of ethical issues in treating cases of child abuse and coercive sexuality.

Leila Dane trained originally as an interpreter and first started counseling under the tutorial of a clinical psychologist in Madras, India, where her husband was serving a diplomatic assignment. On her return to the United States in the early 1970s, she started her formal education in psychology and formed an advocacy group within the State Department to promote a comprehensive program of mental health services. As mental health liaison of the Association of American Foreign Service Women to the State Department and co-chair of the Foreign Service Community Mental Health Committee, she pressed for the establishment of preventive services and training in cross-cultural adjustment, especially re-entry, as well as mental health services covering crisis intervention.

When the Tehran Embassy personnel were taken hostage in late 1979, some of the wives asked for an evaluation of services made available to State Department hostage families compared to military hostage families. They turned to Dr. Dane when the State Department did not respond to their requests. Having received her B.A. in 1975 and her M.A. in 1978, she decided to make the Iran hostage families' coping process her dissertation topic. Dr. Dane received her Ph.D. in 1986. Shortly thereafter, she found the Institute for Victims of Trauma, offering counseling to victims and training to professionals and paraprofessionals.

Rhoda Estep is an Associate Professor of Sociology at California State University, Stanislaus. Her research interests include the mass media, drug use, cross-cultural studies, and sexuality. Dr. Estep's teaching covers a wide range of subjects, focusing most often on research methods and analysis, medical sociology, and computers and society.

Baruch Fischhoff is a Research Associate at Eugene Research Institute and at Decision Research. He received a Ph.D. in psychology from the Hebrew University of Jerusalem in 1975. His research interests include judgment and decision-making, risk perception, risk management, human factors, sexual assault, and public policy analysis.

Ellen R. Fisher, M.S.W., is the executive director of La Casa de las Madres, a battered women's shelter in San Francisco. At the time of the research, she was director of the Center for Battered Women in Austin, Texas.

Lita Furby is a Research Associate at Eugene Research Institute. She received her Ph.D. in psychology from Stanford University in 1969. Her research interests span a wide range of topics in social and developmental psychology and currently include women's decision-making in preventing sexual assault.

Sondra Gardner, Ph.D. is a staff psychologist at American Biodyne, an HMO providing mental health and addiction treatment services. Dr. Gardner received her degree from Case Western Reserve University. Her interests include chemical dependency and its role in perpetuating family violence.

Edward W. Gondolf, Ed.D., M.P.H., is a research professor at Western Psychiatric Institute and Clinic, University of Pittsburgh, and a professor of sociology at Indiana University of Pennsylvania (IUP).

Frank Henry, Associate Professor of Sociology at McMaster University, Hamilton, Ontario, is currently writing a book on corporate violence. He has previously published in journals as varied as *Crime and Social Justice, Victimology, The Criminal Law Quarterly, The American Sociological Review, The Canadian Review of Sociology and Anthropology, Race, Political Methodology and the International Journal of the Sociology of the Family.*

Gerald L. Hutchins was the Urban Studies Center's manager of computer and systems analysis and Director of Student Computer. He received his Ph.D. in political science from the Ohio State University in 1977. Dr. Hutchins has directed several information systems projects and is currently the computer analyst on a study of flood victims funded by the National Institute of Mental Health.

Ranjana S. Jain is an Assistant Professor in the Department of Sociology, University of Rajasthan, Jaipur, India. Her doctoral dissertation was on "Family Relationships and Violence." She has presented several papers on family violence at international meetings and congresses.

Knowlton W. Johnson is director of the Urban Research Institute, a large research component of the College of Urban and Public Affairs at the University of Louisville, Kentucky. He received his Ph.D. in social science from Michigan State University in 1971. Dr. Johnson has extensive research experience in victimology and has published a number of articles concerning victims of crimes and disasters.

Seth C. Kalichman received his B.A. degree from the University of South Florida. He is currently a Ph.D. candidate in Clinical Psychology at the University of South Carolina. His publications are in the areas of professional issues in treating victims of child abuse and personality functioning in sexual offenders.

Irving Kaufman, M.D., has been trained in both adult and child psychoanalysis. He is in full-time private practice, does private supervision, teaches at The Smith College School for Social Work (37th year), and supervises residents in child psychiatry under the aegis of the Harvard School of Medicine. He has consulted for many social agencies throughout New England, such as, The Children's Protective Services of Massachusetts for over thirty years. He has written over 30 published articles starting with "Incest" in 1954. Fifteen of these articles and eight of the eleven chapters in books have been on delinquency behavior, including firesetting, crimes of violence, and child abuse. Other articles include marital adaptation in aging, childhood schizophrenia, and working within mental health and correctional institutions.

J. Stephen Kroll-Smith is Associate Professor of Sociology at the Hazleton Campus of the Pennsylvania State University. He has written several articles on the structure of sectarian belief and ritual. He is coauthor (with Stephen Robert Couch) of *The Real Disaster Is Above Ground: A Mine Fire and Social Conflict* (University Press of Kentucky, 1989) and is currently coediting (with Stephen Robert

Couch) a collection of essays on collective responses to chronic technical disasters (*Communities At Risk*, Peter Lang Publishing, forthcoming 1990).

Heinz Leymann has earned a Ph.D. in psychology and an M.D. in psychiatry. He is associate professor at the University of Stockholm and director of the research program at the National Institute of Occupational Health in Stockholm. He also directs a private institute that helps victims of violence at the workplace.

Jan Lindell has a Ph.D. and is chief psychologist at the Swedish Research Foundation for Occupational Safety and Health in the Construction Industry. There he directs research on psychosocial factors in the workplace.

J. Richard McFerron, M.S., is currently an assistant professor of business at Indiana University of Pennsylvania and assisted with data management while Assistant Director of Academic Systems and Research.

Marcia Morgan is a Project Coordinator at Eugene Research Institute. She has worked in sexual assault prevention for eleven years as a law enforcement officer, consultant, and lecturer. Her work has included developing women's safety programs and school curricula and co-creating the original anatomical dolls now used worldwide for interviewing abuse victims.

Tim Newburn is senior research officer, Research and Planning Unit, Home Office, London, England. He has conducted research into crowd violence, sexual morality, and victims in the criminal justice system. He is presently engaged in research on police-victim liaison.

M. Jean Parks, Ph.D., is a Staff Psychologist in Counseling and Career Services at Trinity University in San Antonio, Texas. She received her doctorate in clinical psychology from the University of Tennessee, Knoxville. Parks began her work with rape victims as a volunteer for the Knoxville Rape Crisis Center in 1978.

Bhanuprasad Pandya is the honorary president of the Indian Research Society for the Welfare of Backward Classes in Ahmedabad, Gujarat, India.

James F. Phifer is a doctoral candidate in clinical psychology at the University of Louisville Research Institute. He has published several articles pertaining to stress and mental health in older adults and has submitted several manuscripts concerning the physical and psychological consequences of natural disasters.

Ronelle Pretorius, M.A., D.Phil., is Professor and Head of the Department of Criminology of the University of Pretoria, Republic of South Africa.

Sarah M. Rieth is an Episcopal priest and a pastoral psychotherapist certified by the American Association of Pastoral Counselors. She received her B.A. in Anthropology from the State University of New York at Albany; she achieved her M.Div. from Colgate-Rochester/Bexley Hall/Crozer Theological Seminary. She did her pastoral counseling training at the Toronto Institute of Human Relations and is a staff therapist at Church Mission of Help, a counseling agency in Buffalo, New York. She is the creator and Clinical Coordinator of the Survivors United crisis and flashback hotline for adult survivors of sexual abuse in Buffalo. She is active in the work of the Erie County Task Force on Sexually Abusing Families.

Helen Warren Ross is a Professor in the School of Family Studies and Consumer Sciences at San Diego State University. She received her Ph.D. in Educational Psychology at Catholic University in Washington, D.C. Prior to moving to San Diego, she worked as a school psychologist and a consultant to Head Start in Montgomery and Howard counties.

In 1979–1980, Dr. Ross spent a year as a Senior Research Fulbright Fellow at the University of Rome, Italy. Her publications address child development and child care issues. She has served as faculty advisor for the Disabled Students Union and as a counselor in the campus counseling center. It was in this capacity that the criminal victimization of the handicapped was brought to her attention.

Her current research interests include victimization of handicapped children and adults as well as victimization of ethnic group members and recipients of mental health services.

Jacquelien Soetenhorst studied law at the University of Leiden, The Netherlands. For many years she practiced as a lawyer, returning to teach at Leiden University in 1972. After the 1975 publication of her thesis, "Tradition and Innovation in the Criminal Justice System," she became a member of the research team of the Social and Cultural Planning Office in The Hague. Since 1982, she has been a professor at the University of Amsterdam. Dr. Soetenhorst is the author of three books and many articles in the field of deviance and social control.

Sarah R. Stanley, M.S., R.N., C.N.A., C.S., is a senior staff specialist in the Center for Nursing Practice of the American Nurses' Association in Kansas City, Missouri. Most recently she was an instructor in the Department of Psychiatry, College of Medicine with a joint appointment in the College of Nursing at the Medical University of North Carolina.

Sandra Murdock Stith completed her Master of Science degree (1982) in Life Span Human Development and Doctor of Philosophy degree in Marriage and Family Therapy (1986) at Kansas State University in Manhattan, Kansas.

She has been active in the area of spouse abuse as a researcher, teacher, and therapist. She conducted a support group for battered women for two years and has made numerous presentations on various aspects of domestic violence.

Jane Timmons-Mitchell, Ph.D. is Assistant Professor of Psychology, Department of Psychiatry, Case Western Reserve University School of Medicine. Dr. Timmons-Mitchell co-coordinates the Incest Families Program through the Center for Human Sexuality, University Hospitals of Cleveland.

James T. Turner, Ph.D., is Director of The Clark Center, a private psychiatric/substance abuse facility. He has many years of experience in terrorism and victimization. He has edited two volumes, *Violence in The Medical Care Setting* and *The Handbook of Hospital Security and Safety*. He has authored handbooks on hostage taking and management of aggressive behavior. Dr. Turner serves as a consultant and expert witness to a wide variety of businesses and attorneys.

Mark S. Umbreit is the Director of Research and Training for the Center for Victim-Offender Mediation of the Minnesota Citizens Council on Crime and Justice (Minneapolis). He also is a Research Associate at the Center for Youth Development and Research at the University of Minnesota in St. Paul. He has provided on-site technical assistance to and mediation training for new programs in more than 30 cities throughout the United States as a consultant for the U.S. Department of Justice. Dr. Umbreit developed and teaches a course on Conflict Resolution at the University of Minnesota; has authored numerous articles and monographs, including his book *Crime and Reconciliation*; and has mediated cases involving a wide range of both non-violent and violent criminal behavior. Dr. Umbreit was a co-founder and former President of the PACT organization in northern Indiana which, along with the Mennonite Central Committee, developed the first VORP program in the U.S. He is the first Chairperson of the U.S. Association for Victim-Offender Media-

tion. Dr. Umbreit is also a Research Associate at the Center for Youth Development and Research, University of Minnesota, St. Paul.

Emilio C. Viano is Professor, Department of Justice, Law and Society, The American University in Washington, D.C., and Editor-in-Chief of *Victimology: An International Journal*. He has been active in the field of victimology and victim/witness services since the early 1970s. He has organized and chaired several national and international meetings in the field, has directed several training and information programs, and has served as a national and international expert on various projects. He has published several articles, books, and monographs in the field.

TABLES AND FIGURES INDEX

TABLES

FIGURES

NAME INDEX

A

B

C

D

E

F

G

H

L

M

N

O

P

Q

R

S

T

U

V

W

Z

SUBJECT INDEX